TOURS of VIETNAM

War, Travel Guides, and Memory

SCOTT LADERMAN

Duke University Press
Durham and London 2009

D1410217

© 2009 Duke University Press

All rights reserved

Printed in the United States of
America on acid-free paper ∞

Designed by Heather Hensley

Typeset in Monotype Janson by
Keystone Typesetting, Inc.

Library of Congress Cataloging-
in-Publication Data appear on the
last printed page of this book.

FOR JILL

CONTENTS

THE NOMENCLATURE OF THE VIETNAM WAR

Language is political. This may especially be so with the Vietnam war.

As a case in point, consider that last sentence. Should we, in fact, call the state of conflict in Indochina before 1975 the "Vietnam war"? Vietnam, after all, has engaged in a number of wars, and the conflict in question was also fought in Cambodia and Laos. To refer to the "Vietnam war" is to thus reveal a certain bias. Should we therefore call it the "American war," which could help to distinguish the conflict from the earlier "French war"? This, too, presents problems. American support for the French before 1954 — financial, military, diplomatic — was considerable. And in using these terms, which denote only the principal Western actor in that phase of the conflict, the Vietnamese themselves — the majority of the combatants and overwhelmingly the majority of the casualties — seem to undergo a linguistic process of erasure. So, too, do the Australians, New Zealanders, Koreans, Filipinos, and other foreign nationals involved in the conflict. Given the extent to which American culture and memory have reimaged the war as a uniquely "American tragedy," to borrow from the title of two well-known American works, this presents a considerable problem.[1]

Some Vietnamese refer to the conflict as the "anti-American resistance war for national salvation." Others prefer the "war against Communism." Yet both of these are fraught with pitfalls. The former overlooks the substantial southern Vietnamese role in the war (a reminder that itself elides the fact that many of those in the south who supported the Saigon government were originally from the north), and the latter overlooks the nationalist fervor that inspired many Vietnamese to take up arms against France and the United States. To refer to the conflict as a Vietnamese civil war, or as a "North–South War," which is how Lonely Planet frames it, falsely implies a comparable legitimacy among the competing parties and a uniformity of opinion in the northern and southern zones. Some scholars, hoping to avoid these linguistic traps, employ the terms First Indochina War and Second Indochina War. This sort of compartmentalization, however, tends to obscure the temporal continuity of the Vietnamese anticolonial struggle and the American commitment, beginning in the 1940s, to combating it.

In short, there is no getting around the many problems inherent in all of these terms. With much trepidation, and fully aware of their shortcomings, in this study I most often use the terms "Vietnam war" and "American war."

The question of nomenclature with respect to the various Vietnamese parties is — in the most important cases, at least — a much simpler matter. Countering their characterization in an untold number of contemporary accounts, throughout this book I generally refer to the forces of the National Liberation Front and the Democratic Republic of Vietnam as the "insurgents" or "revolutionaries" instead of the "Communists" — or as the NLF and People's Army of Vietnam (PAVN) instead of the "Viet Cong," "VC," "North Vietnamese Army," or "NVA." (I recognize that the military units of the NLF were popularly known as the People's Liberation Armed Forces, but I have opted to designate them simply the NLF to avoid even greater confusion.) The word "Communists" not only retains a pejorative and overly broad connotation in the United States, but it is also misleading with respect to the composition of many of those fighting in Vietnam. Although this fact has too often been overlooked since the war officially ended in 1975, there were many non-Communists who resisted the Americans, although the Communist Party in its various incarnations was arguably the most effective and certainly the most dominant segment of the revolutionary movement, often wielding considerable influence or control over southern insurgent decision making.

The terms "Viet Cong" and "North Vietnamese Army" obfuscate far more than enlighten. It is little wonder that the governments in Saigon and Washington found them such useful propaganda contrivances. "Viet Cong," or "VC," predates the formation of the National Liberation Front and originated as part of an effort by the Ngo Dinh Diem regime to portray the war as one waged, in the words of the Saigon authorities, by "communists, traitors, and agents of Russia and China" seeking to "turn Viet Nam into a colony and the Vietnamese into the slaves of Red imperialism."[2] Not only does "Viet Cong" overlook the broad-based opposition to the Republic of Vietnam government and the opposition's origins in the anticolonial movement that opposed the French, but it more easily collapses the Vietnamese revolutionaries into the supposedly bipolar Cold War struggle pitting the "free world" against Communist totalitarianism. And it is simply not true, as several recent guidebooks either imply or directly state, that "Viet Cong" or "vc" — abbreviations for *Viet Nam Cong San* — literally means "Vietnamese Communist."[3] In fact, *Viet Nam Cong San*, which is grammatically incorrect, is a dehumanizing term more closely akin to "Commie." In Vietnamese, a literal translation of Vietnamese Communist would be *Nguoi Cong San Viet Nam; nguoi* gives the term its human dimension. Nevertheless, it must be noted that, in spite of its origins, "Viet Cong" in the years since 1975 has lost some of its pejorativeness among many former insurgents and has in fact been appropriated by numerous individuals for various reasons.

The appellation "North Vietnamese Army," which like "Viet Cong" was a propaganda concoction, was — and often remains — a means of representing the war as an invasion of a country called "South Vietnam" by a country called "North Vietnam." This mythical construction, which may be more widespread among Western tourists in Vietnam than any other myth today, disguises not only the geographical origins of many of those resisting the Americans, but also the fact that among the soldiers of the People's Army of Vietnam — again, what guidebooks casually refer to as the "North Vietnamese Army" — were many southern volunteers who traveled north to be trained, armed, and organized to fight more effectively for Vietnamese independence and reunification.

For several reasons I avoid using "North Vietnam" and "South Vietnam." Having interviewed over 170 tourists during two research trips to Southeast Asia, it is abundantly clear that far too many Westerners believe the war to have been one fought principally between these two entities — so much so that many of those I interviewed were unaware that a southern insurgency even existed. The "Viet Cong" were "North Vietnamese," they told me. In other words, that "South Vietnam" fought "North Vietnam" meant that the southern Vietnamese people fought the northern Vietnamese people. The reality, of course, was far more complex. Yet the tourists' beliefs are emblematic of the widespread ignorance that historians must constantly confront. The crucial southern role in the revolutionary struggle has become so overlooked since 1975, in fact, that even iconic markers of the southern struggle, such as the famous Cu Chi tunnel complex, have become, according to promotional materials for a 2002 trip organized by the Alumni Association of the University of Michigan, "the tunnels the *North* Vietnamese used during the war."[4] Scholars were hardly immune to such misconceptions. One historian, for example, referred in a recently published article to the "National Liberation Fronts of Algeria and North Vietnam."[5] With the emergence of Vietnam war video games, it was inevitable that comparable confusion would arise at a mass level. It did so with "Vietcong: Purple Haze," which promised opportunities to "run reconnaissance missions deep into the jungles of Northern Vietnam to track the Vietcong."[6]

In an effort to sidestep this popular ignorance, I have used not "South Vietnam" and "North Vietnam" but both "southern Vietnam" and "northern Vietnam" and the territories' formal designations: the "Republic of Vietnam," or "RVN," and the "Democratic Republic of Vietnam," or "DRV," respectively. Of course, this also presents problems. The governments of both considered themselves the legitimate authority in all of Vietnam. And my use of "Republic of Vietnam" implies a political legitimacy for the Saigon-based entity that, I believe, was neither justified nor widely embraced. Nevertheless, I believe the inevitable shortcomings in employing these official designations are fewer than those of using "South Vietnam" and "North Vietnam."

Finally, I have not used the diacritics of the Vietnamese language, and, with the exception of the map, I have opted for the American spellings of Vietnamese words (for example, Saigon rather than Sai Gon and Hanoi rather than Ha Noi). In the case of the latter, exceptions appear when I have quoted materials that use a different version; unless otherwise indicated, I have quoted the Vietnamese words in all documents and other sources as they originally appeared. The same applies to the issue of capitalization. When quoting documents or the secondary literature, I have retained the original capitalizations or non-capitalizations, as in "communists" and "Communists."

ACKNOWLEDGMENTS

This project, which began as a Ph.D. dissertation, would not have been published were it not for the tremendous assistance I received along the way. It was my good fortune to work with a community of scholars who consistently provided encouragement, sound criticism, and warm friendship. My indebtedness to the faculty and graduate students in American Studies at the University of Minnesota, Twin Cities, is great. I especially thank my co-advisers, Elaine Tyler May and Patricia Albers; the additional members of my dissertation committee, Hazel Dicken-Garcia and David Noble; and, as an outside member of the committee whose assistance was truly invaluable, H. Bruce Franklin of Rutgers University, Newark. I am grateful for the support offered by my colleagues in the Department of History and the College of Liberal Arts at the University of Minnesota, Duluth.

I was fortunate to have met numerous scholars at other institutions doing work on Vietnam and the wars in Indochina, and I have profited from their knowledge and camaraderie. Ed Martini, who read the entire manuscript, was a valued colleague and critic. Jessica Chapman and I struggled and laughed together as students of the Vietnamese language. Victor Alneng, a Swedish social anthropologist who does work on Vietnamese tourism, provided thoughtful critiques of my study from the other side of the planet.

A great many scholars have provided invaluable assistance by reading and commenting on portions of my work at various stages or by patiently answering my questions about areas in which they hold expertise. Some of these people have already been identified. Others I gratefully acknowledge include Mark Bradley, Christopher Endy, Brett Gary, Jessica Gienow-Hecht, Fabian Hilfrich, David Hunt, Lisa Lowe, Matt Masur, Edwin Moise, Ngo Vinh Long, Viet Thanh Nguyen, Gareth Porter, Richard Price, Emily Rosenberg, and Jeremi Suri. For the instruction I received while studying the Vietnamese language, I thank, from the Southeast Asian Studies Summer Institute at the University of Wisconsin, Madison, Bac Hoai Tran, Dung Thi Dao, Hoan Cao To, Nguyen Linh Chi, Nguyen Thi Thuan, Nguyen Thi Thuy Anh, and Nguyen Trong Hoa. From Chua Phat An in Roseville, Minnesota, I thank Dat Nguyen.

My research in Southeast Asia and the United States was enabled by various sources of funding at the University of Minnesota. For their generous financial support I thank the Graduate School; the College of Liberal Arts on both the Twin Cities and Duluth campuses; the MacArthur Interdisciplinary Program on Global Change, Sustainability, and Justice; the Departments of American Studies and History on, respectively, the Twin Cities and Duluth campuses; the Institute for Global Studies; the Humanities Institute; and the Institute for Advanced Study (IAS). The staff and fellows of the IAS merit a special word of gratitude for their support and feedback as this project was undergoing its transformation from dissertation to book. I also acknowledge the Committee on Institutional Cooperation for two summer scholarships supporting my study of Vietnamese.

The research I undertook was made much easier because of the help I received from numerous people at numerous repositories and institutions. I especially thank John Wilson and Regina Greenwell of the Lyndon Baines Johnson Library in Austin; Richard Boylan, Susan Francis-Haughton, A. J. Lutz, Wilbert Mahoney, and Donald Singer of the National Archives in College Park, Maryland; Ty Lovelady and Justin Saffell of the Vietnam Archive at Texas Tech University; Snowden Becker of the Academy Film Archive and Barbara Hall of the Margaret Herrick Library, both of which are affiliated with the Academy of Motion Picture Arts and Sciences; Haden Guest of the Warner Bros. Archives at the University of Southern California; Stephanie Zeman of the University of Wisconsin, River Falls, Area Research Center; Michael Church of the Kansas State Historical Society in Topeka; Bill McMorris at the Oakland Museum of California; Loraine Baratti of the New-York Historical Society; and various staff members at the John F. Kennedy Presidential Library in Boston and the Minnesota Historical Society in St. Paul.

In Vietnam, I sincerely thank Nguyen Van Kim, Nguyen Quang Ngoc, and Nguyen Lien of the Faculty of History and Vu Van Thi and Nguyen Thanh Hai of the International Cooperation Office in the College of Social Sciences and Humanities at Vietnam National University, Hanoi; Dang Hoa and Trieu Van Hien of the Museum of Vietnamese Revolution in Hanoi; Trinh Thi Hoa of the Museum of Vietnamese History in Ho Chi Minh City; Huynh Ngoc Van, Dinh Van Lien, and Tran Bao Ngoc of the War Remnants Museum; and the staffs of the Vietnam Development Information Center and the United Nations Library in Hanoi. For their assistance as interpreters, I am grateful to Le Quang Canh and Hoang Minh Tien.

A special word of gratitude is owed the interlibrary loan staffs at the University of Minnesota campuses in Duluth and the Twin Cities. Tracy Ellen Smith created the map that appears in this book. My thanks to Valerie Millholland and Mark Mastromarino, my editors at Duke University Press.

Finally, my family. My parents-in-law, Bernadette Torhan, Karen Rae, and Ernie Torres, provided constant support, help around the house, and, perhaps most important, crucial hours of babysitting. My brothers and my sister, Mark, Greg, and Mary Ann, kept me human and, through their example, reminded me that there is more to life than coursework, teaching, and writing. My mother showed me how to be a compassionate and impassioned person. She was also a reliable interest-free lender, coming through with emergency next-day loans whenever they were needed. For my entire life she has offered me nothing but unqualified love. I hope she realizes how much her encouragement has meant to me. My father, who remained furiously in love with my mother until the very end, passed away while I was in graduate school. We often disagreed — and he was always sure to let me know when this was the case — but I have no doubt that I am where I am today because of him. Those who knew him well know that there was nothing more important to him than his family. If today I am not only an able scholar but also a decent father, it is because of his fine example. I miss him.

My greatest debt is undoubtedly owed to my partner and friend, Jill Torres. For her love, her support, and especially for bringing me Izzy and Sam, I dedicate this book to her.

ABBREVIATIONS AND ACRONYMS

ADB	Asian Development Bank
AFV	American Friends of Vietnam
APU	Asian Parliamentarians' Union
ARVN	Army of the Republic of Vietnam
CIA	Central Intelligence Agency
DRV	Democratic Republic of Vietnam ("North Vietnam")
FBI	Federal Bureau of Investigation
FDA	Food and Drug Administration
GVN	"Government of Vietnam" (of the Republic of Vietnam)
IMF	International Monetary Fund
IRC	Indochina Resource Center
MACV	Military Assistance Command, Vietnam
MIA	Missing in Action
NLF	National Liberation Front ("Viet Cong")
NSCVV	National Student Committee for Victory in Vietnam
NTO	National Tourist Office
NVA	"North Vietnamese Army" (People's Army of Vietnam)
OAFIE	Office of Armed Forces Information and Education
PATA	Pacific Area Travel Association
PAVN	People's Army of Vietnam ("North Vietnamese Army")
PBS	Public Broadcasting Service
POW	Prisoner of War
RVN	Republic of Vietnam ("South Vietnam")
TIED	Troop Information and Education Division
UNESCO	United Nations Educational, Scientific, and Cultural Organization
UNICEF	United Nations Children's Fund
USIA	U.S. Information Agency
VC	"Viet Cong" (National Liberation Front)
VNAT	Vietnam National Administration of Tourism
VVAW	Vietnam Veterans Against the War

History, Tourism, and the

Question of Empire

On Pho Hoa Lo in the central section of Hanoi, wedged tightly between Pho Hai Ba Trung and Pho Ly Thuong Kiet, stands what is today a richly complex symbol of modern Vietnamese history. Built by the French in 1896, the Maison Centrale was for years the largest prison in northern Indochina, housing thousands of France's imperial subjects in the decades of colonial exploitation that followed. An important relic of Vietnam's political history, it emerged in the early and mid-twentieth century as an informal school of sorts for the nation's burgeoning revolutionary movement, many of whose members spent years incarcerated between its thick, imposing walls.[1] Within the facility an untold number of Vietnamese were tortured. Some were decapitated by guillotine. One of the machines, in fact, remains today on the prison's grounds as a carefully preserved reminder of this gruesome past. Following the 1954 Geneva Accords that put an end to French suzerainty in Indochina, Hoa Lo Prison, as the institution was called by the Vietnamese, fell under the authority of the Democratic Republic of Vietnam, the independent Vietnamese state proclaimed by Ho Chi Minh in September 1945.

Apart from its obvious political significance, the structure serves as a powerful emblem of the nation's recent economic history. Much of the prison was razed in the 1990s to make way for a high-end business and residential complex that towers over the site, symbolizing the extent to which the government's feverish embrace of capitalist principles has periodically come at the expense of Vietnam's oft-venerated past. No site, it seems, is safe from the march of progress. For visitors looking over the prison's remaining courtyard walls, another modern high-rise, this one a block away, now dominates the skyline: the luxurious Melia Hotel. Not intended for the bulk of the Vietnamese people, for whom its nightly tariffs remain far out of reach, the hotel has housed thousands of foreign tourists and businesspeople who have arrived in Vietnam seeking either holiday pleasure or financial reward. As with much of Vietnam's recent economic development, the building spotlights not only the disparity between host and visitor but also, perhaps less obviously, the mushrooming inequality within one of the world's last avowedly socialist states. A minority of Vietnamese can afford a night at the Melia; the overwhelming majority cannot.

Finally, the prison — and the museum it now hosts — remains a divisive marker of modern international history. To countless tourists in the twenty-first century, the site is known not as the Maison Centrale or Hoa Lo Prison but, unaffectionately, as the "Hanoi Hilton." The widespread Western employment of this moniker suggests the extent to which a narrative of the United States has been placed at the center of Vietnam's recent past. From 1964 to 1973, which constitutes but a temporal fraction of its century of existence, the facility held a number of American captives, most of them pilots whose planes had been shot down over northern Vietnam. Yet these nine years remain seared in American memory. The experiences of the POWs have fascinated millions of the prisoners' compatriots. They were touchingly dramatized in *The Hanoi Hilton*, a 1987 film by the right-wing Hollywood director Lionel Chetwynd that sought to honor the men while almost entirely ignoring the context of their capture: the waves of American aerial bombardment that placed their aircraft in harm's way.[2] The pilots' stories have appeared in dozens of memoirs, print histories, and television documentaries, and rescue tales of POWs in Vietnam constituted a major filmic genre in the 1980s. So enthralled have foreigners been with this element of the American past that, in Vietnam's leading turn-of-the-century travel guidebook, the small museum at Hoa Lo commanded the volume's longest entry of all of Hanoi's museums, surpassing even the entries for the seven national museums found in the city and its surrounding environs. Yet the fascination with Hoa Lo is not with the harrowing Vietnamese experience under the French. Most of the guidebook authors'

attention was devoted, rather, to the relatively brief Vietnamese imprisonment of the Americans.[3] The effacement of Vietnamese history by a narrative of American suffering thus appears to be nearly complete.

In this sense Hoa Lo Prison has come to exemplify a fascinating reality
of contemporary Vietnamese tourism: Many Americans travel to Vietnam
to learn not about Vietnam but about the United States. At its various
historic sites and museums they hope to make sense of their country's
earlier, but still contentious, intervention in Southeast Asia, and they wish
to heal the emotional pain about the conflict that has come to characterize
postwar American life. Some arrive genuinely curious about how Vietnamese have constructed their national past. Others protest the public
Vietnamese narratives that invariably fail, unlike nearly the entire scope
of American popular culture since 1975, to situate the United States at
their center.[4]

Vietnamese tourism, both historical and contemporary, thus provides an
opportune lens through which to examine a multitude of phenomena, from
war and American national identity to what the cultural historian Raymond
Williams would have termed — had he been writing about the United
States — America's "selective tradition."[5] In this book I examine several of
the multiple intersections of tourism with transnational Vietnamese and
American history. I address how, for example, the Republic of Vietnam
(RVN) embraced tourism as a means of furthering its disputed international
legitimacy while at the same time establishing a discursive framework that
appealed to American foreign policy ideals. I explore the U.S. Department
of Defense's concurrent marketing of the promise of exotic travel as a
selling point for American service in Southeast Asia while embracing travel
literature as an effective means of indoctrinating its military personnel.
And I illustrate how Western travel writers — in particular, guidebook authors penning instruments of instruction — elided or rationalized French
and American imperialism throughout the twentieth century.

But my focus is not solely on the period before the war's official end.
Since 1975, too, tourism has been a significant feature of Vietnamese life.
While only a minor phenomenon in the 1970s and early 1980s, since then
millions of foreigners have arrived in Vietnam seeking historical knowledge, cultural enlightenment, coastal relaxation, and, for some men, the
illegal pleasures of youthful prostitution. Accompanying this influx has
been an explosion in travel writing, both creative and referential. While

such literature has not typically interested historians of American foreign relations, the vastly growing distribution of these publications, as well as their influence in shaping perceptions of the United States as an international power, begs for scholarly analysis. Travel guidebooks, for example, have performed a critical role in mediating tourists' understandings not only of recent history — particularly of the American war — but also of Vietnam's location within the hegemonic expansion of late-twentieth-century global capitalism.

Yet it is not only diplomatic historians who have overlooked guidebooks as important primary sources. Significant attention to the publications among scholars more broadly has been, at best, fleeting.[6] From their European origins in the nineteenth century, modern guidebooks — especially since the economic conditions following the Second World War allowed for greater American travel abroad — have enabled millions of people to navigate a world that has seemed at times alternately daunting and exhilarating. Their provision of lodging and restaurant information; their advice on local customs, ground transportation, and when to tip and when not to; and their assistance in overcoming the linguistic hurdles that confront non-native speakers in much of the world have provided a degree of comfort to nervous Americans during their occasional jaunts overseas. By 2000, guidebooks covered nearly every inch of the planet. Even Mars and the moon enjoyed travel publishers' attention.[7]

Guidebooks are hardly uniform or interchangeable, however. They possess different personalities and appeal to different demographics. Some, such as those published by Fodor's, are clearly associated with middle- and upper-middle-class travelers. Others — especially since the arrival in 1973 of Lonely Planet's *Across Asia on the Cheap*, a volume that built on the earlier success of Arthur Frommer's *Europe on $5 a Day* and, even more pertinently, the *Hitch-Hiker's Guide to Europe* published by Pan Books in 1971 — have targeted what Lonely Planet's co-founders, Tony and Maureen Wheeler, dub "independent-minded travelers" or "this huge subversive travel market."[8] These "backpackers," who have taken to Vietnam like a previous generation took to Thailand, often view themselves as a unique and enlightened subculture; they are "travelers," they insist, not "tourists." The latter grouping, in their view, is to be unsparingly derided. Ranging from the benighted masses who stay in chain hotels to those "coach tourists with glazed eyes" who, in the conceited characterization of one guidebook to

France, "obediently plod through a number of over-restored Gothic chapels," these hordes of sheepish "tourists" ruin the apparently more authentic experiences of the armies of non-tourist "travelers" toting a Lonely Planet or a Rough Guide.[9] Or so they claim. It is with a considerable degree of irony, then, that in Vietnam single- or multiple-day tours organized by local travel agencies or cafes (which were often one and the same) had become, by the late 1990s, a preferred method among backpackers of seeing the country.

Probably no single outside force exercised greater influence on late-twentieth-century tourism in Vietnam than the Australian publishing house Lonely Planet. By the late 1990s, its brand was ubiquitous. Employing exclusively American writers throughout that decade, the outfit, by the first years of the twenty-first century, had published not only its standard guidebook for Vietnam but also a volume for Southeast Asia that contained an abridged version of the stand-alone Vietnam guide; separate guides to Hanoi and Ho Chi Minh City; a "world food" guide on Vietnamese cuisine; two phrasebooks (Vietnamese and "Hill Tribes") for non-native speakers; and a guidebook specifically for bicyclists touring Vietnam, Laos, and Cambodia. It is not without foundation that a journalist for the *New York Times* dubbed Tony Wheeler the "trailblazing patron saint of the world's backpackers and adventure travelers."[10] Indeed, by 1999 Lonely Planet's website was reportedly receiving three million hits per day.[11] Yet it is not only for touristic reasons that Lonely Planet guidebooks have been scrutinized. Several Western authors, for example, have used the volumes on Cameroon, Colombia, and Iran to get a "feel" for the exotic locales in which their novels were set. And in a remarkable illustration of the publisher's perceived authority, when the United States invaded and occupied Iraq in 2003, the team accompanying the administrator Jay Garner used Lonely Planet's volume for the Middle Eastern state to compose its list of historic sites to be protected from bombing and looting.[12]

Within Vietnam, unaffiliated businesses have done their best to associate themselves with the brand. The Lonely Planet Cafe had opened in Hanoi by the time the third edition was published in 1995. In Hoi An, a travel agency calling itself the Lonely Planet Office was operating when I was there in 2000. That same year in the central Vietnamese city of Hue, restaurants proudly touted their inclusion in the guidebook's listings. The Mandarin Cafeteria featured a sandwich board and a billboard with a photograph of the Lonely Planet volume (as well as several others), both of which displayed an enlarged excerpt of the guidebook's positive comments about the restaurant's food and gregarious English-speaking owner. A large sign above the business proclaimed, "Lauded in Lonely Planet and the *New York Times*," suggesting a prestige consonant with what is arguably the world's most important daily newspaper. The sign outside the nearby Xuan Trang Cafeteria, as well as the establishment's business card, prominently acknowledged that it was "Listed in the Lonely Planet." "Check the 1999 (5th Edition) of the Lonely Planet," the sign instructed passersby. "They love us[.] We hope you will too." The News Cafe next door seemed modest by way of comparison: "Has Been in the Lonely Planet," its sign casually informed potential customers.

Businesses in Ho Chi Minh City, like their counterparts elsewhere, have recognized the power of the publishing house. Sidewalk vendors sell pirated copies of its titles to not just Vietnam but also to other Asian and Pacific destinations. The women and children who peddle books in the restaurants of the Pham Ngu Lao backpacker district invariably carry, alongside Graham Greene's *The Quiet American*, the latest Lonely Planet wares. And in the city's Linh Cafe, a tour guide from the highland town of Dalat was advertising his services in 2000 with a sign listing, by edition and page number, where the writers for Lonely Planet had said nice things about his business. The words "Lonely Planet" were by far the largest on the sign, and they were the only ones in color.

Whereas Lonely Planet has worked hard to cultivate its image as a progressive outfit for conscientious travelers — in every guidebook, for example, the editors tout the company's contributions to aid projects, human-rights campaigns, and wildlife conservation — its volumes for Vietnam have remained wedded to only the most conventional interpretations of the American war.[13] While perhaps an improvement over the remarkable explanation of the Let's Go guidebook for the basis of U.S. involvement — "With the withdrawal of the French came the arrival of the Americans, who assumed responsibility for the survival of democracy by providing financial aid and military advice to South Vietnam," the New York-based publishing house asserted — Lonely Planet's framework has nevertheless remained deficient by the standards of contemporary scholarly opinion.[14] Understanding of the Vietnam conflict has been forcefully contested for decades, yet no such debates appeared within the pages of the Lonely

Planet (or its competitors). Shunning the view of many scholars that the United States was engaged in imperial aggression, the publishing house opted for a bland, unreliable narrative framed within a mythical construct. The conflict was a "North–South War" in which eventually "enter[ed] the Americans," its Vietnam volume maintained.[15] Given the guidebook's origins, this is perhaps not surprising.

The author of the second through fourth editions, Robert Storey, described himself in an interview as "very anti-Communist"—although this was not disclosed to Lonely Planet's readers—and believed that the war was "absolutely not immoral or even wrong." It "was a mistake because we lost," he claimed, "[b]ut it would have been immoral to have done nothing . . . to have sat back and watched [Vietnam] taken over."[16] The maintenance of such a framework is important. The little scholarship that exists on guidebooks has focused largely on how they present tourism sites and local peoples or contribute to "travel cultures." The recollection of a writer for the *New Yorker* would seem to provide an excellent primary source for this genre, for example. "In the late nineteen-eighties," wrote Tad Friend, "I traveled in Asia for a year, and the Lonely Planet guides were my lifeline."

> I ate and slept where they told me to, on Khao San Road in Bangkok and Anjuna Beach in Goa; I oriented myself by their scrupulous if naïvely drawn maps; and on long bus rides I immersed myself in the Indonesia book's explanation of the Ramayana story. The guides didn't tell me to wear drawstring pants and Tintin T-shirts or to crash my moped—I picked that up on my own—but they did teach me, as they taught a whole generation, how to move through the world alone and with confidence.
>
> I learned to stuff my gear into one knapsack; never to ask a local where I should eat but, rather, where *he* ate; never to judge a country by its capital city; never to stay near a mosque (the muezzin wakes you); how to haggle; and, crucially, when I later went to Mongolia, to shout "*Nokhoi khor!*"—"Hold the dog!"—before entering a yurt. When you spend months with a guidebook that speaks to you in an intimate, conversational tone, it becomes a bosom companion.[17]

Yet while studies of the relationship between guidebooks and tourist behavior are vitally important, almost entirely neglected has been the volumes' influence in constructing or shaping historical consciousness and memory.

It is undoubtedly true that people read guidebooks in different ways and are capable of problematizing their narratives. However, interviews in Vietnam with dozens of tourists reveal that the guidebooks' representations of the past, while perhaps too brief, are by and large considered reliable and reasonably "objective." "I love Lonely Planet," exclaimed an American investment banker in his mid-twenties during a two-week holiday in 2002. The guidebook's synopsis of the Vietnam war was "pretty unbiased" and "informative," he claimed.[18] A thirty-four-year-old American businesswoman living in Hong Kong felt similarly. She "always" relied on Lonely Planet when traveling in Asia, she disclosed. And given the independence of perspective demonstrated in its "good summary" of the American intervention, she was certain, but was mistaken, that it could not have been written by one of her compatriots, who undoubtedly would have revealed a bias.[19]

The comments speak both to guidebooks' ability to present themselves as trusted arbiters of historical truth and of the extent to which the Vietnam war — at least prior to the Iraq invasion of 2003 — had become divorced in popular consciousness from the possibility of U.S. imperialism. While guidebooks do not, of course, provide "objective" accounts of the past for their readers — a seeming impossibility, Peter Novick has asserted — their power of signification resides in their *appearance* of objectivity.[20] As straightforward recollections of the past, according to many tourists, the guidebooks assume unusual importance to foreign travelers whose only other source of information may be the ideologically charged narratives at Vietnamese museums and historic sites. In this way, the socially constructed nature of the guidebooks' accounts is elided, and their efficacy is enhanced. Historical "reality," at least as conveyed in the travel literature, therefore demands scholarly analysis.

Whether in assessing guidebook narratives or examining the touristic experiences of contemporary Western travelers, Vietnam's late-twentieth-century emergence as a major tourism destination raises a host of questions. What can Vietnamese tourism tell us about American memory and national identity? What is revealed by historicizing this social and cultural practice? With tourism and travel writing a "contact zone," to borrow a term from Mary Louise Pratt, what happens when popular American narratives of the war collide with the quite different narratives constructed by Vietnamese?[21] What are the implications of this collision of nationalisms? And how have Vietnamese constructed their tourism sites to accommodate the expectations or desires of American visitors?

The chapters that follow seek to answer these and other questions.

WAR, TOURISM, AND THE UNITED STATES IN VIETNAM

This book was written at a time when we have again been reminded that the Vietnam war is not merely a distant chapter of the American past. The war's inherent imbalance — its pitting of the world's most powerful industrial state against a developing nation of peasants and workers — was reflected in the emotionally charged trade disputes over Vietnam's exportation of catfish and shrimp. Its memory dominated the 2004 U.S. presidential contest, a race that, for the two major parties, pitted a blue-blooded (onetime) antiwar veteran who saw combat in Vietnam against a wealthy oilman who sought to escape the front lines as a (sometime) member of the Texas Air National Guard. At the level of intellectual culture, the Vietnam war's relevance and "lessons" were being passionately debated as the United States, three decades after evacuating Saigon, again found itself mired in two bitter land wars in Asia.

Yet, since 1975, much has also changed. Perhaps most significantly, Americans, following the war's official end, had been subjected to a popular culture offensive that reimaged the Vietnamese conflict as one of U.S. victimization at the hands of inscrutable Southeast Asians. Within the seeming blink of an eye, the Vietnam war of *Hearts and Minds* (1974) had become the "Vietnam" — a war, not a country — of *The Deer Hunter* (1978) and *Rambo: First Blood Part II* (1985). In the wake of this cultural shift, an increasing number of young Americans began traveling to Vietnam, especially after the early 1990s, to see something of the country for themselves. They arrived carrying not just backpacks and cameras but guidebooks and ideological suppositions. They were not seeing Vietnam for the first time; they had seen "Vietnam" already. It had been on the big screen dozens of times and had been discussed ad infinitum by political leaders and the media as a "syndrome" to be overcome or a history to be forgotten. Nor were these intrepid travelers touring the country without direction. They had their trusted guidebooks to help show them the way.

Unbeknownst to most of them, they were blazing a trail that had, in fact, already been blazed many years before. While the 1990s marked the first time that Vietnam began to attract hundreds of thousands of foreign visitors for reasons other than war, the country has a relatively long history of tourism. In the early twentieth century, Europeans and Americans often used Saigon as a point of departure for the Angkor ruins in Cambodia. The city, according to a 1920s guidebook for French Indochina, seemed a "natural halting place at the crossing" of "two of the world's great touristic currents," one of which ran from Europe through India and Java and the other of which ran from the United States through China, Japan, and the Philippines.[22] As the post–World War Two emergence of a broad American consumer class and, in the late 1950s, commercial jet travel made Asian tourism more accessible, the government of the Republic of Vietnam entered the business, publishing guidebooks and pamphlets, sponsoring hotel construction, and attempting to improve the region's primitive infrastructure.[23] The southern state, officials claimed in a promotional pamphlet, was ideally suited to serve foreign tourists as "an 'all year round' vacation land."[24] Of course, this effort, which began in the mid- to late 1950s and continued for over a decade, coincided with the escalation of the American political and military commitment, and the two inevitably became intertwined. The roads that would be necessary to transport tourists were the same roads subsidized and used by the U.S. military. The international-standard hotels built to lodge scores of foreign travelers were quickly occupied by American officials and companies. And the Vietnamese countryside that was central to the south's touristic charm emerged by the early 1960s as a site of widespread insurgency and devastation. All of these affected the once promising tourism industry. War became, in every sense, the principal barrier to Vietnamese travel. Decades later, its memory would ironically serve as one of the country's principal attractions.[25]

Departing from the extant literature on the Vietnam war, this book traverses the intersections of history, tourism, and memory by examining how the West—and, most specifically, the United States—experienced Vietnam as a site of Cold War touristic pleasure and, after 1975, as a "cartography of memory" on which an important chapter of the American (and, of course, Vietnamese) past was written.[26] In doing so, it argues that tourism has been (and, in important ways, has continued to be) intertwined with the projection of American power. I show how tourism's attendant literature—guidebooks, pamphlets, brochures, et cetera—has historically served both to construct contemporary ideological realities in the minds of travelers as well as shape their understandings of the very recent past, almost always in ways favorable to American global ambitions. I contend that, historically speaking, the narratives attached to tourism practices and publications are consistent with an American "selective tradition" evident at the level of popular discourse that since 1975 has largely precluded considerations of the United States as an imperial nation. The book is thus more than just a (very partial) history of American tourism in Vietnam. It is, in a broader sense, a focused case study of history writing. Drawing on twentieth-century travel documents for that country, *Tours of Vietnam* examines the ways in which historical reality became identified and, often, circumscribed for thousands of Americans and other Westerners experiencing Vietnam as a tourism destination.

I take as a starting point two basic assumptions. First, as the Haitian scholar Michel-Rolph Trouillot has persuasively argued, I assume that power and the narrative construction of the past are inextricably linked. The "production of historical narratives," wrote Trouillot, "involves the uneven contribution of competing groups and individuals who have unequal access to the means for such production."[27] I maintain that travel writers, whether official or civilian, have possessed the power to define historical knowledge for thousands of tourists who are generally ignorant of the Vietnamese past other than the discourses deduced from Hollywood films and, in fewer instances, long-ago school study. And second, I assume, as do many diplomatic historians, that the United States is not an exceptional global power. It has, in short, been an imperial actor — one concerned, like others before it and since, with the management of a vast, if at times informal, overseas empire.[28]

Travel and tourism, I believe, provide an excellent interpretive lens for addressing larger issues of ideology and the construction of history. Through tourism we can analyze how states and peoples have crafted historical narratives, how travelers have experienced landscapes riven with memory, and how battles over remembrance can erupt among tourists exposed to alternative stories of the past. Operating at a level that we might call experiential historiography, tourists have debated and embraced various narratives of "Vietnam" just as vigorously as have professional scholars. By addressing these touristic encounters, this book seeks to explore not only the power of the war to notions of American identity thirty, forty, or fifty years ago, but also its continued potency three decades after the conflict officially ended.

I am by no means the first historian to take up international tourism as an issue of academic concern. In *Cold War Holidays*, for instance, Christopher Endy showed how tourism was employed to serve the interests of both Paris and Washington in the years following the Second World War.[29] An official component of the Marshall Plan, American travel to France not only delivered dollars to rebuilding states in need of foreign exchange but, importantly, was intended to help develop a sense of transatlantic solidarity in the emerging Cold War. That tourists themselves often shunned this sort of politically purposeful travel — unless, that is, it was tied to consumerist impulses — inevitably frustrated elites in the United States. Yet in addressing tourism's location within the framework of diplomatic relations, broadly conceived, Endy invaluably drew attention to the ways in which international travel was imbued with ideological meaning. So, too, did Neal Moses Rosendorf. Taking as his focus the efforts by the Franco regime in Spain to use tourism as a means of obtaining dollars and improving its troubled reputation — apart from its dictatorial nature, Madrid had essentially been allied with the Axis during World War Two — Rosendorf skillfully outlined Spain's desire to transform itself from fascist collaborator to holiday paradise after 1945.[30] Cooperation with Hollywood and American travel boosters offered an important means of doing so. While perhaps not as closely associated with the United States as was the Franco regime's campaign in Spain, Nazi Germany also drew on tourism's diplomatic potential, believing it could be used "to improve international relations in Germany's favor," wrote Kristin Semmens. By witnessing the accomplishments of the "new Germany" for themselves, the regime believed, travelers would discover "the truth" behind the negative images "evoked" by what Nazi tourism officials termed the "malevolent press abroad."[31]

Whereas this earlier scholarship focused on the United States and Europe, however, my concern is with American travel in the Third World. The Republic of Vietnam, like a number of European states, employed tourism as a means of furthering its international legitimacy. Several dissimilarities, however, distinguished Saigon's position from those of Paris, Madrid, or Berlin. The issue of nation-building that was so central to the

U.S. enterprise in Vietnam, for example, was not a factor in postwar American relations with France or Spain. Much like Puerto Rico — a subject that has been ably addressed by Dennis Merrill — in southern Vietnam tourism became intertwined with the American desire for Cold War modernization.[32] Yet unlike in the Caribbean commonwealth, it was necessary for the RVN government to negotiate its developmental agenda within the context of a revolutionary insurgency and warfare. *Tours of Vietnam* also departs from most previous studies in that it is not concerned only with the Cold War history of Americans abroad. While past experiences do, in fact, form a substantial part of this book, it also addresses tourism's relevance to contemporary issues of memory.[33] What, in other words, can recent travel in Vietnam tell us about how Americans (and, to a lesser extent, other Westerners) remember, or construct a narrative of, their nation's experience in Vietnam thirty or forty years prior? How is tourism, as a transnational process, implicated in the ongoing battles over American memory? Is there something significant in Americans visiting the site of their nation's most controversial twentieth-century war?

I believe there is. In the United States, where mainstream intellectual culture has tended to be dominated by a story of liberal democracy and benevolent American power, popular historical narratives have generally adhered to notions of a well-intentioned America providing enlightened global leadership. It is true, the basic narrative concedes, that Washington may have installed or supported numerous tyrants throughout the twentieth century, but this was an unfortunate if necessary compromise of American ideals in pursuit of otherwise worthy goals: stability, uplift, or even, paradoxically, democracy.[34] Travel to Vietnam, where tourists often cannot help but be exposed to an alternative narrative of the United States, carries with it the potential to challenge this popular American view. Whether through time spent at the War Remnants Museum, the witnessing of Vietnamese missing limbs, or the sight of still present bomb craters when flying into or out of Hanoi, the ostensibly benevolent nature of American global power has repeatedly been tested through specific reference to the Vietnam conflict.

This test underlies much of the book that follows. Drawing on a wide array of sources from across many decades, its chapters represent an effort to connect the threads of history, memory, and tourism. As a site of Americans' contested national memory, Vietnam offers a unique focus for such a study. For far too many people in the United States, Vietnam represents a war, not a country. But for the thousands of tourists who have begun exploring the Southeast Asian state, the "Vietnam" of American memory may slowly begin emerging as the Vietnam of twenty-first-century reality.

1

Tourism and State Legitimacy

in the Republic of Vietnam

"[Saigon] affects me like a fine wine. There is . . . something in the air, in the rhythm, in the soft water, a somnolence, a richness, something exquisite, a lightness, a quick smile, fleet foot." Thus wrote the American photographer Dorothea Lange during a weeks-long tour of southern Vietnam in 1958. The enchantment Lange experienced in Saigon, she conceded, came as "a great [s]urprise."[1] Such warm sentiments were sure to please the tourism authorities in the newly minted Republic of Vietnam (RVN). Beginning in the late 1950s, as commercial jet travel become possible and Americans took a greater interest in visiting the Far East, the government of the RVN sought, like several of its Asian neighbors, to place Vietnam on the global tourism map. While lacking a single world-class attraction such as the Angkor ruins of Cambodia, Vietnam did offer beautiful pastoral vistas, hundreds of miles of placid coastline, outstanding big-game hunting, several architectural treasures, and a vibrant and — to those from the West, at least — exotic cultural life. The "time has come to develop and promote tourism in Vietnam," a Saigon newspaper urged in 1957.[2] With the proper investment, the potential existed. Whereas the Viet Minh's nearly decade-long war with France after World War Two had created an unfavorable travel environment, within the first few years of the Ngo Dinh Diem era the possibility of international tourism re-emerged.[3]

The reasons for this renewed interest were several. At the most basic level, officials hoped tourism would assist with economic growth, pumping foreign currency into a corner of Southeast Asia battered for years by unrelenting warfare. Yet it was not simply a matter of capturing dollars and francs. As the director of the National Tourist Office suggested in a 1958 report to Diem, tourism's contribution to improvements in technology, transportation, and commerce would aid in the state's development in multiple ways, providing not just economic but political, social, and cultural benefits as well.[4] For a government facing questions both internally and externally about its political legitimacy, this was an important consideration. Born out of the 1954 Geneva Accords that explicitly precluded the seventeenth parallel from serving as a permanent "political or territorial boundary," the Republic of Vietnam — or what became known colloquially as South Vietnam — was essentially a U.S. creation.[5] That it was ruled by a Catholic despot in an overwhelmingly Buddhist nation — one who enjoyed little popular support and routinely employed terror as his preferred method of suasion — only added to the authorities' difficulties. International tourism thus came to assume a notable role in the Saigon government's cultural diplomacy campaign. In particular, tourism carried the potential to generate positive sentiments about the southern state that would translate into popular support and diplomatic goodwill, serving the interests of both America and its client in a variety of ways. Indeed, a motto of the National Tourist Office was "to make the country better known and thus better loved."[6]

This effort by the Saigon government meshed nicely with the American concern for Vietnamese nation building. A functioning tourism industry, after all, signaled state normalcy; this normalcy, in turn, suggested state legitimacy. Given the RVN government's competition with not only Hanoi but, after 1960, the southern National Liberation Front, this question of legitimacy was a paramount concern in both Washington and Saigon. As Vietnamese opposition to the Diem regime spread and, in the early 1960s, as direct American intervention increased, tourism began to serve U.S. and RVN interests at an important symbolic level. Through both its tourism publications and the practical experiences of foreign visitors, Vietnamese authorities presented an image of the southern state that made it seem welcome to U.S. assistance. Suggesting that Vietnam and Vietnamese aspired to be like America and Americans — capitalist, democratic, et cetera — the Vietnamese tourism literature confirmed modernization theorists' prescription for a tumultuous Third World. The intended audience of such publications may have been ordinary American travelers, but it was clear that the political benefits of tourism would accrue to American policymakers as well.

Indeed, the growth of Vietnamese tourism in the late 1950s coincided with Washington's increased interest in American leisure in Asia and elsewhere in the Third World. That travel was a political activity was recognized by both civilian and military officials; tourism's proper development, it was believed, could serve important U.S. geostrategic objectives. Dwight Eisenhower, for instance, remained an enthusiastic proponent of Americans' international travel, repeatedly recognizing its potential contributions to U.S. foreign policy.[7] In a 17 April 1958 report requested by Eisenhower, to cite just one example, Clarence B. Randall, a special assistant to the president and former chairman of the Commission on Foreign Economic Policy, outlined tourism's many benefits. Pointing in particular to "the Pacific area," Randall noted that "Americans are eagerly searching out new areas to visit and their travel expenditures could be of great assistance to the developing countries" seeking "increased dollar earnings." Yet the cultural aspects of travel "may be of even greater importance," he continued. While the media "tell their interesting story" about foreign locales, the "impact of personal experience is deeper and more lasting." The sorts of "direct personal relationship[s]" that travel afforded enriched "the lives of both the traveler and his host," with "each borrowing from the other in customs, manners, and philosophy of life." At a time when American officials were deeply invested in planting the seeds of liberal capitalism in much of the decolonizing world, this was no small concern. In this respect, Randall asserted, "American overseas travelers," if they "measure[d] up to their responsibilities" by comporting themselves honorably, could serve as "ambassadors of good will," developing "effective contacts between Americans traveling abroad and their foreign hosts" while concurrently imparting "a clearer idea of the friendly reception and special attractions to be found in the United States."[8]

Not only, therefore, could cordial personal exchanges bolster the Cold War policies of various American administrations, putting a human face to a nation viewed with considerable suspicion by much of the Third World, but the dollars spent by Americans abroad provided the dollars necessary

for states to import American goods, thus helping to grow the same boom-
ing economy that made leisurely pursuits such as international travel possible. At the same time, however, cultural ignorance or bad behavior by
Americans abroad could potentially prove devastating to U.S. foreign relations. Americans who "assume[d] an air of arrogance" or transgressed "the
common bonds of decency," the State Department warned in a pamphlet
issued to all U.S. passport holders, could "do more in the course of an hour
to break down elements of friendly approach between peoples than the
Government can do in the course of a year in trying to stimulate friendly
relations."[9] Tourism, in other words, was a transnational practice imbued
with political meaning. Respectful comportment was therefore critical.
This was especially the case if, as Francis J. Colligan, an official tasked with
U.S. cultural diplomacy, advised, "further encouragement should be given
to trips to areas of the world which few Americans visit."[10] Vietnam, by
virtually any measure in the 1950s, certainly fit that bill.

MARKETING VIETNAM

Even as Vietnamese tourism peaked in the early 1960s, the number of
international arrivals never reached the level of Japan or India, let alone
that of France or Germany. In part this was a function of the RVN government's lack of serious commitment to the comprehensive and sustained
development of the tourism industry; like its counterpart in the north, it
placed much greater emphasis on rice production and industrialization. In
part the failure to attract large numbers of tourists was a function of the
competition for visitors in which nearby states seemed better positioned.
Vietnam was not usually considered a stand-alone destination but, the
authorities hoped, would attract transit passengers traveling elsewhere in
Asia. And in part it was a function — especially as the 1960s progressed — of
Vietnam's political instability and hazardous travel environment. Yet tourism in southern Vietnam was never merely about luring tens of thousands
of sun-seeking visitors to the fledgling state. Rather, the cultural work
performed by international tourism could contribute to the government's
quest for political legitimization, thus helping to fulfill one of the RVN's
chief diplomatic objectives.[11]

It is not that Vietnam lacked the prerequisites of a successful tourism
outlook. In a 1957 article in *Holiday* magazine, for example, Santha Rama
Rau extolled the virtues of the "stripling Asian nation," with its "French

styles and manners," that contained "all the exotic splendor of the Orient." Saigon retained its pleasant colonial atmosphere: "an ornate opera house, a red brick cathedral, charming homes, boulevards, sidewalk cafes, and the ubiquitous advertisements for *Byrrh* or *Bastos* cigarettes." The beach resort of Cap Saint-Jacques possessed "wide boulevards, shady pastel villas, and French hotels where you can eat the tiny, excellent shrimps and oysters of the China Sea" or "dance in the tepid tropical evenings under the coconut palms by the phosphorescent ocean surf." Elsewhere along the coast, Nha Trang, "with its beautiful harbor and beaches where the tide is like the 'roar of a tiger,'" contained "extraordinary marine life" viewable on one of the glass-bottomed boats that glided over the beds of coral. Hue, "situated on a river the color of celadon," was a "dim echo of the Forbidden City in Peking—imperial palaces and pavilions with lacquered columns, doors painted with golden dragons, huge bronze urns flanking shallow stairways that lead to gardens and pools." Yet "probably the pleasantest resort built by the French," Rau maintained, "is Dalat," which was recognized for two "distinctions": "its excellent hunting (as varied as the more publicized game of Africa and India, and far cheaper), and its extraordinary mountain tribes" whose "strange little villages" and "barefoot and half naked" appearances provided endless fascination.[12]

Two years later, in 1959, *Travel* magazine likewise published an encouraging feature on Vietnam. While war had ravaged Indochina until 1954, wrote Richard Tregaskis, the well-known author of *Guadalcanal Diary*, "the land remained beautiful and various, a bright-colored array of ancient tradition with purposeful overlays of modernity." True, there appeared occasional reminders of the earlier French–Viet Minh conflict as well as a pressing need for infrastructural improvements, but Saigon was "beautiful," Hue was "handsome," and Nha Trang was "dazzling." In general, insisted Tregaskis, Vietnam's sites "were as spectacular as represented" in the artful posters prepared by the National Tourist Office.[13]

Yet the *Travel* essay was not intended to simply extol southern Vietnam's undeniable charms. Much more explicitly than Rau's article in *Holiday*, Tregaskis, who was assisted by the authorities at various times in his and his wife's tour, situated the Republic of Vietnam within the American modernization project, effusively praising its government. For the author, there was no doubt that southern Vietnam was one of four "independent states" to have emerged out of the "colonial domain of French Indo-

China."[14] It was, moreover, "democratic," with a government "elected by universal suffrage" for which the "southern or 'free' Vietnamese are intensely proud." Despite his occasional references to the "wild men" or "half-naked brown savages of the mountain tribes plodding along the road barefoot" — all part of Vietnam's "adventures," he cheerfully noted — Tregaskis was impressed with the RVN's lurching "transition from medievalism to self-determination and modernity." He repeatedly pointed to the infusion of U.S. foreign aid and technical advice that would be happily witnessed by future tourists — he employed "you" in directly addressing his Western readers — from "new patches of waving sugar cane fostered by American agricultural consultants" to "cattle-breeding stations," "rows of young rubber trees of the more productive variety," assembly plants for "Italian-made motor scooters," and "small French taxis" and hundreds of trucks, all built with or supplied by U.S. foreign aid.[15]

Recognizing the contribution of the "promptly created" state-subsidized airline to both Vietnamese tourism and the larger modernization mission, the "patriotic Vietnamese," Tregaskis maintained, hoped to "become prosperous, distinguished independent members of the family of nations." He had no doubt that this goal would be realized. Already "the challenge of setting up a system of tourism was being tackled vigorously" in the "new, proud little nation," Tregaskis wrote.[16] In 1959, for instance, the RVN was represented for the first time by multiple delegates at the annual conference of the Pacific Area Travel Association (PATA), which was held that year in Singapore.[17] The Vietnamese authorities "are working hard," Tregaskis insisted, "and what we feel was sort of a preview peek at its advancement has convinced us that beautiful Vietnam will take its rightful place as a true traveler's goal in tomorrow's world of easy access by jet."[18]

While perhaps not quite as optimistic as Tregaskis, RVN sympathizers and U.S. economic officials were nevertheless hopeful. In 1958, Lieutenant-General John W. "Iron Mike" O'Daniel (Ret.), former chief of the Military Assistance Advisory Group in Vietnam and, after 1955, chair of American Friends of Vietnam (AFV), concluded after a month long visit to the southern state that hotel rooms were in perilously short supply and that new highways would need to be completed before the "tourist business" could "get underway." Yet O'Daniel was encouraged. Having discussed these matters with the director of the National Tourist Office, the AFV leader reported that the director "appears to be aware of the things that need to be done."[19] By 1961, the U.S. Department of Commerce, in a study co-sponsored by PATA, was rating the south's "tourism potentials" as "fair to good." Saigon, considered Vietnam's likely principal attraction, possessed an "unmistakable French atmosphere, French-style bistros, and sidewalk cafes" that lent the city "great appeal," the report concluded. Moreover, its "strategic position with respect to air transportation" rendered it a "convenient and interesting stopping off or transiting point" for travelers.[20] The RVN authorities agreed, issuing a pamphlet in 1961 whose cover advised tourists that they could "discover Vietnam at no extra cost," stopping in Saigon "on [their] way to Hongkong, Manila, Bangkok, Singapore, and Angkor Wat."[21] What was needed to maximize the south's tourism potential, the Commerce Department recommended, was "top-level support by the Government and technical assistance," neither of which, with the south experiencing substantial political unrest, was fully forthcoming.[22]

Nevertheless, tourists did make the trip.[23] Whereas 1957 recorded only 13,250 international arrivals, by 1960 that figure had nearly doubled, to 24,256. The number of visitors increased even further — to 37,783 in 1961 — before stagnating and then falling below 30,000 with the war's gradual escalation.[24] The figure remained there until 1967, when the number of arrivals increased to 34,312.[25] It increased further, to 61,215 in 1969, and then surpassed 72,000 in 1970.[26] The statistics are somewhat misleading, however, because only a fraction of these international arrivals — especially after the Kennedy administration increased its military commitment to the RVN's preservation in 1961 — were persons traveling to Vietnam solely for purposes of sightseeing. By the mid-1960s, most were coming because of their involvement in the war. In 1964, for instance, Americans represented the largest group of visitors, with 8,945 arrivals. (The United States was followed by France, Taiwan, Japan, and the United Kingdom.) But of these Americans, 8,500 were identified as officials, 328 were "businessmen," and only 117 were what might be considered traditional tourists.[27] Even among these non-sightseers, however, many spent their time off touring portions of the country. Indeed, they were generally encouraged to do so. A 1958 booklet for American residents jointly presented by the U.S. Operations Mission to Vietnam and the American Women's Association of Saigon noted that "improvements in security and in the road systems" meant that "more and more of the countryside can be visited by motorists," as well as those traveling by air or rail. The booklet included useful information on various sites, from Long Hai, which was "a favorite spot with Americans," to Nha Trang and Dalat, which were also "favorite recreational spot[s]." With its "delightfully cool climate," the authors wrote, the last provided a "rejuvenating experience after life in the humid lowlands."[28] By 1962, however, motoring the countryside was considered ill advised. The anti-Diem insurgency had escalated, rendering casual sightseeing too dangerous. A revised edition of the booklet thus limited its recommendations for weekend travel to only three southern cities, all of them reachable by air: Dalat, Nha Trang, and Hue.[29] While precise figures are not available, logic suggests that the number of tourists, whether resident foreigners or holiday travelers, would have continued to shrink as the war escalated through the end of the decade. Indeed, as even the director of the National Tourist Office (NTO) — whose job it was to champion Vietnamese tourism — conceded to a journalist in 1967, "It's rather risky to go far from Saigon."[30] This was hardly the stuff from which dreams of exotic travel are made.

Yet, as noted earlier, tourism in the Republic of Vietnam was never solely about earning dollars and cents. It served an important ideological purpose, which the government, with the aid of Western travel writers, did not to hesitate to pursue. Just as the United States saw tourists as "ambassadors of good will" in promoting American foreign policy objectives, so, too, did the Saigon government hope that foreign visitors would champion its cause. The Commerce Department, in fact, had explicitly highlighted this benefit in its 1961 report on travel in the Pacific and Far East, writing that among the forms of wealth that tourism would deliver to the region's developing states was "good will and understanding," something that, with respect to Diem and the RVN, seemed increasingly in short supply.[31] Yet with the news media more and more representing Vietnam as a focus of simmering Cold War tensions, getting people to consider traveling to Vietnam was a challenge. In the late 1950s and early 1960s, therefore, the RVN tourism authorities sought to emphasize the area's evident touristic appeal to a broad global audience. In this vein, the fledgling state produced guidebooks, pamphlets, posters, and brochures that constructed southern Vietnam as an exotic paradise rather than a site of insurgency and state repression. By highlighting the RVN's hundreds of miles of beautiful coastline and coral reefs, its thrilling big-game hunting in the mountainous interior, or its cosmopolitan capital as the "Pearl of the Orient," travel literature provided alternative representations of Vietnam from those too often appearing in Hollywood films or the Western press.

Within this genre, which on the surface appeared to be simply a means of marketing southern Vietnam's many charms, the discursive appeal for political legitimacy was evident.[32] Cognizant that tourists were often interested in history and cultural heritage—and, importantly, that the materials could be distributed abroad by RVN embassies to influence foreigners with no immediate plans to visit Indochina—the authorities used the state-generated travel literature, often in combination with other publications, to subtly suggest that the Saigon regime, as opposed to the revolutionaries challenging it, was the true inheritor of Vietnam's patriotic tradition.[33] The materials' narratives were written in such a way that readers could easily believe the U.S.-created and -supported government to be the sole indigenous force fulfilling Vietnam's historical mandate of national independence. By portraying Hanoi or the southern revolutionaries as Communist interlopers seeking to violently spread the "foreign ideology" of China and the Soviet Union, Vietnamese travel writers presented the RVN authorities as valiantly defending against this unprovoked international aggression.

If Western guidebooks in the 1960s generally felt compelled to address the reality of an escalating Vietnamese war, as will be seen later, the tourism literature generated in the RVN from the late 1950s through 1975 was more ambivalent in confronting the conflict. On the one hand, war is generally bad for tourism—most travelers do not wish to flirt with death while spending their holidays abroad—so the authorities largely sought to mask its visibility in their touristic representations of the south.[34] But on the other hand, the Saigon government faced a severe crisis of legitimacy, and tourism and tourism documents could be one way of spreading its message to a global audience. What one therefore found in many Vietnamese pamphlets, guidebooks, and brochures as the war escalated was a failure to acknowledge its unmistakable omnipresence in much of the RVN coupled with a nod—sometimes subtle, sometimes not—to the Saigon government's military struggle against supposed Communist aggression.

Tourism authorities and the regime's supporters addressed this conundrum through a variety of means. Revealing their transnational sensibilities, for example, tourism publications described the Republic of

Vietnam as committed to modernization — a concept increasingly crucial to American policymakers' objectives for the Third World — yet one that nevertheless adhered to the traditions still governing daily Vietnamese life. "Vast programs of community development, construction, social reform, education, and modernization" were contributing to "a transformation that is taking place so rapidly that it is impossible for the visitor to remain unaware of it," an official pamphlet insisted in 1961. At a time when the Saigon regime was receiving vast quantities of U.S. aid, foreign tourists were assured by the RVN authorities that the southern state, "under the leadership of President Ngo Dinh Diem," was "emerging as one of the most stalwart members of the family of Free Nations."[35]

Yet, it was clear, modernization alone would not entice tourists. Why travel to Southeast Asia, after all, to witness what could be seen in the United States? The RVN's rapid modernization therefore had to be conjoined with the exoticism of Vietnamese traditional life if the authorities hoped to lure international visitors. Whereas modernization and anti-Communism may have provided the ideological template that ennobled travel to the RVN, the conjunction of Vietnamese "tradition" and the region's colonial French heritage would provide its visual appeal. The literature provided a ready means of marketing this facet of Vietnam. For instance, a 1957 volume explained that Saigon owed its designation as the "Pearl of the Orient" to "the verdure in which it is clad, as well as to its exotic character." The public monuments erected in the city in the early twentieth century, the authors wrote, conserved "a national architecture which contrasts with the modern style of the new buildings." This "mixture of the traditional and the modern," they continued, "constitutes the attraction of Saigon."[36] A later National Tourist Office pamphlet offered a similar vision of contrasts. "Broad, shady boulevards bisect modern business centers, but huts stand in the shade of great buildings; tourists," it continued, "shop for mangos and mangosteens in the fascinating markets and visit Cantonese pagodas silent as the centuries" while "big, luxurious cars compete with horse carts," and "Oriental bazaars" abound.[37] In a guide to the capital city, the NTO captured the broader sentiment, insisting, "Visitors will be amazed by [Saigon's] physionomy, a happy combination of old Oriental civilization and blooming modernism."[38] The visible conjunction of the traditional and the modern, then, revealed Vietnam to be an exciting destination for foreigner travelers while, importantly, confirming for Americans that the Vietnamese embraced the modernization mission espoused by the United States.

While in some instances the political nature of the era's tourism publications could be quite subtle — referring to the southern Vietnamese regrouping zone as "Free Vietnam," for example — at other times their political underpinnings were unabashedly explicit.[39] *Your Guide to Vietnam*, a document published by the National Tourist Office at some point between 1960 and 1962, was emblematic of the former. According to its authors, the area below the seventeenth parallel was called the "Free Republic of Vietnam," a name whose adjective ("Free") masked the repression of the Saigon government and was sure to resonate with an American audience (that is, the "free world"), while the use of "Republic of Vietnam" suggested a wholly legitimate state not established in contravention of the 1954 Geneva Accords. Conversely, the northern regrouping zone had no name but simply remained "under Communist control." At no point in the guide could tourists read about an entity called the Democratic Republic of Vietnam.[40] Elsewhere, and consistent with the same sentiment, the two zones were referred to as "the Free Republic and the Communist-held North."[41] And lest any doubt remained about which political entity was the legitimate mantle of Vietnamese nationalist sentiment, Saigon was said by the National Tourist Office — like the government more broadly — to be the capital of "Vietnam" (that is, of all of Vietnam, as opposed to the Republic of Vietnam, or "South Vietnam").[42]

Slightly more explicit was *Visit Fascinating Vietnam*, a pamphlet published to coincide with the designation of 1961 as "Visit the Orient Year." Like other publications, this one spoke glowingly of the "Free Republic of Vietnam," including, importantly, the welcome it offered to "about one million happily resettled refugees" from the north.[43] For Americans exposed to the harrowing plight of these mostly Catholic northerners in the mid-1950s — whether in *Reader's Digest*, secular and Catholic newspapers, Tom Dooley's bestselling book *Deliver Us From Evil*, or the television drama *Navy Log* — the allusion to the happy resettlement of the "refugees" served to link the southern government to the humanitarian impulse that most Americans believed drove U.S. foreign policy.[44] Travel to the RVN could thus be considered a demonstration of one's patriotic commitment to a like-minded Cold War ally. "Vietnam has lived through more than her share of kingdoms and dynasties, colonization and internal partition," the

Visit Fascinating Vietnam authors asserted, "but today, under the leadership of President Ngo Dinh Diem," the RVN was emerging as a devoted member of the American-led "family" of free peoples.[45] For those in the West, venturing to the south could thus serve as a symbolic affirmation of one's support for the anti-Communist struggle.

To entice foreigners, locations were described as attractively exotic yet safely familiar — a slice of Europe in Asia. The highland resort of Dalat was "rather like . . . Geneva, with stately hotels and fashionable villas" as well as "several exclusive little inns of strictly European style" that served food "in the Savoy tradition." Yet in the midst of this Old World comfort, one could still find in the central market "numbers of the many hill tribe people who live deep in the forests."[46] Vung Tau, which "preserves a certain continental charm on its picturesque streets, in its restaurants, and on its beautiful beaches," has, like Nha Trang, "been likened to the Rivera."[47] Similarly, Saigon, where women "patter in French with a Parisian accent," was the "Paris of the Far East" or "the most Parisian city east of the Suez Canal."[48] The RVN capital was "sophisticated" and beautifully adorned; its newest hotel was "decorated with France's St. Gobain glass and Italian marble," and one of its public spaces was constructed like "a typical, spacious French square." And yet,

> everywhere are the street scenes of Oriental life so compelling to foreigners — the rush hour traffic jam, made not by cars, but by scooters; the service station for unlucky bicycles, equipment hanging on a tree or a street corner; the vendors of soup, dried meat, sugar cane juice; the coster mongers with their colorful wares and, *above all, the doe-eyed shapely Vietnamese girls dressed in the most gracious way*.[49]

Saigon, in short, was a city whose "face is French but whose heart is Oriental."[50] With the RVN thus a fascinating blend of the Orient and the Occident, as well as, importantly, a state occupying a "strategic position in Southeast Asia," as the authorities were sure to note, travel there merited tourists' support.[51]

An example of the most blatant sort of politicization of the travel literature was one of the more comprehensive tourism-related volumes of the Diem years. In *A Glimpse of Vietnam*, Bao Dai was characterized as a naïve tool of the French colonialists who sought to "rule through the institution of the monarchy" by "molding it to their designs," rendering the emperor "putty in their hands."[52] The Viet Minh revolutionaries, on the other hand, rode "the shirt tail of the nationalist movement" and attempted "to exploit it to their own advantage." Their undeniable popular support was explained away as rooted in the ignorance of the Vietnamese people:

> The strength of the Viet Minh [immediately after World War Two] was in its appearance as essentially a nationalist movement. French power had been broken and the people were predisposed to support such a successful effort to establish independence. The Communists had gone through the motions of abolishing the Communist Party and making the pretense of pristine nationalism, a fiction which they maintained until 1951 when the Communist apparatus reappeared openly well entrenched in command of the Viet Minh which they had exploited as a front.
>
> It was to a nationalist movement that Bao Dai thought he was rendering the supreme power when he abdicated [to the Democratic Republic of Vietnam in 1945] and it was to such a regime that men like Tran Trong Kim thought they were lending their support. Many found almost too late that they had been duped; some like Bao Dai had a rude and sudden awakening; others realized the true situation only after 1951.[53]

One of those who recognized that the Viet Minh was only "posing as a purely nationalist movement," the authors suggested, was Ngo Dinh Diem. The embattled premier of the south had to contend not only with Communist aggression but also with "a gang of brigands and river pirates" deployed by the French "whose purpose was to thwart and destroy" him. Despite the gravity of the threat, Diem succeeded in overcoming these obstacles while also resettling approximately a million northern Vietnamese who "made their way to freedom in the South," thus "showing their contempt for the Communists."[54]

In its foreign policy, the volume explained, the RVN under Diem had committed itself to "resistance to the Red peril which menaces all free peoples."[55] Domestically, the Saigon authorities had established peace throughout the south, taking over, in "*Operation Liberation*, vast areas of Viet Nam . . . which had been occupied by the Viet Minh," "completely annihilating" the Binh Xuyen rebels, defeating the Hoa Hao sect, and, "in a peaceful way," conducting a "successful all-out campaign against the

Communist underground." Declaring itself a stabilizing presence, the government had established "peace and security . . . for all the territory south of the Seventeenth Parallel, in many instances for the first time since 1945." As a result, "People have drifted back to their villages which they had left years before to begin once more a normal and productive life."[56]

Of course, at an obvious level the corpus of Vietnamese travel literature sought to market the RVN as a land of exotic charm and touristic pleasure, and it did so ably. Yet the literature's deeper purpose in bolstering the Saigon government's legitimacy was unmistakable. Travel publications might be considered a particularly effective tool in the RVN's broader cultural propaganda campaign, as their seemingly apolitical subject matter — tourism and tourist sites — fascinated readers interested in Asia while cloaking the literature's political nature. Toward this end, Vietnamese officials created tourism documents that were widely used for non-touristic purposes. Probably the showcase volume created in this vein was a forty-page booklet published by the RVN's U.S. embassy in 1959 or 1960.[57] Ostensibly a guide for tourists visiting southern Vietnam, the document in fact appears to have been used principally to publicize the appeal of the RVN to the American public, thus promoting the RVN's legitimacy as a sovereign state while engendering political support for the large amounts of aid being provided at the time by Washington.

A Guide to Viet-Nam was a broad overview of the RVN and why it would be of interest to Western tourists. It contained information on festivals, hunting, and beaches, and considerable background on the Vietnamese people and Vietnamese culture. It was also, however, an explicitly political document intended to bolster the Diem regime. The text was bookended, for example, with references to the government's antirevolutionary struggle. Locating Vietnam "at the juncture of East and West," the authors initially distinguished "Communist North Viet-Nam" from the "Free Republic of Viet-Nam in the South," and they concluded their narrative by insisting on the RVN's important role in the global Cold War. "This pamphlet deals primarily with the physical aspects and the picturesque side of Viet-Nam," they wrote. "There is, however, another aspect of Viet-Nam which cannot fail to captivate the tourist: the stimulating picture of the Free Republic of Viet-Nam which remains attached to its ancient heritage while working for economic and social progress." Readers should not dismiss Vietnam as a distant locale of no concern to them, the authors suggested, for "placed at the crossroads of the Far East, and for the time being divided between a Communist regime in the North and a free democratic system in the South, Viet-Nam plays no small part in the ideological contest between the Communist and the Free Worlds."[58]

RVN diplomats cooperated with American Friends of Vietnam, which spearheaded the Vietnam lobby in the United States, in disseminating the booklet to as large an audience as possible.[59] The distribution of the booklets was encouraged in multiple ways. Following a request by the AFV, for example, John Muth of *New York Mirror Magazine* publicized the booklet's gratis availability to the American public in July 1962.[60] In other instances, the publication was distributed to participants in AFV-related events, such as "several hundred" teachers and schoolchildren in 1961.[61] And the *Guide to Viet-Nam* was included in "A Kit for Teachers" prepared by the AFV, for which a thousand copies of the booklet were requested from the RVN embassy in August 1960.[62]

In the case of the last, arrangements were made for the kit to be announced in the Asia Society Calendar, *Social Education, Intercom*, and the UNESCO magazine *Orient-Occident*, as well as over the New York radio station WNYE.[63] Copies were distributed to the Summer Institute for Asian Studies at the State College of Iowa, which administered a summer program for teachers, and to dozens of influential Americans and Vietnamese.[64] By the close of 1962, reported the AFV's executive secretary, sales of the kit had "picked up," with over seventy having been purchased.[65] The guide's inclusion in the teaching kit was certainly ingenious, as the booklet was generously sprinkled with photographs that, unlike the staler verbiage that characterized much overseas propaganda, helped to bring Vietnam to life for school-age children.[66]

Finally, the organization gave the *Guide to Viet-Nam* to interested parties who requested materials with which they could inform others about the Southeast Asian state. One such individual was a Vietnamese student enrolled in a course in the United States on "Education for Mutual Understanding." After initially receiving a complimentary copy of the document (as well as another publication), the student requested five more, as "all my classmates are anxious to know more about Viet Nam" and "I do think that these booklets will help them a lot [in] understanding" the country.[67]

While the RVN generated numerous tourism-related documents intended not only to encourage foreign travelers but to buttress the state's

fragile international legitimacy, the Saigon government was by no means alone in producing tourism materials that sought to cast the RVN's political predicament, as well as the West's relationship with it, in terms favorable to an American audience. Well before the NTO began developing its tourism literature in the 1950s, travel writers had sought to sanitize or even erase the West's imperial dominion over the Vietnamese people. In 1926, for example, author Lucian Swift Kirtland conceded that "French power and authority [in Indochina] are as absolute as any one might care to demand," but added that "the hand of administration wears a velvet glove." Kirtland's view of French colonialism was essentially benign. Considering the "diabolical character of the [region's] climate," he wrote in a discursive reflection of the environment's presumed role in racialized cultural hierarchies, France's "progress of less than a half century [in developing Indochina] is really remarkable."[68]

Even more generously, in 1930 the author of a guidebook to Saigon depicted nineteenth-century Vietnam as a place ravaged by "conflicting forces" until benevolent foreigners acted to put an end to the chaos in 1859. It was in that year that "the French, together with a handful of Spanish volunteers, had to intervene in order to restore peace under the French flag."[69] The action apparently marked the end of Vietnamese history, as, despite seventy years having passed since the intervention, the sentence was the last in the volume's synopsis of the past.

Little changed with the global increase in anticolonial sentiment after the Second World War. While it became possible then to view the French occupation as in fact despised by the bulk of the Vietnamese people, guidebook authors were careful to distinguish the American intervention from that of its European predecessor.[70] For example, Harvey S. Olson, author of *Olson's Orient Guide*, in 1962 divorced the United States from the colonialist ambitions of France while at the same time depicting the Viet Minh as having merely feigned nationalist sentiment:

> The post World War II era has been a troubled, confusing, and unhappy one for these gentle people. The *Viet-Minh* perpetrated a cruel hoax on the Vietnamese people when, under the guise of fighting for freedom and independence for all of Viet Nam, they were, in reality, doing their utmost to lead the country into the open arms of communism. Through a ruse, the old time Communist, Nguyen Ai Quoc, took

the name of Ho Chi Minh and usurped leadership of the *Viet-Minh* which had been founded as a league for the independence of Viet Nam. Instead, it took effective steps to enslave the entire population. During the Indo-Chinese War of 1946–1954, the Vietnamese were faced with horrible decisions. They had either to fight side by side with the *Viet-Minh* whom they knew were Communist in sympathy or refuse to fight for freedom against their own best interests. It may readily be seen that the Vietnamese were never given a clearcut choice between communism and genuine independence and freedom. In their fight for liberation from France, the Vietnamese were inadvertently also striking a blow for communism which the vast majority of them detested worse than the plague.

Ultimately, on May 8, 1954, the French surrendered Dien Bien Phu, and an armistice agreement was signed whereby the French High Command abandoned approximately half of the territory and almost sixty per cent of the population of Viet Nam to the *Viet-Minh*.

This was a sad development for the free world and a dreadful situation for the Vietnamese people.

In the aftermath of the Geneva Accords, Olson claimed, "880,500 refugees succeeded in fleeing to the south[,] abandoning all of their belongings and frequently risking their lives to do so. The *Viet-Minh*," he continued, "did everything possible, including physical violence, to prevent any of the non-Communists [from] escaping." With respect to the reverse flow of regroupees, which by most credible estimates numbered over 100,000, "few if any Vietnamese from the south went north," Olson incredibly stated.[71]

If there was any hope for the Vietnamese people in 1962, according to Olson, it resided in the figure of Ngo Dinh Diem, "a man of great vigor, vision, and iron will" who was "elected President by an overwhelming majority" in October 1955 at the same time that "the Free Republic of Viet Nam was born in all of its glory." As for the southern population, "These sturdy, hardy citizens of the Republic of Viet Nam are democracy's greatest friends and communism's greatest foes. Their country is pleasant, the people warm and friendly, and they love us."[72]

Far less strident, but still accepting the ideological premises of American anti-Communism in the Vietnamese context, was Robert S. Kane's

Asia A to Z. Kane notified his touring readers in 1963 that the United States was "attempting to bring order out of the chaos in Vietnam which might have been averted had the French been more imaginative and far-sighted in their relations with that former colony, particularly after World War II." Vietnam, he wrote, was split in two; half was "in the hands of a Communist regime closely allied to that of neighbor Mao Tse-tung's," and the other half was "a sovereign state." Unlike Harvey Olson, however, Kane was quite critical of Ngo Dinh Diem, offering some praise but also rebuking his administration for its authoritarianism and repression. In his estimation, the anti-Communist perspective of the exiled oppositionist Tran Van Tung, who accused the president of letting "the Communist Vietcong control and terrorize the country right up to the city limits of Saigon" by "purg[ing] himself of all capable anti-Communist leaders" in his broad crackdown on perceived dissent, provided "food for thought." If the United States were to succeed in defeating the southern insurgency, Kane approvingly quoted Tung, it would need to reappraise its "sink-or-swim-with-Diem policy." The author's concern, in other words, was entirely pragmatic.[73]

Among the most popular Asian guidebooks for the English-speaking world in the 1960s were those published by Fodor's. The imprint's naturalized American founder and namesake, Eugene Fodor, was a veteran of the Office of Strategic Services, the predecessor of the U.S. CIA, and he allowed CIA operatives to work as travel writers for the series to furnish them with civilian cover. When the relationship was revealed in 1977, Fodor was unapologetic. "They were all highly professional, high-quality," he said of the agents. "We never let politics be smuggled into the books." It is unknown whether any of the writers who covered Vietnam were intelligence operatives, but that the guidebooks were ideological products is unquestionable.[74]

The company published annual regional volumes that covered Vietnam until 1974, and they were unambiguous in their representation of the Vietnamese conflict: "Vietnam" meant the Republic of Vietnam, a "nation" in which "Communist guerrillas" had been skirmishing with the "legitimate government" of the state "since it was born."[75] Although the rule of Ngo Dinh Diem was admittedly "often heavy-handed," he was an "honest man" who had "succeeded in cleaning up the country, imprisoning the racketeers and warlords, many of whom had their own private armies, and outlawing some of the more militant religions which had been created for the sole purpose of terrorizing the superstitious peasants." Moreover, "Brothels were closed, opium-smoking cut down, land reform achieved, and an attempt made, with massive injections of American aid, to put the country on a sound economic basis." While the RVN was not a "democracy" because "personal rights and liberties" were by no means guaranteed, the Vietnamese accepted this temporary arrangement, particularly in light of "the Communists' well-known ability to utilize freedom of speech and freedom of political opposition to undermine a free but economically weak country." The "people of Vietnam obviously prefer their present form of government to [Communist] dictatorship," the guidebook claimed for years during the 1960s, "but they are waiting for the day when a real democratic system will be inaugurated."[76] That day had still not arrived as the end of the decade approached, although the nature of the conflict remained clear: It was a "war between the Communists and the Free World" in which the "Communist enemy in the countryside" was attempting to "overthrow the free Vietnamese government in Saigon."[77] The critical scholarship of the decade, which viewed the war not in conventional Cold War terms but as a Vietnamese struggle for reunification and independence, appears to have had no effect on the war's representation by Fodor's.

GENDERING VIETNAM

A significant feature of much of the tourism literature was its focus on Vietnamese women. Through photographs, illustrations, and textual references, Vietnam, consistent with widespread Western perceptions of Asia, appeared as feminine, a discursive construction that suggested that manly American protection was necessary. In this gendering of the southern Vietnamese state, women, unlike men, were treated as touristic sights (or sites) in their own right. For instance, *Tourism in Vietnam*, a 1957 publication of Review Horizons, described Hue as "a pre-eminently aristocratic city" in which "the gracefulness and the beauty of its women are proverbial."[78] In the ethnic Chinese city of Cholon, the women were described by the authors as both sexualized objects and emblems of Asian tradition: "Graceful in their gaudy, tight-fitting dresses, *with skilled makeup*, punctilious in their traditional politeness, the girls sing to the accompaniment of a strange and shrill music which, with the relish of Chinese culinary art, contributes to the climaxing of a feeling of zest."[79] The weekly *Saigon Round Up*, meanwhile, alluded to the titillating possibility of exposure in highlighting the "always eye-catching sight" of "two attractive girls" cruising on a motorbike while "wearing colorful traditional dresses, the skirts of which flutter in the wind and threatened to catch in the whirling mechanism a[t] any moment."[80] And for the NTO authors of *Visit Fascinating Vietnam*, Saigon was full of *"doe-eyed shapely Vietnamese girls dressed in the most gracious way."*[81] Even restaurants and bars spotlighted the physical beauty of Vietnamese women, advertising their employment of "lovely," "charming," "attractive," or "graceful" hostesses and waitresses or — combining the exotic with the practicality of the familiar — "lovely English speaking hostesses."[82]

Yet it was not just the Vietnamese-produced literature that drew attention to this remarkable "asset." Writing in *Travel* in 1959, Richard Tregaskis commented on "the inspiring beauty" of Vietnamese women, which gave the people an "advantage in their romantic self-expression."[83] Another American visiting six years later, the actor George C. Scott, was similarly struck by the "exquisitely delicate, superbly feminine Vietnamese women" who "strolled and pedaled in swirling streams of color," revealing, through their *ao dai*, the "padded black brassieres and white panties that were visible in the sunlight."[84] Fodor's likewise drew on explicitly sexualized imagery. "You will enjoy especially the extremely lovely Vietnamese women, whose grace and fine features would be hard to surpass anywhere in the world," the guidebook informed its readers in 1962. "Their costume (high collar, tight blouse, and split skirt over pantaloons) provokes both admiration and criticism, the former because of its sense of elegance and modesty, the latter mostly because of its modesty alone (some people have no imagination)." Among the "assets" of Vietnam, according to the authors, were the "elegance and beauty" of the country's women.[85] Fodor's was certainly not unique in viewing Vietnamese women as a commodity to be exploited. A report published just a year earlier by the U.S. Department of Commerce, in encouraging the creation of an "image" of Vietnam "in the mind of the potential American tourist," suggested women in their "traditional dress."[86]

The NTO concurred. In a 1962 PATA advertisement in *Holiday* magazine, the photograph selected to sell Vietnam to the global travel market featured two young women in *ao dai* beckoning potential tourists from the

Botanical Gardens of Saigon.[87] Vietnam, of course, was hardly alone in deploying representations of women in its national iconography. The scantily clad "hula dancer" served the same purpose for portions of the South Pacific, for example. Yet this feminization, in the context of Vietnam's wartime client-state relationship with the United States, is notable. With their seemingly ubiquitous appearances on the covers of both Vietnamese and foreign travel publications, not to mention their description in often highly sexualized terms, Vietnamese women were used as a touristic lure — both, perhaps, for their sexual appeal as well as to suggest to foreign visitors that the promotion of the RVN's security was synonymous with the masculine protection of traditional Vietnamese womanhood.[88] Vietnamese men were evidently not up to the task. Often described as small and effeminate — one injured Vietnamese soldier was characterized by Scott as having a body as "small as a girl's" — these were not manly men, "heroic" and "courageous" like the Americans.[89] The trope was hardly original. As Kristin Hoganson has persuasively demonstrated, gender politics had decades earlier provoked the expansion of the U.S. empire into the Caribbean and the Pacific.[90] Yet the extent to which Vietnamese women came to represent the face of a fragile southern Vietnam has not received comparable attention.

As for women's service as a touristic lure, the transformation in their perceived utility from the semiotic to the corporeal was being openly discussed among tourism officials by the early 1970s. Highlighting the extent to which they were perceived by the authorities as a resource to be exploited, the director of the NTO disclosed to an American reporter in 1973, "Soon I will send up a proposal for 'sex tourism.' Many people want to visit Vietnam not to see the mountains or the shopping but to try, just once, our girls."[91] Having originally sprouted in response to the foreign military presence, mass prostitution was, by 1973, being enthusiastically touted as one of the waves of Vietnam's touristic future.

TOURISM AND THE WAR

Unfortunately for the RVN government, the potential of southern Vietnam for tourism seriously dissipated with the war's escalation in the 1960s. This was a considerable departure from just a few decades earlier. At that time, the French colonial authorities had touted Vietnam's quiescence as one of the area's great attractions. In a guidebook produced by the Office Central du Tourisme Indochinois in 1938, for instance, "the Indo-Chinese populations" were said to possess such a "quiet state of mind" that "travelers can move about unarmed in the remotest corners of the country in absolute safety, by night as well as in broad daylight." Given that the "traces of our civilization" were still relatively scarce, the volume's French authors wrote, tourists were afforded an opportunity "to see thrilling and unusual things" in a "young country" enjoying "a rapid and steady move towards progress."[92] While liberationist sentiment had certainly been present since the first years of French colonization, by the 1940s and 1950s, it seems, the apparently innate quietude of the Indochinese had been superseded by their unnatural propensity to make revolutionary noise. Whether during World War Two or the three decades following the Allied defeat of the Axis powers, war — or the political instability that accompanied Vietnam's growing nationalist agitation — had threatened to intrude on foreign travelers' pacific enjoyment of the Vietnamese landscape. By the mid-1960s the threat became, in every way, frighteningly real.

While in some instances tourism (or, more broadly, the infrastructure development it demanded) presented opportunities for the United States to prepare more effectively for the eventuality of direct intervention — an obvious example was the assertion of a "purely commercial" cover in building a jet facility outside Saigon that could handle American military aircraft, thus skirting the provisions of the Geneva Accords that prohibited such construction[93] — war also proved taxing on the improvements made to accommodate growing numbers of tourists. Hotel vacancies plummeted as foreign officials and civilian support personnel arrived "in country," roads became clogged with military vehicles and internally displaced peasants, and bureaucratic security measures led to growing frustration among visitors. There was also, of course, the very real possibility of physical harm. One British tourist who arrived in Saigon in 1957, for example, related in a published travelogue how "plastic bombs began exploding" within just "a few hours of [his] arrival," leading the streets to become "burgeoned with police." Amid this tenuous security situation, he was "warned" that he "must not let people think [he] was American" or French. This was not the sort of advice that the disheartened citizens of the United States and France — who, in the late 1950s, together represented the greatest number of visitors to Vietnam — wished to hear. The countryside, through which the tourist, Christopher Pym, journeyed on foot, was quieter than Saigon, but he could not help but feel one of the French–Viet Minh war's legacies. Observed curiously by numerous Vietnamese, Pym wrote, "I might have been mistaken, but into this sullen stare from peasants I read all the unforgotten hatred of the Indo-China war."[94]

Within a few years, the second phase of that conflict consumed nearly all of Vietnam. What one guidebook in 1961 casually characterized as "some terrorist activity in certain parts of the country" had evolved, by the mid-1960s, into a major international conflagration.[95] "This is a tense area," observed one American traveler visiting Saigon in 1964. Just the day before, he recorded in his diary, "three American military advisers were killed" in a town twenty miles outside of the capital. It was "not sane" to venture southwest of the city. "Grenade carriers," he wrote.[96] How the reality of a horrific war came to replace the Vietnam of touristic imaginings with the "Vietnam" that, in the United States, would eventually serve as a signifier of death and national dishonor is significant, not only for what it reveals about the stubbornness of foreigners determined to negotiate a society under stress but also the presumed diminution in tourism's potential to contribute to the RVN's political legitimization.

Perhaps not surprisingly, southern Vietnam, even in the midst of massive warfare, continued to attract curious tourists. It was not until 1967, in fact, that Fodor's began emphatically suggesting to travelers that they cease their visits. Just two years before, Vietnamese tourism — at least according to the American publishing house — still seemed viable. Saigon was deemed "perfectly safe," while Dalat, Nha Trang, and Hue were all reachable by "air transport," thus "eliminating the dangers of roadside ambush."[97] There may be a war "outside" the city, wrote James Reston in the *New York Times*, but Saigon itself is, for the most part, "as calm and available as Boston on the Eastern Shuttle."[98] Yet by 1966, Fodor's reported, "South Vietnam" had become a "place for only the most intrepid travelers." The "best hotel in the country, the Caravelle, in downtown Saigon, had its fourth floor destroyed in a terrorist explosion. The American embassy was bombed. Unwary travelers have been captured by the Communists on the outskirts of Saigon." Nevertheless, the authors still managed to offer helpful advice on the "best time to visit."[99]

By 1967, however, when the publisher added an original essay by the Pulitzer Prize–winning journalist Peter Arnett on the perils of Vietnamese travel, the absurd fiction that one could safely tour Vietnam evidently had become truly untenable. "For years," wrote Arnett, "South Vietnam-ese embassies around the world have been distributing to potential tourists colorful little brochures that tell of the delights of yachting on the Saigon river, hunting tigers in the Central highlands, and fishing in the Ca Mau peninsula. Don't believe a word of it. Vietnam may have at one time provided these pleasures. It may well again at some future date. But cer-tainly not now. This divided nation, torn by war for twenty years, is the most dangerous country in the world for today's visitor." Unless you per-haps "have a close friend [in the capital] who will take care of you," Arnett counseled, "don't ever yield to the temptation" to go.[100] A 1968 guidebook published by Sunset offered a similarly ominous warning. "South Vietnam is not for tourists," it stated. "The country and its capital city, Saigon, constitute the front lines of a major war. Military requirements take prece-dence over pleasure. Security comes before civilian comfort. The curfew is real. So are the sandbag control points and the armed jeeps that range the streets." The volume's section on the RVN was tellingly entitled "South Vietnam: Only for Those Who Have to Go There."[101]

Most Americans heeded the publishers' sage counsel. A 1967 survey for the Pacific Area Travel Association, *National Geographic*, and *Time* found that Vietnam was considered the least safe of twenty-six Pacific destina-tions included in the study, with 29 percent of tourists associating the RVN with "lack of personal security." Vietnam also ranked at the bottom of such destinations in the percentage of travelers (12 percent) who associated the country with "warm, friendly people." It is thus not surprising that it ranked at the bottom of places that tourists who had never been there would most "like to visit."[102] The prognosis for Vietnamese tourism offi-cials was bleak. There was "little or nothing" that could be done to im-prove the situation "in light of the current relations in Vietnam," the survey found. Yet it was possible that the results "might effectively be used for guidance in planning for the day when normal conditions are re-established."[103] Preparing for that day essentially became, in the latter years of the war, the NTO's raison d'être.

Nevertheless, there were occasional Vietnamese nods to the promotion of wartime travel. At roughly the same time that Fodor's warned tour-ists away, the NTO reissued a guidebook to coincide with 1967 as "Inter-national Tourist Year." In its recycling of earlier promotional language about Vietnam "rapidly becoming a 'must see' for thousands of foreign tourists," however, the short volume must have seemed morbidly comical to those who read it.[104] Two years later, the RVN Embassy in Washington produced *An Introduction to Vietnam*, which sought to entice visitors by praising the country as "unexcelled in touristic attractions."[105] And in 1973, a *Vietnam Tourism Guide* was published in Saigon that, like the 1967 guidebook, designated Vietnam a "must see" for international travelers.[106] But for all intents and purposes, tourism officials, receiving minimal state support, had for some time concentrated largely on preparing for a post-war travel boom. Yet in spite of the war's omnipresence, a relative hand-ful of international visitors still wished to see something of the country for themselves. "Amazingly," Arnett reported, "some parties of tourists do arrive."[107] Among this number were the Americans George and Sharon Moudry.

When the young couple decided to honeymoon in Saigon in 1969, the Moudrys knew that they were not traversing popular touristic ground. Vietnam was not their only destination — it was one of many in a lengthy around-the-world trip — but it was undoubtedly their most extraordinary. A major war was, after all, raging in the country, and during the Tet Offensive just a year before, Saigon, generally considered the RVN's safest city for foreign visitors, had come under sustained military attack. But the Moudrys were curious. Sharon, a nurse, wondered about the faraway lo-cale that daily had been all over the news. George, a social worker and former Catholic priest, worked in the San Francisco Bay area with soldiers and sailors recovering from the physical and psychological wounds they incurred in Southeast Asia. He wanted to see the place that had killed or crippled so many young American men. Together they had marched in opposition to the war. Now they wished to witness Vietnam at first hand.

The Moudrys' frustrations with touring the country began as soon as their plane landed. When they tried to receive their visas, they were de-layed by a Vietnamese official who notified them, without explanation, that they could not enter the country if their next stop was Phnom Penh, as their departure tickets indicated. It was not until they agreed to revise their plans and leave for Bangkok several days later that they were finally granted entrance. Once they were in the city, the small hotel where they originally intended to stay had no locks on its doors. On the street outside, George was robbed. Everywhere they went they could see beggars, sand-bagged street corners, and men with guns. At night there was a curfew.

After two days of looking around and meeting with Catholic relief workers, they paid the bribe at the airport necessary to grease the bureaucratic
wheels and left for Cambodia. Vietnam, they said years later, was the only
destination in their travels in which they really felt unsafe.[108]

Other Americans found themselves similarly attracted to the state's
war-induced instability, especially before 1968. One group of American
travelers in Saigon, for instance, "wandered out" to observe "demonstrating students . . . tearing up" a French war memorial, the *New York Times*
reported in August 1964. Following their "rubbernecking at the demolition," the Americans "strolled off to excellent French restaurants to enjoy
some of the best cuisine in this part of the world."[109] Over a year later, a
couple from suburban St. Louis, Harry and Eleanor Foster, "welcomed
the idea" of a meal at the My Canh Floating Restaurant on the Saigon
River, shrugging off any concerns about it having "been blown up by
Vietcong terrorists" just months earlier. For the Fosters, the American
military presence in Vietnam, together with the RVN's struggle to cope,
provided an unusual spectacle. "We wanted to see what this place looked
like," Harry explained. Nevertheless, the Fosters were reluctant to allow
the war to touch too close to home. Relaxing one morning on the veranda
of the Continental Palace Hotel and watching uniformed Americans pass
by outside, Eleanor confessed that, despite her own willingness to travel
there, she hoped her draft-age sons would not find themselves forced to
serve in the southern Vietnamese state.[110]

Visitors such as the Moudrys and the Fosters were in the minority,
however. In 1964, with substantial political unrest in not only Vietnam but
Cambodia, Indonesia, Burma, and Singapore, over half of all scheduled
tours to Southeast Asia were cancelled out of concern for personal safety. A
"large proportion of [American] tourists are retired people who are spending their savings on quests for joy, not turbulence," explained one travel
agent. The "modest flow" of pleasure seekers in Vietnam in 1963 had, by
1964, begun to notably diminish.[111] The National Tourist Office took the
war's effect on international travel in stride. "Our job is to encourage the
development of tourism in this country," Tran Ba Tach of the NTO explained, "but at the moment it's rather difficult. Very, very few people
come here for pleasure. Our service is only encouragement, and since
there's practically nobody to encourage, our efforts are directed toward

helping the hotels and caterers to reorganize their systems to meet the standards of people from other countries."[112]

Adding to the NTO's travails was the fact that, by 1966, the U.S. government was openly discouraging American travelers from even setting foot in Vietnam. Not only was the RVN not safe for travel, but hotel rooms that met international standards were virtually impossible to obtain, given their block occupancy by American corporations and government officials. Managers at the Caravelle, for example, warned prospective guests that they might have to wait one-and-a-half months for a room; at the Astor, the wait was even longer. Corruption was widespread in the RVN, yet efforts to secure a room with bribes of up to one hundred dollars did not meet success. (One Saigon resident claimed, "There's always a hotel room, but one has to bribe with a tape recorder or a camera, not money.")[113] Even travelers with reservations made months in advance could find their rooms already occupied when they arrived.[114] For those people fortunate enough to secure lodging, the corruption (or suggestions of criminal behavior) nevertheless persisted. One visitor recalled that the first thing he saw on entering his "spacious room" at the Hotel Continental was a sign: "The Management warns his Guests against any business offer made by the hotel staff."[115]

Getting to Vietnam was similarly a problem. Ships that had once brought passengers to Saigon through the Mekong Delta had stopped doing so by 1964. Pan American, the only U.S. airline that flew tourists to the RVN, usually had very few seats available, and those travelers who somehow managed to obtain a reservation incurred substantial risk during the flight itself. In 1963, one of Pan Am's planes was hit with a .30 caliber slug, so pilots afterward took to zig-zagging into Saigon in what one observer called "a stomach-torturing series of angles" to avoid being hit by gunfire. Once visitors reached the ground, they found the airport, Tan Son Nhut, quite dangerous. As of October 1966, it had been mortared at least three times, with one incident killing eight people and wounding 128 others. If outbound flights from Saigon were for some reason delayed overnight — Pan Am, given its security concerns in Vietnam, tried to keep its planes on the ground no longer than thirty minutes — transit passengers could not rely on finding hotel accommodations. Indeed, the airline had at times arranged for stranded clients to stay in maternity clinics, in the bunks of a ship in the city's harbor, and in spare beds in the apartments of Pan Am officials.[116]

Many of the attractions once touted by the tourism authorities similarly presented hazards to foreign travelers. A Buddhist institute that was the site of a popular half-day tour had become a convergence point for demonstrations against the RVN government. The My Canh Floating Restaurant at which the Fosters had dined, which was being recommended by the NTO as late as 1965, had repeatedly been attacked. In one incident, thirteen people were killed and more than eighty were injured. Duong Tu Do (Liberty Street), "Saigon's main street on which are found fashionable shops as well as several important Government buildings," according to the NTO's Saigon guidebook, had become "pimpled with honky-tonks," one writer noted, while businesses along the street had installed wire grills to "protect [their] patrons from terrorists' bombs."[117] Saigon as a whole, a *New York Times* journalist wrote in 1966, "is hot, crowded, and dirty" and "smells of rotting fish and exhaust fumes."[118] Indeed, "No one has time to collect the garbage in Saigon streets anymore, the beggars are on the increase, and street riots over politics and food prices can sweep a foreigner up and deposit him, bruised, shaken, and maybe injured, an hour later," Peter Arnett cautioned.[119] Was Saigon, asked *Newsweek* in 1969, the "worst city in the world?" The magazine left it to readers to decide, but its own judgment was unmistakable. In a situation without "modern precedent," the RVN capital appeared to be "plunging headlong" toward "total collapse." The "once-glittering 'Pearl of the Orient,'" the article lamented, "has become a four-star urban planner's nightmare, a present-day paradigm of the gloomiest visions of the 21st-century city."[120]

The pessimism expressed by the magazine was reflected elsewhere. Hunting, which had at one time presented a significant hope for tourism development, was no longer considered tenable under the wartime conditions of the 1960s. The NTO, in fact, was forced to cover portions of its literature describing Vietnam as a "hunter's paradise" with a notice declaring "Temporarily Sustained [*sic*] Under the Present Situation."[121] The same was true of the literature's earlier subtle touting of the Diem regime: A photograph of Ngo Dinh Nhu, the widely despised brother of the deposed president, posing next to a tiger he shot still graced a Dalat travel brochure in 1966, but the caption revealing his identity had been blacked out.[122]

The optimism that had accompanied Vietnam's touristic potential in magazines such as *Holiday* and *Travel* in the late 1950s had given way in subsequent years to a tourism reality treated by observers as a sick joke. Nowhere in the National Tourist Office's "literary output . . . is there any mention of war," *Newsweek* commented sardonically in June 1967.[123] There was something unseemly, suggested the *Times* correspondent Stewart Harris that same year, in enjoying drinks in Saigon while "men were being killed elsewhere."[124] Despite brief efforts after the Paris ceasefire agreements in January 1973 to again promote southern Vietnam's tourism potential — "I hope you come back to Vietnam as a tourist some day," President Nguyen Van Thieu of the RVN once urged departing American troops — it would be decades before the country again occupied the Western touristic imagination.[125] By then, memories of Vietnam's wartime history would be a matter of fierce dispute.

TOURISM'S EFFECTIVENESS AS CULTURAL PROPAGANDA

Returning now to the ideological concerns that opened this chapter, it is worth pondering whether the Vietnamese authorities succeeded in their propaganda objectives. Given the limited evidence available, it is difficult to say. The results appear to have been mixed. Certainly they succeeded in the late 1950s with Richard Tregaskis of *Travel* magazine, who exhibited no hesitation in embracing Diem's "democratic government."[126] They succeeded, too, with George C. Scott, whose visit shortly after his memorable appearance as General Buck Turgidson in *Dr. Strangelove* (1964) resulted in an eight-page meditation in *Esquire*. The "stakes are incredibly high," wrote Scott. In America's larger "war with International Communism," the "Vietnamese conflict is a unique and necessary phase" whose "consequences," he insisted, cannot be "sidestepped, or shirked, or diplomatized under a polished table." The RVN's "cause" was courageous, the actor pronounced.[127]

The following year, the authorities also won over the Follett family of Oak Park, Illinois. "We came because we wanted to see what was happening in Vietnam ourselves," Dwight Follett disclosed to a reporter in 1966. "In the United States everything we read is either black or white." The Folletts thus spent their holiday watching what the press characterized as a "Buddhist riot," visiting a resettlement area for ethnic minorities in the Central Highlands, observing government aid projects in the Mekong

Delta, and, to enliven the trip with something a bit more traditionally touristy, relaxing in the coastal city of Nha Trang. "I'm coming out of this more a hawk than a dove," Dwight Follett insisted. "We must help these people."[128]

But Tregaskis, Scott, and the Folletts were hardly representative. One Australian who visited Vietnam in 1960, Peggy Warner, was convinced at the time of her arrival that "everyone [had] rejoiced" when Ngo Dinh Diem assumed the presidency five years earlier. She had marveled at Diem's contribution to education, refugee resettlement, and land reform, writing that the "hard-working" leader, "a Confucian by temperament and a Catholic in religion," had "pulled the country together." But after conversations with Vietnamese in which "the talk was always of coups" and corruption, and having heard of "dissatisfaction among the peasants and the refugees who had been settled in 'prosperity villages,'" Warner left Saigon convinced that the RVN capital was not only "tense" and "sterile" but "not very democratic." "In South Vietnam," she wrote, expressions of political opinion "can be dangerous."[129]

Dorothea Lange, too, grew disenchanted during her Vietnam tour. Despite the glowing endorsement of Saigon that opened this chapter, Lange did not leave the city praising the American effort to prop up its government. Her experience is revealing. Having emerged as a chronicler of Americans' suffering during the difficult years of the Great Depression, Lange by 1958 enjoyed a reputation as a populist ally of the downtrodden. Together with her husband, Paul Taylor, a labor economist at the University of California and, by the late 1950s, a development consultant for the federal government and private foundations, Lange spent several weeks touring southern Vietnam as part of a six-month excursion that took her throughout Asia and Europe in 1958 and 1959. What she saw in Vietnam both impressed and repulsed her. Saigon was delightful, a "most lovely place" where, with its tree-lined streets and pale yellow buildings that dated to the French colonial era, "time stands still." But outside the capital city, things were appreciably different. Hotels and restaurants were filthy. The food was disagreeable and smelly. The water was fetid. Rural roads were in serious disrepair. People spit. And the regroupees from the north — the hundreds of thousands of mostly Catholic Vietnamese who had been implored by covert American propaganda to make their way south —

lived in wretched conditions. "I wrestle with the ways of Vietnam!" Lange confided to her diary.[130]

Perhaps of greatest alarm to the RVN authorities, however, was the failure to persuade Lange of the ideological necessity for Washington's support for the government. "If we moved out, that is, if American aid moved out of Asia, as in Viet Nam[, the] Philippines[,] and Korea," she wrote, "if they had the courage to stand up to us and deny us our intentions[,] would, in the long run, these countries be in a better position to take their place among nations? Are we weakening them at the source? Are we interrupting the course of their development? The aid program and its mores causes [sic] uneasiness. We are like a conqueror nation."[131] Lange's prescient hesitation, as we know now, proved tragically well founded.

Educating Private Ryan TOURISM AND THE

UNITED STATES MILITARY IN POSTCOLONIAL VIETNAM

> I wanted to see exotic Vietnam, the jewel of Southeast Asia.
> I wanted to meet interesting and stimulating people of an ancient
> culture and kill them.
> JOKER, *FULL METAL JACKET* (1987)

> Greetings & Salutations from the tourist capital of Southeast Asia.
> DAVID L. SARTORI, LONG BINH, 8 MARCH 1969

On 23 July 1962, two American military advisers in Vietnam, together with two allied Vietnamese militiamen, set out on a hunting trip near Phan Thiet, a small town approximately one hundred miles northeast of Saigon. The focus of their excursion was the area's abundant fowl, though larger game remained a distinct possibility. Shortly before dusk, while driving along a jungle road, the party was ambushed by a group of Vietnamese insurgents. In short order, the hunters had become the hunted. One of the RVN (Republic of Vietnam) militiamen evaded capture, and one of the Americans, Master Sergeant Carl E. Brown, somehow managed to escape. The other American was not so lucky. Roque Matagulay, a Californian who spent nineteen years in the armed forces, was held as a prisoner for five months; he was ultimately released in a prisoner exchange on the day before Christmas.[1]

Popular memory does not typically associate the American wars in Indochina with recreational pursuits such as hunting.

Indeed, from the vantage point of the twenty-first century, the idea seems positively absurd. Yet during the early 1960s, when "the war hadn't really become a war yet," as one veteran recalled that "simpler time," the U.S. Department of Defense in fact employed the pleasures of international tourism and travel as a means of selling military service in Southeast Asia.[2] In Danang, the same beaches on which the first official U.S. combat troops splashed ashore in March 1965 were, two years earlier, being warmly touted by the Pentagon as "wonderful recreation spots" for swimming and fishing. Down the coast in Nha Trang, personnel were informed that they could "enjoy all sorts of water sports," such as skin diving and waterskiing, or they could "make a trip to one of the offshore islands in the bay." But "perhaps the loveliest beach of all," the Department of Defense claimed in its first pocket guide to Vietnam, was at Dai Linh, "north of Nha Trang in a spectacular cove backed by high mountains." Unlike at the developed beach resort fifty miles to its south, a "small fishing village at one end of the cove is the only human habitation." For members of the armed forces, the coast offered merely one of several types of touristic pleasure. To the authors of the Pentagon's travel literature, there were abundant opportunities for big-game hunting, the exploration of historic and cultural sites, and, in general, seeing "something of the lovely country you are visiting."[3]

While a small number of Americans had toured Indochina prior to the mid-twentieth century, it was not until the early to mid-1960s, if the Defense Department is to be taken literally, that tens of thousands of Americans truly began "visiting" the area. It is true that these tens of thousands of visitors were military personnel whose primary mission was the decimation of the popular revolutionary movement that had defeated the French colonialists in 1954. But, importantly, the Americans were also implored by their superiors to be more than just agents of the U.S. armed forces; they were to be tourists and cultural ambassadors building "a solid foundation of mutual respect and admiration" between Americans and Vietnamese.[4] Toward this end, the Pentagon published in 1963 — one year after the Kennedy administration initiated the aerial bombardment of the southern countryside and the same year it assented to a coup overthrowing the southern president, Ngo Dinh Diem — the first of its pocket guides to Vietnam. Later editions, with gradually less emphasis on the pleasures of touring the country, were issued in 1966 and 1971. Intended for the use of military personnel, the volumes were at once tourist guidebooks and, of fundamental importance, basic introductions to Vietnamese history, society, and culture.

In the latter capacity the pocket guides assumed a critical role as one element in the Pentagon's larger internal propaganda campaign. That indoctrination would be crucial to maintaining discipline and morale among troops in Vietnam was suggested by the reactions of U.S. personnel to the earliest American assistance in countering the Vietnamese revolution. When the United States took its first steps in supporting the French reconquest of Indochina in 1945, the members of the U.S. Merchant Marine assigned to transport French troops and Foreign Legionnaires to Vietnam objected, with the crew of one ship cabling President Harry Truman and Senator Robert Wagner to protest "the use of this and other American vessels for carrying foreign combat troops to foreign soil for the purpose of engaging in hostilities to further the imperialist policies of foreign governments when there are American troops waiting to come home [from service in the Second World War]." They were not alone. Once in Saigon, the entire crews of four of the Merchant Marine troopships drafted a resolution decrying U.S. assistance to the impending French efforts "to subjugate the native population."[5]

As the American intervention escalated over the next two decades, concerns increased that personnel arriving in Vietnam were insufficiently persuaded about the gravity of the situation. By 1962, officials were readily acknowledging that some GIs were "not sure why they are in Viet Nam or why it is in the U.S. national interest for them" to be there.[6] Troop information officers tasked with ideological instruction had, until then, focused on the theme of "personalism versus communism" in their educational outreach. There was a problem with this focus, however: "No one understands personalism," the unusual ideology developed by Ngo Dinh Nhu and adopted by his brother, RVN President Ngo Dinh Diem.[7] A "timeless indoctrination or orientation" would therefore be necessary, one that framed the struggle in Vietnam as an instance of global Communist aggression and not, to be sure, as indigenous resistance to the Diem regime, let alone what the Merchant Mariners called "the imperialist policies of foreign governments."[8] Yet it was important, officials recognized, that their propaganda efforts not be identified as such. "Troops tend to shy away from 'indoctrination,' particularly if formal, mandatory instruction is involved. They prefer 'information' and are sensitive to any hint that it may be colored by propaganda."[9] The pocket guides authored that same year thus seemed ideal instruments in this "information" campaign. Their seemingly innocuous purpose — providing information on where and how to enjoy oneself while serving in Vietnam — masked their insidiousness. While they hardly represented the Americans' first exposure to Cold War ideology, they certainly helped to reinforce it.

The military's tourism publications, as will be made clear, provided a context for the American presence that divorced it from the taint of French colonialism, associating it instead with the promotion of freedom and a righteous defense against Communist expansionism. The pocket guides' publication followed years of attempted indoctrination by military officials as well as Hollywood's explicit connection in the 1950s of the American anti-Communist gospel to the political situation in Vietnam. The guidebooks thus emerged out of a political and cultural milieu that sought to mediate America's growing confrontation with revolutionary nationalism in much of the Third World while bolstering Washington's efforts to promote an international system consistent with the tenets of liberal capitalism.

At this broader analytical level, the travel documents fused the state's need to instill ideological conformity with the troops' desire for information on places to visit while serving overseas. The pocket guides therefore assumed an important role in the military's larger effort to properly educate Americans sent to Indochina. They were, in essence, an early and implicit acknowledgment of the manner in which travel literature could be embraced to further crucial political and ideological ends. As such, the guidebooks serve as revealing documents in generally examining how culture — in this case, the culture of tourism — became intertwined with U.S. foreign relations and, more specifically, the American involvement in postcolonial Vietnam. They illustrate, moreover, the critical importance of language to international politics and how particular discourses were employed to construct America's global mission for thousands of military personnel.

"SERVICE WITH SATISFACTION":
PROMISING PLEASURE WITH THE PAIN

At a time when Americans called to serve in Southeast Asia were being asked to temporarily forgo the supposed consumer abundance of middle-class domestic life, the Department of Defense promised these men that pleasure would accompany their sacrifice. "If you are bound for Viet-Nam, it is for the deeply serious business of helping a brave nation repel Communist invasion," its 1963 guidebook began. "This is your official job and it is a vital one." But for American personnel it was not just about the "deeply serious business" of fulfilling their military duty. For these early pioneers, the guidebook declared, the exotic otherness of Vietnam presented "opportunity unlimited." According to the Pentagon authors, the "dangers of ambush and raid will make sightseeing impossible in some places; but, when security restrictions permit, be sure to see something of the lovely country you are visiting and get acquainted with the charming — and tough and courageous — people who call Viet-Nam home." While opportunities were in fact limited by the presence of the war, these "advisers" would nevertheless "certainly have the chance to explore the colorful markets and shops of Saigon and Cho Lon." They might "be able to visit the traditional capital of Hue or cool, hill-encircled Dalat," and they might "even get in some good swimming or deep-sea fishing from the quiet beaches of the South China Sea or a hunting trip on the high plateaus inland."[10]

The colorful imagery invoked in the guidebook, which was typical of the idyllic visions of Vietnam appearing in the broader tourism literature, helped to mask the violence of the Americans' antirevolutionary campaign. "The Republic of Viet-Nam is a study in contrast," the authors mused.

> The brown waters of the canal between Saigon and Cho Lon versus the sky-blue Perfume River as it flows past the imperial tombs in the city of Hue. Rice in the delta; coffee, tea, kenaf, and ramie on the high plateau. Water buffalo dragging plows through mud paddies on the plains; elephants toting bundles in the highlands. Fragile girls in colorful *ao dai* costumes strolling gracefully along city boulevards; loin-clothed tribesmen with ivory plugs in their earlobes trotting along forest trails. The grey threads of incense in a Buddhist temple and the red joss sticks in a jar in front of a spirit house on a lonely mountain curve. . . .
>
> Boys drying black fishnets suspended from bamboo frames three stories high, and fishermen straining to beach their boat after a day at sea. Militiamen armed with muskets and tribesmen carrying crossbows. French pillboxes; Cham towers. Pagodas and modern depart-

ment stores. The new steel and concrete bridges on the Saigon–Bien Hoa Highway, and the pontooned planking across the Tra Khuc River in Quang Ngai. Sampans decorated with painted eyes; ocean-going freighters unloading military equipment and powdered milk along the quay.[11]

But for the brief allusions to armed militiamen, French pillboxes, and arriving military equipment, U.S. personnel reading this description might have thought they were embarking on a taxpayer-funded vacation to exotic Southeast Asia.

It was an impression reinforced elsewhere in the volume. "For a small country, Viet-Nam has a great variety of attractions—none of them far away from wherever you are," its authors promised. Saigon offered "fascinating shops and markets," as well as museums, theaters, cafes, and "excellent restaurants." Hue, too, provided "great sight-seeing possibilities," from the remains of the citadel—portions of which "the Communists blew . . . up in 1945 in an attempt to sever Viet-Nam from its past"—to the imperial tombs and sampan rides on the Perfume River. For those inclined toward outdoor pursuits, there were "tiger and elephant hunting in the high plateaus, and sunning and bathing at the quiet white-sand beaches along the country's thousand miles of coastline." While in the mountains, personnel could "visit a tribal village" or "test" their "climbing skill"; while at the beach, they could fish, water-ski, or "skin-dive from an island in the South China Sea." Pleasurable activities were promised as well to those who ventured to Vung Tau, the "exquisite mountain resort" of Dalat, and other popular Vietnamese destinations.[12]

The general impression a casual reader might have received from the flowery descriptions in the pocket guide was that southern Vietnam in 1963 was more of a holiday destination than a war zone. While the authors explicitly sought to emphasize Vietnam's attractions, however, they were careful to do so while connecting touristic pleasure to civic and martial responsibility. "You won't find life dull in Viet-Nam if you stay tuned in on the wave length of people around you," they wrote. "You will see exotic places, build lasting friendships, and be of service to a young democracy—while fulfilling an important duty to your own country."[13] Yet the pocket guide went even further. Through its provision of ideological instruction on how to interpret the growing anti-Diem insurgency, it sought both explicitly and implicitly to reinforce the crucial importance of the Americans' mission. For instance, the same section in which personnel were told they would "see exotic places" — "Service with Satisfaction," it was headlined — noted that "as long as there is danger of Communist agents prowling its streets, Saigon necessarily is a tensely guarded 'pearl of the orient,' and until the last Viet Cong sniper has been smoked out of the bamboo thickets, much of the beauty of the provinces will be hidden from visitors." But "there are compensations," the authors continued. "You who help the Vietnamese maintain their freedom will have many fine things to remember about the people and the country. You will have the satisfaction of sharing the experiences of a staunch and dedicated nation in a most critical period of its history. In a broader sense, you will be helping to block the spread of communism throughout Southeast Asia."[14]

When these words appeared in 1963, the unit of the Pentagon that produced the pocket guides had already been tasked for years with identifying the Vietnamese insurgency as evidence of global Communist expansionism. And while the publications were merely one of many vehicles that the Department of Defense exploited to reach its ideological charges, they were, to my knowledge, the only ones that sought explicitly to conjoin the pleasures of international travel with the often painful realities of overseas military service.[15]

THE POCKET GUIDES AND THE OFFICE OF
ARMED FORCES INFORMATION AND EDUCATION

The pocket guides to Vietnam were part of a larger series of such publications produced by the Office of Armed Forces Information and Education (OAFIE). Among other pocket-guide titles, which by 1963 numbered twenty, were Korea, the Philippines, Germany, and Japan. The guides, OAFIE explained, were "illustrated booklets about a country (or group of countries) where a sizeable number of our Service persons are stationed or will visit frequently." They were conveniently small, literally of a size — approximately five inches by four inches — that could easily be carried in one's pocket. Like all OAFIE publications, the guides were to elide complexity in their articulation of often complex matters, focusing on presenting information at an "eighth grade level of understanding."[16] The textual structure of each volume was the same. It included sections on history and geography, "information about the people, their religions and customs," and their "system of government" and armed forces. In addition to practical assistance in understanding foreign weights, measures, and monetary systems, as well as "pointers on conduct, hints on shopping, the most historic and scenic places to visit, hotels and restaurants, and suggestions about recreation," the pocket guides crucially included explanations of "why our military personnel are in the area."[17]

The identity of the pocket guides' authors was never disclosed, but, according to OAFIE, the guides were prepared "by a person who is well acquainted with the country and who has been there recently." To ensure their accuracy and their conformity with the needs of the U.S. government, the manuscripts were reviewed before publication by representatives of the different armed services (Army, Navy, Air Force, Marines, and Coast Guard), by the "State Department expert dealing with that geographical area," by "official representatives" of the country concerned, and by "United States military personnel in that country."[18]

The Office of Armed Forces Information and Education essentially served as the internal indoctrination unit of the American military, rendering it critical to the success of U.S. objectives in Southeast Asia. A July 1953 memorandum from Assistant Secretary of Defense John A. Hannah to the secretaries of the Army, Navy, and Air Force clearly articulated what was meant by its policy of "information and education": While the "primary mission" of the military was to train its members to be "the most effective combat forces it is possible to develop," if "at the same time we can include in our programs values that will carry over into civilian life and contribute to making better citizens and better Americans, we have a special obligation to do so." As such,

> It is desirable that we make adequate provision for inculcating in each serviceman and woman: the highest ideals and sound practices of good citizenship; deep faith in the principles of our form of representative government; full confidence in the future of the United States of America as a nation and as a world force for honest dealing and fair play; a firm sense of mission based on understanding of the world situation which has made their military service necessary; a willingness and eagerness to serve as a member of the team which is training and fighting for the ideals of freedom as contrasted with those in a totalitarian state — all with the primary objective of making them better and more

efficient members of the Armed Forces, and better fitted to return to their communities as mature, thoughtful, and responsible citizens.

All information and education programs were thus to, among other objectives, make "each serviceman fully conscious of (1) national and international problems and issues which may and do have [an] impact on his life and upon his attitudes and conduct both at home and overseas; (2) Soviet Communism, its meanings, its aims, its objectives, and where it is so strongly in conflict with the free world's concept and practical application of decency, integrity, fair play, the worth of the individual, and the rights assured the individual by our form of representative government."[19]

OAFIE, in other words, was charged with instilling in military personnel the ideological assumptions of American global anti-Communism. If there was any doubt in the early 1950s about the unit's Cold War mandate, OAFIE staff had only to recall the experience of their counterparts several years earlier. In April 1948, two congressional subcommittees organized a joint hearing on a weekly publication created by OAFIE's predecessor, the Troop Information and Education Division (TIED) of the United States Army's Special Staff. The immediate impetus for the hearings was concern over a specific issue of TIED's pamphlet series, *Armed Forces Talk*, on organized labor, an undoubtedly sensitive topic given that the mid-1940s witnessed the largest strike wave in U.S. history. Various concerns were expressed on the subject by legislators, such as whether service personnel, having read about labor unions in the TIED publication, would be encouraged to "organize among themselves, to limit their hours of duty, and to force bargaining with military authorities as prevails in private industry." Another problem, according to Walter Judd of Minnesota, was that the labor issue of *Armed Forces Talk* mentioned abuses by employers but not by unions; the latter abuses, he insisted, "exist and are disturbing our national welfare."[20]

However, the hearings were not confined to TIED's treatment of the labor movement; they broadly addressed matters ranging from racial prejudice in America — the general counsel of the Subcommittee on Publicity and Propaganda, Frank T. Bow, and Representative Forest A. Harness of Indiana, respectively, credited a different issue of *Armed Forces Talk* with potentially "inflam[ing]" or "incit[ing]" African Americans who had earlier claimed that they would refuse to bear arms in defense of the country as long as they were treated as second-class citizens — to the federal legislature's response to Puerto Rican self-determination. There were even objections by congressmen to whether or not the United States should be described by TIED as a "democracy." (In the opinion of at least two of the members present, that designation should not have been used. "This is not a democracy at all," Representative Harness maintained. "Our forefathers debated pure democracy and rejected it because it had never worked up to that time, and never will," opined Congressman Judd. They preferred that the United States be called a "republic.")[21]

Consistent with the larger anti-Communist hysteria then gripping the nation, including the acceleration of House Un-American Activities Committee investigations in the late 1940s, the congressional subcommittees were concerned that the Army, in engaging in political-education activities, was inevitably rendering itself susceptible to Communist subversion of its education organs. For the congressmen, the dissemination of information was itself not particularly troubling. What concerned them was TIED's attention to "controversial issues," which they viewed as crossing a barrier separating information from propaganda. For Representative Harness, for example, "Lectures being made in military schools on patriotism and Americanism and the Constitution and our system of government" would make for "some mighty fine pamphlets." Vigilance was necessary in the preparation of *Armed Forces Talk*, however, as "the personnel preparing these talks, or other propaganda," could be "infiltrated or dominated by people with a foreign ideology," warned Congressman Judd. "What we are getting at here is that we respect you gentlemen," Judd's colleague, Wint Smith of Kansas, told the TIED witnesses, "but we are very much afraid that down along the line someplace [in the TIED hierarchy] there is going to be somebody creep [*sic*] in that is going to start indoctrinating the Army with subversive lines."[22]

A former director of the education program, Brigadier-General Charles T. Lanham, was adamant that TIED sought "to teach that this is a great and good country and the last hope of man and everything we stand for," but his assurances about Communist penetration of the unit apparently failed to satisfy the subcommittees' membership.[23] While there was hardly any doubt as to the loyalty of TIED's leaders, the congressional hearings almost certainly had a chilling effect on the military's treatment of various subjects, and they served as a subtle lesson for future authors and editors of military education documents: Toe the official line or risk being called before Congress. The fact that senators Joseph McCarthy and William E. Jenner — the former representing the Senate Permanent Subcommittee on Investigations, and the latter, the Senate Internal Security Subcommittee — both inquired about OAFIE's authors, editors, and consultants in 1953 and 1954 must have served as a powerful reminder to the unit's staff of its hysterically anti-Communist mandate.[24]

By the early 1950s, when TIED had been reorganized as the Office of Armed Forces Information and Education, Cold War tensions were in full bloom, and OAFIE was advising service members to be constantly vigilant against Soviet designs on "the destruction of freedom everywhere." Echoing NSC-68, the important Cold War blueprint generated by the National Security Council, the American fighting man was to be trained not only in the "offensive and defensive techniques of ultra-modern warfare and armed with the most effective military weapons," but he "must be prepared as never before to parry unrelenting assaults on his mind and spirit." The "enemy soldier fighting us in this age is not always in uniform," personnel were cautioned, "for enemy assault squads operate behind our lines — even in the United States — aiming to develop disunity, apathy, indecisiveness, and muddled convictions. Among their tools are propaganda, subversion, and sabotage."[25] One such tool in the Communists' arsenal, OAFIE learned in 1953, was I. F. Stone's *Hidden History of the Korean War*. On discovering the volume in the troop information and education library of the Army's Second Infantry Division, the "anti-American red propaganda" was promptly removed, its ability to "destroy a man's faith, not only in his military leaders, but in his country as well," safely excised.[26]

Yet simply taking publications out of circulation was not enough. Cognizant of the need for a powerful offensive, OAFIE produced films and posters, published pamphlets and magazines, created radio programming, and authored pocket guides imbued with the American ideological foundations of the Cold War.[27] Its efforts were wide ranging, as was its reach. Not confined to military personnel, OAFIE's literature was used to educate public-school students (including in lessons about Vietnam) and missionaries, provide material for republication in local newspapers, and serve as a source for public lectures and public-service radio and television programming.[28] Copies of OAFIE's publications were requested by universities and public libraries, as well as by organizations such as the Foreign Policy Association and the American Geographical Society. At times, the office clearly aimed to promote responsible citizenship practices, as when it published an issue of *Armed Forces Talk* that dealt largely with the ways that off-duty servicemen could reduce their disproportionate contribution to the nation's incidence of traffic accidents.[29] Attention was also periodically paid to service members' career choices, retirement planning, and financial peace of mind.[30] Even subjects that appeared to be fairly innocuous, such as the 1952 Olympic Games, could be contextualized with explicit references to Soviet nefariousness.[31] Most common, however, were OAFIE publications addressing the perceived threat to everyday life posed by international Communism.

The Communists, service members were warned, must either "storm us from the outside" or "tear us apart from within."[32] To defend against this possibility, the Pentagon supplied a steady stream of instructive pamphlets describing Communist propaganda and how to immunize oneself from its threat to order and democracy, tips on how to identify and counter the spread of harmful rumors, and how to employ truth as a weapon in "the battle for men's minds."[33] Yet vigilance was not the publications' only objective. Issues of *Armed Forces Talk* were also devoted to celebrating the "American way of life," the "ABCs of democracy," and "what's *right*" with the United States.[34] OAFIE, in other words, sought not only to prepare servicemen for national defense but also to instill in them why they should be willing to sacrifice their lives for such a calling.

The reception to the military's publications during the early years of the Cold War, at least as registered through correspondence to OAFIE, was almost universally positive. Members of the armed services and the public wrote gushing letters about "splendid" and "very fine" articles and a "Job Well Done."[35] One serviceman found *Armed Forces Talk* "the most practical and most informative literature I've ever had the pleasure of reading."[36] Another believed an issue of the same publication to be "the best objective analysis of Communism that I . . . have ever read."[37] The pocket guides were especially popular with readers of the OAFIE literature, according to one Army information officer, for they provided "valid, accurate, and authentic information" in a "handy, useful form" that personnel could "take with them." "We have all learned to look for and depend" on the guides, Colonel Clair E. Towne maintained.[38] Although rare, there were occasional voices of political dissent. For example, one Air Force captain, with some fear of the consequences that might ensue — he specifically mentioned being "reported to the FBI and fired from my job for possessing dangerous ideas"—objected to the fact that "anything labeled 'Communist' is evil [and] anything 'democratic' or 'U.S.A.' is good. I can't believe that."[39] For the most part, however, OAFIE's publications appear to have been very warmly received.

In the early 1950s, at a time when Vietnam and other Southeast Asian states were largely unknown to most Americans, OAFIE sought to bring Indochina to the attention of U.S. military personnel. Its early descriptions of American support for the French in their post–Second World War effort to re-conquer Indochina were framed wholly in Cold War terms. In an essay on the "free world's allies," for example, "French Union forces and the Vietnamese" were said to be "battling Red Vietminh forces in Indochina."[40] In distinguishing the "Red Vietminh" from "the Vietnamese," the authors used a practice, replicated elsewhere, in which those hostile to American objectives were essentially denationalized, consequently delegitimizing their authority as representatives of indigenous concerns while more easily portraying them as agents of an organized global menace.[41]

A later issue of *Armed Forces Talk* devoted exclusively to the "situation in Southeast Asia" described the manner in which the French "tried to play ball" with Ho Chi Minh and the "Vietminh Reds" after the Second World War, only to be rebuffed by Ho's demand for "complete independence." But enlightened Vietnamese, OAFIE suggested, recognized that they "can never achieve freedom under Communist leadership." As for why this distant conflict should matter to Americans, the Defense Department offered a concise explanation:

> To take the best-known and oldest fact first, *Southeast Asia is rich in natural resources needed by the rest of the world, including the United States.* Second, *most of the countries of Southeast Asia are going through a phase of revolutionary change—from colonies of Western powers to independent nations.* Third, *Communist China (backed by the Soviet Union) is taking more and more advantage of this revolutionary movement to keep Southeast Asia in a turmoil and soften it up for the kill.*

If the Communists were to "succeed in capturing Southeast Asia," the publication warned, "the rest of Asia could not long hold out—and we, and what would be left of the free world, would be in the most dangerous situation in our entire history."[42]

Probably OAFIE's most extensive written examination of the Indochina conflict came in March 1953 when it devoted an entire issue of *Armed Forces Talk* to the French campaign in Vietnam, Cambodia, and Laos, a combined "battlefront where the free world fights one of the 'hot wars' against Red aggression." Indochina, the publication maintained, "is the key to Southeast Asia," yet it was being imperiled by Ho Chi Minh, "a determined, cautious little man who has had long service as a communist." The cleverness of Ho and the Viet Minh, OAFIE insisted, was in "hammering at the idea of national independence — which they knew would win popular support, and they soft-pedaled any mention of communism — since this then had, and still has, little appeal for the Indochinese." But, the publication continued, "There isn't any doubt now about the real nature of the Viet Minh. It is a communist-dominated group," which by definition meant it was incapable of sincere liberatory impulses.[43] Instead, as OAFIE explained elsewhere, Communists were interested only in the surreptitious establishment of totalitarian rule.[44] As such, to support the French in Indochina was, ipso facto, to support freedom. The importance of the war to U.S. military personnel was helpfully described in a "discussion pointer" at the end of the magazine: "France and the United States are proving to the people of Asia that we will assist genuine nationalist movements toward independence and will help to prevent communism from destroying national freedom." What this meant in real terms was that the conflict "is not a local shooting match. Nor is it, as the communists say, a war to restore French rule. Seen in full perspective, the war in Indochina is a vital part of the free world's struggle against the expansion of an aggressive communist empire. The people of Indochina want to work out their future in freedom rather than under the slave chains of communism." The United States, service members were told, is "sharing in Indochina's effort because we recognize that this is part of the struggle for our own freedom as well."[45]

The sentiment resonated with at least some American military personnel. The "taxpayers' money is being put into a very worthy cause," Humbert Roque ("Rocky") Versace wrote home from Vietnam in 1962. The United States was helping to "[free] the Vietnamese people from an organized Communist threat aimed at the same nasty things that all Communists want": "denying" Vietnam and "its wonderful people a chance to better themselves" and "denying them a chance to choose a system a lot better than Communism."[46] As late as 18 October 1963, just weeks before Ngo Dinh Diem was overthrown in a U.S.-backed coup, Versace "esti-mate[d]" that "Diem has his people[']s good at heart and much good is being done for the people in the countryside."[47] This would be the last time the American expressed such views to his family. Captured by the National Liberation Front less than two weeks later, Versace was report-edly executed in 1965.

The effort to shape young Americans' minds was not strictly a military endeavor, however. In the 1950s, OAFIE was aided by the American culture industry when Hollywood took up the conflict in Vietnam in a number of cinematic and televisual productions. The first films to deal with the Southeast Asian country — then part of French Indochina — were released as early as 1929, but it was in the 1950s, with the Viet Minh challenge to France, that Hollywood began to seriously employ film in support of French and American power.[48] As Jack Warner Jr. noted of *Jump Into Hell*, a 1955 effort by Warner Bros. to "show the magnificent battle of French democracy as exemplified" in the siege at Dien Bien Phu, his studio was producing not "a mere commercial venture . . . but a genuine effort to impress on the free people of the world the value of fighting for free-dom."[49] It was a message important not only to the broad American pub-lic but specifically to the young American men who would soon be sent abroad. Against this backdrop of military propaganda and Hollywood fan-tasy, the United States gradually increased its presence in southern Viet-nam, moving from massive financial and military support of the French to, eventually, direct military intervention. Indeed, by 1962 the number of troops — still officially classified as "advisers" — had increased to the point that OAFIE decided to undertake a guidebook for Vietnam. It would be the first of three such publications.

INFORMATION, MEDIATION, INDOCTRINATION

Broadly speaking, for military officials the pocket guides served at least three necessary purposes. First, as travel guidebooks are intended to do, they provided information about various sites of interest in southern Viet-nam. Second, they introduced Vietnamese culture and the Vietnamese people to service members who, in many cases, had previously had little or no contact with foreign peoples or societies. And third, they sought to persuade their readers of the dire necessity for American military involvement in Southeast Asia. Unlike other items that were more obviously intended to serve as official propaganda, however, the pocket guides cloaked their creators' ideological designs in publications ostensibly meant to assist military personnel simply seeking touristic pleasure.[50]

CONSTRUCTING VIETNAM

As the opening pages of this chapter illustrate, the mellifluous language that often characterizes traditional travel writing was not foreign to Defense Department documents in the 1960s and 1970s. Narratively mapping the landscape of southern Vietnam with poetic descriptions that could easily have been mistaken for civilian tourism literature, the 1963 pocket guide outlined the many pleasurable diversions available to American personnel serving in the region. In the highlands they could hike and go big-game hunting. In the cities they could shop, eat, and visit temples and other cultural sites. Along the coast they could sunbathe, water-ski, and dive. Photographs throughout the guidebook reinforced both southern Vietnam's charms and its government's competence.[51] The Republic of Vietnam, the guidebook suggested, was not only a burgeoning democracy but a wonderful place to fulfill one's military duty. "You and I could really enjoy a holiday here," one U.S. Army doctor wrote to his wife upon arriving in Saigon in April 1964.[52]

By the time of the second edition's appearance in 1966, however, tens of thousands more troops had been sent to Southeast Asia, and the ground invasion of Vietnam had officially begun. Not surprisingly, the concurrent pursuit of recreational enjoyment became substantially more dangerous. Just months before the landing of the first official ground troops in March 1965, for instance, three Army officers "were shot at while water skiing on the Saigon River and another, sent to investigate the incident, was wounded by a grenade," *Newsweek* reported.[53] The revised OAFIE publication thus reflected these changed circumstances for pleasure-seeking GIS. No longer were Americans informed about the possibilities for "tiger and elephant hunting in the high plateaus" or told that they might "be able to visit a tribal village in a remote mountain area."[54] Instead, the guidebook mentioned only southern Vietnam's urban and coastal attractions, and it warned that, while some sites were "always accessible," for others it "depend[ed] on the military situation."[55] Whereas American readers were notified in 1963 that they could travel to the highland resort of Dalat "from Saigon by auto in about a half a day's drive, or by bus, taxi, rail, or air," such information was excised from the 1966 text, presumably on security grounds. Gone, too, was the first edition's comments on Dalat's relatively inexpensive hotels. Consistent with the diminished focus on Vietnamese tourism opportunities and the constricting secure areas for U.S. personnel, the town was transformed in the two publications from "the center of a grand sightseeing area" to "the center of a small sightseeing area"; removed altogether from the 1966 edition was the original volume's promotion of hiking and hunting opportunities in the nearby mountains.[56] The revised language may have been rooted in the climate of increasing civilian hostility to the American military presence. On 4 April 1966, for example, thousands of students in Dalat demonstrated against the RVN government and Dalat's use as a recreation center for U.S. troops, occupying a Vietnamese–American military police facility and reportedly seizing a radio station operated by the RVN authorities.[57]

One new feature of the 1966 edition was that sites identified by their French names (or by both their French and Vietnamese names) in the 1963 guidebook were now referred to only in Vietnamese or English. No longer did OAFIE acknowledge that Danang was "formerly called Tourane" and that what was earlier the Marché Central Saigonnais was now the Saigon Central Market.[58] The reason for the changes may have been the editors' desire to erase France's colonial history for American readers, although this history was briefly acknowledged, albeit in remarkably sterile terms, in an earlier section of the guidebook. After all, recalling decades of French colonialism and the post–Second World War effort at re-conquest — and thus, implicitly, the U.S. inheritance of the French imperial project — placed the Vietnamese struggle in a substantially different context than the protection of freedom or defense against Communist aggression that, by 1966, had become the oft-repeated public explanations for the American intervention.

If the 1963 pocket guide read like literature for a working holiday, and the second edition in 1966, while much more subdued, still acknowledged southern Vietnam's limited tourism potential, the third edition in 1971 was a very different document. By the time of its publication, hundreds of thousands of Americans had served in Indochina, tens of thousands had been killed or wounded, and dissent and insubordination were increasing among the troops. The notion of "domestic" military tourism was, by the early 1970s, a thing of the past. Apart from the obvious fact of poor security throughout the south, it is also the case that some of the sites touted in the 1963 and 1966 pocket guides could not any longer be said to exist *as* tourism sites. For example, Hue, the "former royal capital" where U.S. personnel were earlier encouraged to learn "about the background of Vietnamese civilization and culture," experienced a combination of heavy American bombing and intense ground combat during the 1968 Tet Offensive that left the city and many of its architectural wonders a shambles.[59]

The reality of the war's omnipresence was reflected in the third edition's photographic imagery, which was heavily militaristic and, for the first time, featured a large number of Americans. In many instances, the U.S. personnel were portrayed as benevolent forces whom the Vietnamese were grateful to have present. The images included one of a young woman handing an American an item ("U.S. troops get gifts on International Assistance Day at Dak To"); another featured U.S. sailors on a ship next to dozens of Vietnamese ("U.S. Navy aided refugees fleeing Communist North Vietnam in 1954"); a third showed American and Vietnamese personnel cooperating with one another ("In the field, Vietnamese and Americans make professional teams"); a fourth showed "Montagnard villagers greet[ing] an American advisor with a toast"; and a final image showed two Americans speaking with a Vietnamese man while a couple of young children looked on ("Marine civic action officer talks over new school for Son Thuy").[60] Other photographs seemed intended to demonstrate the competence or professionalism of the RVN military at a time when "Vietnamization" was accelerating, including a picture of a Vietnamese man steering a boat ("Vietnamese petty officer takes the wheel on a waterway patrol") and a photograph of two men inspecting a control board ("With crew chief watching, Vietnamese pilot checks out helicopter").[61] A third type of image implied that democracy was flourishing in the south, such as one showing a voting booth with a caption that stated, "Freedom of choice in elections is guaranteed South Vietnamese."[62] Notably absent from the 1971 pocket guide were the sorts of touristic images that graced the pages of the first edition. To millions of Americans, "Vietnam" had become strictly a war.

While "domestic" Vietnamese tourism had largely become impossible for Americans by the third edition's publication, OAFIE did not entirely write off the pleasures of escape; instead, it simply shifted the destinations. Under the heading "Take Time To Travel," the 1971 guidebook suggested to service members that the "highlight of your tour in the Republic of Vietnam may well be your trip under MACV's (Military Assistance Command, Vietnam) rest and recuperation (R&R) program" to Bangkok, Sydney, Tokyo, Taipei, Hong Kong, Singapore, or Honolulu, all cities outside Vietnam.[63] This was the only mention of travel or tourism in the third edition of the guidebook.

MEETING THEIR HOSTS: BILL AND JOE'S EXCELLENT ADVENTURE

With respect to the second of the pocket guides' three general purposes — introducing U.S. personnel to the Vietnamese people and Vietnamese culture — proper and respectful behavior was encouraged of all troops. This was not simply a matter of encouraging graciousness for its own sake; there was a clear recognition that American servicemen were, whether wittingly or not, grassroots propagandists whose actions could undermine the anti-Communist crusade. Edward Lansdale, the legendary counterinsurgency specialist, cogently articulated this reality with respect to personnel assigned to "critical areas" such as Vietnam. "It isn't a question of how practicable it is for officers and enlisted men to be propagandists against Communism and for freedom, with indigenous counterparts," he wrote in a memorandum for an advisory committee on non-military instruction.

> I don't believe they should be specifically tasked to act as propagandists, simply because they would then become self-conscious and do it badly. However, as I told the Committee verbally, whether the U.S. military stationed abroad like it or not, every last one of them is a living, breathing propagandist. Our overseas military are down at the grassroots all over the world. They are, for good or bad, knowledgeable or unknowledgeable, walking, talking propagandists. If they behave as decent human beings, know and believe in our political heritage, and are aware of the enemy, then we will have trained them adequately for today's half-hidden battleground where we are placing them. This we owe them.[64]

In a problem that extended far beyond those men assigned to duty in Southeast Asia, OAFIE was aware in the 1950s and 1960s that many young Americans had no experience with international travel or with foreigners.

To overcome the potential for hostility that could result from Americans behaving as if they were at home (or worse) when in actuality they were stationed in what were, culturally, often very different lands, the unit began producing a generic *Pocket Guide to Anywhere* in 1953. The booklet featured the story of Bill and Joe, two fictional Americans who assume the role of unofficial American ambassadors when they "find themselves for the first time among alien people, whose ways are not our ways, whose language and customs are different from ours, whose religion may be different, [and] whose skin may be of different color."[65] The publication offered guidance on how to negotiate military service abroad. With respect to addressing local resentment at the American troop presence, for example, the guide provided the following lesson:

> Bill is well-meaning, but thoughtless. He doesn't quite understand why he is where he is, and he is disgruntled. Joe, on the other hand, is a little older, and has done a lot of reading about the problem, and a lot of thinking. He understands why the frictions with the people have developed.
>
> Bill and Joe are going to town on a bus for a week-end of recreation. They get no smiles from the other passengers — all local people. Bill turns to Joe:
>
> "Joe, these foreigners are beginning to get on my nerves. You'd think they'd show some appreciation of what we're doing for them."
>
> "Well, now," says Joe, "just a minute. In the first place, they're not the foreigners here. We are. This is their country and we're here as guests. If the people here don't seem too friendly, maybe we're partly to blame. Maybe we're doing a lot of things that irritate them.
>
> "And in the second place, Bill, we're not here to do these people a favor. We're here for only one reason. We're here to do a job for the United States. Our Government believes that the security of this country we're stationed in is tied up with the security of our own country.
>
> "Any way you look at it this job of holding back Red aggression is just too big for one nation. The free nations have got to work together. The people in this country right here realize that. That's why they're willing to let us occupy bases and quarter troops on their soil."
>
> "Sometimes, I think they just want us to bail them out," Bill objects.
>
> "No," says Joe, "you're wrong there. It was a hard blow to their pride to have to accept help from us, to let us build camps and installations all

over their country. You can hardly blame them for wishing they didn't have to have us around.

"We'd feel the same way, Bill, if the tables were turned. You know, since the days of George Washington, we've never had to bring in foreign troops to help defend our soil. How would you like it if a lot of foreign soldiers were camped all over the United States?"

"I don't think I'd like it," says Bill.[66]

After further conversation, Bill agreed that he, too, would be resentful if forced to rely on foreigners' assistance, thus helping him understand the somewhat frosty reception that he and Joe experienced.

The 1963 pocket guide to Vietnam offered a more direct plea for humility and graciousness. "Wherever you go, remember that Viet-Nam is a land of dignity and reserve," the authors wrote. "Your good manners, thoughtfulness, and restrained behavior will be appreciated by the Vietnamese." If the personnel abided by these cultural norms, they were told, "Viet-Nam and the Vietnamese are prepared to welcome you officially and unofficially. Meet them halfway and you'll be glad you did." Yet at the same time that scores of Americans were arriving in Vietnam with such counsel in hand, thousands of southern insurgents were actively engaged in resisting the Saigon government essentially created by the United States—a Vietnamese regime that, with American acquiescence, had already executed, tortured, and imprisoned tens of thousands of its opponents. But the sentiments of these Vietnamese did not factor into the travel writing of the Pentagon authors. Instead, the insurgency in the countryside was neatly subsumed within the rhetoric of global Communist subversion: "By helping the people of this proud new nation repulse the aggression of the Communist Viet Cong, you will strike a telling blow for democracy. By doing it in a spirit of friendship you will be adding greatly to the strength of the bonds that unite freedom-loving people throughout the world."[67] The clear association of personal behavior with the success of America's global mission was constantly reinforced.[68]

SELLING A WAR: REINFORCING THE ANTI-COMMUNIST CONSENSUS

The Defense Department guidebooks, like their private counterparts, were ideological products. And as in many civilian publications, the OAFIE authors provided their readers with a synopsis of the Vietnamese past. It was this history writing that stood at the center of the pocket guides' third general purpose: reinforcing for U.S. service members why it was necessary for them to risk their lives in Vietnam. Whether OAFIE succeeded in this objective is unknown (and, thirty to forty years later, probably unknowable). Regardless, it must be noted that the guidebooks were only one element of the larger ideological struggle that developed during the war. Americans were not unthinking automatons merely waiting to be injected with the pocket guides' dose of anti-Communist history. Instead, the political and popular cultures of post–Second World War America had conditioned the U.S. citizenry about the ideological foundations of the Cold War, and the guidebooks, like other OAFIE creations, helped to mediate Americans' roles within it. The Vietnamese revolution thus became subsumed within broader Cold War concerns for policymakers and for thousands of military personnel alike. But the publications were products of their precise historical moments, such that by 1971, when the third edition was published, the pocket guide almost certainly would have been treated with far greater skepticism by service members than the first edition in 1963. Official claims were being subjected to constant critical scrutiny by the mid- to late 1960s, and the enormous antiwar movement, both civilian and military, fostered a climate of distrust with respect to self-serving government pronouncements.

It is also important to recall that not all members of the armed forces — such as, I suspect, the anonymous authors of the various OAFIE publications —were privy to the high-level communications or studies in which many of the most honest assessments of the Vietnamese revolutionary movement could be found. The division is thus not always clear between conscious efforts to instill in service members a distorted version of the Indochinese past and an unconscious reflection of official ideology.[69] It is also not certain to what extent this division clearly existed for many members of the military. There is probably no greater burden than being asked to kill or be killed, so those called on to assume this position naturally desire to believe, however desperately, that they are justified in taking the lives of other human beings or would be heroes in losing their own. Consequently, during the war in Vietnam, there was an obvious incentive for service members to accept the official narrative of northern Communist aggression against a democratic government in the RVN. Whether or not this narrative was genuinely embraced by the authors of the OAFIE pocket guides, the publications clearly parroted the official line while ignoring the growing voices of dissent, both scholarly and popular, that marked the shattering of the American liberal consensus during the 1960s and 1970s.

With respect to the guidebooks' historical narratives, the second edition was only slightly modified from the first. The 1971 pocket guide, conversely, was almost entirely rewritten. Quickly gliding over ancient Vietnamese history, centuries of Chinese domination, the Cham civilization, and a Vietnamese "golden age" under the dynasty founded by Emperor Le in the fifteenth century, the coverage in the 1963 guidebook devoted to the period after 1863 — the year marking the beginning of French colonial control — received approximately twice the attention as the two thousand years preceding it. The pre-1863 history received even less coverage in the second edition, with four-and-a-half of the thirteen paragraphs that appeared in the 1963 publication removed by 1966.

Broadly speaking, the Pentagon authors used the guidebooks' historical background to render the RVN leadership the inheritors of Vietnam's patriotic tradition, thus lending legitimacy and purpose to the mission of those Americans assigned to counter the threat posed by Communist interlopers who, it was suggested, were aggressively seeking to undermine the genuine liberatory impulses of the Saigon government. As the actual history of Indochina found the United States on the side of French colonialism, OAFIE sought to cloak the U.S. collaboration with the French (or to ascribe it simply to anti-Communism) and to accentuate what it considered the positive legacies of this colonial past. The 1963 pocket guide, moreover, suggested that Vietnamese aggression or intransigence inspired the French colonial presence: "Conflicts between the Viet-Nam people and French missionaries are said to have sparked the French military action that resulted in the takeover of the province of Cochin China by the French in 1863."[70] Overall, the guidebook framed the French imperial project as largely selfless and, while admitting to Vietnamese frustration with French domination, nevertheless beneficial in important respects:

> Although their administrative policies led to deep resentments by the Vietnamese, the French did much to advance the standards of living of the country. They built roads and railroads, canals, dikes, churches, hospitals, and scientific institutions, and sent many Vietnamese to France for advanced education. The famous Pasteur Institutes, estab-

lished in various cities to aid in public health problems, were largely instrumental in stopping the recurrent outbreaks of epidemics of small-pox, cholera, and other diseases which had plagued the nation.[71]

The description should be considered within the context of the American presence in the south. Like France, the United States was viewed by most Vietnamese as a domineering foreign party. But also like the French, the Americans rationalized their presence by claiming to be improving the lot of the people. Such assistance presumably served as the humanitarian carrot sating the consciences of those Americans concurrently wielding a painful military stick.

Postcolonial Vietnamese history — or, at least, that portion of it experienced by those living north of the seventeenth parallel — was either neglected or, in describing the events that led to Vietnam's temporary partition in 1954, implied to be emblematic of Communist duplicity. The Pentagon authors observed, "After the fall of France in 1940, the Japanese occupied French Indochina. This occupation continued until 1945 when Japan granted Viet-Nam independence under a puppet emperor, Bao Dai. Meanwhile, by the time of the Japanese occupation, a group of expatriate, anti-French Vietnamese had formed in South China." The guide continued,

> One of these was Ho Chi Minh, a dedicated Communist, who entered Hanoi secretly in 1944. A year later, after Japan's surrender to the Allies, Ho's forces became the "Vietnam Liberation Army" and the shadow government set up by Japan under Emperor Bao Dai soon fell before the Communist leader's well-organized onslaught. The emperor abdicated, handing over his powers to Ho Chi Minh. At the same time, a "Provisional Executive Committee for South Vietnam[,]" with seven Communists among its nine members, took control of Saigon.

The final sentence was immediately followed in the guidebook by a new section heading: "Communists Show Their Hand."[72]

Whether out of ignorance or purposeful neglect is uncertain, but whatever the reason, the authors failed to mention Ho and the revolutionaries' active collaboration with the United States against the Japanese during World War Two, the Americans' favorable impression of Ho at that time, and the symbolically important U.S. presence in Hanoi's Ba Dinh

Square during his declaration of Vietnamese independence before approximately four hundred thousand cheering supporters on 2 September 1945. The explanation for the omission may lie in OAFIE's need to represent these respected previous allies contemporaneously as de facto members of the international Communist conspiracy who were cleverly manipulating the sincere aspirations of the Vietnamese people. Under the heading "Communists Show Their Hand," the authors addressed the undeniable popularity of the revolutionary forces by simply designating them "pretend[ers]":

> Like many other colonial people, the Vietnamese wanted national independence above all. That is why many followed Ho Chi Minh and the Communist-directed Viet Minh which pretended to be a league for the country's independence.
>
> When the French tried to regain a foothold in Viet-Nam in 1946, Viet Minh forces attacked them on a wide front, supported by many people who had only one purpose in mind; that was, national independence for their country. So began the costly 8-year Indo-China war that ended with the division of Viet-Nam at a Geneva conference table in July 1954. The southern part of the country struck out as a free nation — the Republic of Viet-Nam — under [the] leadership of Ngo [D]inh Diem, with Saigon as its capital. The northern part of the country became the Communist-controlled Democratic Republic of Viet-Nam, with Hanoi as its capital.[73]

The fact that the Geneva Accords explicitly identified the "independence, unity, and territorial integrity" of a single Vietnamese state that was to be only temporarily divided into separate military "regrouping zones" — one for the French colonialist forces, the other for those of the Democratic Republic of Vietnam — until the country's reunification following a nationwide election in July 1956, and that the "military demarcation line" at the seventeenth parallel was to be strictly "provisional" and "should not in any way be interpreted as constituting a political or territorial boundary," was ignored by the Pentagon authors.[74] Instead — under the heading "A Free Nation Emerges" — they addressed the "legality of the present Republic of Viet-Nam Government" by insisting that it was "confirmed in October 1955 by a referendum which offered the people of the nation a choice between Emperor Bao Dai as chief of a state patterned on the old regime, and Ngo [D]inh Diem as chief of state of a republic." The "vote was overwhelmingly in favor of the latter," the authors noted, "and the Republic was proclaimed with Ngo [D]inh Diem as President."[75]

But the Defense Department's treatment of the "legality" of the Republic of Vietnam must be understood as an elision. Under the Geneva Accords, there was to be a nationwide election in 1956 — that is, in both the northern and southern zones — to determine a national government. This vote was denied by the Saigon authorities with the support of the United States. The 1955 southern referendum, which was by all credible accounts fraudulent, had no legal basis in the settlement ending the French war. Moreover, the guidebook's affirmative comment that the vote "overwhelmingly" favored Diem seems risible when the results of the referendum are considered in context. In Saigon, for example, the Diem ticket claimed more than 605,000 votes, but the city contained only 405,000 registered voters. Throughout the south, Diem improbably purported to have received 98.2 percent of the vote, despite being told by U.S. advisers that 60 percent would be an adequate majority.[76] American officials were well aware of the referendum's procedural and structural shortcomings. In a confidential dispatch, the U.S. ambassador in Saigon characterized the electoral campaign as a "completely one-sided" endeavor in which "no support for Bao Dai or opposition to Diem was permitted" as "the government carried out a most intensive and efficient propaganda campaign for Diem and against Bao Dai." While claiming shortly after the referendum that "no solid evidence has yet turned up to substantiate charges of fraud" in the actual voting process, the ambassador nevertheless concluded that the election was a "travesty on democratic procedures, since the Diem forces maintained absolute control over all avenues of propaganda and did not permit the opposition to make its case." Moreover, the referendum was designed in such a way that "voters who wished to depose Bao Dai without voting for Diem had no way of registering such a vote." In sum, the referendum could not have been considered "a truly democratic election."[77]

Diem's unpopularity, as well as his authoritarianism, was hardly a secret to American diplomats and military officials, although this reality was not disclosed to the larger readership of oafie's publications. The description of the rvn as a "free nation" must thus be interpreted within the context of the military's campaign to persuade its charges of the justice of its Vietnam mission. At approximately the same time that the first pocket guide was released, American policymakers were contemplating the overthrow of the southern government, an eventuality to which they secretly assented in October 1963. However, Diem's antidemocratic ways had been well known for years. For instance, as early as February 1956, in an intelligence brief prepared at the State Department, Diem was described as "almost pathologically sensitive to criticism and potential opposition, with the result that the regime is becoming increasingly autocratic despite his democratic principles," which were generally asserted but never clarified.[78] Similarly, in an October 1961 secret memorandum from the chairman of the State Department's Vietnam Task Force to Maxwell Taylor, the president's military representative, Diem was said to be "cast in the mold of an oriental despot" and someone who ruled in "the oriental despotic tradition."[79] How these internal assessments squared with the RVN's public description in the guidebook as "a free nation . . . under [the] leadership of Ngo [D]inh Diem" was not explained, although a former aide to John Foster Dulles would several years later provide some clarification. Lamenting in 1966 the American decision to abandon Diem in 1963, John Hanes informed the journalist Richard Crowl that Diem represented America's best hope in establishing "a free government" in Vietnam. "In this case," he continued, " 'free' means non-communist, because 'free' in Vietnam doesn't mean a democracy of the United States type, any more than it does in Cuba or in Ghana or in any place that's at a different stage of development."[80] The usage suggests the extent to which the pocket guides were intended to serve as tools of ideological indoctrination that paid little heed to the internal realities of various states' political systems.

Apart from its efforts to establish the credibility of the political leadership chosen by the United States to rule the south, OAFIE also was tasked with the important role of explaining the undeniable opposition to the Saigon government. It did so by writing recent Vietnamese history to the RVN's political and moral advantage. The immediate origins of the Second Indochina War — that is, the American war — were ascribed in the 1963 guidebook not to the repression of the Diem regime but, instead, to the threat Hanoi allegedly perceived in the south's "progress":

South Viet-Nam's progress under President Ngo [D]inh Diem irked the North and, during 1959, Communist guerrillas began an intensified campaign of terror in the remote countryside of South Viet-Nam. Village, district, and province chiefs, policemen, people's defense militiamen, civil guardsmen, school teachers, malaria eradication workers, and Government officials were assassinated; roads and trains were destroyed; and bridges and schools were burned. The tactical objective of the Communists was then and still is to destroy the people's confidence in their Government and its ability to protect them. By sabotaging the nation at its roots in the rural and mountain areas, they hope to achieve the strategic goal of toppling the Diem regime and turning the south to communism.[81]

It is clear that the Defense Department believed that the morale of U.S. service members, and thus their effectiveness as a fighting force, was tied to their belief that they were defending against Communist aggression. Pentagon officials only had to recall, for instance, the opposition displayed by members of the U.S. Merchant Marine when assigned to transport French troops and Foreign Legionnaires to Vietnam in 1945. In the years since then, therefore, the promotion of anti-Communism became crucial to the military's mission.

The pocket guides were products of this ideological campaign. The 1963 edition described the conflict as an outside effort to topple the Diem government to which the southern peasants were implied to be loyal, directly stating that "increasing numbers of Viet Cong guerrillas were infiltrating into South Viet-Nam through Laos and by sea," forcing the United States to "furnish the aid so seriously needed" in strengthening "South Viet-Nam's defense against the Communist guerrilla aggression directed by the North."[82] When the second edition was published in 1966, the insurgents were designated "a subversive network the North Vietnamese had left in the South after the country was divided."[83] Like the 1963 pocket guide's comments on the 1955 referendum, which were slightly revised in the second edition, these statements contradicted internal American evaluations of the Diem government and the nature of the southern struggle.[84]

The discrepancies were several. First, despite the publication of two State Department white papers (in 1961 and 1965) arguing for precisely such a framework, many U.S. officials were aware that the notion of aggression by the Democratic Republic of Vietnam (DRV) was in fact quite fragile, as one leading scholar termed it.[85] Presidential adviser Walt W. Rostow, for example, wrote to Secretary of State Dean Rusk in July 1961: "As I see it, the purpose of raising the Viet-Nam issue as a case of aggression is either to induce effective international action or to free our hands and our consciences for whatever we have to do. . . . At the minimum we put ourselves in a political position to salvage South Laos and save Viet-Nam with a more rational military plan than we now have."[86] Or, as conceded by the *Pentagon Papers* analysts, "Most of those who took up arms [in the 'structured rebellion' that began in 1957 and 1958] were South Vietnamese, and the causes for which they fought were by no means contrived in North Vietnam." Moreover, they wrote of the period before 1960, "No direct links have been established between Hanoi and perpetrators of rural violence," and they opined that captured documents suggesting "the communists plotted and controlled the entire insurgency" were "difficult to take at face value." The "official U.S. position" that "the DRV manipulated the entire war . . . can be supported," the analysts concluded, but "the case is not wholly compelling, especially for the years 1955–1959."[87]

Second, it was accepted among American policymakers that the Diem regime — that is, "their Government" — was widely despised by the people of the south, particularly in "the remote countryside." Indeed, the assassinations carried out by the National Liberation Front (NLF) in most instances were credited by observers with bolstering the popularity of the insurgents. On the matter of southern Vietnamese opinions about the Diem government, U.S. Ambassador Eldridge Durbrow cabled Secretary of State Christian A. Herter from Saigon in March 1960 about the worsening security situation in the south, noting that "signs of general apathy and considerable dissatisfaction . . . have become more evident among the people in rural areas." There was, Durbrow wrote, resentment toward the government "because of the methods which are all too often employed by local officials," including coercion, involuntary labor, torture, extortion, favoritism, and corruption.[88] So detested was Diem and his nepotistic government that, by the fall of that same year, Durbrow notified Herter that if Diem failed to initiate "proper political, psychological, economic, and security measures, it may become necessary for [the] U.S. government to begin consideration [of] alternative courses of action and leaders in order [to] achieve our objective."[89]

Third, the statement that the guerrillas sought to "[turn] the south to communism" was contradicted by the NLF platform announced over Liberation Radio in February 1961, which expressed the revolutionaries' desire for "a government of national and democratic union . . . composed of representatives of all social classes, of all nationalities, of the various political parties, of all religions."[90] While Communists certainly played a dominant role in the coalition, the diversity of the NLF, as disclosed by a *Pentagon Papers* analyst in 1968, was nevertheless known to Defense Department officials:

> It is clear that the NLF was not intended as an exclusively communist enterprise. Rather it was designed to encompass anti-GVN [anti-RVN] activists, and to exploit the bi-polar nature of politics within South Vietnam. In the period 1954–1960, prior to the NLF's "creation," the objectives of insurgents in the South, other than the overthrow of My-Diem, were vague. Communists in the South no doubt shared the overall objectives of the DRV, and were aiming at unification of all Vietnam under the Hanoi government. Some rebel nationalists were no doubt aware of the communists' ambitions, but would have regarded such an outcome as acceptable, if not desirable. Others, disillusioned by the actions of the Diem regime after 1956, simply looked toward the establishment of a genuine democratic government in the South. Some peasants may have been fighting to rid themselves of government, or to oppose modernization, looking only to village autonomy. The sects, if not struggling for a democratic regime, were fighting for their independence, as were some of the tribal groups who chose to join the NLF. The National Liberation Front formulated and publicly articulated objectives for all these.[91]

At the level of foreign policy, the NLF sought a neutralist position in the global Cold War — for Washington, neutralism was essentially synonymous with Communist appeasement — and expressed its desire to stay out of "any military bloc" and "refuse any military alliance with another country." For the members of the NLF, a great many of whom were not Communists, the southern Vietnamese zone created by the 1954 Geneva Accords, to be gradually reunified with the northern zone, would pursue "diplomatic relations with all countries, regardless of their political regime, in accordance with the principles of peaceful coexistence adopted at the Bandung Conference," the gathering of nonaligned states from Africa and Asia in 1955.[92]

And fourth, the 1963 pocket guide made no mention of the widespread repression by Diem of the revolutionaries and their sympathizers who remained below the seventeenth parallel after 1954. It was this repression — which was hardly a secret to American policymakers — that, by all scholarly accounts, inflamed southern opinion in the late 1950s and inspired the official turn to southern armed opposition.

By 1966, with the publication of the guidebook's second edition, Diem had been overthrown and assassinated in a U.S.-backed coup. The intense opposition to his administration that had been evident among southern Vietnamese since the mid-1950s was finally, if only subtly, conceded by OAFIE, which, after all, had to somehow account for the removal from power of this longtime American client. The 1966 pocket guide thus inserted a new paragraph into its section on the RVN government:

> From 1956 to 1963 South Vietnam was governed under a constitution modeled in many respects on those of the United States and the Philippines, which provided for a strong executive, a unicameral National Assembly, and a judicial system. The Diem government, however, became increasingly personal and dictatorial. Opposition was suppressed; there were charges of injustice and corruption against members of his family, particularly his brother, Ngo [D]inh Nhu; and President Diem lost in part the confidence and loyalty of the people. In 1963 serious political conflicts arose between the Government and the Buddhists, the largest single religious group in the country. Other non-Communist oppositionists to Diem made common cause with the Buddhists, and, on 1 November, 1963, the Diem government was overthrown by a military *coup d'etat*. Diem and his brother, Ngo [D]inh Nhu, who exercised great power in the regime, were killed.[93]

In other words, what in 1963 had been described by OAFIE as a "free nation" with "dedicated leadership" making "progress under President Ngo [D]inh Diem" — in whose defense the United States was "strik[ing] a telling blow for democracy" — was rhetorically transformed, by 1966, into a corrupt and dictatorial regime inhibiting southern Vietnamese national aspirations.[94]

The Pentagon authors were careful, however, to ascribe the problems in the south to faulty Vietnamese leadership rather than to faulty American policies. To have done the latter — that is, to have called into question the attempt by the United States to establish by force a separate anti-Communist state south of the seventeenth parallel — was inconceivable.

As for the succession of coups that for nearly two years followed the assassination of Diem, OAFIE described it somewhat mildly as "a series of changes of government" that had, admittedly, resulted in "considerable political instability." (The brief period from November 1963 to February 1965 witnessed more than a dozen different governments.)[95] The authors reminded U.S. service members, however, that "two things should be kept in mind":

> One, that the Vietnamese had little preparation for self-government and are struggling to develop unity and stability during a very dangerous internal security crisis caused by Communist aggression; and two, that not one of the groups competing for political power is in favor of accommodation with the Viet Cong.[96]

The second claim is notable for its failure to acknowledge that advocacy of "accommodation with the Viet Cong," including even "neutralism," carried great personal risk. Moreover, such accommodation was formally forbidden under a revised RVN constitution — Article 4 proscribed any activity "designed to publicize or carry out communism" — just one year after the second edition of the guidebook was approved by U.S. military officials.[97] Most important, however, the National Liberation Front, which was one of only two groupings that enjoyed a substantial degree of popular support in the south (the other, which emerged on a considerable scale in 1963, was the organized Buddhist movement), was prohibited from formally "competing for political power."

As for the first claim, the racialist conviction of American policymakers that the Vietnamese were inherently incapable of "self-government" until, one presumes, sufficiently mentored by the United States had deep roots. The historian Mark Bradley has documented how the prevalence of this belief dates to the moments when Vietnam and the Vietnamese first began seriously occupying the strategic thinking of American officials in the years surrounding the Second World War.[98] But in fact, as Bradley notes, the notion of indigenous incapacity is thoroughly ingrained in the imperial ideology of U.S. policymakers, and it was used to justify the expansionist policies of the United States well before the first American steps to prevent Vietnamese independence under the Viet Minh.[99] What, in this case, the pocket guide implied to be an innate Vietnamese inability to govern themselves should in actuality be interpreted as a failure by the United States to create competent authorities sufficiently subservient to its wishes. The southern Vietnamese people were not given the opportunity to demonstrate their capacity for "self-government" by freely developing their own political institutions, for U.S. officials were aware that, if given the choice, they would almost certainly have elected members of the revolutionary movement or other opposition groups as their representatives. But rather than acknowledge this reality, U.S. officials ascribed their clients' failure to genuinely secure the support of the southern people to a Vietnamese lack of "preparation for self-government."

If the little support that existed for the RVN leadership was centered largely in the urban merchant classes benefiting from U.S. aid and in those individuals profiting from official corruption, sustained or meaningful allegiance to the Saigon authorities was virtually impossible to locate in the countryside. The United States expended considerable resources in assessing southern rural opinion, and its findings were consistently unfavorable to its hopes for popular support. But rather than frankly concede this conundrum, OAFIE sought to cloak it by claiming that the National Liberation Front was responsible for the government's deficit of support, and that the insurgents, like the Saigon authorities, were also unpopular:

> Political activity has been confined chiefly to the cities and has had little impact on the great bulk of the population living in the countryside. These people — the villagers, the rice farmers, the rubber plantation workers — have had little feeling of identification with either the Viet Cong or the central Government. The Vietnamese farmer lives in a small world limited by the bamboo hedge around his village. His loyalties are to his family, his land, and his spiritual world. The Viet Cong have neutralized the people's support for the Government in some rural areas by a combination of terror and political action. One of the continuing programs of the central Government has been to provide better security and living conditions to convince the villagers that the Government the Communists seek to destroy is *their* Government.[100]

There is no doubt that at least part of the guidebook assessment was accurate: Rural Vietnamese did not identify with the Saigon authorities. But that they did sympathize with the NLF was known — albeit often denied — by U.S. officials. Putting aside the authors' condescending suggestion about the peasants' lack of political sophistication, one need not have looked far to gauge the people's identification with the revolutionaries. Numerous Americans recognized, and bemoaned, the relative political strength of the southern insurgents. For example, Robert Scigliano, formerly a member of the Michigan State University Vietnam Advisory Group, reported the estimate of "American officials in Saigon at the end of 1962" that "about one-half of the South Vietnamese support the National Liberation Front."[101] Discussing American assessments in 1963, the *Pentagon Papers* analysts conceded that "only the Viet Cong had any real support and influence on a broad base in the countryside."[102] The U.S. official probably most knowledgeable about the south, John Paul Vann, wrote in 1965:

A popular political base for the Government of South Vietnam does not now exist. . . . The existing government is oriented toward the exploitation of the rural and lower class urban populations. It is, in fact, a continuation of the French colonial system of government with upper class Vietnamese replacing the French. . . . The dissatisfaction of the agrarian population . . . is expressed largely through alliance with the NLF.[103]

Similarly, in 1966 the head of the RVN Military Directorate acknowledged the NLF's widespread popularity: "We are very weak politically and without the strong political support of the population which the NLF have."[104] Given the broad acknowledgement of the revolutionaries' political appeal, OAFIE's effort to deny the southern peasants' identification with them must be interpreted as disingenuous in the extreme.

Whereas the 1963 and 1966 editions of the Vietnam pocket guide appeared to be subtle manipulations of the historical record in order to buttress the legitimacy of the American intervention, the third edition in 1971 represented a nearly unabashed assault on the minds of military personnel. The publication of the *Pentagon Papers* that same year would demonstrate to millions of Americans the extent to which government officials had deceived the public for well over a decade about the realities of the Vietnamese political situation and their effects on the U.S. military campaign. But even before the secret Defense Department history was exposed by Daniel Ellsberg, the U.S. armed forces appeared to be in a state of grave peril. Desertion and racial tensions were widespread, drug use was endemic, and troops were periodically "fragging" their superiors and refusing to obey orders. The situation had become so dire that, in June 1971, Colonel Robert Heinl concluded in an essay in the *Armed Forces Journal* that, "by every conceivable indicator, our army that now remains in Vietnam is in a state approaching collapse, with individual units avoiding or having refused combat, murdering their officers and noncommissioned officers, drug-ridden, and dispirited where not near-mutinous."[105] While the United States had been attempting for years to win the "hearts and minds" of the Vietnamese people, it was clear by the early 1970s that American policymakers had lost the broad support of even their own military charges.

The 1971 pocket guide reflected the U.S. government's deteriorating political and military control. Dispensing with the subtle nuances that had appeared sporadically in the first two editions, the historical narrative of 1971, an almost total fabrication of the post–Second World War Vietnamese past, signified a full rejection of the critical scholarship of the late 1960s and a desperate embrace of the crumbling official narrative. In the Pentagon's version of history, in mid-December 1946 the "Communists launched attacks against the French and those Vietnamese leaders who were working with them," thus sparking the First Indochina War; ignored entirely in this tale of revolutionary aggression was the major French bombardment of Haiphong just weeks before that killed an estimated 6,000 Vietnamese civilians, not to mention the *Pentagon Papers'* conclusion that the "issue of who was the aggressor" in initiating the anti-colonialist insurgency "has never been resolved."[106]

Concerning electoral matters, the "Communists who controlled the north had no intention of complying with the provisions of the Geneva Accords, especially that article which called for free elections," the pocket guide asserted.[107] The purposes for which the publication was intended become clearer when compared to the historical narrative disclosed in the *Pentagon Papers*, which was completed at least two years earlier. Thus, the *Pentagon Papers* analysts concluded in a study not intended for public consumption that the DRV "repeatedly tried to engage the Geneva machinery, forwarding messages to the Government of South Vietnam [GVN] in July 1955, May and June 1956, March 1958, July 1959, and July 1960, proposing consultations to negotiate 'free general elections by secret ballot,' and to liberalize North–South relations in general. Each time the GVN replied with disdain, or with silence."[108] Referring specifically to the political leadership in Saigon after 1954, OAFIE discussed a "constant" goal in the "history of democratic government in the Republic of Vietnam": "freedom of the individual to elect his representatives by secret ballot and in that manner decide his own future." "Freedom of choice in elections," the authors wrote, "is guaranteed South Vietnamese."[109]

But the most recent presidential elections in the south, held in 1967, were deeply flawed, according to U.S. officials. As it became clear that the RVN leadership was determined to exclude from the ballot both Duong Van Minh ("Big" Minh) — the candidate most likely to pose a significant challenge to the incumbent ticket of Nguyen Van Thieu and Nguyen Cao Ky — and Au Truong Thanh — the only candidate advocating a ceasefire and negotiated settlement to end the war — the State Department cabled the U.S. Embassy in Saigon expressing its deep concerns. "Denial of Minh's candidacy in our view so deeply affects the election process," Secretary of State Dean Rusk wrote, "that we believe we have a legitimate reason for entering into discussions about it" with Thieu and Ky. As it appeared unlikely that RVN officials could come up with a "convincing case" for Minh's exclusion, the State Department feared that his absence from the ballot would "undermine present strong GVN position based on its offering South Vietnamese people opportunity to make free choice, and will jeopardize internal benefits expected from elections. Adverse reactions on U.S. and world opinion also predictable." Rusk concluded, "We fear that Directorate's position on Minh's candidacy may be seriously damaging to chances of elections making contribution to our objectives in Viet-Nam and, perhaps, even to political development process."[110] The same was true of Thieu's and Ky's exclusion of Au Truong Thanh. The stated justification — he was alleged to have "communist or neutralist associations" — seemed "exceedingly dubious" in light of his service in several cabinets since the coup against Diem. The prevention of his candidacy would "be another clear sign that Directorate does not intend to permit a genuinely free election" while presenting Tri Quang of the organized Buddhist movement "with ready-made protest issue."[111] In the end, neither Minh nor Thanh was allowed on the ballot, highlighting the incongruity between the pocket guide's assertion that "freedom of choice in elections is guaranteed South Vietnamese" and the State Department's internal assessment that a "genuinely free election" was not possible in 1967 without the inclusion of Minh and Thanh.[112]

With respect to the 1955 referendum between Diem and Bao Dai, the OAFIE authors wrote that "free elections were held in the southern half of the country in October 1955," contradicting the confidential finding of the U.S. Embassy that the vote was "a travesty on democratic procedures."[113] The *Pentagon Papers* analysts were less blunt but still frank, describing Diem's incredible margin of victory as "dubiously overwhelming," although they believed that he "plainly won nevertheless."[114]

Similar distortions were presented about the nature of the early southern struggle. According to the pocket guide narrative, "Thousand [*sic*] of Communist sympathizers had remained in the Republic of Vietnam after the partition of the country," and when "it became evident that the newly formed nation was not going to fall of its own accord, these Communists — or Viet Cong — shifted from subversion and terrorist tactics to open warfare."[115] But this statement flatly contradicted a *Pentagon Papers* assessment, written no later than 1968 but not publicly disclosed until after the pocket guide's publication, that the "stay-behinds" were "by no means . . . all dedicated communists in the doctrinaire sense," and that many even "reported that they resented and feared the communists in the Viet Minh." Moreover, they "apparently might have been willing to serve the GVN [that is, the RVN] faithfully had it not hounded them out of the society."[116] Likewise, the OAFIE guidebook insisted, the "Liberation Army" of the National Liberation Front "consisted of hard-core Viet Cong," contradicting the admission in the *Pentagon Papers* that the NLF was not "an exclusively communist enterprise."[117]

The United States, according to OAFIE, wished only for peace in Indochina, not the war into which it had implicitly been forced. "The United States has consistently stated its readiness to negotiate peace in Vietnam on the basis of the 1954 Geneva Accords and in a manner which would insure the security and territorial integrity of the entire Southeast Asian region," the pocket guide insisted.[118] The *Pentagon Papers* analysts noted a decidedly less accommodationist view. "The Geneva Settlement of 1954 was inherently flawed as a durable peace for Indochina," they wrote, "since it depended upon France, and since both the U.S. and the Republic of South Vietnam excepted themselves." At a prescriptive level, the "Southeast Asia policy of the U.S. in the aftermath of the Geneva Conference was conservative, focused on organizing collective defense against further inroads of communism, not on altering *status quo*. *Status quo* was the two Vietnams set up at Geneva, facing each other across a demilitarized zone."[119] In other words, Washington had no intention of adhering to the most fundamental element of the 1954 accords: the unity and territorial integrity of the single Vietnamese state only temporarily partitioned in the aftermath of the French war.

Whereas the first two editions of the pocket guide had portrayed the Saigon authorities as the genuine nationalists of the south, the third edition in 1971 escalated the rhetoric surrounding this issue by repeatedly distinguishing "communists" from "nationalists"—a distinction much clearer in the minds of American policymakers than in those Vietnamese revolutionaries who saw no contradiction in believing themselves to be both—and suggesting that the NLF was the former while hostile to the latter. Probably the most explicit articulation of this larger framework was OAFIE's description of the various parties to the French war:

> The war which followed [the Communist "attacks against the French and those Vietnamese leaders who were working with them"] was actually a three-way struggle. On one side was [*sic*] Ho's Communist forces which sought to impose a dictatorship on the country. On the other side were French forces seeking to regain control of a former colony and those Vietnamese nationalists who chose to fight militarily with the French against the Communists but who wished neither French nor Communist domination.[120]

The true nationalists, in other words, were France's military collaborators rather than the Vietnamese forces, organized under the Viet Minh, who enjoyed the admiration and support of the bulk of the Vietnamese population. The early RVN leadership, whose state, according to the *Pentagon Papers*, "was essentially the creation of the United States," assumed OAFIE's nationalist designation following the Geneva Accords: "The political portions [of the documents] only served to heighten the tension between the Vietnamese nationalists and the Communists."[121]

For the OAFIE authors, "Freedom's Long Road," as traveled by the Saigon government, began more than twenty-one centuries earlier with "a simple goal — freedom from foreign rule." It was an objective "celebrated in the folklore of a people who have as their heroes the men and women who inspired and led them in struggles against conquerors and invaders." This patriotic mantle, according to OAFIE, had been inherited by the post-1954 southern regimes. "This desire for freedom from foreign rule is as strong today as it was centuries ago," the authors wrote. "Eighteen million citizens of the Republic of Vietnam are determined to fight against an enemy whose political theories and practices would destroy the culture and way of life of their nation as surely as has been done in the Communist-controlled portion of the Vietnamese homeland."[122] To preserve the democratic foundations of the RVN, they claimed, "that nation's leaders and people have asked one of the world's oldest democracies to assist in their struggle against Communist aggressors. What they are fighting for is one of man's fondest dreams — freedom."[123] Surely, OAFIE hoped, this was an objective for which all American personnel would be willing to risk their lives.

The pocket guides for Vietnam underwent a number of evolutions that tended to mirror the changing military predicament of the United States. Although mired in an escalating conflict, the war seemed sufficiently small in 1963 — to most Americans, at least — that the original Defense Department guidebook was in many ways a rosy introduction to the touristic marvels of Vietnam. By the time of the last edition's publication in 1971, however, the authors had, not surprisingly, abandoned any pretext that Vietnam might serve as a holiday site for military personnel. Rather than an overview of ideal places to hunt, fish, and sunbathe, the pocket guide was transformed into a primer on martial responsibilities. In this respect it differed from the RVN travel literature of the era, which continued to foreground the attractions of southern Vietnam instead of the overwhelming reality of the war being experienced by most Vietnamese. All of the guidebooks, pamphlets, and brochures shared a common attribute, however: They were ideological products that employed travel, or touristic imaginings, as a means of shaping their readers' impressions of Vietnam. In this sense there would be a continuity with the numerous Western guidebooks that appeared in the 1990s.

It is to two case studies of these more recent publications that we now turn.

"They Set About Revenging Themselves on

the Population" THE "HUE MASSACRE" AND

THE SHAPING OF HISTORICAL CONSCIOUSNESS

For tourists the story was simple. During the 1968 Tet Offensive, American and Army of the Republic of Vietnam (ARVN) troops were taken aback by the extensive military campaign waged by the combined forces of the National Liberation Front and the Democratic Republic of Vietnam. Nowhere was the warfare more sustained than in the former imperial capital of Hue. Drawing on "detailed plans to liquidate Hue's 'uncooperative' elements," the Lonely Planet guidebook reported, thousands of people were "rounded up in extensive house-to-house searches conducted according to lists of names meticulously prepared months before."[1] During the following three and a half weeks of "Communist control," either 3,000, "at least" 2,800, or 14,000 people — depending on which guidebook one was reading — were "massacred" as the "North Vietnamese Army," according to *Fodor's Exploring Vietnam*, "set about revenging themselves on the population."[2] The campaign targeted "anyone considered remotely sympathetic to the Southern regime."[3]

"Foreign aid workers," "merchants, Buddhist monks, Catholic priests, intellectuals, and a number of travelers, as well as people with ties to the South Vietnamese government," were "summarily shot, clubbed to death," or buried or burned alive, various guidebooks reported.[4] Others were "beheaded."[5] The "victims were buried in shallow mass graves, which were discovered around the city over the next few years."[6] Following a massive bombing campaign, the story continued, the United States "regained Hue at the cost of destroying it. The North Vietnamese had attempted to indoctrinate Hue residents," the Moon guidebook maintained, "and had killed most of Hue's government officials. Neither side won any appreciable number of Hue hearts or minds."[7] As of the late 1990s, the Moon writer continued, tourists could "still see symbols over doorways indicating where residents were killed."[8]

In its calculated planning and ruthless execution, the "Hue Massacre" typified Communist governance. As, by definition in the United States, Communist movements could not enjoy popular support in a truly free society, a resort to widespread terror — or what in American parlance became known as the "bloodbath theory" should the Vietnamese insurgents prove victorious — was a necessary precondition for political control. For tens of thousands of Western tourists reared in conventional Cold War ideology and reading about the episode in their guidebooks — publications whose background historical information was typically characterized by a mundane and strictly factual style — the "cruelest retribution" exacted against the people of Hue would seem to have merely confirmed this axiom. For these individuals, it might then have come as something of a surprise to learn that the accounts of the massacre presented in the travel literature were a matter of academic dispute. According to one scholar of the episode, they represented a "complete fabrication."[9] Rather than established facts, the details of the Hue Massacre — by which, through the use of capital letters, I am referring to the conventional narrative of what transpired — have in actuality been vigorously contested since at least 1969. Countering those who, during the war, viewed the episode as a harbinger of what might follow a revolutionary victory, a number of scholars, many of them active in the antiwar movement, believed the official account of the atrocities to be a largely unsupported instance of prowar propaganda. Foremost among them was the political scientist D. Gareth Porter. For Porter, whose 1974 critique of the atrocities narrative has been influential in informing much postwar scholarship, the "enduring myth" of the Hue Massacre "bore little resemblance to the truth, but was, on the contrary, the result of a political warfare campaign by the Saigon government, embellished by the [U.S.] government, and accepted uncritically by the U.S. press."[10]

Like the public memory of Nat Turner, whose violent 1831 uprising against white slaveholding families has for decades been a matter of bitter contestation, the meaning of the events in Hue has been fiercely disputed for well over thirty years.[11] Exactly what happened in 1968 remains uncertain. However, uncertainty about precise details should not be confused with affirmation of the claim, reported uncritically in most of the leading Western guidebooks, that thousands of civilians were methodically executed by the Vietnamese insurgents. There is no credible evidentiary basis for this version of events, and even its foremost Western architect had in later years backed away from his earlier allegations about the scale of the atrocities. Nevertheless, for reasons that are perplexing, the dubious origins of the Hue Massacre have not tarnished the narrative's reliability in the tourism literature and in a number of works of historical scholarship.

Originally a discursive construction of the Tenth Political Warfare Battalion of the Army of the Republic of Vietnam, the Hue Massacre was given its respectable veneer in a controversial 1970 document authored by Douglas Pike for the U.S. Mission in Saigon.[12] According to Pike, an employee of the U.S. Information Agency (USIA) and a staunch proponent of the bloodbath theory, the "meaning of the Hue Massacre" seemed "clear." If the insurgents were to "win decisively in South Viet-Nam (and the key word is decisively)," a succession of events would follow. "First, all foreigners would be cleared out of the South, especially the hundreds of foreign newsmen who are in and out of Saigon. A curtain of ignorance would descend." Then—and here Pike conjured an explicit allusion to Nazi Germany—"would begin a night of long knives. There would be a new order to build. The war was long and so are memories of old scores to be settled. All political opposition, actual or potential, would be systematically eliminated." For Pike, Communist movements appeared to be monolithic:

> Stalin versus kulak, Mao versus landlord, Hanoi communist versus Southern Catholic, the pattern would be the same: eliminate not the individual, for who cares about the individual, but the latent danger to the dream, the representative of the blocs, the symbol of the force, that might someday, even inside the regime, dilute the system. Beyond this

would come communist justice meted out to the "tyrants and lackeys." Personal revenge would be a small wheel turning within the larger wheel of Party retribution. But little of this would be known abroad. The communists in Viet-Nam would create a silence. The world would call it peace.[13]

Given the undeniable force of the author's language and its utility to prowar partisans, the report seemed destined to reach an audience far broader than diplomats and military planners, as indeed it did. Perhaps most significantly, *Reader's Digest*, the nation's highest-circulation general-interest magazine, excerpted the study just months after the American invasion of Cambodia — and the explosion of antiwar agitation it sparked — in its September 1970 issue.[14]

Yet if the Hue Massacre narrative found a welcome reception within certain quarters at a time of tremendous national polarization, its foundational document has not fared as well in the years since 1975. In one of the most serious analyses since the war's official end, for example, the historian David Hunt noted the logical inconsistencies in the conventional accounts and characterized Pike's study for the U.S. Mission as constituting, "by any definition, a work of propaganda."[15] Indeed, in 1988 Pike readily conceded that he had earlier been engaged in a conscious "effort to discredit the Viet Cong."[16] Yet given the politics and perceived credibility of the narrative's foremost wartime critic — Gareth Porter was an outspoken opponent of American policy in Southeast Asia and, before 1978, one of the principal skeptics concerning the earliest evidence of the Khmer Rouge genocide in Cambodia — the tenability of the conventional massacre narrative has remained a matter of bitter contestation.[17] This is in spite of what has amounted to, in essence, a nearly wholesale scholarly rejection of Pike's study — as David Hunt observed, only one of the authors (Guenter Lewy) he covered in his analysis of Vietnam war survey texts actually cited the USIA analyst — and the emergence of further support for Porter's wartime critique through the postwar research of historian Ngo Vinh Long.[18] No such dispute over the atrocities existed within the Western tourism literature, however. In nearly every foreign guidebook to Vietnam at the end of the twentieth century the basic structure of Pike's account persisted. Not a single travel author acknowledged the presence of a counter-narrative.

It is important to note that whether or not there were executions in Hue is not a matter of dispute; Porter and other scholars are in agreement that NLF — but not People's Army of Vietnam — troops killed noncombatants during the Tet Offensive, and these certainly merited tourists' attention.[19] However, the most reliable enumerations of those killed range from 300 or 400 to a more precise 710; in either case, the estimates are 10 to 25 percent of the approximate figure of 3,000 cited in nearly all of the guidebooks, which is a figure from which even Douglas Pike had distanced himself by the late 1980s.[20]

Whereas the reality of the executions is acknowledged by scholars on all sides, the available evidence suggests that they were nothing like the indiscriminate slaughter presented in the travel guidebooks, and by all accounts they represented a stark departure from previous NLF policy — a point, conceded by Pike, that would be forgotten or ignored in later statements on the potential for a postwar bloodbath. In addition to "far exceed[ing] in numbers any atrocity by the communists previously in South Viet-Nam," Pike wrote, the "difference was not only one in degree but one in kind." While still assuming that the executions were ordered by the NLF leadership, he concluded that the "character of the terror that emerges from an examination of Hue [was] quite distinct from communist terror acts elsewhere."[21] Porter agreed but framed the issue differently, maintaining that "Douglas Pike's notion of an NLF plan to purge Vietnamese society through mass executions is so bizarre and unrelated to the reality of NLF policy that it tells us more about Pike's own mind than it does about the movement he claim[ed] to be describing."[22]

While a number of individuals undoubtedly were killed immediately after the insurgents' occupation of Hue, the bulk of the scholarship on the issue since the first iterations of the conventional narrative has provided a very different portrait from that reported in the tourism literature. According to Porter, the NLF, which sought to create a revolutionary administration in the city, entered Hue with lists containing certain residents' names and dividing them into several categories. These included persons who had worked for the RVN's secret police apparatus, those who were high civilian or military officials, and those who were ordinary or low-level civil servants in the RVN government. Many of these individuals were slated for temporary imprisonment outside the city or for "reeducation" under the revolutionary authorities, although others — in particular those from the first category, who were personally involved in the repression of the resistance movement — were summarily executed.[23] Citing interviews with "most of the people involved," Ngo Vinh Long, who concluded after years of research that a total of 710 people lost their lives at the hands of the revolutionaries, claimed that most of the killings occurred "at the last minute" as the insurgents were leaving the city. "They were afraid their organizations in Hue were exposed," he explained, and if the captives were allowed to live, the guerrillas believed, they would have sought vengeance against the clandestine revolutionaries remaining in Hue.[24] Somewhat similarly, Porter and Len Ackland claimed in the first study critical of the conventional massacre narrative that the bulk of the executions "were not the result of a policy on the part of a victorious government but rather the revenge of an army in retreat," referring to the disposition of persons originally identified for "reeducation" but executed when, following U.S. attacks, it became "increasingly apparent that the [National Liberation] Front would not be able to stay in Hue indefinitely."[25]

A prominent feature in many accounts of the "Hue Massacre" is the "shallow mass graves" said to contain the revolutionaries' victims — an image that penetrated U.S. popular consciousness in the 1980s in Stanley Kubrick's *Full Metal Jacket* (1987).[26] In the film, the uncovering of the Vietnamese corpses offered one of the few moments in which the protagonist, Joker, appeared truly repulsed by the bloodshed in Vietnam. A lieutenant on the scene explained to him: "Well, it seems the NVA came in with a list of gook names. Government officials, policemen, ARVN officers, schoolteachers. They went around their houses real polite and asked them to report the next day for political re-education. Everybody who turned up got shot. Some they buried alive."[27]

While civilian reporters were shown to be examining a mass grave in *Full Metal Jacket*, Gareth Porter found that, in actuality, investigation of the sites by independent journalists was strictly prohibited and that official claims about the graves were often contradicted by the available evidence. For example, the only Western physician known to have been given access to the sites, the Canadian doctor Alje Vennema, wrote that the number of bodies in the graves he examined was inflated sevenfold by the United States and the Saigon authorities and that most of the victims appeared to have been killed as a result of the combat in Hue, with many of the corpses clothed in the threads of military uniforms.[28] Indeed, the claims about the excavated bodies offered by the ARVN's political warfare department were considered so outrageous that they were met with skepticism even by the RVN government's minister of health. "The inconsistencies and other weaknesses of the various official documents, the lack of confirming evidence, and the evidence contradicting the official explanation," Porter wrote, "all suggest that the overwhelming majority of the bodies discovered in 1969 were in fact the victims of American air power and of the ground fighting that raged in the hamlets, rather than of NLF execution." The "undeniable fact," Porter asserted, "was that American rockets and bombs, not communist assassination, caused the greatest carnage in Hue."[29] In support, the Magnum photojournalist Philip Jones Griffiths — whose photographs of the city during the Tet Offensive have provided a harrowing portrait of the war's devastation — concluded that the majority of the fatalities in Hue were caused by "the most hysterical use of American firepower ever seen," and that afterward, in an "unprecedented propaganda campaign," thousands of those killed by the United States were presented as "the victims of a Communist massacre."[30]

The 1968 battle for Hue was, by all accounts, bloody and intense. Robert Shaplen, a board member of American Friends of Vietnam, wrote in the *New Yorker* in March 1968, "Nothing I saw during the Second World War in the Pacific, during the Korean war, or in the Vietnam war so far has been as terrible, in terms of destruction and despair, as what I saw in Hue." Most of the thousands of civilians killed during the siege, he claimed, perished as a result of "the American air and artillery attacks that were called upon to dislodge the North Vietnamese and Vietcong forces, which held the city stubbornly as long as they could."[31] Approximately three out of every four houses were completely destroyed or seriously damaged by bombs and artillery, while there were "bodies stacked into graves by fives — one on top of another." Bomb craters forty feet wide and twenty feet deep were "staggered" in the streets near the walls of the ancient Citadel.[32] Under such circumstances it would hardly have been surprising to find the insurgents burying the dead in mass graves; the disposal of bodies is always a dire problem for those administering cities under siege.

Inexplicably, none of the contemporary guidebooks revealed that among those executed in Hue were victims of RVN assassination teams that moved throughout the city during and after the final days of NLF/DRV control. The "surfacing" of many supporters and others who cooperated with the revolutionary administration — among them students, university faculty members, and priests, many of whom openly sympathized with the NLF — rendered such individuals particularly susceptible to violent retribution following the insurgents' retreat.[33] According to the historian Marilyn Young, "In the last days of the NLF occupation of Hue, teams of Saigon government assassins fanned out through the city with their own list of targets, underground NLF supporters who had revealed themselves in the course of occupying the city."[34] The Italian journalist Oriana Fallaci, citing a French priest from Hue, claimed that 1,100 people were killed following the American and RVN reoccupation, while Stanley Karnow wrote that the bodies of those executed by these "clandestine South Vietnamese teams" were thrown "into common graves with the Vietcong's victims."[35] Yet no RVN executions were disclosed in the Western guidebooks.

THE EXECUTIONS IN HISTORICAL AND
INTERNATIONAL CONTEXT

It has credibly been suggested that some of the killing attributed to the revolutionaries was "the result of individual acts by the Front's cadres, long suspicious of and resentful toward the city people whom they had associated with the enemy and now further embittered by defeat and by the loss of many of their comrades in the battle" — acts for which the cadres were reportedly "severely criticized by their superiors for excesses which had 'hurt the revolution.' "[36] Assuming the suggestion is accurate, it is possible, indeed probable, that some of the insurgents in Hue had experienced the systematic devastation wrought by the United States in large areas of central Vietnam during the months preceding the Tet Offensive. For example, Jonathan Schell has documented how, by August 1967, approximately 70 percent of the villages in Quang Ngai province — "which means seventy percent of the houses" — had been destroyed by U.S., Korean, and RVN forces, and thousands of noncombatants killed.[37] The "cumulative effect" of the "full force of the Americans' overwhelming firepower," Schell maintained, "had been to bring disruption, destruction, and death to the countryside on an immense scale, and to leave among the people an indelible bitterness that no new [U.S.] program — unless it were a program to raise the dead — could hope to overcome."[38] At a more retail level, investigative reporting in 2003 uncovered a seven-month program of systematic atrocities by the so-called Tiger Force of the 101st Airborne Division against "hundreds of unarmed civilians" in Quang Nam and Quang Ngai provinces in 1967. According to the journalists who exposed the depredations, children were sexually assaulted and decapitated, civilians were killed when hand grenades were dropped into their underground bunkers, and farmers and other villagers were summarily executed. The Americans kept trophies of some of the atrocities — severed ears and scalps — as souvenirs.[39] Nicholas Turse, drawing on internal Defense Department records and other documents, has revealed the pervasiveness of even more American war crimes.[40]

It is almost certain, moreover, that many of the revolutionary troops in Hue had been affected, whether personally or through members of their families, by the systematic policies of torture, political imprisonment, and execution practiced for years by the Saigon regime. Indeed, its Law 10–59 explicitly prescribed a sentence of death or a lifetime of hard labor for people who participated in virtually any meaningful way in the resistance against the Diem government, which designated "those who adhere to the illegal organizations secretly left behind in south Viet Nam by the Viet Cong or set up by them after the signing of the Geneva Agreements" as, "without exception, elements who deliberately help the *Viet Cong*, and work for the interests of foreign communist imperialists, Russian or Chinese, carrying out activities of subversion, espionage, and betrayal."[41] These included not only party members and armed insurgents but also individuals associated with groupings such as the "Peace movement," as the RVN leadership identified one illegal and particularly "treacherous [organization]."[42] Among those not executed, many tens of thousands were tortured while being held for years in horrific conditions of imprisonment, including in the notorious "tiger cages" of Con Son Island in the Con Dao archipelago. Of the three "special military courts" established by Law 10–59 to adjudge those accused of subversion, one was located in Hue. Given the 1968 siege of Hue's context, and judging from historical precedents in Europe, North America, and elsewhere, it would hardly be surprising that years of repression engendered acts of retaliation against government officials, informers, and others in the city whom the revolutionaries viewed as responsible for their — or their families' — suffering.

Yet no context appeared in the guidebooks' accounts of the Hue Massacre; the authors suggested no possible impetus for the executions other than simple Communist malevolence. This was in stark contrast to their synopses of the Son My (My Lai) massacre. In prefacing their rendition of the latter episode, the authors for Lonely Planet noted that "Son My subdistrict was a known vc stronghold, and it was widely believed that villagers in the area were providing food and shelter to the vc (if true, the villagers would have had little choice — the vc was known for taking cruel revenge on those who didn't 'cooperate'). Just whose idea it was to 'teach the villagers a lesson' has never been determined. What is known is that several American soldiers had been killed and wounded in the area in the days preceding the 'search-and-destroy operation' that began on the morning of 16 March 1968."[43] Likewise, the Fodor's Gold Guide reported: "Although the full truth concerning the events of My Lai remains shrouded in controversy, what is known is that the area around Son My was considered by the U.S. military to be a stronghold of the Vietcong and that a number of American soldiers had been killed and wounded in the area in the days preceding 16 March 1968."[44]

The lack of context in describing the events in Hue while contextualizing, however minimally, the massacre at Son My is especially notable given its reinforcement of a troubling cultural trend. With respect to the executions in Hue, tourists reading the guidebooks might have interpreted the atrocities as emblematic of an innate Vietnamese cruelty that successive Hollywood films — from the critically acclaimed *The Deer Hunter* (1978) to the immensely influential *Rambo: First Blood Part II* (1985) — have instilled in Western historical consciousness. In other words, the Hue Massacre occurred because the Vietnamese revolutionaries were inherently demonic or cruel — forcing, for example, young working-class Americans to play Russian roulette or torturing secretly held American POWs well into the 1980s. If interviews with Western tourists about atrocities in Vietnam are indicative of larger national sentiments, however, the American actions at Son My were viewed more sympathetically; they represented the tragic but explicable response of frightened young men to a war in which U.S. personnel were unable to identify their enemies from those they were purported to be assisting. In other words, the Americans appeared to many tourists to be moral human beings who, reacting to circumstances usually imposed upon them by outsiders, were nevertheless capable of losing touch with their basic humanity and occasionally perpetrating horrendous deeds. As one elderly woman from California confided, despite their actions she did not believe that the American troops responsible for civilian atrocities were "evil people."[45]

Moreover, the guidebooks' failure to explain that many of the executions in Hue were apparently acts of vengeance by individual insurgents, and not official policy, must be contrasted with guidebook treatments of a perhaps comparable — though far bloodier and more organized — case of widespread retribution less than twenty-five years earlier: the repression of Axis collaborators in Europe during and after the Second World War. In the years surrounding the Allied victory in France, for example, thousands of alleged Nazi collaborators were summarily executed during its *épuration*, or purge, from 1944 to 1945, many of them during the period in which General Dwight Eisenhower exercised "supreme authority" in the country. The most reliable scholarly estimates place the French figure at approximately 9,000 killed "without any legal procedure."[46] Another 767 individuals were shot following convictions by the victors' "courts of justice," with "around 800" others executed after being condemned to death by military tribunals.[47] However, the major Western guidebooks for France failed to acknowledge, let alone graphically convey, the French executions, suggesting that France and Vietnam were subject to different standards when determining which events merited historical narration.[48]

In the case of France, it may be significant that the atrocities were committed by the victors during and following what is popularly remembered in the West as a "good war." Yet with respect to Vietnam, the executions were carried out by the southern revolutionary forces that contributed to the ultimate defeat of the United States and the Saigon government in the midst of a conflict still vigorously contested in American memory. Apart from the identity of the perpetrators, also significant may be the identity of the victims. In the case of France, those executed were collaborators, or people alleged to have been collaborators, with the Nazis; in the case of Vietnam, however, the victims were people associated with the RVN authorities and thus the United States. Complicating the way in which race often determines the perceived worthiness of victimhood, Europeans in this instance have apparently been deemed less worthy than Asians of contemporary moral reprobation. Similarly notable in considering the different standards for narrative inclusion is that France, as a European state, is regarded by most Americans — despite their evident distaste for the French people and government — as one of the cradles of modern

Western civilization. Vietnam, conversely, has long been viewed by people in the United States through a predominantly Orientalist lens.

The conflicting treatments of the two cases may also be viewed in the manner in which the wars' outcomes were designated in the tourism literature. When alluding to the Allied defeat of the Germans, constant references were made in a number of leading guidebooks to the liberation — without quotation marks — of France from the Nazi invasion and occupation.[49] Yet in the case of Vietnam, several guidebooks repeatedly placed the word "liberation" in quotation marks when describing the revolutionary victory; in doing so, tourists were presumably meant to question the propriety of the term as a descriptor of the American defeat.[50] While the French and Vietnamese histories are by no means identical, there are, nevertheless, important parallels. In both cases, for instance, a nationalist resistance movement vanquished foreign invaders (although with respect to France, outside assistance was far more determinative) and the local population with whom they forged an alliance. Where they significantly differ, to be sure, is within postwar Western views of the two conflicts. The collaborationist Vichy government led by Marshal Philippe Pétain, which enjoyed widespread French support (or, at least, acquiescence) during the war, is today regarded with nearly universal revulsion, while American — and to a lesser extent Western, judging from interviews of European and Australian tourists — memory of the war in Vietnam is still a matter of contestation. The successive military governments in Saigon prior to 1975 have continued to be viewed favorably by certain elements of the American populace as forces for Vietnamese "freedom" rather than as brutal and corrupt dictatorships unwilling to adhere to the 1954 Geneva Accords that mandated the peaceful reunification of the northern and southern regrouping zones.

THE HUE MASSACRE AND THE BLOODBATH THEORY

The appearance of the Hue Massacre in twenty-first-century Vietnam guidebooks was perhaps not surprising. As a narrative construction, its roots stretch back to the first reports by American embassy officials during the NLF's capture of the city, and for over three decades it has been cited by opponents of the revolution as evidence of the insurgents' malevolent designs.[51] During the war itself, the atrocities were repeatedly exploited to powerful effect.

Perhaps because of the greater confusion in 1968 about exactly what transpired in the former imperial capital, the Johnson administration was less aggressive than its successor in highlighting the atrocities' propaganda value to American and RVN officials. Nevertheless, before the fighting had even ended in Hue, the State Department drafted a presidential statement for dissemination in southern Vietnam that celebrated the "military valor" of the U.S. and RVN forces while decrying the revolutionaries' "incredible brutality and terror against civilian officials and an innocent populace which accompanied their attack on a sacred city at a sacred time."[52] For months afterward, the events were addressed by the Vietnam Information Group, a White House unit intended to make "the most effective use of the information coming in from Vietnam to put out our position over here at home," whether in presidential speeches, in press briefings and leaks, or in "background material" for Johnson's "use on the Hill."[53] However, it was not until late in 1969, months after Richard Nixon assumed the presidency and when reports of the Son My (My Lai) massacre first began to appear in the American press, that the executions in Hue achieved considerable political currency.[54]

From that time until shortly after the war officially drew to a close in 1975, the Hue Massacre was employed by supporters of U.S. policy to buttress their claims that a bloodbath would occur if the Vietnamese revolutionaries defeated the United States and the Saigon government. As such, in the view of the war's proponents, to oppose the American intervention was, ipso facto, to endorse the mass slaughter of thousands or even millions of Vietnamese.[55] The total number to be killed was a matter of dispute. The "lowest estimate," Senator James Eastland noted in 1972, appeared in what Eastland referred to as Stephen Hosmer's "superbly researched study of terror as an instrument of Communist policy."[56] According to Hosmer, an analyst for the Defense Department–affiliated RAND Corporation, the number would likely not be "much less than 100,000" persons, and it could very well be "considerably higher." Other estimates, such as P. J. Honey's speculation that the "minimum number of those to be butchered will exceed one million and could rise to several times that figure," were widely accepted by supporters of the American war. Indeed, Eastland maintained, "that there would be a massive bloodletting is something that is taken for granted by virtually every serious student of Vietnamese affairs."[57] The debate was simply over numbers.[58]

To the war's proponents, the Hue Massacre — a chilling narrative in which thousands of noncombatants were mercilessly slaughtered in a mass collection of the victims' "blood debts" to the Vietnamese people — was a crucial piece of evidence substantiating the bloodbath hypothesis. And for some it illustrated what they perceived to be blatant media bias. The atrocities were cited repeatedly in Congress, in the press, and among pro-war activists to justify the American intervention. Undoubtedly the most prominent articulation along these lines was President Richard Nixon's major television and radio address on 3 November 1969. Citing the specter of a "precipitate [American] withdrawal," Nixon insisted to his compatriots, "We saw a prelude of what would happen in South Vietnam when the Communists entered the city of Hue last year. During their brief rule there, there was a bloody reign of terror in which 3,000 civilians were clubbed, shot to death, and buried in mass graves. With the sudden collapse of our support," he continued, "these atrocities of Hue would become the nightmare of the entire nation — and particularly for the million and a half Catholic refugees who fled to South Vietnam when the Communists took over in the North."[59] The White House had actually been notified by a National Security Council staff member two days before the speech that, "in all, approximately a thousand civilian men, women, and children were executed in the Hue area" during the Tet Offensive, yet Nixon nevertheless claimed in his address that three times this number had been killed.[60] Other figures he cited in support of the bloodbath theory — in this case involving the land-reform atrocities of the mid-1950s — apparently became a matter of internal White House concern.[61]

The 3 November speech, in which the president proposed his "Vietnamization" plan and famously invoked an American "silent majority," was considered a great success by the administration. The A. C. Nielsen Company notified the White House that over 72 million people had viewed the address on the three television networks, which was more than three times greater than the number who had watched Nixon's inauguration, and by late January 1970 approximately 400,000 persons had responded to the speech with letters, telegrams, or postcards sent to the president. Ninety percent of these reportedly expressed support for the administration.[62] Among the correspondents, some specifically drew moral encouragement from the president's bloodbath comments. In Oregon, Governor Tom

McCall issued a press statement immediately following the speech, which he duly sent to the White House, in which he warned that "our immediate capitulation" in Vietnam would "scar our souls with the remorse of a people who, wearily after 200 years, first stamped their approval on genocide."[63] And Vice Admiral W. R. Smedberg III, writing for the 117,000 members of the Retired Officers Association, applauded Nixon's "enduring efforts [to bring to a close this nation[']s military participation in the war in Vietnam] in a manner that will not only illiminate [sic] American casualties but prevent wholesale slotter [sic] of the Vietnamese."[64] A number of editorial writers similarly adopted the bloodbath argument; those at the *Orlando Sentinel*, for example, predicted massacres following an American withdrawal that "might approach the genocide of Hitler's Germany in the 1940s."[65]

Yet not all Americans embraced Nixon's address. Among those dissenting were dozens of soldiers at Fort Bliss, Texas. "No one wants to witness a 'blood bath' in Viet Nam," they wrote to the president.

The slaughter which you predict will occur upon our withdrawal is certainly an ugly possibility. But the slaughter in which we are now participating has already cost 40,000 American lives and hundreds of thousands of Vietnamese lives. Also, over a million South Vietnamese have been left homeless by the war and presently live in "refugee camps," a polite term for what we call concentration camps when they are set up by our enemies. Perhaps the killing will continue in Viet Nam after we leave, but it is time for us to end our participation in that killing. From the kill-ratio figures released by our army, it is plain that it is the United States and not the Viet Cong that are doing most of the killing in Viet Nam today. We urge you to end our part in this massacre.[66]

In the pages of the *New York Times*, George McT. Kahin, the influential co-author of *The United States in Vietnam* and director of the Southeast Asia program at Cornell University, charged that Nixon's warning of a potential bloodbath was not only misleading but that the facts the president alleged in support of the theory — in particular, the "appalling misunderstanding" of the DRV exhibited in his statement that the Viet Minh in the mid-1950s "murdered more than 50,000 people and hundreds of thousands more died in slave labor camps" — were "contrary to the historical record."[67] Nevertheless, the hundreds of thousands of messages that poured into the White House in support of the speech must have bolstered Nixon's confidence in the course he had chosen.

For the administration, the Hue executions continued to serve as an important rhetorical tool. When press accounts of the 1968 Son My massacre increased in the weeks following the 3 November address, Nixon's national security adviser, Henry Kissinger, suggested that the White House had to deal with the "Roman circus" enveloping the affair.[68] The strategy would assume several approaches. In light of the right-wing "backlash" that had begun to emerge following the media's focus on the U.S.-perpetrated atrocities, Kissinger proposed instituting "a program designed to contribute to the backlash which could not be attributable to the White House."[69] He also suggested highlighting the "humanitarian actions taken by U.S. military forces" in the RVN. Finally, Kissinger believed it was important to remind Americans about "Communist terror tactics in South Vietnam." Among these, he wrote, were the executions during "the three-week occupation of Hue in 1968" in which "an estimated 3,500 citizens were shot, strangled, or clubbed and buried alive." Thus far, he added, "some 2,600 bodies have been discovered in a series of mass graves."[70]

In furtherance of this last objective, the presidential aide and speechwriter Pat Buchanan drafted a response for Nixon to media queries about the Son My incident, which clearly distinguished American atrocities from those of the revolutionary Vietnamese forces:

> If what is alleged to have occurred did occur, a tragedy has happened. But if it is true, it was done *against* the policy of the American government — and *against* the explicit directives and orders of the American armed forces serving in South Vietnam.
>
> Any atrocity which ever occurs at the hands of America's armed forces in combat is an exception to the rule of their conduct. It is not in accord with our policy — but against everything we stand for and are fighting for. It will be investigated and anyone guilty will be prosecuted. As for the charges of our enemies in the field, they should be treated with utter contempt. *A policy of atrocity is the policy of the enemy* we confront in Vietnam. What happened in the city of Hue, the indiscriminate massacre of three thousand civilians, was on the direct orders

of those people against whom the United States army is engaged. The thousands of village leaders, and teachers, and ordinary citizens who have been systematically slaughtered by the enemy in Vietnam, that is inherent to the character of our enemies — and that is an approved tactic of their military strategy.

Any individual who cannot see the difference between the isolated acts of members of the American army, and the premeditated and systematic atrocities of its Communist enemy in the field[,] does not know what this war is about — or what his society is about.[71]

For the administration, then, the Hue Massacre could be used to remind Americans that, in moral terms, the Vietnamese revolutionaries, unlike U.S. officials, had no concern for the sanctity of human life.

Yet when Nixon finally addressed the Son My atrocities in a news conference on 8 December, he offered a much briefer response than the one drafted by Buchanan. "One of the goals we are fighting for in Vietnam," he declared, "is to keep the people from South Vietnam from having imposed upon them a government which has atrocity against civilians as one of its policies. We cannot ever condone or use atrocities against civilians in order to accomplish that goal."[72] If Nixon ultimately opted for brevity rather than precision in deflecting Americans' attention from the Son My incident, the same cannot be said for the Department of Defense, which that same day briefed dozens of members of Congress on the Hue executions. The purpose of the Pentagon presentation, according to Richard H. Ichord, chairman of the House Committee on Internal Security, was to place the Son My massacre "in proper perspective." Ichord confessed to being "deeply concerned" about the media, which he said was presenting a "distorted and definitely one-sided picture of the relative values placed on human life" by the opposing sides in Vietnam. At Son My, the "alleged acts of individuals are in violation of official regulations," Ichord explained, whereas in Hue the executions were "systematic."[73]

In spite of Nixon's failure to explicitly cite the Hue atrocities on 8 December, the White House was by no means hesitant in further exploiting the executions for propaganda purposes. Months after the December news conference the administration placed the atrocities at the center of its effort to sell anti-Communism to the Vietnamese (and American) people when, in August 1970, Buchanan recommended to the president that the executions be employed in an unambiguous ideological offensive. "Elections, critical elections, come up in Vietnam next year," he wrote to Nixon.

> Anti-Communism, hopefully, will carry the day — but it would be utter folly to rest on our "hopes" after so many lives have been lost. A correspondent suggests that the Saigon Government begin now — with our help — a massive anti-Communist advertising campaign, portraying the atrocities of Hue, the horrors visited on Catholics and all religions by Communists, right now in preparation for those elections. Anti-Communism, like Cadillacs, is a good commodity — but one does not see General Motors let Cadillac sell itself — it advertises all over America that Cadillac is the finest car in the country.

"Should we do less with 'anti-Communism'?" he asked. "This seems to me the best way to set the stage for running into the ground any 'peace' candidates." Nixon agreed, calling it a "good" proposal, and he asked Buchanan to set it in motion.[74]

The White House had many allies in conjuring the Hue Massacre in pursuance of the country's anti-Communist campaign. In the halls of Congress, Representative John Rarick had taken to the floor eight months before Nixon's 3 November speech to criticize the media's alleged tendency to ignore the atrocities of the Vietnamese revolutionaries. "While U.S. leftists shout and proclaim a gospel of dissent against all throughout our land," he proclaimed, "their counterpart, the Communist Vietcong, slaughter thousands of innocent men, women, and children in South Vietnam, if for no other reason than the victims reject communism and are not yet under party control."

> Yet, loudmouths in the United States continually spout their false propaganda, which is repeated by "cooperative and sympathetic" pinkos in the communications field and passed on to the American public for mental conditioning to accept the promises of winds of change.
>
> The fact that Communist atrocities are not covered by the same media with similar exposure for the same American public is unquestioned.

"Brutal acts of slaughter reminiscent of the 1917 Communist revolution continue," Rarick announced, "yet there is no indignant outcry from so-called antiwar protesters, moralists, pacifists, and their sympathetic cronies in the news profession."[75] He then placed on the record an article and an editorial on the Hue Massacre.

Several months later, Representative William Springer bemoaned the amount of press attention being afforded the recently disclosed atrocities at Son My. While "reams have been written about the Green Berets" with "first page articles [to] no end," Springer claimed, he was concerned that the "assassinations, kidnapings [sic], and injuries done to civilians by the North Vietnamese in South Vietnam" were not receiving a similar level of coverage. He thus entered into the record a newspaper column by Jack Anderson discussing, among other incidents, the Hue Massacre.[76] Springer's colleague, Senator George Murphy, was similarly displeased with the discrepancy in press coverage. Placing on the record a piece published in the *Los Angeles Times* that drew almost entirely on the work of Douglas Pike, Murphy sought to distinguish the "alleged" atrocities of "one American group" from the "known, proven actions committed by the Vietcong Communists [at Hue] that are too terrible for civilized people to imagine." Whereas the massacre at Son My, "if true," was "committed against all instructions of the American government," Murphy maintained, the atrocities at Hue "were carried out as part of the officially ordered plan and design to establish a Communist government in South Vietnam."[77] Indeed, the conviction that Americans needed to be reminded that the atrocities at Hue were far worse than those perpetrated by the U.S. soldiers at Son My was not lost on the media. Chet Huntley asserted as much during the *Huntley-Brinkley Report* on 28 November 1969, and John Wheeler of the Associated Press followed his lead several days later.[78]

For many supporters of U.S. policy, it became apparent as early as 1968 that the atrocities could serve a valuable propaganda function. Visual imagery of bodies being excavated from mass graves, and the devastated relatives of these victims mourning their heartfelt losses, was circulated in a brief film presented by the psychological warfare unit of the RVN armed forces after the Tet Offensive.[79] Attempting to lend weight to the bloodbath theory, the RVN diplomat Ta Quoc Tuan prepared a manuscript on "Vietnamese Communist terrorism" in January 1970 that devoted considerable space to the "Hue precedent." "If the massive and systematic killings which the Communists have been and are performing wherever they can control are any indication of their intentions if they [succeed] in imposing their totalitarian rule on South Vietnam," Tuan maintained, "then the estimates that they may kill from 1,000,000 to 3,000,000 South Vietnamese are not exaggerated. And in the years that followed this initial bloodsetting [*sic*] there would come further waves of terror and mass killings that might add many hundreds of thousands more to the final toll of victims. . . . Organized terror, of a ruthlessness and on a scale that defies civilized comprehension, has been a cardinal aspect of Communist policy."[80]

That same year, the RVN Embassy in Washington published a special issue of its *Viet-Nam Bulletin* on the Hue Massacre. It reproduced two articles from *Vietnam Magazine* on the "red mass murder" or "red massacre," and the sympathetic counsel offered the relatives of the "red victim[s]" by RVN President Nguyen Van Thieu. "Look at these sad faces, then look at these coffins," Thieu pleaded in a eulogy for the deceased. "Is this the final freedom offered by the Communists — to lie in a coffin in the ground?" The editors of the publication also included a tabulation of the victims based on "the judicious calculations of an authority, Mr. Douglas Pike." According to the embassy, Pike's findings had "borne out the worst fears entertained by the Vietnamese with regard to the 'humanity' of the Communist enemy. Most of these victims were led away under the pretext of going to attend 'education sessions'[;] little did they realize that the Communists meant these 'sessions' to be their last in this world."[81]

Among U.S. civilians, the AFV issued a pamphlet in June 1969 on the "slaughter of the innocents" in Hue and elsewhere throughout the south. The group reprinted portions of a publication by the India Vietnam Humanitarian League containing an essay on the "tragedy at Hue" by Trong Nhan, which, with its focus on the grisly discovery of corpses and their identification by relatives, lent the document a sentimentality certain to resonate with many Americans. Embedded within the AFV pamphlet was a larger message, however. Cautioning that the "massacres at Hue . . . were only the most outrageous in a long history of such Communist atrocities" in which "tens of thousands of persons have been murdered in this Communist bloodbath," the AFV drew attention to the RVN's valiant resistance in an implicit appeal for continued U.S. support. With "the Communists hav[ing] again stepped up their program of premeditated atrocities" in 1970, and "despite this inhuman pressure and the unprecedented slaughter of innocent people that has resulted from it, the free people of South Vietnam have not yielded. Their heroic and steadfast resistance to Communist terrorism has been truly remarkable. It demonstrates their amazing tenacity in defense of their civilization and their right to determine their own political future." As such, the group insisted, "this heroic nation deserves the support of all free men in the hour of their most urgent need."[82]

For proponents of the war, widespread student hostility to the conflict presented a great challenge, so efforts were undertaken to influence popular opinion on the nation's campuses. The Hue Massacre, it was believed, could benefit this campaign. The National Student Committee for Victory in Vietnam (NSCVV) thus published a pamphlet in March 1970 entitled "The Massacre at Hue," most of which was devoted to reproducing a lurid and lengthy Copley News Service report that was essentially a rehash of the Douglas Pike narrative. The newspaper piece was prefaced, however, by comments from the student committee. "Seldom has a military force utilized terrorism, directed exclusively at the civilian population, to so great an extent as has the National Liberation Front (Viet Cong) in South Vietnam," the NSCVV claimed. Stating that thousands of "innocent civilians are being murdered every year by the Communist National Liberation Front as part of a calculated program aimed at instilling terror in the minds of the people," the pamphlet's creators maintained—without citation to any evidence—that "Communist leaders boast that a communist victory would bring [the] fate [of Hue] to all of South Vietnam."[83] It is not difficult to comprehend the atrocities' appeal to those attempting to mobilize support for the war. The attraction was clearly explained in a 1970 proposal from another prowar organization, American Youth for a *Just* Peace, for a "National Student Conference on Vietnam and World Freedom." "The basic issues involved in the Vietnam war must be explained to the American people in understandable terms," the organizers wrote. "And we must seek to put the prime emphasis on those issues which are the clearest, the most easily understandable, and the most morally compelling." The "massacre at Hue and the human cost of a Vietcong victory" was one of three issues "which best meet these specifications," the activists believed.[84]

It was in November 1969 that the first published critique of the Hue Massacre narrative appeared in the United States, providing a more nuanced account of what transpired than the "easily understandable" story of indiscriminate brutality that was being circulated by prowar activists and American officials in Vietnam, the White House, and Congress. Written by Len Ackland and Gareth Porter, the article in the *Christian Century*, which was part of the authors' larger engagement with the bloodbath hypothesis, did not deny that there were NLF executions.[85] Instead, it contested their nature and scale, claiming that they totaled in the hundreds, not the thousands, and that, contradicting the bloodbath theory, the Hue atrocities "were not the result of a policy on the part of a victorious government but rather the revenge of an army in retreat."[86] Shortly after its publication, and to the certain chagrin of the bloodbath hypothesis's proponents, the article received a far greater audience than its original distribution allowed when it was cited in other venues.[87] Tran Van Dinh, a former RVN diplomat and member of Ngo Dinh Diem's National Security Council and Cabinet, favorably discussed its findings in the *New Republic*, relating as well his own experience of having been told by authorities in Saigon that his younger brother and nephew had been executed by the NLF in Hue only to much later learn from his family that they had been killed by American bombs. The reason his brother and nephew were "buried in a temporary grave," he wrote, was that "Hue was under siege" and "nobody could get out of the area to buy a coffin for a decent burial."[88]

Undoubtedly the most explosive reference to Porter and Ackland's study was made by *New York Times* columnist Tom Wicker in a May 1970 commentary critical of Richard Nixon. Charging the president with falsifying history, Wicker noted that, in addition to scholarship refuting the notion that there had been massive political reprisals in the northern Vietnamese zone in the mid-1950s, which Nixon had claimed in his major televised address the previous November, Porter and Ackland had demonstrated that "most of these wicked executions [in 1968 in Hue] took place in the heat of battle and as 'the revenge of an army in retreat' and were not the deliberate policy of Hanoi."[89] The column sparked a firestorm of outrage among backers of the war. William F. Ward, national chairman of the AFV, sent the *Times* a letter accusing its columnist of rewriting history in a "futile and pathetic rationalization of the bloodbath potential in Vietnam if the North Vietnamese prevail." For Ward, Wicker's allusion to the Hue atrocities being perpetrated by an "army in retreat" was analogous to "saying that there were not millions of German Jews and Polish Catholics exterminated in Poland in World War II, but only in parts of Poland such as Treblinka, Auschwitz, and Katyn." For "appropriate research on the Hue Massacre," Ward counseled, "I recommend Douglas Pike's work."[90]

In Congress, Senator Gordon Allott denounced Wicker's criticism as "entirely false" and "dead wrong." That "Communist domination of South Vietnam would bring about hideous massacres" was a "very real danger," Allott alleged, dismissing Porter and Ackland's conclusion that the Hue executions occurred "in the heat of battle" — which was actually Wicker's phrase — as "pernicious twaddle."[91] The senator insisted that "neither Mr. Wicker nor the men who wrote for the *Christian Century* can possibly know the full reality about the Hue massacres because the full grim reality is still being explored." The statement, which was in many respects fair (but also irrelevant, as neither Porter and Ackland nor Wicker claimed to know the "full reality" of what had occurred two years earlier) was logically undercut, however, by the fact that it immediately followed Allott's enunciation of "the facts," which for him was the contested Douglas Pike version of what transpired.[92]

Two years later, the column was still being disputed in the U.S. Senate. When a subcommittee of the Committee on the Judiciary published its compendium of documents intended to demonstrate the potential for a bloodbath in the event of a revolutionary victory, the collection included an essay by the RAND Corporation consultant Anita Lauve Nutt that rebutted Wicker's *New York Times* commentary.[93] Accounts of the Hue Massacre were a prominent feature of the compendium. In addition to printing excerpts of Pike's 1970 monograph for the U.S. Mission in Saigon, its editors included numerous other documents that accepted without question the conventional narrative popularized by the USIA analyst.[94]

At times in Congress the Hue Massacre was used as a rhetorical device with which to directly challenge the moral compass of policy critics. For example, when John Sullivan of the American Friends Service Committee, who had just returned from a humanitarian trip to northern Vietnam, was invited to testify before a Senate subcommittee examining the plight of bombing victims in the DRV in 1972, Senator Hiram Fong, a supporter of the war and a proponent of the bloodbath hypothesis, became bothered by Sullivan's criticism and sought to reframe the discussion by arguing that responsibility for American aerial warfare lay with Hanoi. "I just want to present a balanced picture here," Fong told Sullivan. "I want to present a picture that the present situation is the result of the massive invasion of the south by the north." Clearly unhappy with the attention Sullivan was affording the victims of the U.S. bombing campaign, Fong went on the offensive by recalling the Hue executions and challenging the witness to unequivocally condemn "the massive massacre of 3,000 to 4,000 people in Hue."[95]

Barbed comments such as Fong's were not only directed at people invited to testify before Congress. In some instances, members of the House and Senate cited the Hue Massacre to also rebuke their legislative colleagues for criticizing American policy. In the midst of a presentation on Vietnamese, Cambodian, and Laotian refugees by Senator Edward Kennedy in May 1972, for example, Senator William Saxbe interrupted Kennedy in mid-sentence to challenge his suggestion that the United States bore a considerable share of responsibility for the civilians' plight. "This situation has been caused by North Vietnam," Saxbe argued, reminding Kennedy that "we know what happened the last time they went into Hue. They murdered approximately 7,000 people. They seem to be getting ready to do the same thing." While Kennedy took issue with Saxbe's charge that his "entire [prepared] statement tends to make it appear that America is flooding the roads with casualties and killing the old women and children," he joined his colleague in deploring "the killings in Hue"—which, according to Saxbe, totaled approximately seven thousand victims.[96]

By early 1973 a detailed critique by Gareth Porter of the conventional massacre narrative had begun circulating among scholars.[97] Arguing that for years "the political warfare agencies of Washington and Saigon have been shaping American attitudes toward the Vietnamese revolution by systematic disinformation in support of U.S. intervention," Porter charged that the official accounts of the executions in Hue must be understood within this context.[98] His then unpublished study was destined to receive a fairly broad hearing—at least by the standards of antiwar scholarship—when it was extensively cited by two leading dissident scholars in a book published in 1973 that devoted considerable space to challenging the Hue Massacre.[99] However, as the volume, *Counter-Revolutionary Violence: Bloodbaths in Fact and Propaganda*, by Noam Chomsky and Edward S. Herman, was being printed in the days preceding the annual meeting of the American Sociological Association in 1973, at which it was to be sold, nearly its entire run was ordered destroyed by the president of Warner Publishing, the parent company of the academic unit, Warner Modular, that had commissioned the book. Its intra-corporate suppression was reportedly justified by Warner Publishing's chief on the grounds that Chomsky and Herman's study, while admittedly not libelous, was "a pack of lies, a scurrilous attack on respected Americans, undocumented, a publication unworthy of a serious publisher."[100] At Warner Modular, the staff and the publisher, a nineteen-year veteran of the academic book industry, disagreed with this assessment and the challenge to their professional judgment; they immediately resigned. With *Counter-Revolutionary Violence* essentially censored, it was not until 1974 and the publication of his article in the *Indochina Chronicle* that Porter's critique of the Hue Massacre — and, in particular, its detailed challenge to the widely cited claims of Douglas Pike — appeared in print.

Although the war officially ended shortly afterward, the Hue Massacre — as a potent symbol and rhetorical device — did not disappear once its utility in mobilizing support for the American conflict dissipated in 1975. As the fighting drew to a close, Pike cited the atrocities — the toll in 1968 was "more than 3,500 civilians" executed, he claimed — in an interview with *U.S. News and World Report* on the potential for a postwar bloodbath.[101] In Congress, Representative John Ashbrook took to the floor just days after the cessation of hostilities to rail against the "liberal press and those apologists who blindly belittle the possibility of large-scale reprisals," insisting that they "not be permitted to forget the mass slaughter at Hue."[102] Even as late as the early 1990s the atrocities were still being cited or exploited by American elected officials. In 1988, Republican Representative Newt Gingrich, speaking on "the human cost of Democratic failures," chastised a member of the opposition who had earlier "engaged in self-deception" by suggesting that "some of the people buried in the trenches at Hue may have been killed by American bombs." In "other words," asserted Gingrich, "this particular liberal Democrat had to blame America for the bodies which virtually every historian agreed were the deliberate acts of the Communists in Hue."[103] And when, in 1990, Toan Truong recalled "footage of Vietnamese wailing over the bodies of loved ones who were buried alive in huge mass graves by the Viet Cong" in commentaries in the *New York Times* and one of Seattle's daily newspapers, two legislators placed the columns in the *Congressional Record*.[104]

Like their legislative counterparts, right-wing activists and authors outside Congress have periodically drawn on the Hue Massacre since the hostilities in Vietnam ended to criticize the left, the mainstream press, and the antiwar movement—which are synonymous, many of these critics believe—for their alleged inattention to revolutionary terror while focusing on atrocities perpetrated by American troops. Reed Irvine of Accuracy in Media wrote in 1975 that the difference in press coverage given the "bloodbath in Hue" and the "attack on the village" of My Lai was emblematic of "how the media helped defeat us" in Vietnam. Indeed, that the Hue Massacre serves as a blatant illustration of media bias has been a common refrain from Irvine for well over two decades, including in a documentary produced by his outfit in response to *Vietnam: A Television History*, the extensive 1983 series by PBS that, ironically, accepted the Pike version of the 1968 massacre.[105] James Clifford, a former reporter with United Press International and the Associated Press, expounded a similar position in arguing that the divergent media treatment of the atrocities at Hue and Son My suggested a "cover-up" by journalists in deciding "what does or does not become part of our national memory."[106] And according to another author, Gerard Jackson, what transpired in Hue was not unusual but was merely "the most shocking example of the North's barbaric policy" of "terrorism by mutilation and massacre." The "cold-blooded business of calculated mass murder" in Hue, Jackson's headline writer concluded, was "the massacre the left wants us to forget."[107]

Contradicting these critics, Leo Cawley, a political economist and infantry squad leader while with the Marine Corps in Vietnam, conversely claimed that elements of the antiwar movement encouraged media scrutiny of the Hue Massacre but were rebuffed because of the controversies such an examination might engender. Discussing his own experience with the issue, Cawley wrote:

> At the end of the war, Richard Nixon was using the need to prevent a bloodbath as the only excuse for continuing the war and citing the "Hue massacre" as proof that this would happen should the other side gain control. At the time, I was active in Vietnam Veterans Against the War (VVAW). A CBS file clerk sent to the offices of VVAW an outline of a documentary project that had been killed. The proposed project had located a number of credible (that is, non-Vietnamese) sources who said that what the Marine Corps claimed were massacre victims were in fact killed by the Marine Corps bombing raids during the retaking of Hue. As the Vietnamese forces held out against the Marines for weeks

after Tet, the corpses became a health hazard and the city's residents pushed the dead into mass graves. . . . Armed with internal documents, VVAW staged a sit-in at CBS headquarters at "Black Rock," where it became clear that CBS would give no ground and would soon call the police. We gave in. But the episode exposed me to the thinking at CBS. I was told that they "had taken so much heat over My Lai" that it was just impossible to go with another story like the one we were then proposing. As Barry Richardson, then vice-president for public relations, told me, "One of these is enough." So one of those was all America was permitted to have.[108]

Rather than American journalists consciously suppressing a story that might have tarred the reputation of the Vietnamese revolutionaries, as a number of right-wing observers have suggested, Cawley maintained just the opposite: that at least one television network killed a project because it might have invited the sort of flak the company had earlier received in response to its coverage of the American atrocities at Son My.

Despite repeated efforts by American politicians to smite the bitter contestation of the war's memory, debates about the conflict have tenaciously stuck around. With Jane Fonda, military service, and antiwar veterans arising as divisive issues in the 2004 presidential contest, it seemed inevitable that the Hue Massacre would emerge at some point in the election. It did. In a *National Review Online* column accusing Democratic presidential contender John Kerry of lying about American war crimes in Vietnam, Mackubin Thomas Owens, a veteran of the conflict and a professor of strategy and force planning at the Naval War College in Rhode Island, wrote that the "NVA and VC frequently committed atrocities . . . as a matter of policy. While left-wing anti-war critics of U.S. policy in Vietnam were always quick to invoke Auschwitz and the Nazis in discussing alleged American atrocities, they were silent about Hue City, where a month and a half before My Lai the North Vietnamese and VC systematically murdered 3,000 people."[109] Greg Lewis of the *Washington Dispatch* also drew on the Hue Massacre in a column critical of Kerry's 1971 opposition to the conflict. Noting that the Democrat "was a principal in one of the most virulent antiwar groups [that is, VVAW] this country has ever known," Lewis claimed that, following Kerry's "testimony about supposed atrocities committed by our troops in Vietnam," the "media bought it hook, line, and sinker." Moreover, "while lapping up Kerry's witness about [sic] American atrocities, they all but ignored the Hue massacre committed by the North Vietnamese against the South." According to Lewis:

> The Hue massacre of more than 3,500 Vietnamese civilians, you'll recall — wait, you probably won't recall, because Walter Cronkite et al. hushed it up — was perpetrated when the battle for the town of Hue turned against the Vietcong, who proceeded to slaughter the men, women, and children of several villages surrounding the besieged city when they discovered that South Vietnamese support for their cause was less than expected. After the Hue massacre it was understood among the South Vietnamese that, as local provincial chief Le Van Than said at the time, "the Vietcong would kill them, regardless of their political belief."[110]

Among elements of the Vietnamese diaspora, the Hue Massacre has come to symbolize the malign intentions of the revolutionary movement, in effect justifying the exiles' earlier support for the RVN government. For many of these members of the overseas community, the factual basis of the atrocities narrative has remained beyond reproach; the critical scholarship challenging it is either unknown to them or has been ignored or dismissed. The editors of a book published by the Vietnamese Laity Movement in the Diaspora, for instance, sought to "collect fragments of the truths available to remind one another and to advise the younger generations that the 1968 massacre at Hue is the most barbaric and worst crime of all in our country's historical tragedies."[111] The editors did not address the work of Gareth Porter or other scholars who have challenged the conventional accounts. Their principal concern was the education of those too young to have experienced the war at first hand. Even more than the authors of *The Vietnam War for Dummies*, whose attempt to enlighten the uninformed also subscribed to the Douglas Pike narrative, the "horrific atrocities" at Hue provided a crucial lesson.[112] "The facts in this book are not unfamiliar [to] most Vietnamese who kept themselves abreast of the situation when the war was going on," they wrote. "But for those who live under the communist rule and are affected by the communist propaganda, especially the younger generations, and for a vast majority of foreigners who, for a time, could only have access to secondhand sources of information that were brutally tampered and distorted by the anti-war reporters and journalists, these are the truths that they need to know."[113] The exiled Buddhist activist Le Huu Dan agreed. Drawing for factual support on the documentary produced by Accuracy in Media, he published a volume in 1998 that in considerable part focused on the "savage killing of thousands of Hue's civilians with tremendous cruelty." The Hue Massacre, he wrote, was a crime "unprecedented in the history of human kind" which exceeded even "Pol Pot's crime[s]," for the NLF, according to Dan, killed a Buddhist monk, a transgression of which, he said, not even Pol Pot and the Khmer Rouge had been accused.[114]

Solemn remembrances of the Hue atrocities among overseas Vietnamese have been common. During commemorations of the thirtieth anniversary of the Tet Offensive in 1998, Vietnamese in the Washington, D.C., area broadcast radio interviews with relatives of some of those killed in Hue, sponsored prayers for the victims in local churches and pagodas, hung a banner reading "In Memory of Hue Massacre's Victims" at a commercial center in Falls Church, Virginia, and held a demonstration next to the Vietnamese embassy.[115] In Canada, a commemorative service was held at approximately the same time in Edmonton to recall the "over 10,000 innocent people [who] were reportedly killed by Communist North Vietnam's troops during their short-lived occupation" of Hue.[116] It has not been unusual to find online enumerations of those killed that exceed the approximately three thousand executions said to have been carried out in most conventional accounts. On a website devoted to the deceased ARVN veteran Ngo The Linh, for example, one could find excerpts of Douglas Pike's *Viet-Cong Strategy of Terror* after a statement memorializing "the 7,600 civilians murdered in Hue by Vietnamese communists." Identical figures have appeared elsewhere.[117]

In 2003, the Hue Massacre emerged as a public issue with the dispute between elements of the overseas community and the curatorial staff at the Oakland Museum of California. During the institution's preparations for a historical exhibit tentatively entitled "Next Stop Vietnam: California and the Nation Transformed," Mimi Nguyen, a Vietnamese American staff researcher, was dismissed days after her submission of a memo complaining about various shortcomings she perceived in the exhibition's initial organization. Among these was an insufficient examination of the Hue atrocities. "For the 1968 section in the exhibit," she wrote of the plans, "we may have someone talk about an ancestral altar rather than hearing

Hue Massacre survivors living in California. If we do include the Hue tragedy, it has to be a quote on the wall, [and] only if 'it is really good.' Why must we suppress what actually happened?" she asked.

> Nguyen Ly Tuong chronicled an entire text (in Vietnamese) on the Tet Offensive survivors. San's father was captured and buried alive with some 4,000 students, professors, doctors, government officials, and their families in the mass graves. San was captured and bound, but managed to escape. Why must we deny this voice from reaching the American public? Wouldn't this story teach our audience about the atrocity of war?[118]

Nguyen's dismissal — which museum officials denied was related to the memo but declined to explain, telling reporters they could not discuss personnel matters — led to outrage within the Vietnamese diaspora.[119] Letters were sent to the museum, and within days an online petition criticizing the exhibition and Nguyen's termination had gathered hundreds of signatures. While most signatories simply lent their names to the document without providing additional comments, among the minority who did offer their remarks were two individuals who specifically referred to the need for the museum to publicly memorialize the atrocities in Hue.[120]

THE FUNCTIONS OF THE HUE MASSACRE IN AMERICAN MEMORY

In spite of uncertainty about exactly what transpired in 1968, the Hue Massacre has persisted as an uncontested historical reality in the contemporary tourism literature. Its fin-de-siècle representations appeared to serve several purposes. Not only did the massacre's ruthlessness confirm the inherent malevolence attached to "Communists" in American popular culture, but the episode also demonstrated to tourists the inability of postwar Vietnam to come to terms honestly with its own recent history. In this respect, the Hue Massacre served as what Dean MacCannell designated a "truth marker," knowledge that functions "to cement the bond of tourist and attraction by elevating the information possessed by the tourist to privileged status."[121] By virtue of its absence in Vietnamese war museums, tourists were reminded of the selectivity of Vietnamese representations of the conflict, which arguably had the effect of casting doubt on the remainder of the nation's official historical narrative.[122] This was critical, as, contrary to many popular accounts in the United States, the conflict has been framed by most Vietnamese as a nationwide revolutionary and anti-imperialist struggle for reunification and independence, and not, as *Newsweek* characterized the war during the twenty-fifth anniversary of its official end, as an effort by "well-intentioned policymakers in Washington" to "save" the RVN from its "North Vietnamese invaders."[123]

Several of the guidebooks explicitly made this connection between the massacre's absence in interpretive exhibits and the consequent unreliability of Vietnamese public history. "There is, of course, nothing about [the massacre] in Hue's War Museum," the writer for Fodor's observed, suggesting the purposeful forgetting of Vietnamese curators and historians.[124] Nor, for that matter, was the event acknowledged in the popular War Remnants Museum in Ho Chi Minh City, whose "one-sided propaganda," according to another Fodor's guidebook, failed to include "information about some of the horrors perpetrated by the National Liberation Front, particularly the 14,000 people massacred in Hue during the 1968 Tet Offensive."[125] In writing about the disclosure of the atrocities at the same institution, the authors for Lonely Planet were less precise, simply stating that "of course" there was "official amnesia when it comes to the topic of the many thousands of people tortured and murdered by the VC."[126] For tourists turning to guidebooks to learn about the country's history — a majority of those people independently traveling in Vietnam, my fieldwork suggests — there were many such reminders of the official historical narrative's shortcomings in museums and at war-related sites. And the guidebooks' employment of "of course" to characterize the lack of information on revolutionary atrocities implied that one should naturally expect an inaccurate depiction of the war at Vietnamese tourist attractions. The inverse of this caution, never stated but nearly always implied, was that popular Western accounts were devoid of such ideological constraints, providing for their readers an "objective" representation of historical reality.

The communication scholars Laurel Kennedy and Mary Rose Williams addressed this perceptual conundrum in their examination of touristic narratives in postwar Vietnam, such as those evident at war-related sites and in travel brochures. "Observers may bring at least a little skepticism to reconstructions of the past offered by the (identifiable) state," they wrote, "while accepting more readily narratives whose anonymous authorship does not alert their critical faculties."[127] Their admonition is important; however, when specifically considering the role performed by travel guidebooks, it seems that authorial anonymity has not necessarily been a positive attribute. While perhaps not personally invested in the detailed individual biographies of guidebook authors, interviews reveal that many tourists chose their guidebooks precisely because they trusted the publisher "brand." This was overwhelmingly the case with Lonely Planet, which many travelers referred to as "The Bible."[128]

Kennedy and Williams explored the manner in which "the stories in brochures . . . mediate tourists' travel experience [in Vietnam] even before it has begun."[129] But contemporary Western guidebooks, with the contested historical narratives they must address, have not, for the most part, received similar scholarly consideration.[130] There do, however, exist theoretical models for such an undertaking. For example, in her semiotic analysis of the Lonely Planet guidebook for India, Deborah Bhattacharyya employed, among other theories, Erik Cohen's notion of communicative mediation.[131] As Bhattacharyya applied Cohen's term, communicative mediation involves the "selection of sights to be seen, providing information about these sights, and interpreting the sights for the tourist." She asserted that "while a guidebook shapes the image of the destination through both selection of sights and providing information about them, it is the process of interpretation that is perhaps most crucial in this regard." The process of interpretation to which she referred "is a combination of contextualization and evaluation." This is especially critical as a result of the perceived authority guidebooks claim to possess, for language, according to Bhattacharyya, is used in such a way as "to present a particular representation as the sole legitimate one." In other words, the portrait of Vietnam that emerged in travel guidebooks could be considered "a straightforward, self-evident description of reality rather than . . . a socially constructed representation."[132]

This notion of communicative mediation is fundamental to understanding the historical synopses provided by the Vietnam guidebooks. Consider the volume published by Lonely Planet, which field research I conducted in 2000 and 2002 indicated was the most widely used by Western tourists in the country.[133] One of its authors, Robert Storey, stated in an interview that, despite having an opinion of the war, he strove for a "neutral" and "unbiased" account that would "describe exactly what happened." He asserted, "For me, I think it's very important actually to get to the real facts." Yet Storey admitted to disregarding an influential segment of the historical literature because he found it ideologically unpalatable. This included not only the work of Noam Chomsky—a "supporter of the Khmer Rouge" who was "very pro-Communist, very pro-North Vietnam" and whose publications seemed like "endless propaganda," Storey maintained—but also studies emanating from the Indochina Resource Center (IRC), which published Gareth Porter's critique of the conventional Hue Massacre narrative. The IRC was "too left-wing," in the Lonely Planet author's estimation, and its "left-wing garbage" was "giving you the wrong impression of what was happening [in Vietnam]."[134] While at first glance admirable, Storey's nod to "neutral[ity]," then, clearly overlooked problems with the "objectivity question," as the historian Peter Novick characterized it, and with the selection of an explanatory framework as itself a subjective construction.[135] Indeed, Storey's admitted preclusion of certain sources graphically illustrates the problem of representing *the* history of a tourist site after selecting only those background materials that express a favored view. When one considers the extent to which travelers have come to rely on Lonely Planet's authority in developing their understanding of the Vietnamese past, the grave implications of this constricted perspective become apparent.

MYTHS AND MEMORY FOR AMERICANS COMING TO TERMS WITH THE WAR

Given its longevity, its wide circulation, and its perceived moral force, the Hue Massacre must rank among the most successful psychological warfare projects instituted by U.S. officials during the war. In spite of the fact that what occurred in Hue remains contested, it is abundantly clear that the disputed tale of wanton Communist slaughter has become enshrined as historical truth in the minds of many Americans and overseas Vietnamese. That this narrative persisted in the travel literature over thirty years after it was first constructed by ARVN's political warfare unit and then recycled by the U.S. authorities in Saigon may be a testament to the limits of critical scholarship in effectively penetrating popular discourse. After all, even some academic historians, relying on the secondary literature, have internalized the narrative's basic structure.

Why an abiding faith in the Hue Massacre remains is an important question, and one for which scholarship on historical myths in American popular consciousness may provide some illumination. In his analysis of the collective memory of spat-upon Vietnam veterans, for which he argued that no contemporaneous evidence exists, Jerry Lembcke wrote that myths may function "to reverse the verdict of history, to find the innocent guilty and the guilty innocent."[136] While it is important that "innocence" not be ascribed to those NLF insurgents who did, it must be recalled, execute at least several hundred noncombatants, this is nevertheless an important consideration when contemplating representations of the Hue Massacre as a historical actuality in both travel guidebooks and the popular historical literature. The representation of atrocities, wrote Sandie Holguín in discussing the depiction of one particular instance of indiscriminate killing during the Spanish Civil War, "is not a debate about which side committed more acts of savagery; rather, it is a question of narrative shaping and of how those stories would be used to convince international tourists — and, by extension, the international community — of the necessity for a Nationalist victory."[137] The Hue Massacre must be considered in a somewhat comparable context. Over twenty-five years ago, Edward Herman and Gareth Porter wrote that belief in the Hue Massacre was necessary, for it "permitted the creation of a massive bloodbath if the revolutionaries were to win in South Vietnam, which . . . in turn provided an important moral basis for [the] continued [U.S.] intervention as the 'lesser' evil."[138] This message was not lost, for example, on the authors of the Footprint guidebook, who were explicit in noting that the episode, which they did not question, "lent support to the notion that should the north ever achieve victory over the south it would result in mass killings."[139]

Yet at the same time that it justified continued U.S. military intervention in Southeast Asia, Herman and Porter maintained, the alleged massacre also diverted attention from the "real and massive bloodbath" sponsored and executed by the United States in which, by the end of the war, an estimated one million to three million Vietnamese had been killed. In other words, the Hue Massacre "was *needed*," they wrote, "to help convince us that even if we were not quite as kindly toward the Vietnamese as in the rhetoric of intervention, *they* were worse."[140]

In much the same way, the Hue Massacre today serves as a means of reversing — or, at least, balancing — the brutality of the war in American memory.[141] From their wartime image in certain quarters as an embattled resistance movement, the Vietnamese revolutionary forces have since been transformed in the American popular imagination into perpetrators of atrocities in Hue against "anyone connected with, or suspected of being sympathetic to, the [U.S.-backed] government in Saigon," as the Footprint guidebook identified those thousands of noncombatants allegedly subjected to the NLF's organized slaughter.[142] While all sides in the war engaged in acts of terror, the conventional Hue Massacre story, wrote David Hunt, represents "a Cold War narrative construction purporting to demonstrate that enemy terrorism was qualitatively different from GVN [Government of Vietnam, or Republic of Vietnam] and U.S. attacks on civilians and that it resulted in the most heinous atrocity of the war." Within this narrative construction, "The guerrillas killed more than the Americans and the GVN," and "they killed with a uniquely blameworthy premeditation and relish." The revolutionaries' violence was thus " 'systematic,' " Hunt continued, "meaning that it was constitutive, inevitable, and limitless in scale, in contrast to reactive violence on the other side, intended to halt the depredations of the Foreign Other." In other words, Hunt asserted in response to Douglas Pike's original account of the alleged massacre, "only 'fiends' could have committed the acts that [Pike] describes, pinpointing thousands of victims in advance, torturing and executing them, and dumping their corpses into mass graves."[143] If the Hue Massacre in fact unfolded as the leading travel guidebooks claimed, it is not difficult to speculate about the "fiendish" impression of the revolutionaries with which tourists reading about the atrocity would have been left.[144]

To be sure, Americans hardly arrived in Vietnam as tabula rasae entirely unfamiliar with their nation's history in Indochina. Rather, if it was true that — as my field research suggests — tourists had largely internalized the historical discourses extant in their travel guidebooks, it was probably because these guidebooks presented discourses consistent with many of the representations of the war in most standard U.S. history texts and in American popular culture.[145] Or, to borrow a concept from Raymond Williams, they conformed to the American "selective tradition," which had constructed the conflict as a tragic but well-intentioned mistake rooted in Washington's benevolent intentions for Southeast Asia.[146] At its core, this selective tradition has been shaped, H. Bruce Franklin maintained, by "those myths, celluloid images, and other delusory fictions about 'Vietnam' that in the . . . decades [since the war] have come to replace historical and experiential reality."[147]

By the time they visited Vietnam, Western tourists had usually watched any number of the hundreds of Hollywood films or television programs that dealt with the war, or perhaps they had heard stories from friends and relatives. Some possessed lived memories — as combat veterans, members of the antiwar movement, Vietnamese exiles, or merely disinterested observers. For most first-time visitors, their experiences in Vietnam were extraordinarily formative occasions influenced by the people they met, the sites they saw, the things they read. And for many, if not most, travel guidebooks were instrumental in framing and shaping their touristic experiences and the memories with which they departed. It is with an awareness of this context that we must interpret the guidebooks' repetition of accounts describing an indiscriminate slaughter, meticulously planned months before, of thousands of civilians in Hue during the 1968 Tet Offensive.

The years since 1975 have witnessed a remarkable re-imaging of the war in American memory. From the nefarious barbarism of the Vietnamese in *Missing in Action* (1984) and *The Hanoi Hilton* (1987) to the heroic bayonet-wielding American warriors in *We Were Soldiers* (2002), the United States has, in the decades following the conflict, projected what some have adjudged its own wartime criminality onto the elusive Other it failed to subdue in Indochina. At the same time, the nation has allowed its soldiers to finally emerge victorious — or, at the very least, heroic. The Hue Massacre, in this respect, has provided a necessary salve for America's wounded collective conscience. Over thirty-five years after the United States led a devastating drive to recapture Hue, travel guidebooks continued to present the gruesome details of a massacre that remained fiercely contested by a number of Vietnam specialists. In this respect, the episode continued to serve as a neutralizing agent, reminding Americans that as horrible as "we" acted during the war, "they" most certainly were worse.

4

The New Modernizers NATURALIZING CAPITALISM

IN *DOI MOI* VIETNAM

Tourists seeing Hanoi as the twentieth century drew to a close chose an auspicious moment for their visit. Just fifteen years earlier, their guidebooks suggested, Vietnam's capital had been a dull, gray cityscape bled of vitality and life. It was, the travel literature implied, a dreadfully despondent place. But then something magical happened. Following the 1986 Party Congress, capitalism arrived in Vietnam — and none too soon. From out of the darkness emerged the first hint of light; the transformation was astonishing. "No longer is a shopping trip in Hanoi a journey to a large state owned department store specializing in empty shelves," the Lonely Planet authors rejoiced. Replacing this bleak scenario, "color and liveliness [have] returned to the streets."[1] Indeed, "Hanoi's prosperous shop owners exemplify Vietnam's new economic reforms," the authors asserted, implying that the urban merchants of the capital city, vastly outnumbered by the country's rural peasantry whom most tourists would never meet, were in fact representative of the reforms' effects.[2]

Fortunately for the Vietnamese — or so one must have concluded from the guidebook's descriptive language — the "geriatric revolutionaries in the prime of senility" who advocated Vietnam's continued adherence to socialist principles were "being forcibly retired." In their place had emerged a "younger generation — with no romantic attachment to the past — [that]

is only interested in the side of the bread that is buttered."[3] Thanks to this "economic resurgence, . . . buildings are being repaired and foreign-owned companies are now investing in everything from joint-venture hotels to banks and telecommunications." Hanoi, and "the rest of the north," according to Lonely Planet, "has great potential to develop export-oriented manufacturing industries," a euphemism for low-wage assembly platforms that critics have, more cynically, derided as "sweat-shops." It was "a potential now only beginning to be realized," the authors surmised as the twenty-first century rapidly approached.[4]

Lonely Planet was hardly alone in its effusive celebration of the capital-ist reforms. Remarking that "the Hanoi government immediately turned southern Vietnam into a Soviet-style economy" following reunification, the leadership's policies, according to the authors of the Insight guide-book, "nearly left a carcass of a nation." By the mid-1980s, they main-tained, "the country's economy was destitute. Inflation exceeded 800 per-cent. Large parts of the rural population were starving or nearly so." Gratefully, however, "saving face is not an obsessive concern of the Viet-namese," so "admitting that their socialization of the South was in error, the government shifted course towards a free-market economy with its *doi moi*, or new reform, policy." The move was "essential," the guidebook informed its readers.[5]

For the travel publisher Fodor's, among whose authors could be counted the former executive director of the American Chamber of Commerce in Ho Chi Minh City, the changes in Hanoi were viewed similarly. Following the government's 1986 proclamation of "the move to a market economy," foreign investors "started preliminary explorations." Over time, "more and more foreign investment started coming." In the late 1990s, the guidebook contended that "few can argue that the last decade of change in Hanoi has been [nothing] short of a godsend," with the city "now cordially welcoming both billions of dollars of foreign investment and the many foreign visitors eager to see this city—this nation—in the midst of re-newal."[6] To the author of another Fodor's guidebook—one apparently written for more historically minded tourists—Vietnam represented a "dinosaur of Marxist–Leninist rhetoric . . . now letting chinks of free-market economy lighten the gloom." The Vietnamese, the author be-lieved, were in the process of finally "rediscover[ing] their identity, buried for decades under the dust of war and Communist dogma."[7] Capitalism was thus not only economically imperative but also integral to the nation's spiritual rebirth. For Vietnamese, it seems, its arrival was life-saving.

TOURISM, GUIDEBOOKS, AND THE MEDIATION OF EXPERIENCE

In the years following Vietnam's introduction of the capitalist reforms popularly known as *doi moi* (renovation), international tourism emerged as one of the country's principal growth industries. In 1993, according to the Vietnam National Administration of Tourism, approximately 515,000 foreigners visited Vietnam. By 2001, the total had increased to over 2.3 million.[8] For many of these non-Vietnamese-speaking tourists, and especially for independent travelers from the West, guidebooks, as I argued earlier, performed an instrumental role in mediating their travel experiences, helping them to negotiate not just Vietnamese history — such as the 1968 Tet Offensive in Hue — but also the state's evolving economic system. "It is the travelers' (backpackers') 'Bible,'" confessed a British woman in her early thirties when referring to the Lonely Planet volume for Southeast Asia.[9] The sentiment was echoed elsewhere — by backpackers and non-backpackers alike.

The cultural historians Christina Klein and Melani McAlister have addressed the important ways in which cultural items such as films, novels, and essays in mainstream publications have helped to shape popular perceptions of Asia and the Middle East for Americans and other Westerners.[10] Although they do not receive nearly as much scholarly attention, travel guidebooks have performed a similar function, not only identifying what tourists could or should see but also articulating how such places should be interpreted. In the case of Vietnam, which as the twentieth century drew to a close found itself in a state of tremendous economic flux, the publications provided readers with immediate guidance about the turbulent world they were witnessing. This provision of an ideological template for the wrenching changes being experienced by Vietnamese was crucial, for with its government seeking increased integration into an economic world order dominated by the United States and other powerful "market" proponents, tourists were navigating a physical space that was both fiercely contested and highly contentious.

Guidebooks thus assumed considerable influence. As a "country of memory," in the memorable words of Hue-Tam Ho Tai, the word "Vietnam" itself still evokes in American and Western consciousness powerful images of brutal warfare and political friction.[11] Since 1975 few images have emerged to replace them. Tourists' experiences—and the guidebooks that mediate them—have therefore proved of critical import for hundreds of thousands of Westerners experiencing Southeast Asia for the first time. The Vietnamese travel literature not only fosters and shapes how international tourists conceive of the pre-1975 conflict with which the memory of "Vietnam" is so inextricably intertwined; it also frames the economic policymaking in the country since that time, cueing visitors in particular to the efficacy and sapience of the economy's capitalist transformation. Despite scholarly and popular dissensus on the overall wisdom of the doi moi reforms, the discourses pervading the guidebooks have generally been favorable to the capitalist policies, representing them as positive, sensible departures from what the most popular guidebook for the country —that published by Lonely Planet—referred to in 1999 as the "ideologically driven policies . . . followed after reunification."[12] In this sense, "Vietnam" has become not just a signifier of aggression and destruction or, for many in the United States, American victimization, but also, for some in the West, an object lesson in the brilliance of global capitalism.

Perhaps it should not be surprising that travel publishers, themselves profit-seeking institutions dependent on the growth of international tourism, would look favorably on the official embrace of capitalist principles in an avowed socialist state. Given the global hegemonic position of capitalism as essentially synonymous with "objective" economic laws, it seems only natural that guidebooks would view doi moi through a predominantly approving lens. Nevertheless, by the late 1990s the negative human consequences of the reforms for millions of Vietnamese had generated substantial internal debate, and they were the focus of increasing attention from historians, journalists, economists, and other scholars of Asia. For the most part, however, the critical perspectives within both Vietnamese society and the extant literature appear to have escaped inclusion in the leading Western guidebooks.

This is by no means shocking when considered in the context of twentieth-century international history, for the travel authors' embrace of the capitalist transformation is essentially an extension of the modernization ideology that predominated among American policymakers and academics after the Second World War.[13] Whereas Cold War modernizers viewed the strength of the U.S. economy after 1945 as an affirmation of the American global mission's moral and intellectual legitimacy, the sense in guidebooks of the late 1990s that capitalism was the appropriate economic path for Vietnam to pursue appears rooted in the market triumphalism that has characterized the period following the Soviet Union's collapse. Today, as the historian Nelson Lichtenstein argued in 2004, the "triumphalism of the free market" may be "the single greatest legacy of the end of the Cold War."[14] Consistent with this celebratory impulse and the diffusion of American power, the naturalization of capitalist principles has percolated into nearly every region of the planet. It was certainly evident in the discourses of the Western guidebook authors, who implied that doi moi, as a marvel of rational economic thought, would transform a nation of economic primitives into modern human beings.

In the broadest sense, these guidebooks constructed Vietnam's capitalist policies as natural, necessary, and overwhelmingly beneficial. In doing so, their authors established a specious dichotomy between ideological socialism on the one hand and non-ideological capitalism on the other, neglecting the complexity of the Vietnamese experience since the American war officially drew to a close in 1975. Improvements in economic performance were almost uniformly ascribed in the guidebooks to capitalist policies rather than, for example, the cessation of war in Cambodia or the lifting of the international embargo, and, with several notable exceptions, the reforms' contribution to growing inequality was minimized or even entirely overlooked. The same was true of doi moi's effects on the health-care system, infant mortality, and educational opportunities, which received virtually no detailed appraisal in the travel literature.[15] The cumulative result was the confirmation for many Western tourists visiting a self-proclaimed "socialist republic" that accession to a rigid International Monetary Fund (IMF) model and full integration into the U.S.-led neoliberal world order were not only natural but, from the perspective of economic justice, possibly even imperative. As one guidebook approvingly reported, "After suffering impatiently through 10 years of high socialism," Vietnam at the close of the twentieth century was "ushering in a stampede of venture capitalists ready to bless the Vietnamese with free enterprise."[16]

To propagate the wisdom of Vietnam's accession to "market" principles, several of the guidebooks misrepresented Vietnamese economic history prior to 1986, the year the doi moi reforms were largely solidified as official policy.[17] The authors for Lonely Planet, for example, claimed that the Vietnamese economy "started growing in the late 1980s, reversing the trend of the previous decade when it experienced precipitous negative economic growth."[18] Yet according to the economist Masahiko Ebashi, the gross domestic product grew at an average rate of 7 percent from 1981 to 1984.[19] In fact, in 1985 — that is, before doi moi was described by Lonely Planet as having "really got[ten] underway" — the Vietnamese economy experienced its second highest gain of any year between 1984 and 1991, and, with the exception of trade, the period from 1981 to 1985 experienced higher growth than the period from 1986 to 1990.[20]

In other instances, the misrepresentation of the past was more subtle. The Indochina guidebook published by Moon, for instance, observed that by 1985 "inflation was running at 700 percent, and radical economic reform was required if Vietnam was to survive."[21] Yet in highlighting the astronomical inflation rate of the mid-1980s the author implied that it was "hard-liners" — his appellation for those resistant to capitalist principles — who were primarily responsible. In fact, the opposite was true. It was, the scholarship reveals, the country's "market" reformers who introduced the currency measures in 1985 that exacerbated the already serious difficulties and culminated in a hyperinflationary disaster, not the "hard-liners" derided by the guidebook.[22] The travel writer's insistence that survival depended on further "radical economic reform" — identified in the next sentence as "capitalist market principles" — thus seems misplaced. Nevertheless, there were grounds for optimism, tourists learned. With the introduction of these capitalist principles, the guidebook noted in a presumed testament to the economy's success, Vietnam found itself "included [by 1995] in the list of the world's most promising emerging markets for U.S. business," according to a Department of Commerce announcement.[23]

In addition to misrepresenting Vietnamese economic realities prior to 1986, the guidebooks offered sweeping judgments about the reforms that elided their complexity and the popular and scholarly debates they spawned. Moon, for instance, reported, "Since 1986 and the dawn of doi moi (new thinking), Vietnam has pursued capitalist market reforms and made remarkable economic progress."[24] As the passages that opened this chapter attest, the unambiguously positive sentiment was hardly unique. It is difficult to determine the criteria employed by the guidebook's author in reaching this judgment, but it seemed to follow the belief of the IMF and other global actors that growth should serve as the primary determinant of economic success.[25]

Yet whatever the logic in employing words like "remarkable" and "progress," most of the guidebooks omitted or minimized critical information that might have provided tourists with a more nuanced understanding of Vietnamese economic life. For instance, even if one were to employ the principal IMF criterion of success, it is not universally accepted that the rise in gross domestic product was rooted in the capitalist principles underlying doi moi. At least one eminent scholar has argued forcefully that the lifting of the international sanctions imposed after the Vietnamese invasion of Cambodia and the success of the state oil industry largely explain much of the economic growth since the late 1980s.[26] But perhaps even more significant, either ignored or minimized in most of the guidebooks was the reforms' contribution to growing class and social stratification. To be sure, such inequality was hardly unanticipated. As the World Bank economist Bradley Babson conceded to a Western journalist in 1995, "I think it's fair to say that Vietnam in the past has had more equality than many other countries, and that the reforms necessary for economic growth will bring greater inequality."[27]

Yet recognition of this growing stratification was not a prominent feature of the guidebooks' economic discursions. The volumes thus failed to enlighten travelers about the region's complex social geography. And when one considers that the reforms were often prompted by multilateral institutions acting at the behest of the major capitalist powers — the United States, Japan, France, and the United Kingdom, among others — from which many of these tourists originated, the significance of this failure becomes particularly acute. With "globalization" the object of increasingly critical scrutiny as well as the focus of major worldwide opposition throughout the 1990s, it is curious that not a single guidebook located the Vietnamese state's embrace of capitalist reforms within this framework. Whether or not their authors agreed with the critiques of the IMF, the World Bank, and other global bodies seeking structural adjustment in much of the developing world, it would have seemed only natural that they acknowledge the scholarly and popular debates concerning Vietnam and other impoverished states' accession to this contested global model. That they did not reveals much about the power of capitalist discourses in the late twentieth century and their implications for international tourism.

The relative weight given to various explanations for Vietnam's economic difficulties after 1975 is a matter of dispute among scholars. There can be no doubt that Vietnamese authorities committed serious errors in managing the economy in the decade following the American war. However, often overlooked by economists from the IMF and other lending institutions, and inexplicably minimized by a number of guidebook authors, was the legacy of the war's devastation and its implications for postwar development. It is questionable, at best, whether any economic system in and of itself could have led to the rapid and successful reconstruction of the country, or whether the north and south could have been reunified painlessly.[28] Moreover, most of the guidebooks seriously downplayed what the historian Gabriel Kolko claimed was "the principal cause of the post-1977 economic crisis: Vietnam's protracted war with the Pol Pot regime [of Cambodia] and then the brief but terribly costly conflict with China in 1979."[29]

Consider the synopsis by Lonely Planet. In evaluating Vietnam after 1975, its authors claimed that the economy went "straight down the toilet after reunification." While they conceded that Vietnam "was hurt by wartime infrastructure damage (not a single bridge in the North survived American air raids, while in the South many bridges were blown up by the vc)," the guidebook maintained that "by the government's own admission the present economic fiasco is the result of the ideologically driven policies followed after reunification, plus corruption and the burden of heavy military spending." The recent "intense intra-Party disagreements over the path Vietnamese Communism should take," the authors observed, had pitted "changing coalitions of conservatives and dogmatists squaring off against more pragmatic elements."[30]

The assertion that the Vietnamese economy collapsed after reunification — indeed, it went "straight down the toilet" — implied that a healthy (or, at least, healthier) southern economy was undermined by the government's postwar ideological rigidity, which in this instance the authors ascribed to "those two white guys, Marx and Lenin."[31] Yet given the tremendous structural defects of the economy under the wartime Saigon regime — it was essentially a corrupt U.S.-subsidized shell reliant on high rates of consumption without corresponding productive capabilities — the guidebook's suggestion was extremely misleading.[32] And unclear about why socialists were "dogmatists" while capitalists were "pragmatic," the presumed authority suggested by the government's "admission" that it was responsible for the "present economic fiasco" was instructive.[33] In lending it credence, the guidebook failed to consider the so-called admission's possible impetus. According to Kolko, official Vietnamese accounts of the economy in the decade following 1975 "exaggerated its failures to justify the new economic strategy" under doi moi.[34] The authors for Lonely Planet provided no indication that such was even a possibility.

Another guidebook, the Southeast Asia volume published by Moon, baldly claimed that the Vietnamese leadership after the American war "inflicted on the nation one of the world's most disastrous economic models." To be sure, there are numerous grounds on which analysts have criticized Vietnamese planners. Yet the author's comment appeared to be little more than a reflexive iteration of the received wisdom given his failure to mention, let alone examine, how the country's infrastructure was devastated by years of conflict, how billions of dollars in reconstruction aid promised by the United States was withheld, and how an international embargo imposed by Washington isolated Vietnam globally. In fact, these last two factors, the historian Edwin Martini argues, represented two planks of a punitive post-1975 U.S. policy that amounted to a continuation of the war "by other means."[35] Whatever the Moon guidebook might have failed to acknowledge, however, there can be little doubt, according to its author, that capitalism promised a more sensible future. "Twenty years of failure seems finally to be having an effect on the rulers of Vietnam, who announced a policy of economic doi moi (new life) in 1991," he wrote, misstating the timing of the capitalist reforms' introduction by at least half a decade.[36]

A similar discourse pervaded the volume published by Let's Go. "With the memories of failed hard-lined communism in mind," its authors wrote, "it would appear as though [the] party is committed to an open market economy," which the leadership was "willing to liberalize . . . to a prosperous end." According to the guidebook, however, the fact that party leaders had embraced capitalist reforms while concurrently disallowing political liberalization rendered them "not-so-hard-lined-but-still-communist," implying that socialist goals were innately "hard-lined" while capitalist objectives were not.[37] The basis for the characterizations was left unarticulated, but to tourists inured to the "free-market faith," as Thomas Frank labeled the prevailing economic consensus of the 1990s, no clarification would presumably have been necessary.[38]

The degree to which most guidebooks adhered to the ideological presuppositions of international financial institutions can be discerned by the extent to which they welcomed Vietnam's strengthened relationship with various multilateral lenders. For the author of Moon's Indochina guidebook, "Rapprochement with the United States has meant a tremendous boost for Vietnam's economy," for it led to "the International Monetary Fund, the World Bank, and the Asian Development Bank all pledg[ing] new funds."[39] While numerous analysts dispute that agreement to the terms of IMF or other loans represents a "tremendous boost" for any state given the painful strings normally attached to such fund disbursement in terms of reduced social spending, this caution did not appear in the Moon guidebook. Instead, it advised tourists that light industry "has a bright future" in the country, as the "combination of an educated, highly skilled workforce and low wages is attractive to foreign investors," maintaining — perhaps naïvely given the realities of the late 1990s — that "Vietnam could become one of Asia's leading producers of computer software."[40]

Moon was not the only publisher to draw positive attention to Vietnam's cheap yet skilled labor. Rather than viewing the relative poverty of the working class as a shortcoming in need of upward adjustment, however, the travel writers generally framed it as a comparative advantage begging for exploitation by foreign investors. In fact, some guidebooks seemed to gauge the country's willingness to open up to predatory foreign investment as a measure of its economic promise. Lonely Planet, for instance, remarked that "low wages and the strong Vietnamese work ethic (when offered incentives) bodes well for Vietnam's export industries," while *Fodor's Exploring Vietnam* noted how the country's "Asian neighbors" — to the apparent detriment of late-arriving Western corporations — had been "eager to profit from a young, well-educated, and low-paid work force."[41]

For their part, Vietnamese officials did not hesitate in extolling this phenomenon. In outlining his vision for the country's development, Nguyen Xuan Oanh — a collaborator with the Japanese during World War Two, a former functionary of the IMF, and a onetime acting prime minister in the

RVN who became an influential economist at the local (Ho Chi Minh City) and national levels after 1975 — disclosed that foreign investors were free "to roam around the country to find out for themselves areas in which they might have a comparative advantage[, t]o be in the best position to produce with efficiency and low cost, to draw raw material[s] locally or from overseas to keep production costs to a minimum." In fact, he boasted, "you can come in with 100 percent foreign capital and full foreign management — simply transplanting an enterprise to our country. Only here you have the benefit of the relatively lower costs of labor, abundant raw materials, and a low corporate income tax — between 10 and 25 percent, which [is] the lowest in the world."[42]

Yet tellingly for the government's stated commitment to principles of economic justice, even the "low wages" trumpeted by the guidebooks did not appear to be low enough for certain Vietnamese advisers. Do Huu Hao, director of the Ministry of Industry's Institute for Industrial Policy Studies, observed in a 2002 interview that "labor costs in urban areas are constantly on the rise, reducing competitiveness in the textile, garment, and footwear sectors. Meanwhile, international markets for these products are expanding rapidly, creating greater demand for cheaper products." A shift to "rural locations [in Vietnam] will capture the full benefits of cheap labor," Hao thus counseled.[43] Indeed, such mobility on a domestic scale may serve as a microcosm of the "race to the bottom" that various critics have described on a global scale — a phenomenon in which states compete to provide international capital with the most attractive investment climate through a downward leveling of wages and environmental, health, and labor standards.[44] The guidebooks did not locate Vietnam within such an analytical model — nor, for that matter, did they hint at its existence.

COMMODITY EXPORTS: THE CASES OF RICE,
COFFEE, AND CATFISH

As revealing as the guidebooks could be in the information they imparted, equally telling could be what was left unsaid. This is especially so with respect to Vietnam's experience in several of the export drives on which the country placed great emphasis. In Lonely Planet's attempt to represent the capitalist reforms as a positive departure from earlier socialist planning, for example, the guidebook, like several of its competitors, omitted crucial information that would have provided a more complex portrait than that offered to readers. Perhaps in no case was this more true than in its treatment of commodity agriculture.

With respect to rice — or what one guidebook referred to as "white gold" — Lonely Planet extolled Vietnam's elevation "from . . . a rice importer in the mid-1980s to . . . the world's second largest rice exporter in 1997," claiming that the transformation was a "direct result" of the Vietnamese reforms.[45] The exports were possible, its authors explained elsewhere, because the Mekong Delta alone "produces enough rice to feed the entire country," leaving "a sizable surplus" available for international trade, and by 1997 northern Vietnam, "for the first time in its history," had "excess" stocks that could be sold abroad.[46]

The basis for these assertions is unclear. In fact, export targets under doi moi were determined before the harvest and regardless of actual production levels, not afterward. Vietnamese reports on output had consequently been "exaggerated" to justify the international sales. And there had never been an adequate amount of rice to satisfy the country's basic human needs. Indeed, in the 1990s, while some of those who prospered from the capitalist reforms found themselves suddenly having to contend with problems such as obesity, malnutrition remained a major problem in much of Vietnam.[47] In short, a synopsis disclosing that rice had been exported for profit rather than distributed to satisfy continuing domestic needs might have provided a lesson in the shortcomings of capitalist principles, not the positive attributes suggested by several guidebook authors.[48]

Similar complexities were apparent in the Vietnamese experience with coffee. Consistent with international financial institutions' unremitting advice to increase the share of agriculture destined for export, the Vietnamese government began providing farmers with subsidies in the 1990s to encourage their transition to coffee beans, a crop whose end product enjoyed minimal popularity in the country.[49] While Vietnam's massive entry into the international market initially may have seemed promising for Vietnamese farmers — by 2000 they collectively constituted the world's second largest producer — the result was a collapse of global coffee prices. This collapse proved beneficial for roasters in the United States and Europe who watched their profits soar, but in Vietnam the effect was calamitous. In Dac Lac province, the heart of Vietnam's coffee-growing region, Oxfam found that farmers in early 2002 were recovering only 60 percent of their production costs, while "the income derived by the worst-off farmers, dependent solely on coffee," was "categorized as 'pre-starvation.'" Hunger was "particularly acute" in households that "opted to dedicate a higher proportion of land to coffee than to other subsistence crops," creating conflicts between women "responsible for feeding their families and men keen to earn a higher cash income." In addition to generating substantial class and ethnic tensions in the Central Highlands, the coffee crisis negatively affected areas of public welfare such as education and health. Many farmers disclosed that coffee prices were "a problem in ensuring a decent education for their children," a growing worry in Vietnam given the imposition of school fees under doi moi, while the "combination of falling coffee incomes" and "rising health demands" was "having devastating impacts on health care."[50] Exacerbating the difficulties for these families, with the introduction of capitalist principles the government cut spending on public health, and user fees became the norm.

Still, these "coffee plantations" were touted by several guidebooks as attractions meriting tourists' attention, while the developments in Dac Lac had generated "newfound coffee-bean prosperity" in the provincial capital of Buon Me Thuot, according to the writer for *Fodor's Exploring Vietnam*. This prosperity, she maintained, was "having positive repercussions."[51] The authors for Lonely Planet similarly ascribed the city's "current prosperity" to the coffee industry, failing, like their counterpart, to reveal how farmers had fared since being encouraged to pursue the export market.[52]

The Vietnamese experience with catfish and, to a lesser extent, shrimp could similarly have raised questions about the travel literature's rosy portrait of the capitalist transformation and the government's decision to subscribe to the global trade regimen developed by the major capitalist states. Broached in a special boxed section in the sixth and seventh editions of the Lonely Planet guidebook, the case of catfish offers a sobering reminder of the "market" system's practical imbalances in light of the power differential enjoyed by the developed world.[53] It is worth examining in some detail.

The roots of Vietnam's catfish exports date to the last decade of the twentieth century, when Vietnam began to emerge as a major catfish producer. With seafood representing the country's third largest export earner in 2002, industry officials hoped to produce as much as five billion dollars in seafood exports by 2010. Catfish would make up a considerable share of that total. The American response was mixed. Congress resisted the market penetration by the Vietnamese, fearing its ramifications for domestic producers. Yet at the same time, the endeavor was openly encouraged by certain authorities, including, in 2002, the vice-consul general in Ho Chi Minh City.[54] As recently as 1998, Vietnamese catfish shipments to the United States amounted to only about 575,000 pounds per year. Exports grew rapidly, however, particularly after the ratification of a bilateral trade agreement in 2001. By 2002, they soared to as much as 20 million pounds, capturing approximately 20 percent of the U.S. market for frozen catfish fillets.[55]

American industry players took the offensive. Hoping to stem the tide, U.S. producers successfully persuaded Congress to bar the Vietnamese exporters from calling their product "catfish." It was their position that only the North American variety—one of approximately two thousand types of catfish worldwide—could be designated as such. When the U.S. Food and Drug Administration (FDA), which officiates naming rules, sought expert counsel, it turned to Dr. Carl J. Ferraris Jr., an adjunct curator of ichthyology at the California Academy of Sciences whose field of specialization was global catfish species. Unfortunately for the American producers, Ferraris sided with the Vietnamese. "The FDA wanted some indication of whether there was any justification for limiting the term catfish to North American catfish," he told a reporter, "and the answer was there's no justification, historically or scientifically, for such a statement."[56] A frustrated Congress thus simply ignored the FDA, forcing the Vietnamese to label their exports, which by most accounts looked and tasted the same as the American product, "basa" and "tra."[57]

Following this success on the naming front, U.S. producers sought country-of-origin legislation requiring that the national origins of all fish be identified. Despite the double standard this effort made apparent—as the *Economist* noted, "In many labeling arguments—particularly those over genetically modified foods in Europe—America is making exactly the opposite case, decrying enforced labeling as protectionist"[58]—the industry embarked on a broad public-relations campaign that tapped into popular American images of the Third World by referring to the Vietnamese exports as "dirty, even toxic, and definitely un-American," according to a report in the *New York Times*.[59] An advertisement issued by one group, for example, drew on presumed fears of developing states as sites of filth and contamination. "They've grown up flapping around in Third World rivers and dining on whatever they can get their fins on," the advertisement claimed. (The same ad contained even more explicitly xenophobic language, warning wholesale buyers — it appeared in the national trade weekly *Supermarket News* — to "never trust a catfish with a foreign accent" while quipping that "those other guys probably couldn't spell U.S. even if they tried.")[60]

Representative Marion Berry, an Arkansas Democrat whose state was among the largest domestic producers of catfish, went so far as to warn that the Vietnamese exports could be contaminated by Agent Orange and other toxic defoliants sprayed extensively during the war by U.S. forces over southern and central Vietnam. "That catfish is produced in disgusting conditions on the Mekong River," Berry maintained, "which is one of [the] most polluted watersheds in the world." Moreover, he continued, "that stuff [Agent Orange] doesn't break down. Catfish are bottom feeders and are more likely to consume dioxins that were sprayed as defoliants."[61] To be sure, no evidence was produced to support the allegation of contaminated fish, and the charge was rebutted by the U.S. Embassy in Hanoi: "In the case of catfish," it reported, "the embassy has found little or no evidence that the U.S. industry or health of the consuming public is facing a threat from Vietnam's emerging catfish export industry. . . . Nor does there appear to be substance to claims that catfish raised in Vietnam are less healthy than [those raised in] other countries."[62]

In its final attempt to undermine the Vietnamese export market, the industry sought import duties for the Vietnamese based on American "anti-dumping" laws.[63] Vietnamese officials countered that their prices were lower not because they dumped their product but because Vietnamese feed and labor was cheaper — precisely the sort of comparative advantage that international lenders had encouraged developing states to pursue. Yet in a controversial finding in 2003, the Bush administration nevertheless ruled that the Vietnamese farmers dumped their products at unfairly low prices and that the imports would be subject to tariffs ranging from 44.66 percent to 63.88 percent.[64] The lesson for Vietnam and others in the developing world could not have been more obvious: The planet's most powerful states need not adhere to the same principles as those dependent on their patronage. The American departure from "free market" theory as it pertained to Vietnamese catfish — a theory with little basis in global economic reality—was frankly conceded by Representative Berry: "We have to protect the agriculture in [the United States], whatever it takes."[65] In other words, while one standard was exploited by the powerful—such as the American corn industry, which was encouraged through enormous government subsidies to export its crop to Mexico at prices up to 25 percent lower than its cost, thus devastating small Mexican growers—developing states had to abide by a different standard: They could not employ their comparative advantage in the labor market to compete with influential interests in industrialized nations.[66] For U.S. policymakers, low wages were desirable if they benefited corporations such as Nike, reportedly "the leading source of private employment in Vietnam" by the turn of the twenty-first century, but they were intolerable, one must conclude, if they threatened the viability of an established American industry.[67]

ABANDONING EQUALITY

Economic indicators, which fail to sufficiently capture people's levels of life satisfaction, are, of course, an inadequate means of measuring overall well-being. While the data are important, social realities are defined by far more than how much money one earns or one's access to public benefits. Nevertheless, such indicators are useful, particularly in a nation undergoing rapid economic and social transformation. Within the framework of such measurements, how one was to adjudge Vietnam's economic performance since 1986 largely depended on the criteria one chose to employ. If, following what became known as the "Washington consensus," rates of growth were considered the most important criterion of economic health, there could be no doubt that Vietnam flourished during most of the doi moi period. Yet the Vietnamese economy, as noted earlier, also demonstrated impressive growth in the early to mid-1980s—that is, prior to the solidification of its IMF-influenced structural adjustment—and there was scholarly dissensus about whether the capitalist reforms sufficiently explained the economic expansion since the late 1980s.

Some, alternatively, may have chosen to evaluate Vietnam's economic health by gauging its rate of privatization. This was certainly the case with a number of guidebooks, which implied that such privatization was integral to economic progress. Yet few, if any, disclosed the 1996 finding of the IMF—no ally of public ownership—that "the [state-owned enterprise] sector has surpassed the non-state sector in several respects," and that its performance had been "broadly favorable." In fact, despite widespread corruption, such enterprises had served as a "significant net contributor to the state budget," often registering higher growth rates than the private ventures — an enormous percentage of which were guilty of tax evasion — the guidebooks and the emerging capitalist class routinely celebrated as the engine of Vietnam's economy.[68]

For most people, however, a determination of economic health is about far more than rates of growth or privatization. Yet such other criteria received virtually no sustained attention in the tourism literature. For example, one relevant indicator that the travel writers could have considered, but largely did not, was the country's growing class stratification. "Economic development has occurred at the cost of social equity," Gabriel Kolko observed, with the wealthiest stratum frequently attaining its riches through nepotism or party membership. In fact, he noted, "income [in Vietnam] is already significantly more unequal than in Western capitalist nations." In the United States, for instance, World Bank data indicate that the richest fifth of the population received 41.9 percent of income in the mid-1990s; in supposedly socialist Vietnam, the richest fifth received 44 percent.[69] And according to the country's 2001 *National Human Development Report*, "New recent evidence suggests that income disparities may be widening more significantly than previously believed," as "inequality appears to have increased significantly in almost all provinces" between 1995 and 1999.[70]

The implications were serious. Employing the United States as a model — and for many Vietnamese, the American economy was one to which their country aspired — Ichiro Kawachi and Bruce P. Kennedy argued that "growing inequalities threaten the various freedoms that economic development is supposed to bring about: freedom from want, freedom from ill health, freedom to exercise democratic choice, as well as freedom to pursue leisure and the activities that [people] have reason to value." While it may be true that policies that raise everyone's incomes without regard for distributional concerns could increase societal welfare in states that "have not yet reached the level of development necessary to satisfy basic needs such as adequate nutrition or shelter," they provide a poor long-term model. The "relative income hypothesis" — which posits that "a person's level of well-being depends not just on their own level of income, but on everybody else's" — predicts that "among societies that have passed that [minimum] threshold, . . . doubling everyone's standard of living without altering the underlying distribution of resources will not necessarily result in improvements in the average level of well-being." The greater the disparities in the distribution of income, for instance, "the lower the health achievement of that society." Such findings led Kawachi and Kennedy to counsel that, rather than attempt to emulate the American model, other states "should heed the lessons of the destructive forces wrought by social inequalities on American society," such as high rates of crime and incarceration, relative declines in health, and the slow disintegration of civil society.[71]

Within Vietnam, income inequality in the 1990s was disproportionately borne by what the state refers to as "ethnic minorities." This was particularly true of the indigenous peoples of the highlands — a popular tourist attraction for Westerners enamored by their Otherness — who have suffered the continued colonization of their homelands, as well as the dislocations such a process engenders, under government policies both socialist and capitalist. In the first years of the twenty-first century, "ethnic minorities" made up approximately 14 percent of the country's total population, yet they accounted for 28 percent of the poor in 1998, according to a 2002 study by the Asian Development Bank (ADB).[72] The rate undoubtedly would have been higher if the largest minority group, the Hoa, or ethnic Chinese, who disproportionately benefited from the capitalist reforms, were excluded from the calculation. According to the ADB, the incidence of poverty in the Central Highlands only decreased from 92 percent to 91 percent from 1993 to 1998; the Northern Highlands recorded a slightly less marginal decline, from 84 percent to 73 percent, during the same period. But even these small reductions masked the increasing gap between the areas' native and settler populations. And in a troubling portent of what may have awaited the indigenous peoples, many of whom had already been forced by the settlers' presence to radically alter their traditional practices, the Central Institute for Economic Survey predicted that the proportion of poor "ethnic minorities" would increase to 34 percent from 28 percent "if the current economic model is applied for the next 10 years."[73]

In spite of the disproportionate impact on indigenous groups, income inequality broadly affected the well-being of people throughout Vietnam.

For instance, whereas the country's mortality rates for infants and children under five "were among the lowest in the developing world" by the mid-1980s, and by international standards "inequalities . . . between poor and better-off children were extremely low" until the early 1990s, "marked inequalities" had since emerged in the survival prospects of children. "Reductions in child mortality [under doi moi] have not been spread evenly" in recent years, World Bank researchers found in 2002, but were instead "concentrated among the better-off." Poorer children, they wrote, did "not appear to have seen any appreciable improvement."[74] The researchers identified various reasons for this disparity, such as "differential changes in mother's education and access to safe water." However, they found the largest contributory factor, at least among impoverished people "experiencing less advantageous changes in the determinants of child survival," to be "differential changes in health service coverage."[75]

As the World Bank and others have noted, Vietnam under doi moi suffered "a reduction in the scale and quality of public health services (at least in some areas)," with the government introducing user fees as it encouraged a private health sector.[76] The changes were in many respects devastating. Using data from 1997, the World Health Organization assigned Vietnam a ranking — with one being the highest — of 160 out of 193 countries in terms of the overall performance of its health system.[77] The decline must be contrasted with the health system's contribution to Vietnam's earlier "generally impressive health indicators," which were "much better than would be expected for a country at its level of income per capita." This was "probably a consequence of its socialist character," the World Bank conceded. In fact, the country's reductions in infant, child, and maternal mortality in the previous three to four decades brought Vietnam to levels comparable to states earning two to three times its per capita income. And these improvements were achieved with little external assistance, a situation owing in part to the country's ostracism while under a U.S.-imposed international embargo.[78]

Yet under doi moi, Vietnam's solid foundation of equalitarian health facilities and programs disintegrated, generating "considerable dislocation" in the "immediate years of the reform program." Funds for "infrastructure, equipment, drugs, and training were drastically reduced and the quality of health services at the local level deteriorated significantly." Indeed, concluded the World Bank, "the country's extensive network of grassroots health facilities and community-financed health workers, which formed the backbone of the national health system since the 1960s, faced imminent collapse." In an effort to halt this precipitous decline, the government began to undertake various measures in the early to mid-1990s in an effort to strengthen the public health services, although the effects of these actions tended to reflect both capitalist principles, in which health is viewed as a commodity, and the growing inequalities in Vietnamese society. The national health insurance program established in 1993, for instance, covered only a tiny minority of the population — approximately 12 percent as of the late 1990s — and disproportionately benefited higher-income families. Moreover, the user fees instituted under doi moi — which increased between 1993 and 1998 by, in some instances, as much as 1,400 percent — severely affected the poor, consuming a considerable proportion of people's nonfood expenditures and, in the case of a catastrophic illness, potentially wiping out a lifetime of savings and driving them into debt.[79]

Given this reality, inequities increased in the use of public hospitals — which claimed from 75 percent to 87 percent of the recurrent state health budget — with a plurality (36 percent) of all hospital users in 1998 drawn from the top income quintile and only 8 percent from the bottom quintile. This 8 percent, moreover, represented a decline from 1993, further exacerbating the gap between the poorest and wealthiest strata of Vietnamese society.[80] None of this came as a surprise, suggested the World Bank, for in a "market-oriented health care system," it noted, "high income elasticity for secondary and tertiary care and for privately provided health services means that the disparity in utilization rates between the poor and the better-off will increase."[81]

One consequence of this development was a dangerous reliance on drug vendors as health care providers — approximately two-thirds of all individual health-service contacts across income groups, according to surveys — despite their "insufficient competence in clinical pharmacology and clinical pharmacy." As a result, the incidence of self-medication "spiraled out of control," especially with respect to antibiotic drugs, causing "antibiotic resistance levels in Vietnam to reach epidemic levels." The developments threatened to derail the country's earlier, significant achievements in the health sector, according to the World Bank, as Vietnam lost "the ability to control and prevent the spread of many infectious diseases" and had to rely on more expensive, later-generation drugs in treating common infections. Even with these medicines, however, Vietnam experienced low compliance levels by the ill with rational treatment guidelines — such as a failure to abide by complete prescription regimens — as the introduction of user fees meant that poor patients often lacked the money to buy a full course of drugs.[82] Until 1989, pharmaceuticals were available without charge through the public health network to whoever required them, although the country's international isolation and economic straits meant there were often severe shortages of necessary medicines. At the dawn of the new millennium, however, drugs — in a paradox hardly unique to Vietnam's increasingly stratified class society — were generally abundant but remained unaffordable to millions of the country's most impoverished people.

The guidebooks' record in disclosing the existence of growing inequality — in income, health care, education, and so on — was mixed, and most shirked assessing its implications for Vietnamese society.[83] On the contrary, nearly every author, to the extent he or she even alluded to the disparities, framed the problem as a tragic but inevitable side effect of Vietnam's otherwise impressive economic achievements, which were portrayed as both necessary and generally beneficial. Neither the Moon guidebook for Indochina nor its volume for Southeast Asia acknowledged the enormous rise of inequality in their synopses of Vietnam's economy and history, although the latter — placing the touristic experience at the center of Vietnamese life — did identify what it referred to as "startling" recent changes "on a social level": "Today, you can purchase war-era Zippos in Hanoi, listen to the Doors wail in Saigon's Apocalypse [Now] Cafe, or sign up for the annual surfing contest at China Beach."[84] The guidebook produced by Let's Go also failed to address the negative social indicators; however, its section on Ho Chi Minh City recognized "such side-affects [*sic*] of modernity as pollution, overcrowding, and fast living" while noting that the "metropolis is home to more beggars, thieves, and prostitutes than any other city in the country." Nevertheless, no causal relationship between the capitalist reforms and the latter phenomena was suggested. When the guidebook did outline how the "economic changes . . . are already affecting the daily lives of Saigon's inhabitants," the examples proffered included visions of "school girls in flowing white *ao dai*'s peddl[ing] down broad boulevards, oblivious to the din around them, while delivery boys, their faces hidden behind sunglasses, zip through mid-day traffic on Japanese motorbikes."[85]

Explicitly embracing the capitalist reforms, *Fodor's Exploring Vietnam* nonetheless acknowledged "a rapidly expanding gap between the rural poor and *nouveau riche* city-slickers, and between those who can profit from bribes and those who cannot," while its introductory information contained a short section on the "imbalances" generated by the country's "economic momentum." However, the author identified those left "out on a limb" as "much of the rural population," largely ignoring substantial urban poverty and rural inequality. Her characterization, in other words, did not preclude the implication that perhaps the problem was the capitalist reforms' failure to sufficiently penetrate the countryside, not that they had already done so.[86] The Rough Guide and Insight guidebooks represented the introduction of capitalist reforms as a positive step while conceding — probably better than most others — the "problems" rooted in the increasing differentiation.[87]

In some guidebooks the acknowledgment of negative consequences assumed rather unusual forms. The only mention, accompanied by much praise for doi moi, of its resultant inequities in the introduction to Fodor's Gold Guide came in a three-word reference to Vietnam's "growing moneyed class" that liked to frequent Saigon's "better markets and chicer shops filled with more contemporary-looking goods." In the guidebook's section on Ho Chi Minh City, the disclosure that "the flip side of all [the metropolis's] success is rank failure," in which "many are being left behind in the struggle for self-enrichment," almost appeared like a warning to tourists rather than an acknowledgment of global capitalism's inherent class stratification:

> Homeless children roam the downtown streets, sometimes earning a living by shining shoes or by begging or pickpocketing. Limbless war veterans hobble behind wealthy tourists badgering them for small change. Women desperate for tourist dollars carry comatose infants and endlessly shuffle through the streets like specters. And after twilight prostitutes cruise downtown on their Hondas prowling for foreign customers. But, oddly, you grow accustomed to these tragic sights.[88]

Lonely Planet's single comment on inequality in its economic synopsis was framed as an act of denial on the part of the Vietnamese leadership rather than as a phenomenon demanding careful consideration by tourists. "Another fact that the government doesn't like to admit," the authors wrote, "is that the urban economy is improving much faster than the rural, widening the already significant gap in Vietnamese standards of living. The Vietnamese government fears what China is already experiencing — a mass exodus of countryside residents into the already overcrowded cities."[89] When the guidebook addressed the Vietnamese health system, it claimed that the economy's "significantly improving . . . has brought with it some major improvements to the medical situation." To support this assertion, the authors cited, in part, a decrease in malnutrition, which they asserted "is not a huge problem anymore."[90] The statement was important because it indirectly justified Vietnam's decision to invest in food production for export, and it supported the guidebook's claim — discussed earlier in greater depth — that the Mekong Delta alone "produces enough rice to feed the entire country, with a sizable surplus" available for international trade.[91]

As with all guidebooks, it is generally difficult to determine the sources employed by their authors, as the texts are not accompanied by footnotes or a list of references. Nevertheless, Lonely Planet's dismissal of malnutrition as no longer "a huge problem" was directly contradicted by virtually every study on the issue, and even the slight overall statistical improvements masked the trend's increasing inequalities. The incidence of adult malnutrition in 1998 was 28 percent, and according to several researchers commissioned by the World Bank, "Vietnamese children are among the most malnourished in the developing world."[92] In fact, a 1999 study conducted jointly by UNICEF and the official National Institute of Nutrition found that 39 percent of children under five were malnourished in terms of weight for age, and 34 percent were undernourished in terms of height for age.[93] Surveys conducted over the previous two decades — most of them in the period of the country's "[significant] improve[ment]" — had identified "mixed results," with a "sluggish rate" of decline during the previous fifteen years. Indeed, the greatest decrease in underweight malnutrition occurred before the 1990s, which is the decade widely celebrated in the travel literature for its substantial economic growth.[94] Furthermore, there were "large differences" in the rates of child malnutrition across economic groups; the decline was "much greater" among the top quintile than among the poorest, highlighting the emergence under doi moi of widespread social differentiation. As the World Bank concluded in 2001, the "economic disparity in child nutrition appears to have widened over the last five years."[95]

VIETNAM UNDER CAPITALISM:
"NOTHING SHORT OF A GODSEND"

In their assessment of the capitalist reforms, the guidebooks might have contemplated not only class and social stratification but also the status of land ownership in the countryside. For those millions of Vietnamese who sacrificed during the war to support the revolution, land redistribution had always been considered one of its greatest achievements. During the two decades following the introduction of doi moi, however, laws instituted to govern the agrarian transformation had, in practical effect, dispossessed poor peasants of their land, forcing many to work as hired laborers under conditions that increasingly compared to those prior to the revolution. The Vietnamese Ministry of Agriculture and Rural Development estimated that nearly 5 percent of peasant households in southern Vietnam were landless in the mid-1990s; however, the "political sensitivity" of the issue to policymakers in Hanoi suggests that the estimate "might not represent the real magnitude of the problem," wrote Hy Van Luong and Jonathan Unger.[96] World Bank data, which are probably more reliable, recorded rates of landlessness in 1998 ranging from 2.6 percent in the Central Highlands to 21.3 percent in the Mekong Delta and 28.7 percent in the southeast.[97] In the north, where rural conditions are somewhat different and collectivization was far more entrenched, landlessness was less widespread but was increasing, with estimates of 3.7 percent in the Northern Highlands, 4.5 percent in the Red River Delta, and 7.7 percent in the northern central panhandle.[98] Having renounced its commitment to socialist principles, it became the party's official position that land concentration was desirable "to accelerate both industrialization and export agriculture." In short, whatever the defects of collectivization, the transition away from it was "beset by the emergence of a rural class structure, exploitation, and corruption."[99]

Across the country, the Vietnamese leadership had "lowered . . . taxes on corporate income and international trade, and interest, rent, and dividends [were] excluded from personal taxation." Spending on health and education had been slashed despite the fact that, in the mid-1990s, "the wealthiest fifth receive[d] 45% of the public subsidies for both these fields," and user fees were introduced. In Vietnam's formerly egalitarian health service, access became "a function of income rather than need."[100] The 2001 *National Human Development Report* observed that, with respect to overall expenditures on social welfare, the "general lack of public funds" was "exacerbated by the gradual decline of tax revenues in recent years. In light of the expected fall in revenues related to import duties," the report noted, "this trend is not expected to reverse in the near future."[101] Perhaps in an effort to stanch the slide, in January 1999 the government — following the advice of the IMF and World Bank — introduced a regressive value-added tax that Vietnamese economists predicted would lead "lower income households [to] suffer and rich households [to] gain."[102]

Poverty rates had decreased but were still high in 2001, and "the easy gains in poverty reduction are probably over," the report continued, with what remained being "increasingly difficult to eradicate."[103] Moreover, many of those previously classified as poor remained barely above the official poverty line, and the gains, according to the Asian Development Bank, "remain quite fragile."[104] As the 2001 Vietnamese study cautioned, "The risk that people will fall back into poverty is serious."[105] Yet had income inequality not increased since 1992, the IMF concluded, "Vietnam would have been able to reduce poverty by an additional 8 percentage points."[106]

In other words, judging from the basic social indicators by which most individuals assess their economic well-being, millions of Vietnamese would likely have concluded in the late 1990s that the economic reforms under doi moi had been imposed at an unacceptably high cost. Many might have concurred with Le Thi Quy of the Center for Scientific Studies of Women and the Family in Ho Chi Minh City, who complained that "something very serious is happening to our society," in which "traps are being laid at the gates of profits." While the "market economy is about mechanism," she noted, she wished "to speak for humanitarian values":

> If we affirm that development can only be achieved by sacrificing these values, which have been long pursued by mankind and give us hope for freedom, democracy, and equality, it means that we reject the most basic factors that link people together as a community. It is an insult to our humanity to maintain that people only have economic demands,

and therefore economic development must be made at all costs. To live is not enough. People must seek many things to make their lives significant.[107]

Policy analysts such as Le Thi Quy were not alone in lamenting the mad rush for personal wealth.

Fiction writers similarly reflected the unease surrounding the radical change in values spurred by the capitalist reforms. For example, in his popular short story "The General Retires," Nguyen Huy Thiep described a household on the outskirts of Hanoi in the late 1980s, as doi moi was firmly taking hold, in which the quest for profits by the narrator's wife, Thuy, deeply troubled her father-in-law, a recently retired general in the Vietnamese armed forces. A medical doctor at a maternity hospital, Thuy raised Alsatian dogs for wealthy residents of Hanoi seeking increased personal security, a business that had become the primary source of income for her and her physicist husband. When the retired general learned that the dogs were being fed aborted fetuses that Thuy brought home from the hospital, he exploded: "Vile! I don't need wealth that's made of this!" In response, Thuy seemed troubled not by what she had done but, rather, by the failure of her boarder, Mr. Co, to conceal the practice. "Why didn't you put it [the meat from the fetuses] through the meat grinder? Why did you let Father see it?" she asked Mr. Co. Thuy's husband, whom the general insisted must put an end to the practice, emerged in the story as a figure emblematic of the amoral foundations of the capitalist reforms. He disclosed to the reader, "I had in fact known about this [the use of human fetuses to feed the dogs], but overlooked it as something of no importance."[108] Given his advanced age and—as a lifelong member of the military—his close association with the Vietnamese revolutionary struggle, the general seemed to represent a nostalgia for the sorts of values that many Vietnamese believed were being lost under doi moi in the frenzied rush to acquire individual wealth. A similar sense of nostalgia was observed by journalists covering the remarkable popularity in 2006 of an exhibition on pre–doi moi Hanoi at the city's Vietnam Museum of Ethnology.[109]

For countless workers and peasants, frustration with doi moi's inequities sparked an explosion of grassroots unrest. In the northern provinces of Thanh Hoa and Thai Binh, where decades earlier the revolutionary movement had so effectively mobilized the peasantry against colonial exploitation, people took to the streets in protest throughout the 1990s. "The farmers and people who work in the fields have been forgotten in the drive to modernize the country," complained one frustrated Vietnamese who quit his farm to seek work in Hanoi.[110] Others resisted the government's appropriation of land for large private investment projects that, for generations, had been worked by peasant families. Hundreds violently objected, for example, when the Korean conglomerate Daewoo, with the government's acquiescence, sought to build a golf course outside Hanoi that, observed one critic of the project early in 1997, would serve as a "playground for foreigners."[111] Whether in the cities or the countryside, the tide of international investment promised by doi moi contributed to appalling working conditions for Vietnamese laborers. By the mid- to late 1990s, such conditions had fueled numerous demonstrations of worker discontent. In an assembly plant for the footwear company Nike, for instance, hundreds walked off the job in March 1997 to protest their treatment by a subcontractor for the American corporation.[112] Approximately three thousand workers went on strike just a few weeks later.[113]

Such dissent received little notice in the guidebook literature, however. To the authors for Lonely Planet, critics of the capitalist policies and their institutionalization of class differentiation were dismissed as "geriatric revolutionaries in the prime of senility," while readers of the Moon guidebook learned about the "hard-liners" futilely (and foolishly, one must have presumed) challenging Vietnam's "remarkable economic progress." For one Fodor's guidebook, "The last decade of change . . . has been [nothing] short of a godsend." For another, "chinks of free-market economy" had been "lighten[ing] the gloom."

The descriptions say much about the ideological triumph of global capitalism and the increasing naturalization of "market" principles. The guidebook discourses presumed that states adhering to the dominant economic paradigm were following objective economic laws, while those resisting the prescriptions of the IMF and other lending institutions were rejecting or denying that which was immutable and scientifically rational. Unlike their capitalist counterparts, such states (or people), it was frequently suggested, were driven not by pragmatism but by ideology. Within the broader intellectual culture of the West, the often considerable shortcomings of existing socialist policies were presented as tangible evidence of an inherently terminal system; however, massive economic crises in states such as Mexico,

Turkey, Argentina, and Indonesia were viewed merely as aberrational set-backs owing to country-specific maladies, not as illustrative of the neo-liberal model demanded by international lenders.

Vietnam's leadership, enabled by its authoritarian grip on power, had by the late twentieth century largely abandoned socialist principles by sub-scribing nearly wholesale to the precepts of global capitalism. For count-less Vietnamese — although perhaps not for many party members and their newly wealthy families — the reforms were immensely destructive. Yet hundreds of thousands of Western tourists were being encouraged by their guidebooks to view the capitalist transformation as both rational and, as one author described it, "essential." As such, presuppositions were confirmed, and reigning orthodoxies persisted. Whereas the case of con-temporary Vietnam could have offered tourists a graphic illustration of capitalism's inevitable deficiencies, instead, guidebooks suggested to their readers, the miracle of the "market" was setting the Vietnamese free.

5

"The Other Side of the War"   MEMORY AND MEANING

AT THE WAR REMNANTS MUSEUM

When George H. W. Bush implored Americans during his inaugural address in 1989 to ignore one of the seminal events of
twentieth-century international history, he connected his nation's greatness to its embrace of collective amnesia. "The final
lesson of Vietnam is that no great nation can long afford to be
sundered by a memory," he proclaimed.[1] The plea — that the
United States forget its (and, by implication, Vietnam's) history
— would not be the last time Bush spoke of the Vietnam conflict.
When the United States went to war with Iraq two years later,
the president promised that "this will not be another Vietnam."[2]
And when the war ended, he was jubilant: "By God, we've
kicked the Vietnam syndrome once and for all."[3]

Yet with the more recent escalation of warfare in Iraq and the
ubiquitous allusions to "another Vietnam," not to mention the
omnipresence of the Southeast Asian conflict in the 2004 U.S.
presidential contest, it was made abundantly clear that Bush
could not have been more wrong. The United States had not
"kicked" the troubling memories to which the president referred. In the twenty-first century, Americans clearly remained
conflicted about the meaning of the war and its implications
for national identity. For the right, the U.S. intervention was a
"noble cause" whose warriors were shamefully betrayed when
Washington bureaucrats and the antiwar movement hindered
the American fighting machine.[4] For liberals, the war repre-

sented a tragic "mistake" in which the United States deviated from its national values and ideals. And for the left, the Americans invaded Vietnam in furtherance of Washington's post–Second World War efforts to establish a global system of liberal capitalism that furthered the interests of various elites. The irreconcilability of these interpretations ensured that the debates would continue.

Indeed, among tourists in Vietnam they had been raging for years. Whereas the war erupted in American political culture somewhat episodically, foreign travelers, who began arriving in Vietnam in exponentially greater numbers in the 1990s, never stopped disputing its memory. No site better captured the explosive emotions engendered by this popular conversation than the War Remnants Museum in Ho Chi Minh City. The institution provided a space in which foreigners often remarked about being exposed for the first time to a narrative of the war with which they were previously unfamiliar, a narrative that, in its most basic focus, placed Vietnamese rather than American experiences at its center. As a result of witnessing through photographs, illustrations, and textual displays the suffering endured by millions of Vietnamese, many of these tourists sought contrition. "I am very sorry for what our country has done to [the Vietnamese] people," wrote a former Australian soldier in January 2002.[5] "I regret the part I played in it," added another. "Normally, I am proud, grateful, and even blessed to be an American living the good life that I do," a visitor from San Francisco commented. "However, today I feel a sense of shame at what my country did to this part of the world in pursuit of folly." Among the displays at the museum in 2002 was a set of combat medals donated by William Brown, a veteran from the United States. "To the people of a united Vietnam," he wrote, "I was wrong. I am sorry." He was far from alone. "This museum may be a hard pill for many American visitors to swallow," another returning American veteran noted in 1994, "but [the] truths underlying these exhibits [are] as important to our history as [they are] to that of the Vietnamese people."

Other tourists responded by defiantly expressing their rejection of the official Vietnamese narrative, accusing the museum of bias and historical inaccuracy. "If you believe half of what you read here your [sic] a fool. U.S.A. all the way," an anonymous tourist, presumably an American, insisted in March 2002. "The war was a tragedy for everyone involved," commented an entry signed "Asian-American" that same month, "but what you see here is a bias [*sic*] viewpoint. Ho Chi Minh should not have invade [*sic*] South Vietnam. If the communist government is so wonderful, why would millions of Vietnamese flee Vietnam after the war[?] They don't talk about that. Think about it." The museum was "a little biased," another visitor — this one from Australia — wrote in January 2002. "The Americans were here to give freedom[;] they too lost a lot."

What the responses at the museum collectively reveal is both tourism's potential to briefly denationalize travelers, placing them within an ideological universe in which the power of their inherited beliefs becomes at least temporarily suspended, as well as many tourists' persistent hold on such beliefs as shields with which to fend off alternative historical perspectives. As such, an examination of the War Remnants Museum and visitors' responses to it provides a temporal snapshot in the social history of international postwar memory. This intersection of memory and culture — in the present case, the culture of tourism — deserves the attention of international historians. Tourism as a practice can be implicated not just in diplomatic relations, as Linda Richter, Christopher Endy, and others have ably shown, but also in sustaining or destabilizing the cherished myths of those nations from which many tourists originate.[6] Travel can allow, in other words, for a decentering of the United States from many Americans' understanding of the Vietnam war, introducing them (and others) to a narrative of the conflict that places Vietnamese experiences at its center.

The War Remnants Museum is a particularly significant institution, as it engages a popular audience whom most historians have clearly failed to reach, sparking reactions among tourists of various nationalities that arrive with a multitude of frequently conflicting experiential or acquired memories. By addressing these tourists' responses, the museum itself, and the ways that travel writers have mediated the site for foreign visitors, this chapter sets out to explore the continued potency of the war to notions of national identity nearly thirty years after the RVN's remaining leadership surrendered to its revolutionary foes in Saigon.

MAPPING THE MUSEUM: IMPERIAL AGGRESSION
FROM FRANCE TO THE UNITED STATES

Once known as the Exhibition House of American and Chinese War Crimes, later rechristened the Exhibition House of Aggression War Crimes, and now officially called the War Remnants Museum, the institution had become, by the turn of the twenty-first century, the most popular in the former Saigon, welcoming hundreds of thousands of visitors every year.[7] As of early 2003, according to Vietnamese media, attendance at the museum had reached unprecedented numbers, with approximately 1,300 foreign visitors coming to the site every day.[8] Yet most Western tourists, judging from dozens of interviews conducted in 2000 and 2002, arrived knowing little or nothing about the recent Vietnamese past.[9] Indeed, the effort after 1975 to essentially forget the conflict had left a void in historical understanding that became filled with popular culture representations (generally of U.S. origin but made international by the global profusion of American culture), unfounded myths, and distorted memories rooted in the political battles and emotional pain that characterized postwar American life. For many of these tourists, travel to Vietnamese museums and historic sites thus provided not only a basic introduction to the history of the war — albeit one that many visitors found sorely deficient — but also a sobering revelation about the sacrifices borne by the Vietnamese people during their long struggle for independence.

How foreigners ultimately viewed the museum was often determined by their moral assessment of the U.S. intervention. Many of those inclined, like Ronald Reagan, to adjudge the campaign a "noble cause" rejected the photographs and other displays at the site that were inconsistent with their vision of American benevolence. Conversely, those tourists confused or undecided about the war found and often embraced a narrative to which they had previously not been privy. The museum's tone and emotional thrust were evident from the moment visitors entered the exhibition space.[10] Adjacent to the entrance to a room designated "Historic Truths" intended to offer tourists background information on the war was a photograph of Robert McNamara, the U.S. secretary of defense in the Kennedy and Johnson administrations; he was sitting alone and surrounded by empty chairs and a lectern. Below the photograph was a case containing English- and Vietnamese-language editions of *In Retrospect*, his controversial 1995 book. A glass plate next to the case rested between two jagged blocks, as if they had been ripped or torn apart, symbolizing, perhaps, Vietnam's division for over twenty years. On the plate, as well as in the museum's official pamphlet, was transcribed probably the most famous line from the publication: "Yet we were wrong, terribly wrong. We owe it to future generations to explain why."[11] "It was that mistake," the curators added, "that has caused severe results toward the country and people of Vietnam."

In a move replicated elsewhere, the museum staff employed American or other Western sources — in this case the concession by one of the war's major architects that the United States was "wrong" — as framing devices through which to examine the contested subjects being addressed. As such, it was not necessary for the curators themselves to inveigh against the war, consequently inviting charges of "anti-Americanism" or explicit curatorial bias. Quoting Robert McNamara, Representative William Clay, the U.S. Declaration of Independence, or other prominent figures and documents sufficed for this purpose. Indeed, the citation of such sources rendered opposition to the intervention a decidedly American position.

What was perhaps most striking and ultimately divisive about the room devoted to "Historic Truths" was its departure from most popular Western accounts in either Hollywood films or Vietnam travel guidebooks. Whereas, to cite one recent cinematic production, Mel Gibson's character in *We Were Soldiers* (2002) explained the U.S. intervention to his young daughter as having to simply stop "some people" from "try[ing] to take the lives of other people," the curators located the Geneva Accords of 1954, and their acknowledgment that Vietnam was a single nation, at the center of their rendition of the past.[12] From around this discursive foundation the remainder of the exhibits were constructed. The displays covered wartime weaponry, the imprisonment of revolutionaries at Con Dao, the antiwar movement in the United States and around the world, and "hostile forces against the Vietnamese revolution," which was a euphemism for Vietnamese anti-Communists. There were also rooms devoted to the work of photojournalists killed in the conflict, to the photographs of Ishikawa Bunyo and Nakamura Goro, and to drawings by Vietnamese children on war and peace.

For many tourists, the most troubling portion of the museum was the room documenting the suffering of those whom a sign outside referred to as "war victims." The exhibits graphically illustrated the American atrocities at Son My (My Lai), where U.S. forces massacred hundreds of unarmed women, men, and children; the widespread use of the herbicide Agent Orange and its alleged repercussions for Vietnamese and Americans; the U.S. destruction of schools, hospitals, and other civilian structures; and the employment by the United States of napalm and white phosphorus bombs. A sign recorded the 1995 findings of the government in Hanoi on the human costs of the conflict to Vietnam: "Nearly 3 million people killed, over 4 million injured, over 2 million affected by chemicals, about 500,000 infants malformed," and, in one of those statistics that has rarely surfaced in scholarly accounts of the era, "170,000 old people [who] get lonesome [because] their children or relatives [were] killed during the war." What was perhaps most shocking to many tourists about such numbers was that, as the anthropologist Victor Alneng observed, "[three] million Vietnamese *people* were killed—in the movies there were only gooks, vcs, and hookers."[13]

Like all such institutions, the War Remnants Museum offered visitors a necessarily incomplete narrative. Beyond basic limitations of space and resources, the museum exemplified the struggles that have been waged for decades in Vietnam over issues of memory and narration. One could certainly find a "version of the past" that, as the historian Hue-Tam Ho Tai characterized it, "inscribes [the party] as the legitimate inheritor of the Vietnamese patriotic tradition and the dominant force in the recent history of the country," although such a narrative was less starkly evident than at other major historical sites, such as the Museum of Vietnamese Revolution in Hanoi.[14] At the War Remnants Museum, the strictures of official ideology accounted for only part of the publicly presented story. In fact, the demands of international tourist consumption had generated a historical narrative that was surprisingly nuanced in its treatment of the United States.

Visitors learned, for instance, of the American alliance with the Vietnamese revolutionary forces during World War Two, including the cooperation of U.S. intelligence with Ho Chi Minh. Moreover, there had been numerous displays, since first emerging in 1993, on the American antiwar movement, both civilian and military. Several resisters were prominently featured, among them Michael Heck, a U.S. Air Force pilot who refused to bomb northern Vietnam; Hugh Thompson and Lawrence Colburn, two of the three helicopter personnel who intervened in the American massacre of civilians at Son My (the third was Glenn Andreatta, who was killed in April 1968); and the deserters Terry Whitmore, John Michael Barilla, Richard D. Bailey, Michael A. Lindner, and Craig W. Anderson. There was an exhibit devoted to two Americans about whom most of their compatriots had almost certainly never heard: Norman Morrison and

Roger LaPorte, both of whom immolated themselves in November 1965 to protest the war. Taken together, the exhibits on the antiwar movement served as a powerful institutional reminder that many Vietnamese recognized, although perhaps too simplistically, the distinction between the American political leadership and the American public.

Also given voice at the museum—without critical comment, it should be added—was what has been called the "official view," or the U.S. government's "public explanation," for the intervention; the English translation of a large quote said, "In August 1953, President Eisenhower, while briefing the Domino Doctrine, said Burma, India, and Indonesia would be easily oppressed if the Communists [achieved] victory in Indochina. He emphasized that the U.S. economic and military aid to the anti-Communist forces in Indochina was the best way [to combat] the severe threat [to] . . . U.S. security." Elsewhere in the same room, visitors learned that "the U.S. policy gradually strongly supported [the] Diem regime, eliminated French influence, and changed South Vietnam into a bunker against communism."[15]

Since 2000 and the installation of the Requiem exhibit featuring the work of photojournalists killed in the war, there had been numerous photographs and testimonials to the wartime suffering and pain of American combat troops, from Henri Huet's images of a wounded American medic assisting a fellow soldier to the photographs shot by Sam Castan minutes before the Vietnamese attack that claimed his life.[16] In the area of the museum devoted to Agent Orange, among the victims portrayed by the curators were a young American boy, a former U.S. Air Force electrician, and two American parents and their young daughter. A sign noted that veterans from the United States, Australia, and New Zealand were awarded compensation for their exposure to Agent Orange, and it maintained that a "medical check carried out on Australian vets confirmed that at least 10 [percent] of them were so seriously affected that their spouses suffered miscarriages and that [one-quarter] of their new-born children had malformations." The sign also alluded to a demonstration for compensation by former Korean soldiers who had served on behalf of the Americans in Vietnam and claimed that, "according to them, nearly 5,000 veterans had been affected" by their exposure to chemical agents. And the museum's gallery of photographs by Nakamura Goro contained an image from a 1994 demonstration by those referred to as "Agent Orange victims and war widows" in Washington, D.C. The photograph was dominated by the presence of an American woman with the words "Widow of Agent Orange Victim" in large print across the front of her sweatshirt.

In other words, one found at the War Remnants Museum a remarkable willingness by the conflict's principal victims to acknowledge the human travails of their foreign adversaries. While certainly not identical as historical analogies, one might wonder, for instance, whether similar treatment has been afforded the Japanese invaders of China or the German occupiers of France at Chinese and French sites devoted to displaying the histories of those mid-twentieth-century military ventures, or whether in Kabul today one could locate exhibits on the undeniable hardships endured by Soviet troops in Afghanistan.

To be sure, the Vietnamese institution was not without its problems. A number of tourists complained, for example, about there being far too little historical context, including almost no attention given to the origins, composition, and appeal to many Vietnamese of the Republic of Vietnam and its anti-Communist government. In a similar vein, the museum also failed to remind visitors that among those who perished before 1975 were tens of thousands of members of the RVN armed forces; killing, in other words, was attributable to all sides in the conflict. And while its absence should not have detracted from the force of the museum's exhibits, an examination of a number of the insurgents' gravest shortcomings, such as the execution by National Liberation Front insurgents of hundreds of noncombatants in Hue in 1968, would only have strengthened the site's historical richness.

Whereas the curators constructed a narrative that was remarkably nuanced in its acknowledgment of American suffering, they were less sympathetic to right-wing visions of the conflict as a necessary defense against Communist aggression. To the museum's staff, the Vietnamese insurgents were fully justified in their resistance against France and the United States, which they depicted as a mass struggle for national liberation opposed by hostile foreign powers. It naturally followed that if there was merit in the revolutionary movement, as the exhibits suggested, then the moral basis for the American intervention was implicitly undermined. For visitors who were convinced that Washington's involvement was inspired by the enlightened support it lent to an embattled democratic government (that is, the RVN), the unbridgeable tension between these interpretations was certain to generate conflict. That it did so was demonstrated, as will be seen, by the reactions of numerous visitors. But first, it would be useful to map the ideological terrain traversed by foreigners in mediating their visit to the museum.

MEDIATING THE MUSEUM EXPERIENCE

Any examination of tourists' displays of memory at the museum must account for the fact that most visitors arrived there neither accidentally nor wholly uninformed. The site was brought to tourists' attention by their guidebooks and other media, by tour companies (some of which still referred to it as the "War Crime [sic] Museum"), and by other travelers.[17] What they learned from these sources contributed to their understandings of how the Vietnamese depicted the past. At a broader level, American films also performed a role in mediating tourists' firsthand experiences, providing the "Vietnam" template against which reality would be judged.[18] Years of Hollywood fictionalizations had, after all, placed American combat and suffering at the center of postwar historical memory. Actual Vietnamese — be they combatants, politicians, or civilians — in most cases served as little more than backdrops through which to evaluate the strategic or moral quandaries of the accounts' American protagonists.

Perhaps most crucial, however, was the broad genre of travel literature, which tourists said they viewed as a trusted repository of factual information. It was within this genre that many foreigners were first notified — and warned — of the museum's existence. For example, the Asia catalog of Intrepid Travel, a tour company that identified itself as an outfit for "real" travelers, for several years promised a visit to "the infamous War Remnants Museum" (the adjective was changed to "famous" in the 2003–2004 brochure) as part of its twenty-one-day Vietnam itinerary.[19] Journalists for some U.S. publications adopted a comparable tone. A writer for the *Morning Call* of Allentown, Pennsylvania, for instance, asserted that the site "illustrates the old maxim that the victors write the history books," as the museum presented an "entirely one-sided view of the war."[20] And while not going so far as Intrepid's charge of infamy, an article in the *Pittsburgh Post-Gazette* nevertheless bemoaned the curators' failure to acknowledge the atrocities of a number of revolutionaries by invoking an analogy to Japanese imperialism. The site "is reminiscent of the peace museum in Hiroshima," the writer intimated, "an emotionally wrenching memorial that nevertheless suggests that, one fine day, the Americans just happened along and, with nothing better to do, dropped an atomic bomb." He added, "Interestingly, [the Vietnamese museum] includes a 'Hiroshima Stone for Peace,' a gift from people in the Japanese city to the president of Vietnam. It is as if one lack of context is saluting the other."[21]

Yet the last statement seems misdirected. The accounts all suggest not a frustration with a *lack* of context, as the *Post-Gazette* claimed, but, rather, a disagreement with the curators' *choice* of context. The museum did, after all, include an explanation for the American intervention. What it did not do was treat the revolutionary struggle as Communist aggression, which is how many Americans, including travel writers, have preferred to frame the conflict. The accounts thus seem indicative of what the historians Christian Appy and Alexander Bloom designated "the myth of 'external aggression.'"[22] As numerous scholars have noted, the belief that the war was, at its foundation, an invasion of a country called "South Vietnam" by a country called "North Vietnam" is widespread in the United States and has been posited in numerous popular histories and Hollywood storylines.[23] It is, however, a view largely rejected by academic specialists. Still, so dominant is the "external aggression" framework that most of those I interviewed in Vietnam in 2002 were either unaware that there was a southern insurgency or told me that the "Viet Cong" were "North Vietnamese." Even those Vietnamese who were featured in the museum as having been victimized by Americans, including those who were clearly from the south (apart from pilots and those involved in covert operations, no American personnel were active in the north), were, according to one American who later wrote of her visit, "North Vietnamese."[24]

Probably no sources were more important as daily instruments of touristic mediation than Vietnam travel guidebooks. Their authors' synopses of the museum are themselves revealing markers of memory, recording the responses of some foreigners — none of the publishers used Vietnamese writers — to a narrative of the war not often seen or heard in cultural accounts outside Southeast Asia. More crucially, however, interviews with numerous tourists attest to the guidebooks' importance in influencing visitors' itineraries and, in many cases, their perspectives. "Everything is from the guidebook," emphasized a young German traveling with her Lonely Planet.[25] Likewise, when a Briton in his late thirties noted that the site's exhibits displayed a "Vietnamese bias," he added that his opinion "probably [came] through the guidebook."[26]

The extent to which tourists' reactions to the museum appear to have been colored by guidebook accounts was graphically demonstrated in 1998 in a comment book entry by a British tourist. The complaints about the site voiced by the Briton were almost identical to the language then being used by Lonely Planet in its synopsis of the institution. Whereas the tourist wrote, "This museum really drives home the point that war is horrible and brutal," the guidebook claimed that "there are few museums in the world which drive home the point so well that modern warfare is horribly brutal." When the tourist observed, "I do feel, however, that *this museum is one-sided*," the statement paralleled the observation in the guidebook that many Americans "complain that the museum is one-sided." And there was a remarkable similarity between the two sources on the issue of NLF atrocities. The Briton asked, "What about the thousands of people murdered and tortured by the Viet Cong? Where are the pictures?" According to the guidebook, "Of course, there is official amnesia when it comes to the topic of the many thousands of people tortured and murdered by the VC."[27] The British tourist was certainly voicing a legitimate complaint, and it is one that other visitors had expressed without mimicking the author for Lonely Planet. However, the resemblance to the publication, suggesting that it may have impelled his displeasure, is striking.

While guidebooks have been instrumental in mediating tourists' experiences in places other than Vietnam, their importance in understanding late-twentieth-century Vietnamese tourism and its relationship to American memory cannot be overstated. With respect to their coverage of the museum, which has emerged as ground zero for the touristic contest over postwar memory, most of the publications demonstrated a certain degree of ambivalence. All conceded — some explicitly, some implicitly — that the United States had been responsible for gruesome acts of violence in Vietnam. However, several seemed to take umbrage at the Vietnamese curators for displaying this record. The Moon guidebook for Southeast Asia, for example, drew its readers' attention to the museum's "crudely rationalized propaganda."[28] Similarly, the author of *Fodor's Exploring Vietnam* warned, without elucidation, that the site was "an eye-opener on both the atrocities of war and on the manipulative language of propaganda," while the same publisher's Gold Guide suggested, "You'll probably come away with mixed feelings about the one-sided propaganda—ashamed of the U.S. actions, angry about the Vietnamese inaccuracies in depicting them, or both." Even with the facility's change of name to the War Remnants Museum, the guidebook insisted, the "coverage continues to be skewed."[29]

Yet in a paradox unnoted by any of the same foreign publications that charged the museum with serving as a vehicle for misleading "propaganda," the Vietnamese authorities apparently sought to minimize Western tourists' awareness of the institution's existence. The two most recent editions of the English-language guidebook published by the Vietnam National Administration of Tourism (VNAT), a state entity that was created and placed directly under the prime minister in 1992, failed to acknowledge the War Remnants Museum either in their listings of sites of interest or on their maps of the city's principal tourist attractions, a curious omission given its position as the most popular museum in the metropolitan area.[30] However, the site *was* included in the Vietnamese-language edition of VNAT's guidebook, suggesting the museum's political consonance with what Hue-Tam Ho Tai identified as "the single most important theme in Vietnamese historiography"—that of "national unity achieved through heroic sacrifice."[31] Although one can only speculate, the basis for the mixed record in VNAT's guidebooks was almost certainly the desire by officials to avoid exposing Western visitors to graphic reminders of the war. Such an exposure, after all, could diminish the pleasantness of a Vietnamese holiday, affecting consumer spending and, perhaps, the state's international reputation as a vacation destination. The tourism authorities had, in fact, made a conscious effort for years to revise Western perceptions of Vietnam, for they were well aware that many tourists continued to view the country largely through the prism of the American war.[32] A publication launched by VNAT in 2002, for example, insisted on the first page of its inaugural issue that Vietnam is "More Than a War."[33] The second issue actually offered an implicit plea. Move "Beyond the War," it begged its foreign readers.[34]

With respect to probably the most influential tourism resource for Western travelers in Vietnam, the Lonely Planet guidebook, like those of Moon and Fodor's, offered a brief objection to the museum. Ironically, its complaint was first leveled in 1995 in the third edition, two years after a younger generation of curators had begun taking steps to professionalize the site's exhibition space by adding new displays and updating old ones. Their work included, for example, revising captions that had been written by members of the institution's original staff, some of whom, according to the vice director, had been more personally affected by the American conflict.[35] Reflecting the fact that readers' mail to Lonely Planet partially inspired the changes in the third edition, the guidebook's criticism was initially displaced onto others: "The main objection to the museum," Robert Storey wrote, "comes from, not surprisingly, American tourists, many of whom complain that the museum is one-sided." There are "some unnecessary crude comments placed under the photos," he continued, "such as one of an American soldier picking up a horribly mangled body to show the photographer, and a caption saying 'this soldier seems satisfied.' And[,] of course, there is official amnesia when it comes to the topic of the many thousands of people tortured and murdered by the vc."[36]

The "crude comments" mounted below the photograph cited by Lonely Planet, which the guidebook misquoted, were in fact those of the Japanese photographer who shot the image, not the curators, as an apparently overlooked citation at the bottom of the caption made clear.[37] Yet what the objection illustrates is the extent to which one's ideological convictions, which can be deeply embedded in one's national origins or cultural background, might affect one's interpretation of the displays. When the curators are viewed not as public historians navigating contentious ideological terrain but simply as ideologues unconcerned with historical accuracy, then one becomes more willing to ascribe to them disreputable motives. Storey evidently believed that Americans were incapable of deriving satisfaction from Vietnamese suffering, so he dismissed as "unnecessary" and "crude" the suggestion by Ishikawa—which he mistakenly attributed to the museum—that the soldier he photographed had done so. Rather than viewing the photograph as a primary document by a Japanese witness to the war, in other words, Storey interpreted it as evidence of the curators' propagandistic intent—as well as the photographer's, as Storey asserted in an interview that the image was "staged"—that discredited the document's symbolic force.[38]

Other guidebooks deduced a similar sort of malevolence. Consider the volume in Fodor's popular Gold Guide series. "Conspicuous in its absence," the writers for Fodor's maintained, "is any mention of the division of the country into South Vietnam and North Vietnam throughout the

Vietnam War. (The Communist government tends to overlook this division; instead it claims a puppet government backed by American imperialists illegally ruled in the South against the will of the people.)"[39] While the first sentence was in fact false, its empirical untenability masked something much deeper: a lingering anxiety concerning how the war would be popularly remembered.[40] The authors' frustration was clearly rooted not in the museum's alleged failure to acknowledge the country's division for over twenty years, which it unambiguously did, but, rather, in the curators' seeming embrace of the sentiment expressed in the guidebook's second sentence.[41]

Indeed, the travel literature often struggled in addressing the issue of the 1954 partition, as this reframed the nature of the American conflict. For the notion of Communist aggression to retain its plausibility, its adherents had to believe that the southern Vietnamese people supported the RVN authorities and opposed the revolutionary movement. The dilemma for those accepting this framework is that all credible evidence indicates just the opposite — that is, the United States and the successive Saigon governments consistently rejected a political settlement with the insurgents precisely because they knew that their popular support was minimal and could translate into unfavorable terms. America, in other words, was fighting a counterrevolutionary rather than a defensive war. For a people whose nation was born out of its own eighteenth-century revolution, this presented something of an ideological conundrum. To cloak the inherent contradiction between American rhetoric and the Vietnamese reality, U.S. policymakers (and some travel writers) overlooked the RVN's lack of political appeal and ignored the recent past, preferring instead to minimize the importance of the 1954 Geneva Accords in favor of a more simplistic, but largely unsupported, narrative of Communist aggression.

Countless visitors — guidebook authors, tourists, journalists — decried the lack of attention to revolutionary atrocities at the site. This omission, and the consequent suggestion that human-rights violations during the war were a one-sided affair, is arguably the museum's most egregious fault. While some critics offered views so expansive that even the killing of American military personnel fell under this umbrella — missing from the displays was any "record of North Vietnamese atrocities to U.S. and South Vietnamese troops," wrote the authors for Footprint — most critics seemed to hold a more traditional view of what merited inclusion.[42] Still, the allegation that the museum ignored violence against U.S. personnel is notable. Apart from the fact that it is untrue, the charge suggests that Hollywood's depiction of American suffering as perhaps the central experience of the war had become so powerful that its alleged nonacknowledgment emerged as a legitimate criterion for gauging other accounts' historical credibility. Reflecting the degree to which a focus on the United States had become normative, however, this test did not seem to apply in the inverse. For instance, of the two exhibits dealing with the war at the National Museum of American History in Washington, D.C., in 2002, neither addressed the war's consequences for the Vietnamese people.[43] However, this "one-sidedness" did not stimulate any guidebook objections.[44] The same held for the capital's Vietnam Veterans Memorial. While the Wall has been recognized by millions of Americans as a painful site of remembrance — indeed, "possibly the most poignant sight in Washington," one travel author observed — the absence of any Indochinese names from its compendium of "fallen heroes" was met only with silence in the guidebook literature.[45] In fact, it was virtually impossible to discern from guidebook accounts that museums in the capital had for years been contested political spaces. With respect to the highly publicized Enola Gay controversy at the National Air and Space Museum, for example, only one major guidebook acknowledged the debate that erupted over the proposed commemorative exhibit in 1994 and 1995.[46] What this double standard suggests is the naturalization of American suffering as the symbolic embodiment of the Vietnam war. To locate the Vietnamese people at the center of the narrative was, for many from the West, to reveal an ideological bias. Yet to locate Americans at the center of this narrative was perceived as ideologically neutral — indeed, it was perfectly natural. As such, Vietnamese museums and historic sites were treated in the guidebook literature as highly political spaces. In contrast, American museums and historic sites did not merit a comparable level of critical scrutiny.

At a more prescriptive level, the guidebooks' critiques of the War Remnants Museum collectively illustrate the extent to which many Westerners believed there was a need to somehow balance Vietnamese depictions of what was, by virtually all historical accounts, an inherently unbalanced war. It is clear that this call for balance resonated with some American tourists. "Very graphic pictures. War is always full of these pictures," one wrote in a comment book in 1998. But "there were a lot of casualties on both sides! Each country has a lot of horror stories." A resident of Louisiana concurred. "A terrible war," he intoned. "I only [wish] that the displays had some balance." Demonstrating the extent to which the comment books often became an interactive means for visitors to rebut the opinions of other visitors, someone wrote in response to the Louisianan, "Really? Four million dead vs. 55,000! Flechettes, napalm, phosphorous bombs — balance!!!"

It was not only in the relative anonymity of the comment books that complaints about "bias" were expressed. Interviews revealed a wealth of similar perspectives. For instance, one American traveler, after decrying the "silly bias" of the museum, which he said was so "one-sided" that "you don't take it seriously," explained that the site could have showed "the POWs in Hanoi," the "atrocities committed against the POWs." But like most tourists whose knowledge of the war's history was scant, he qualified his statement by adding that he was not actually certain any such mistreatment occurred. The American, a thirty-one-year-old Navy veteran from California, acknowledged that Hollywood movies had been the leading source in his own education on the conflict.[47]

While American prisoners were in fact tortured by the Vietnamese as late as 1969, his comments nevertheless speak to the power of popular culture to shape Western historical consciousness, as American POWs have for years been a regular staple of cinematic treatments of the war. From *The Deer Hunter* (1978) and *The Hanoi Hilton* (1987) to *Uncommon Valor* (1983) and *Rambo: First Blood Part II* (1985), the plight of captured Americans has served in the United States as one of the most potent symbols of the suffering caused by the U.S. intervention.[48] But this remembering — or, more accurately, reimaging — has found a necessary correlative in forgetting. With only two exceptions, no major American filmic productions have seriously addressed the hundreds of thousands of people imprisoned and tortured by the RVN authorities, many of whom were left physically crippled or psychologically devastated after years of confinement.[49] Indeed, one forty-three-year-old American woman confided that, before learning at the museum about the torture of Vietnamese insurgents and civilians, "in the past [she] probably would have thought it was just the opposite."[50]

One of the most remarkable aspects of the War Remnants Museum is the extent to which the site has combined official public history with multinational mourning and dialogue. Its comment books in particular have allowed tourists to record their impressions for the curators, to respond to other travelers, to address the Vietnamese or American people, or to discuss larger global issues of war and peace. For some visitors, the books are a means of expressing their deep emotional pain about the war and the suffering it caused. For others, they have provided a venue in which to denounce the American intervention and, at times, the continued exercise of U.S. global power. For a minority of visitors, the comment books have allowed them to criticize what they consider the museum's skewed narrative of the war. Perhaps more than anything else, however, the books have emerged as a site of witness. Countless visitors want to simply record their presence and their revulsion at the suffering caused by the war.[51] The Vietnamese people, they suggest, had demonstrated why aggression should be denounced at every turn.

TOURISM AND NATIONAL IDENTITY

Within the comment books, a multitude of discourses emerged. Among these were some visitors' acknowledgment of a sense of culpability—generally national rather than personal—in the suffering of the Vietnamese people. Whereas a number of Americans criticized the museum's focus on these Vietnamese hardships, many more tourists, including Americans, transformed their presence into an act of atonement. As one veteran pleaded, "May God forgive us." Another American simply wrote, "I'm sorry, Vietnam." Such expressions demonstrated the museum's potential, however symbolic, for transnational reconciliation. While many Americans have focused since 1975 on healing the wounds caused by the war in domestic social life, many tourists—a group more traditionally associated with the quest for pleasure rather than for contrition—have sought to transcend the spatial constraints of national healing by using their holidays to request forgiveness from the Vietnamese. For a visitor from the Midwest, for example, the comment book afforded an opportunity to offer a collective apology: "I want to express the sorrow I feel for the horrors presented in this museum. On behalf of my prayer community in Chicago, Illinois, U.S.A., I want to apologize for the violence committed here in Vietnam."

A recurring theme among mostly non-American travelers was a perceptible continuity between the conflict in Vietnam and postwar U.S. foreign policy. A February 2002 entry by an Italian visitor read, "Yesterday in Vietnam (Laos-Cambodia). Today in Afghanistan." The following month his comment was echoed by a German at the site: "Bush = Nixon? Afghanistan = Vietnam? Muslims = Communists? What's the difference? Never again?!" While there were and are, in fact, great differences between the wars in Vietnam and Afghanistan, American power and the country's continued resort to military force nevertheless left many tourists unsettled. Shortly after the invasion of Afghanistan, for example, one visitor lamented, "I am from the U.S., a country so proud & so ignorant. I leave here today saddened & confused why our country refuses to educate itself." The sentiment was mirrored by "An Anonymous American": "It[']s really sad to see that nearly forty years later my country and the world has not learned that killing is wrong." In its political ambiguity, the last comment reflected a pacifist strain that ran through many of the entries. While many tourists made pointed comments about the United States in the books, for others they provided a more metaphysical venue. "Can we live without killing each other?" asked an American traveler in January 2002. "No more war," wrote another.

That different interpretive lenses were employed by different peoples could be seen in the entries by visitors from, on the one hand, settler states or states that had been twentieth-century colonizers and, on the other hand, those from states that at one time had been colonized. The former seemed more inclined to focus on the tragedy of war or the "mistakes" made by the Americans. Conversely, most of the comments celebrating Vietnamese resistance — that is, foregrounding Vietnamese agency rather than the repercussions of the American intervention — were written by individuals from the latter. Typical of the first group was the entry of an Australian woman: "Thank you for giving the new generations & those from other countries the opportunity to see the tradegic affects [*sic*] of such a brutal war. May we all learn & move on to make a better society." An Indian visitor was more representative of the second: "After viewing all these photographs, all my credit goes to the valiant people of Vietnam who had the courage and guts to face such a mighty military as a U.S. Army who always boast they are almighty. My kudos & best wishes to Vietnamese in their struggle to build up a strong nation." Likewise, the Vietnamese who faced "horrifying brutality committed by the aggressors," opined a Malaysian in July 1995, were "freedom fighters" on a quest "for unification and liberation." For a Singaporean immigrant to Canada, "To say no more war is naive," he wrote in March 2002. "You have to fight for your rights and freedom. I admire the Vietnamese people for defeating foreign powers to regain their dignity and stand proudly as an indipendent [*sic*] nation in the world."

The greatest diversity of opinion among visitors, however, was intranational. This was particularly the case with Americans. In some instances, tourists from the United States employed the comment books to make statements certain to invite the scorn of others. When a Californian claimed in a 1998 entry, for example, that "war is a good experience for those who do not get killed or wounded," an Irish national retorted underneath, "*Some* Americans never learn." Another visitor added in response, "A thoughtless, idiot[ic] comment. Fortunately few Americans would think that. Moron!" It is unclear whether the Californian was being genuine or to whom he was referring, but the sentiment tapped into a larger cultural trend in the post-1975 United States that depicted war as a positive form of male bonding. In a slew of films and other cultural productions, military combat was portrayed as physically awful yet spiritually ennobling. The effect, argued the feminist scholar Susan Jeffords, was the "remasculinization" of America, a phenomenon crucial to Washington's continued interventionism — in Latin America, the Middle East, and elsewhere — after the earlier, ignominious experience in Vietnam.[52]

While the predominant sentiment among Americans was undoubtedly an embrace of the alternative narrative displayed at the site — from the veteran who, in 1996, confessed to being "devastated by the exhibits and feel[ing] tremendous sympathy for all Vietnamese and hope that there can be healing for all of you" to the third-time visitor six years later who, noting that the museum is "just as moving and horrifying as ever," counseled that "*all should* visit this place" — most of the signed entries critical of the institution were written by tourists from the United States. For example, in response to an anonymous comment in March 2002 that "this museum is outrageously biased . . . a disappointment," an American echoed and expanded on the sentiment:

> I can't agree more with the above comment. This ought to be a museum about the atrocity of war. BOTH sides are at fault. I feel as though I've been fed a ton of bullshit propaganda so that the N. Vietnamese can justify what they too did to thier [*sic*] own people. Rather than blame one side we ought to blame both. But then again, I suppose this is a testimony from a non-democratic country which is afraid of the *whole* truth.

Similarly, two women who felt in 1998 that the museum "paints a picture about the Americans that is untrue" and that "we were not the only people killing others in this country" — "Where are the pictures of the HORREN-DOUS things done by the Viet Cong???" they asked — signed their entry "Proudly AMERICAN!" Even the widely acclaimed Requiem exhibit came in for criticism. "A moderately interesting collection of *Life* photos presented in a largely distortative [*sic*] context," remarked a traveler from the United States in January 2002.

The comments demonstrate a national discomfort with the sorts of actions often ascribed by mostly white Americans to people whose tongues betray a foreign accent or whose skin is of a darker hue. That seemingly wholesome young men could be responsible for the inhuman deeds shown at the site was such an unsettling notion to some visitors that a form of denial was embraced. To be sure, it was not an explicit denial; in most instances, the tourists in question did not gainsay the reality of the actions depicted, as did some Americans during the war. Rather, they deflected their touristic gaze by complaining about the museum's lack of attention to revolutionary atrocities or by simply ascribing the American atrocities to the tragedy of war. The responsibility of the United States for extensive Vietnamese suffering represented such a devastating blow to some Americans' sense of national identity that, as one of the travelers quoted above insisted, "BOTH sides" had to be "at fault." Other tourists retorted by citing the hellishness of war. "Sick anti-American propaganda does not further the cause of world peace!" wrote one visitor in response to a 2002 entry lamenting the continued American reliance on military force as an instrument of state policy. "Unfortunately there were horrible atrocities from both sides," he continued. "War is hell!" The sentiment was echoed in January 2002 by a visitor from Texas: "These pictures showed the horror of war, but let us not forget the atrocities and horror committed by the North Vietnam Army." The disjointed attribution of responsibility evinced by the last entry is notable. With respect to the American actions, the remarks suggest, the "horror of war" was responsible, not the U.S. armed forces. Conversely, the "North Vietnam Army," and not the "horror of war," "committed" "atrocities and horror."

The tourists' remarks were not without historical precedent. Countless Americans reacted similarly in 1969 following the public revelations of the Son My (My Lai) massacre, the March 1968 incident in Quang Ngai province in which American soldiers indiscriminately executed, and in some cases raped, hundreds of unarmed Vietnamese civilians, most of them women, children, and elderly men. One contemporaneous account based on more than two hundred interviews across the United States found that, while opponents of the war tended to recoil at the reports of the atrocities, seeing them as confirmation for why the United States should withdraw from Vietnam, supporters of the war largely responded with a combination of explicit denial, deflection, or dismissal.[53] In another account—this one approximately one month after the details of the Son My incident became publicly known and the first photographic images of the atrocities appeared—a poll in Minnesota of six hundred adults indicated that nearly half (49 percent) did not believe "the charges of mass murder are true." According to an elderly Minneapolis woman, the story was "a lot of propaganda to divide our country with."[54] A Los Angeles salesman agreed, telling the *Wall Street Journal* that the reports of the massacre were part of an antiwar conspiracy: "I don't believe it actually happened. The story was planted by Vietcong sympathizers and people inside this country who are trying to get us out of Vietnam sooner."[55]

Other Americans in 1969, foreshadowing a number of their compatriots three decades later, sought to deflect attention away from the episode by suggesting that the revolutionaries were either equally guilty or were worse. An elderly resident of a Philadelphia suburb, for example, insisted that Americans "wouldn't do something like that deliberately—but the other side would." Another Pennsylvanian maintained, "If people here could see what the Vietcong do, no one would be saying our soldiers are such bad guys." Indeed, the theme that "the North Vietnamese and the

Vietcong are much more ruthless than U.S. soldiers," reported the *Wall Street Journal*, "was sounded by people" in nearly every one of the twelve cities in which the newspaper conducted interviews, suggesting the extent to which Americans imbued with a sense of national innocence struggled to retain their notion of a benevolent United States by insisting that, whatever the nation's faults, others were clearly worse.[56]

And like their touristic counterparts more than thirty years later, some proponents of the American intervention sought to justify the Son My atrocities in 1969 by dismissing them as mere casualties of war. Removing the incident from the realm of individual or national responsibility, it became subsumed within the encompassing explanation that "war is hell." Such was the response of a retired nurse in Los Angeles: "Oh fiddle! Every war has that. War is war." Her remarks were echoed, with the addition of an explicit approbation, by a fifty-five-year-old elevator starter in Boston. "It [the massacre] was good," he disclosed in an interview. "What do they give soldiers bullets for — to put in their pockets? That's the way war is." For a woman in Cleveland, the incident reflected a sense of moral equivalence in the conflict. "It sounds terrible to say we ought to kill kids," she confessed, "but many of our boys being killed over there are just kids, too."[57] Indeed, when *Time* polled 1,608 American households in December 1969 about the atrocities, 65 percent of respondents "shrug[ged] off My Lai, reasoning that 'incidents such as this are bound to happen in a war.'"[58]

Among those whose responses were recorded in the American press, it became increasingly clear that their denial (whether explicit or through deflection or dismissal) had little to do with the credibility of the proffered evidence but, rather, with how Americans perceived U.S. foreign policy. As one mother from Ohio confessed, "I can't believe that a massacre was committed by our boys. It's contrary to everything I've ever learned about America." Others, such as a contractor from Memphis, concurred: "I can't believe anyone from this country would do that sort of thing." And a resident of Philadelphia expressed a similar lament. "I can't believe that our boys' hearts are that rotten," he said.[59] That all three respondents refused to recognize the massacre's actuality because they could not "believe" Americans were capable of such things testifies to the power of American national identity. The incident at Son My was so at variance with the carefully cultivated perception of the United States as a global champion of freedom and human rights that to accept its reality was inherently to challenge the moral justification for the war — and even, perhaps, of U.S. foreign policy itself. It thus became necessary to dismiss the atrocities as a singular aberration or to deny them altogether.

For its part, the Nixon administration left open the possibility of the latter — it was publicly ambiguous about what actually had occurred, counseling patience while the military investigated the episode — but explicitly embraced the former. Most pertinently, the White House attempted to minimize the atrocities and differentiate them from those of the revolutionaries. When the American actions at Son My were graphically revealed to be innately contrary to the enlightened ideals for which the United States was ostensibly fighting, the president was advised to remind the public that, if true, the incident was "*against* the policy of the American government" while "*a policy of atrocity is the policy of the enemy* we confront in Vietnam."[60] His advisers specifically alluded to the Hue Massacre of 1968, which Nixon had highlighted only weeks earlier as a "prelude" to "the nightmare" the people of the RVN would face if the United States were to withdraw from Indochina.[61] For the administration, in other words, there was not just a nonequivalence in both sides' employment of violence but, more important, a fundamental qualitative difference between American and revolutionary atrocities. Those of the United States were aberrations; those of the insurgents were a matter of policy.

When, decades after the Son My incident, the curators at the War Remnants Museum implied that violence against civilians by the Americans was widespread, a number of tourists, such as the two "proudly *AMERICAN*" women cited earlier, sought moral solace in Nixon's and their compatriots' earlier defenses. Complaining about the "untrue" picture generally painted of "the Americans" at the site, they did not hesitate to broadly ascribe "*HORRENDOUS*" atrocities to "the Viet Cong." The insurgents, that is, were collectively guilty of barbarous deeds that could not be ascribed to the hell of war, let alone the politics of terror in national liberation movements. The United States, conversely, employed an armed force of individuals with individual stories and individual experiences; some Americans may admittedly have engaged in unwarranted violence, but no collective generalizations were possible. These were not, after all, "Communists."

These were "our boys." To therefore suggest that the United States, as a collectivity, was responsible for much Vietnamese suffering was to engage in anti-American propaganda of the most vicious sort.

While a number of American tourists interpreted the museum as an inherently anti-American affront and pursued a discursive strategy similar to that of years earlier, other travelers found in its images a more complex and textured story. With the opening of the Ishikawa Bunyo photography exhibit in 1998, for example, an anonymous visitor remarked, "In these photos we can see that not all Americans were evil, but simply soldiers, young men put into a tragic situation by stupid leaders who were so arrogant that we must question all politics." Rather than reflexively deriding as anti-American a museum that displayed images of American atrocities in addition to images of American suffering and noncombat experiences (the last ranging from a photograph of marines during an outdoor Christian prayer service to one featuring a solitary young soldier laying in a grassy field while reading a book), the tourist viewed the troops within the larger context of war and state power. Individual responsibility for atrocities would not be excused in this sort of analysis, but the culpability was understood to be not just personal but collective. The actions of the Americans, that is, were rooted in a national ideology of "empire-building" and the political calculus of U.S. officials.[62]

Through the children of veterans one could detect the personal struggles that young people confronted in coming to terms with the sorts of actions for which they possessed no lived memory but for which their parents may have been responsible. For some, such as a twenty-one-year-old woman from Australia, the horror visible in the displays explained her father's reticence to discuss the conflict. "My father was an Australian soldier in the war," she wrote in January 2002. "He doesn't talk about it very much at all. I can see why. I hope everyone can see why. I hope this cruelty will never happen again." For two others, their 1998 visit afforded an opportunity for contrition. "My wife and I come here representing the U.S. and our fathers who fought in the war," they wrote. "We wish to ask for your forgiveness for the crimes committed against the Vietnamese people."

Some veterans' children sought to ascribe benevolent aims to their parents, as if to distinguish the loving individuals who raised them from the troops responsible for the brutality evidenced at the site. "My dad served in the Vietnam War," wrote a woman from Texas in March 2002. "Now 29, I have the opportunity to visit this country [on] which the war has laid a path before my time. People don't pay much [attention] to how it starts, but to how it ends. Please remember who helped." Other children, reflecting a perhaps broader psychological reaction, asserted a moral equivalence between the principal belligerents and pled openly for mutual atonement. As an eighteen-year-old veteran's daughter from Oregon wrote in February 2002:

> Having American GIS as friends my first reaction is to harden my heart and firmly declare that this all can't be true! But these pictures are a testimony.
>
> True, the U.S. made mistakes. Mistakes that cost lives, futures, and security. But what happens when mistakes are made? Forgiveness needs to follow.
>
> The side that isn't displayed in this museum is what the Viet Cong did to our boys. They made many mistakes too — mistakes that cost American mothers their sons and our country a good deal of money. But mistakes need forgiveness.
>
> Today I choose to first forgive the Viet Cong for what they did and secondly forgive my fellow countrymen for what they did. Forgiveness is the only way healing can begin and from what I see, both sides need a lot of healing.
>
> Remember what you have seen but don't become hardened or sad[;] instead choose to forgive the wrong and move on to make a future full of right.

The young woman's entry, rich with both humanitarian idealism and ideological conviction, starkly evinces the moral crisis that confronted many visitors when contemplating what meaning to deduce from the war's horrific violence. Should, in other words, the conflict be understood as a meaningless orgy of bloodletting and cruelty? Or should it be considered at a deeper political level? Rather than reject the Vietnamese narrative as a propaganda fabrication, as did some of her compatriots, the Oregonian acknowledged its merit. Yet uncomfortable with the curators' greater attention to Vietnamese suffering, she sought refuge in the charge that *American* suffering "isn't displayed in this museum."

Perhaps most provocatively, in choosing to forgive the Vietnamese —

most of whom would probably be puzzled by the idea that an American believed they sought forgiveness—she equated the actions of the United States with those of the Vietnamese insurgents. Both forms of violence were "mistakes," she suggested, rejecting a moral distinction between foreign aggression and national resistance. Her embrace of forgiveness was no doubt genuine and, in its own way, quite moving, but it points to a larger sense of denial on the part of many Americans. It remained a fervent belief that some Other had to be culpable for the tens of thousands of American deaths suffered in Indochina. For many on the right, government bureaucrats, the mass media, and the antiwar movement had assumed this role. The "Viet Cong" did so for the veteran's daughter. Whereas most Vietnamese regarded the insurgents as patriots who fended off the latest in a succession of foreign invaders, the young Oregonian clearly did not draw such a distinction. The politics of national liberation was absent from her entry; the violence that accompanied the Vietnamese independence struggle instead assumed the moral equivalence of the American invasion. There was no difference, in other words, between just and unjust wars or between just resistance and unjust aggression. When the revolutionaries killed the foreigners who were trying to kill them, these were "mistakes" that "cost American mothers their sons and our country a good deal of money." Forgiveness thus followed.

In stark yet subtle ways, therefore, the entry in essence erased the unique politics of imperial violence, detaching the war—or, indeed, much modern warfare—from any deeper meaning. If only the acts of killing were considered contemptible, and not the motivations or conditions that engendered the mutual bloodletting, then something was being lost historically. If, that is, modern warfare were to be contemplated in a world shorn of norms and values, how, it could be asked, were any "lessons" to be derived from the American experience in Vietnam?

THE MUSEUM AS SYMBOL: A MULTINATIONAL DIALOGUE

At times, the entries in the comment books transcended the immediate focus of the Vietnam war, with the museum essentially becoming a site at which an international dialogue on peace and justice could be entertained. But unlike in most such forums, the discussion took place among "ordinary" people, not the elites or government officials who staff the United Nations, the Organization of American States, and other multilateral bodies. The museum, in other words, became a space more akin to the World Social Forum than the World Economic Forum. While the discussion was not truly representative—it was limited, after all, to people who could afford to be tourists—its broad international participation rendered it unusual by most standards. The focus of those remarks that transcended the temporal and spatial boundaries of the Indochina wars was wide-ranging, covering everything from the Israeli–Palestinian conflict and the war in Afghanistan to corporate power and the politics of McDonald's hamburgers.

The Vietnamese themselves did not emerge from this discussion unscathed. In addition to complaints about the absence of exhibits acknowledging revolutionary atrocities, some writers expressed concern about the country's contemporary human-rights violations. Represented in the museum as the victims of American aggression, the Vietnamese revolutionaries were taken to task by at least one visitor for the government's recent repression of indigenous peoples in the interior mountainous provinces.[63] This touristic concern with state power, however, was more often directed across the Pacific. Incensed by a perceived hypocrisy in light of the visible record at the museum, countless tourists mocked the profession by U.S. officials that America's global ambitions were strictly humanitarian. A number of travelers consequently wrote critically about the Western campaign that, by 2002, had replaced anti-Communism as the reigning orthodoxy in international affairs: the "war on terror." Thus reflected a Briton in March of that year: "I'm amazed and humbled by the tolerance, forgiveness, and pragmatism of the people I have met during my two visits to Vietnam. I hope that people seeing the exhibition can—each in their own small way—oppose our current surge of world domination, where atrocities are approved in Palestine, Kashmir, N. China, etc. under the guise/pretence of the 'War Against Terrorism.' And[,] in particular, to cry foul when the perpetrators (here the U.S.) claim the status of victims!" One of his compatriots felt similarly, stating at approximately the same time that "these photographs are an indictment of war, from whichever side you were on, and whatever way you choose to look at it. It didn't stop after Vietnam[;] it continues to this day. Why is it," he asked, "that people using car bombs and suicide bombers are terrorists and those using jets, tanks, etc. are soldiers[?]" In then suggesting that people "please always try to look at things from the two sides that exist, not just the one the media (in general) tells you about," the British tourist raised a troubling prospect.

Just as decades earlier the war in Vietnam had been framed by policy-makers and, in most instances, by the press as a war against Communist aggression, what if, in 2002, the policies of the United States, the United Kingdom, and others in the West were being misleadingly ascribed to anti-terrorism? Indeed, it was precisely the ease with which visitors viewing the museum's historical exhibits drew connections to the present that lent the site its symbolic power.

What the comments illustrate is the transnational solidarity felt by many tourists with respect to issues of peace and justice. Allegiance to humanistic principles was expressed by visitors on the basis of their shared beliefs, not their shared citizenship. In fact, in some cases travelers even urged others to resist the actions of their own governments, as when a Briton asked that the world "oppose our current surge of world domination" in March 2002. The objective was a peaceful coexistence that crossed national borders. How to achieve this peace was not always certain, but by engaging people from Vietnam and across the planet, the tourists in Ho Chi Minh City thought they were taking a first step.

THE MUSEUM IN AMERICAN POLITICAL DISCOURSE

If the museum emerged in the twenty-first century as a symbol of multi-national dialogue and cooperation, it became a symbol of an entirely different sort during the 2004 U.S. presidential contest. A portion of the room in the museum largely devoted to the global antiwar movement featured photographs of Vietnamese and Americans engaged in peaceful dialogue after 1975. Some showed former architects of the war in conversation rather than confrontation, such as Robert McNamara and Vo Nguyen Giap in the mid-1990s. Other images showed the American organization Heart to Heart International delivering humanitarian aid to post-war Vietnam. But it was the photograph of a meeting between the Vietnamese official Do Muoi and a group of American politicians and veterans that contributed to something of a political tempest in 2004. The caption next to the photograph was simple: "Mr. Do Muoi, Secretary General of the Vietnam Communist Party[,] met with Congressmen and Veterans Delegation in Vietnam (July 15–18, 1993)." But in the context of the presidential contest, the image proved explosive, for one of the people who appeared with Do Muoi was Senator John Kerry, the Democratic nominee.[64]

American veterans angered by Kerry's earlier activism with Vietnam Veterans Against the War — especially his testimony in 1971 on American atrocities before the Senate Foreign Relations Committee — had organized to oppose his campaign for the White House, and they seized on the photograph to advance their efforts. An entire chapter ("Kerry's Communist Honors") of *Unfit for Command: Swift Boat Veterans Speak Out Against John Kerry*, the bestselling book by John E. O'Neill and Jerome R. Corsi, was devoted to the image. As Jeffrey M. Epstein of Vietnam Vets for the Truth explained,

> This photograph's unquestionable significance lies in its placement in the American protesters' section of the War Crimes [sic] Museum in Saigon. The Vietnamese communists clearly recognize John Kerry's contributions to their victory. This find can be compared to the discovery of a painting of Neville Chamberlain hanging in a place of honor in Hitler's Eagle's Nest in 1945.[65]

The photo, wrote the senator's critics, "corroborates" the charge that Kerry was a "traitor," as it "demonstrates the extent to which the Vietnamese communists acknowledge that he supported them during the Vietnam War."[66] Kevin McManus, a former prisoner of war, cited the photograph as clear evidence of Kerry's treasonous behavior. "I think John Kerry is probably the first man in two hundred years of American history to make Benedict Arnold look good," McManus opined in a controversial program aired by the Sinclair Broadcast Group shortly before the election. "Arnold — to compare the two — Arnold had a long and illustrious military career prior to his betrayal, and George Washington actually singled him out for his actions. In the case of John Kerry," McManus continued, "he had a short career but he also was singled out by the Vietnamese Communists and placed in a hall of honor in their revolutionary war museum."[67]

The comments unambiguously illustrate the bitterness felt by American veterans who supported the war and believed that Kerry had betrayed the honor of their military service. Yet the charges surrounding the photograph were wildly misleading. Kerry, formerly the chairman of the Senate Select Committee on POW/MIA Affairs, met with Do Muoi during an official trip to Vietnam with fellow legislators John McCain, John Glenn, Lane Evans, Douglas "Pete" Peterson (who became the first U.S. ambassador to Vietnam after diplomatic relations were normalized in 1995), and

Dana Rohrabacher.[68] Together with representatives of AMVETS, Vietnam Veterans of America, and the Veterans of Foreign Wars, as well as family members of deceased American servicemen whose bodies had yet to be recovered, the delegation sought further cooperation on the POW/MIA issue.[69] After evidently having been reminded of this fact, the anti-Kerry veterans conceded that it was "reasonable that Senator Kerry would seek to meet with the communist leaders of Vietnam" in the "course of pursuing the POW and MIA issue." But the "critical issue," they insisted, was that "the Vietnamese communists have chosen to honor Senator Kerry in their War Crimes Museum for his assistance in helping them achieve victory over the United States." They noted, for example, that the "sign outside the entrance to the room where Kerry's photo is displayed reads 'The World Supports Vietnam in Its Resistance.'" And "exhibited inside the room are protest banners and emblems from various nations and photographs of international leaders who supported North Vietnam's cause."[70]

The veterans' argument was weakened by the fact that the curators chose not to identify Kerry by name — an unusual choice, given their ready identification of others, if the intention was truly to "honor" the senator. But even more significant was the veterans' failure to disclose that the room was not exclusively devoted to the antiwar movement or to those who actively supported Vietnam's resistance to American intervention. It contained, for example, an exhibit on the Viet Minh's alliance with U.S. intelligence agents during the Second World War. And of critical import, the room also featured an exhibition space on postwar reconciliation; the photograph that showed Kerry was just one of several that the curators displayed to illustrate the development of peaceful relations between Americans and Vietnamese. Other public figures from the United States whose photographs with Vietnamese officials were mounted on the same wall included Admiral Elmo Zumwalt Jr. (Ret.) of the U.S. Navy, Secretary of State Warren Christopher (who was shown with his Vietnamese counterpart, Nguyen Manh Cam, signing the document normalizing diplomatic relations), and former Secretary of Defense Robert McNamara, as well as business executives, politicians, former agents of the Office of Strategic Services, and representatives of U.S. veterans' organizations.

The images, in other words, were not intended by the Vietnamese to honor Americans who supported their wartime struggle or "help[ed] them achieve victory over the United States," as the anti-Kerry veterans alleged.

Zumwalt and McNamara, for instance, could hardly have been considered sympathizers of Hanoi or the National Liberation Front.[71] Rather, the photographs were simply meant to demonstrate the postwar movement toward the peaceful coexistence of former enemies. That the image containing Kerry was located in a museum dismissive of the celebratory American narrative embraced by many prowar veterans clearly lent the photograph its emotional weight, demonstrating how a small institution halfway around the world could exert an influence on American electoral politics far out of proportion to what its relatively modest number of visitors would suggest. Indeed, its exhibits have regularly contributed to discourse in the United States.[72] In this way, the War Remnants Museum not only performed a role in the reelection of George W. Bush in 2004 but, surprisingly, has continued to serve as a transnational memorial institution.

COMPETING PASTS, COMPETING FUTURES

History museums are inherently political spaces. In providing narratives about the past, they inevitably comment on both the present and the future. Visitors are exposed not just to artifacts and recorded experiences, but also to implicit signals about history's contemporary meanings. When, in January 2004, officials at the National Museum of American History disclosed their plans to address the U.S. experience in Vietnam within a larger exhibit called "The Price of Freedom: Americans at War," they seemed to be suggesting that the Indochina wars were a cost to be paid in defense of one of America's most cherished ideals.[73] To be sure, freedom is a fundamental tenet of American national identity, and it is one whose meaning, as Eric Foner has richly demonstrated, has been vigorously contested since the country's inception.[74] But the struggle for freedom would strike many Vietnamese as a curious interpretive framework for the American campaign in Southeast Asia. For them, the conflict was self-evidently an imperial crusade, one of several interventions — a painfully tragic one given that many revolutionaries had initially viewed the United States as a guarantor of self-determination[75] — intended to undermine their decades-long quest for national liberation and unification. While these American and Vietnamese views would appear to be mutually incompatible, both countries do, however, share experiential terrain.

It is this shared history that was on display at the War Remnants Museum. What made the site so disconcerting to a number of tourists were precisely these connections between the American military and the Vietnamese people. The curators decentered the United States from the conflict, reminding travelers that the war deeply affected millions of Vietnamese. The reminder shocked countless travelers whose views had been shaped by popular narratives that focused almost exclusively on the travails of the foreign invaders. "Finally I was able to see the other side of the war," an American visitor wrote in March 2002, signing his name next to a peace symbol. Or, as an Australian tourist observed in 1998, "A number of people who have written in this book have complained about this museum not providing a balanced view of the war. I, like most of them, come from a Western society and I can honestly say that after my visit here a balanced view is exactly what I *now* have." The comments, which allowed for a multinational conversation among visitors who otherwise probably never would have conversed, were revealing for their implicit acknowledgment that tourists' views had previously been limited. While not offering a full or complete narrative, the museum nevertheless forced Western travelers to confront some of the realities of a conflict that for years had remained shrouded in celluloid fantasy and myth. No longer could Vietnamese perspectives be ignored.

More broadly, the museum provided a sobering reminder that war is much more than the technological spectacle — or what *Newsweek*, referring to the Persian Gulf conflict of 1991, called the "bloodless unreality of the Nintendo-game air war" — that, as the new century dawned, had seemed its defining feature on American television screens since at least 1991.[76] In actuality, the curators implied, war is an impersonal force that causes unspeakable destruction and death. For travelers who embraced Washington's continued resort to armed interventionism, the museum was thus interpreted as a bastion of anti-American propaganda. For a far greater number of tourists, however, the site's images of suffering served, they suggested, as an important and timeless corrective.

Tourism and the Martial Fascination

The story of Shosei Koda's visit to Iraq is an ultimately tragic story. It starts innocently enough: a journey by bus from Amman to Baghdad, a popular route covered over the years by many a seasoned traveler. What was unusual about Koda's experience was its timing: October 2004, or nineteen months into the American counterinsurgency war that followed the deposition of Saddam Hussein. Despite the violence tearing the country apart, the twenty-four-year-old Koda, a Japanese national, was determined to tour Iraq, stubbornly rejecting the counsel of both locals and diplomats aware of the grave danger tourists could face. His stay in the war-torn capital was brief. Unable to find lodging in an inexpensive hotel — such facilities had, for security reasons, ceased accepting foreigners — and unable to afford a room in one of the more secure international hotels in the city, Koda reportedly whiled away the time by wandering about, waiting for a bus that would eventually return him to Jordan. It was not long before he was kidnapped by forces hostile to the American occupation. Following the release of an online video in which he unsuccessfully pleaded for the withdrawal of Japanese troops from Iraq, Koda's journey reached its end: His headless body was discovered in central Baghdad resting under an American flag.[1]

Orfeo Bartolini was an older and more experienced traveler than Koda. A middle-aged Italian, Bartolini embarked in March 2003 on a motorcycle excursion from his home in Rimini to Calcutta, India, where he apparently intended to visit the grave of

Mother Teresa. Had he completed his journey, the trip would have taken him through Turkey, Iran, Afghanistan, and Pakistan. But Bartolini never reached Calcutta. When his motorcycle broke down in southern Afghanistan, he hired a taxi to transport him from Kandahar to Kabul. Along the way the car was stopped by two alleged Taliban militants traveling on a motorbike. Bartolini was fatally shot, reportedly at point-blank range.[2]

In many ways, the twenty-first century has thus far appeared to be little different from the one preceding it. People seem to be just as fascinated with war-ravaged states or sites in this century as did earlier generations of travelers in the last. John Lennon and Malcolm Foley called this phenomenon "dark tourism."[3] Its draw is unmistakable. Consider the case of Rory Stewart. While to him the regional conflict did not appear to be the destination's principal lure, Stewart became "Afghanistan's first post-Taliban trekker," according to the *Observer* newspaper, when he set out on a six-hundred-mile journey across the country in January 2002, just weeks after the collapse of the Islamist regime. It was not the twenty-nine-year-old Scotsman's first experience with a state in conflict. He had spent part of his childhood in Vietnam, where his father, a diplomat, was posted during the American war. For Stewart, the danger in traveling across Afghanistan so shortly after the Taliban leadership fled Kabul was apparent, but he remained undaunted. "It would be a pity to be killed, of course," he told a reporter. "But I'm willing to take that chance."[4]

Stewart may have been the first foreign tourist to visit Afghanistan in what the United States surely hoped would be the post-Taliban era, but he was certainly not the oldest. Only sixteen months after Orfeo Bartolini was shot on the Kandahar–Kabul highway, a dozen American senior citizens — their average age was seventy-four — began a journey of their own, despite the anti-American insurgency raging in the countryside. "We want to see Afghanistan before they start putting up Hiltons and McDonald's. We want to get out and smell the land," claimed seventy-nine-year-old Richard Glenn of California. In Kabul, a car bomb was detonated just half a mile from their guesthouse, claiming the lives of three Americans and at least nine others. When the group later traveled to Herat, they learned that the city had nearly "been engulfed in a battle between the governor and a rival warlord" just two weeks before their arrival. "My kids think we are nuts," Glenn acknowledged.[5]

The ongoing Taliban insurgency apparently did little to stop the American travelers, just as decades earlier the war in Vietnam failed to prevent the tours of their compatriots. Whereas the stubborn determination to see something of the world connected these intrepid tourists, it was not their only connection. Although they began their journeys at least thirty years apart, they were nevertheless begun in a climate of comparable discourses. A guidebook's admonition to travelers that "there was some terrorist activity [at the end of the previous year] in certain parts of the country" such that "you should take advice from travel agents . . . before settling on your plans for seeing the interior" could as easily have been a description of Afghanistan in 2004 as of Vietnam in 1961.[6] That it was a warning about the latter suggests how little our vocabulary for identifying touristic threats — or the identity of those hostile to the exercise of American power — has changed.

It remains to be seen whether Afghanistan and Iraq will, like Vietnam, emerge as popular tourism destinations years after the current combat ends.[7] If they do, how will their histories be constructed for Americans and other travelers? Will the United States have bombed Afghanistan to liberate its women from the Taliban regime? Will America have invaded Iraq to implant democracy in the Arab world? Will travel writers recall the extensive U.S. support for the Islamist mujahedeen — "freedom fighters," the Reagan administration called them — that resisted the Soviet Union in Afghanistan but later turned against their American benefactors? Will tourists learn about Washington's close ties with, and material assistance to, Hussein and the Baathists before 1990? Will the war in Iraq have become a mere tragic "mistake"? How, in other words, will the tourism industry construct the imperial past for those who, twenty or thirty years hence, will either have been too young to have lived through it or were too indifferent to have paid much attention? It is too early to say. However, given the passionate debates surrounding the Afghanistan and, especially, Iraq wars, tourism in Vietnam and its contemporary attendant literature may provide some indication.

Since 1975, millions of Americans have experienced difficulty in coming to terms with the devastation their government visited on the Vietnamese people. Some sought simply to forget the war. Others lamented it as a regrettable error. A minority, aided at times by Hollywood and the broader culture industry, reimaged the conflict as a "noble cause" in which the United States defended democracy against a global Communist menace. To gauge the immorality of the threat the Americans confronted, tourists needed only to have considered the "Hue Massacre," a disputed story of lurid Asian cruelty that persisted as an indisputable reality in the late-twentieth-century travel literature. As a rhetorical device it reminded tourists that the Vietnamese insurgency could be inhumanly ruthless and cruel — how else could one explain the premeditated executions of thousands of noncombatants? — and that the American intervention may thus have been driven by deeply moral concerns.

This was certainly the lesson imparted to thousands of American troops in the 1950s and 1960s. Through its broad educational program the Department of Defense sought to construct the anticolonial insurgency in Vietnam as an aggressive menace that imperiled all of Southeast Asia. Rather than the nationalist movement with which American intelligence had collaborated during the Second World War, the Vietnamese revolutionaries were metamorphosed by the Pentagon into a tentacle of the Communist octopus seeking global domination. Such was the message, I have argued, for thousands of young Americans "visiting" Vietnam in the mid-1960s. In asking these men to forgo the consumer abundance that was said at that time to characterize middle-class domestic life, the Pentagon promised them compensations. Vietnam, they were told, was not only a dangerous battleground; it was also a stunning nation of big-game hunting and deep-sea fishing, of cultural exoticism and coastal familiarity, all of which would be accessible to them as military tourists. There would, in other words, be pleasure to accompany their pain.

Tourism officials in the Republic of Vietnam sought to construct a similarly idyllic vision. However, whereas the U.S. military authorities concurrently acknowledged the realities of martial danger, RVN officials — at least before 1965 — attempted to represent their state as a safe and welcoming destination, an exciting outpost in the growing Asian travel market that promised foreign tourists fascinating architecture, natural beauty, and countless attractive women. For these officials, tourism served a dual purpose. First, it generated the foreign exchange crucial to the RVN's development. And second, it endeared travelers to southern Vietnam and, the Saigon government hoped, to the notion of the RVN as a bastion of democracy and America's greatest friend. With the aid of the United States, it was suggested, the Vietnamese authorities were determined to vanquish the Communist threat.

As tourists would learn years later, many of the Vietnamese revolutionaries were hardly doctrinaire Communists, as they came to fervently embrace neoliberalism in the years after the war's official end. For foreign travelers in Vietnam amid the "market" worship of the late twentieth century, lessons thus abounded in the country's postwar economic history. With "globalization" reputed to be the answer to many of the world's problems, Vietnam guidebooks constructed a narrative of progressive economic improvement that began with the state's embrace of capitalist principles in the 1980s. Similar to the popularity of modernization theory during the Cold War, the Vietnamese economic reforms were touted as a non-ideological accession to global reality, a maturation of a Vietnamese worldview that had earlier been mired in the myopia of socialist dogma. Capitalism, it was implied, was shorn of such ideological baggage. The "market" would make the Vietnamese people free.

Freedom, as Eric Foner has argued, has long been an animating principle in American political culture.[8] That the concept would be embraced by travel writers in the mid-twentieth century as the basis for the American intervention should not be surprising. During the war, as we have seen, the tourism literature largely accepted at face value the proposition that policymakers in Washington were driven by enlightened ideals. This was true of the pocket guides published by the Department of Defense, and it was true of the various guidebooks and pamphlets published independently or by the government in Saigon. As one author reported, with the Viet Minh attempting to "enslave the entire population" it was no wonder that the "sturdy, hardy citizens" of the Republic of Vietnam "love us." These courageous Vietnamese were, after all, "democracy's greatest friends and communism's greatest foes."[9] That most southern Vietnamese were in fact hostile to the U.S.-backed authorities in Saigon was immaterial. In the logic of Cold War ideology, these same southerners had to oppose the revolutionaries, as the insurgency was led by Communists and Communists were, by their very nature, unpopular and evil.

Time has done little to soften this view among a considerable number of tourists. As the debates about the past at the War Remnants Museum reveal, the presentation of a Vietnamese narrative — a view of twentieth-century Vietnam in which the wartime aggressors were the United States and France rather than Ho and his comrades in Hanoi — is still capable of inflaming the passions of countless Americans. The placement of Vietnamese experiences at the center of the war's history proved so unsettling to tourists accustomed to remembering the war as, above all, an *American* tragedy that the museum inspired a backlash. Derided as a bastion of vicious anti-Americanism and one-sided propaganda, the War Remnants Museum has been held by tourists and travel writers to a standard quite different from that for American institutions. The singular focus in the United States on American suffering has always seemed entirely natural, such as, in Washington, D.C., at the Vietnam Veterans Memorial or the National Museum of American History. However, the greater attention in Vietnam to Vietnamese suffering, such as at the War Remnants Museum, has been angrily and repeatedly denounced because, I argue, it serves as an inherent affront to American collective memory and many Americans' sense of national identity.

Tourism can thus be quite revealing in examining the contentious history of American foreign relations. Through travel Americans are provided the opportunity to learn about the global role of their nation from what, for most of them, is an astonishingly unique perspective: that of its subjects. What they learn, and how they learn it, has been the focus of this book. As is evident from its limited scope, the study was not intended to be an exhaustive history of Vietnamese tourism. Much important work remains to be done in this area, and scholars will have no shortage of topics to address in coming years. Rather, what I have sought to demonstrate are the discursive intersections of tourism and American power. It is, after all, at precisely this level that tourists often engage the foreign peoples and cultures that are the objects of their travels. Within such a discursive universe, the Vietnamese suffer from the unfortunate reality that their state invokes for many Americans images of war rather than pleasure. The "Vietnam" of the American imagination — a mélange of blood and guts and American suffering that has in fact achieved transnational currency — has yet to become the Vietnam — a state of seventy million people — of the twenty-first century. The tension between these competing visions has been reflected in years of tourism publications. How to mediate the Vietnamese past, and thus the present, for those hundreds of thousands of people traveling to Southeast Asia has for decades been a highly delicate matter. If tourism has revealed anything, it is that the tensions are not likely to be resolved anytime soon.

NOTES

RGC	Ronald Garrison Collection
VA	Vietnam Archive, Texas Tech University
WBA	Warner Bros. Archives, School of Cinema–Television, University of Southern California
WCC	William Colby Collection
WHCF	White House Central Files
WHS	Wisconsin Historical Society

PREFATORY NOTE

1. Kaiser, *American Tragedy*; Taylor, *Nuremberg and Vietnam: An American Tragedy*.
2. "Excerpt from the Official Text of Ngo Dinh Diem on 'The Policy of the Government of the Republic of Viet Nam with Regard to Former Resistance Members,'" in Pham Van Bach et al., *Fascist Terror in South Viet Nam*, 79.
3. Buckley, *Vietnam, Cambodia and Laos Handbook*, 63; Colet and Eliot, *Vietnam Handbook*, 338; Dodd and Lewis, *Vietnam*, 406, 464; Florence and Storey, *Vietnam*, 6th ed., 25.
4. Advertisement for "Global Volunteers" trips to Romania and Vietnam, Alumni Association of the University of Michigan, *Michigan Alumnus* (Winter 2001): 23; emphasis added. A separate brochure for the same organized trip to Vietnam referred to the "matrix of North Vietnamese tunnels used during the war." I am grateful to Anne Martinez for providing me with both of these documents.
5. Suran, "Coming Out Against the War," 467.
6. "Vietcong: Purple Haze," *Movie Gallery Video Buzz Magazine* (August 2004): 7. I am indebted to Melanie Steinman for bringing this material to my attention.

INTRODUCTION

1. On the role of French colonial prisons in mobilizing nationalist and revolutionary sentiment, see Zinoman, *The Colonial Bastille*.
2. *The Hanoi Hilton* was one of the few Hollywood productions to enjoy an explicit presidential plug by Ronald Reagan: "Every American should see this powerful and moving film as a tribute to our POWs and as an exercise in sheer understanding of history." A portion of Reagan's statement was reprinted on the jacket of the home video; for the full quote, see Gruner, *Prisoners of Culture*, 61–62.
3. Florence and Storey, *Vietnam*, 6th ed., 202.
4. By 2005, claimed the *New York Times*, American tourists had begun to kick their "Namstalgia," preferring to journey to Vietnam for its "palm-fringed beaches, tropical waters, and championship golf courses" rather than for "a cathartic trip down a sometimes guilt-ridden memory lane." James Sullivan, "A Former Enemy Rolls Out the Welcome Mat," *New York Times*, 24 April 2005.
5. Williams, *Problems in Materialism and Culture*, 38–39.
6. Among the most notable exceptions are Bhattacharyya, "Mediating India," 371–

89; Koshar, *German Travel Cultures*; idem, "What Ought to Be Seen," 323–40; McGregor, "Dynamic Texts and Tourist Gaze," 27–50; Siegenthaler, "Hiroshima and Nagasaki in Japanese Guidebooks," 1111–37.

7. "The Holiday Issue: The Story of Tourism," *Independent* (London), 15 July 2004.

8. Philip Shenon, "The End of the World on 10 Tugriks a Day," *New York Times Magazine* (30 June 1996): 35, 37.

9. Gray et al., *France*, 730–31.

10. Shenon, "The End of the World on 10 Tugriks a Day," 34.

11. Stephen Wyatt, "Lonely Planet in Global Link-Up," *Financial Times*, 24 May 1999. A lower number of hits per day, one-and-a-half million, was reported in John Shaw, "Planet Circles the Globe," *Europe Business Review*, vol. 2, no. 7 (January–March 1999): 26.

12. Tad Friend, "The Parachute Artist," *New Yorker* (18 April 2005): 79.

13. Laderman, "Shaping Memory of the Past," 87–110. On Lonely Planet's financial contributions to various progressive projects, see, e.g., Florence and Jealous, *Vietnam*, 8.

14. Yang, *Let's Go*, 730.

15. Florence and Storey, *Vietnam*, 5th ed., 25–26.

16. Interview of Robert Storey, 30 May 2000, Jiafeng, Taiwan.

17. Friend, "The Parachute Artist," 80.

18. Interview no. 17, 6 February 2002, Hoa Lo Prison, Hanoi.

19. Interview no. 33, 15 February 2002, Hoa Lo Prison, Hanoi.

20. Novick, *That Noble Dream*.

21. Pratt, *Imperial Eyes*. Pratt employed the term to refer to "the space of colonial encounters, the space in which peoples geographically and historically separated come into contact with each other and establish ongoing relations, usually involving conditions of coercion, radical inequality, and intractable conflict." Ibid., 6. My use of the term is slightly different.

22. Hue Touristic Office, *Travelling and Tourism in Annam*, 1.

23. On Americans' increased interest in Asian tourism after World War Two, see Klein, *Cold War Orientalism*, 100–42.

24. *Visit Fascinating Vietnam*, folder 1, box 1, RGC, VA, 3.

25. Ironically, the war as a tourist attraction was almost entirely ignored by the World Tourism Organization when it developed a master plan for Vietnam in the early 1990s. World Tourism Organization, *Tourism Development Master Plan*, 6–17.

26. For more on the Vietnam war and its "cartography of memory," see Nguyen, "Memorializing Vietnam," 153–63.

27. Trouillot, *Silencing the Past*, xix. I am indebted to Jason Stahl for his recommendation of this book.

28. For two excellent sources on American empire and its denial, see Appy, "Struggling for the World," 1–8; and Kaplan, "Left Alone with America," 3–21.

29. Endy, *Cold War Holidays.*

30. Rosendorf, "Be El Caudillo's Guest," 367–407.

31. Semmens, *Seeing Hitler's Germany,* 129–30.

32. Merrill, "Negotiating Cold War Paradise," 179–214.

33. For studies addressing the Vietnam war and American memory, see Hass, *Carried to the Wall*; Lembcke, *The Spitting Image*; Sturken, *Tangled Memories*; Tai, *The Country of Memory*; and Turner, *Echoes of Combat.*

34. See, e.g., Schmitz, *Thank God They're On Our Side.*

1. TOURISM AND STATE LEGITIMACY

1. Dorothea Lange, Vietnam Notes (1958), DLC. Several of the photographs Lange shot in Vietnam were published in Lange, "Remembrance of Asia," 50–59. According to an editor's note introducing Lange's photographic essay, a larger selection of images from her Asian tour appeared in an exhibition a year earlier at the San Francisco Museum of Art. The scholar Pierre Borhan did not mention the San Francisco show but wrote that the photographs were exhibited at the Siembab Gallery in Boston. Borhan, *Dorothea Lange,* 254.

2. *Times of Viet Nam,* quoted in Masur, "Hearts and Minds," 165.

3. Unlike the government in Saigon, officials in Hanoi did not seriously enter the tourism business until relatively late, establishing a tourism department only in 1974. Lynch, *All-Asia Guide,* 573.

4. Masur, "Hearts and Minds," 165.

5. "The Final Declaration on Indochina," in U.S. Department of State, *Foreign Relations of the United States, 1952–1954,* 1541.

6. Gregory et al., *A Glimpse of Vietnam,* 99.

7. For an excellent overview of the political importance attached by the United States to American mass tourism in the 1950s, to which my own analysis owes a considerable debt, see Klein, *Cold War Orientalism,* 100–42. On, specifically, Eisenhower and international tourism, see ibid., 108.

8. Randall, *International Travel,* 2–4.

9. Department of State (which was itself quoting a Congressional committee report), quoted in Francis J. Colligan, "Americans Abroad," *Department of State Bulletin,* vol. 30, no. 775 (3 May 1954): 664. The political implications of Americans' actions when out of the country were addressed by President Eisenhower in letters later issued with all civilian and military passports. See "Letter of President to Be Included in U.S. Passports," *Department of State Bulletin,* vol. 37, no. 946 (12 August 1957): 275–76. On earlier sentiments in the popular press, see George Kent, "How to Be an American Abroad," *Travel* (May 1949): 10–11, 32; and idem, "How to Be an American Abroad," *Reader's Digest* (June 1949): 116–18.

10. Colligan, "Americans Abroad," 667.

11. For an important overview of the RVN's cultural propaganda offensive, including tourism, see Masur, "Hearts and Minds."

12. Santha Rama Rau, "The Strange Beauty of Vietnam," *Holiday* (August 1957): 63, 114, 118. Rau also briefly praised sites in northern Vietnam but lamented that the lack of diplomatic relations with the United States meant that "the American tourist cannot now, nor probably for some time to come, visit the north." Ibid., 119.

13. Richard Tregaskis, "Vietnam Visit," *Travel* (March 1959): 41–42, 44, 46.

14. Ibid., 41. The others were Laos, Cambodia, and, he wrote, "the Communist-oriented People's [*sic*] Republic of Vietnam." Ibid., 42.

15. Ibid., 42–45, 47.

16. Ibid., 42, 44.

17. The Republic of Vietnam continued to be represented by multiple delegates until 1964, when, for the first time since 1957, none were present. The RVN's representation rebounded in 1965, however, before again dropping to zero in 1966. One delegate was present in 1967. Pacific Area Travel Association, *Sixteenth Annual Conference*, 26.

18. Tregaskis, "Vietnam Visit," 47.

19. Confidential report of Lieutenant-General John W. O'Daniel (Ret.), 8 October 1958, folder 19, box 1, DPC: OM-AFV, VA.

20. Clement, *The Future of Tourism in the Pacific and Far East*, 147.

21. *Visit Fascinating Vietnam*. This version of the pamphlet did not contain any publisher information, but it can be found on a slightly different version of the document—with different advertisement placements and no reference to 1961 as "Visit the Orient Year"—in folder 1, box 1, RGC, VA.

22. Clement, *The Future of Tourism in the Pacific and Far East*, 147.

23. While the focus of this chapter is not northern Vietnam, it should be noted that over two hundreds Americans—most of them journalists or antiwar activists—traveled to the DRV during the war, as Mary Hershberger has recorded. Hershberger, *Traveling to Vietnam*, xv. For at least some of these visitors, such as the Catholic peace activist Marianne Hamilton, the trips also provided brief opportunities for more traditional tourist activities. On her journey, see "Hanoi Diary," box 3, "Hanoi Diary 1972" file, Marianne Hamilton Papers, 1945, 1964–75, MHS, St. Paul, 3, 8. According to Hershberger, "There were many other visitors to Hanoi from countries traditionally allied with the United States—Canada, England, France, the Netherlands, West Germany—who went to see the war first-hand." Hershberger, *Traveling to Vietnam*, xix. On the difficulties encountered by the Vietnamese in hosting foreign travelers, see ibid., 75–76. For a collection of interviews with two dozen Americans who traveled to the DRV during the war, see Clinton, *The Loyal Opposition*. For several contemporaneous accounts of travel in

northern Vietnam, see Cameron, *Witness*; Fox, *Friendly Vietnam*; Phoebe L. Friedman, "Life Today in North Vietnam," *Nation* (10 December 1973): 626–28; Sontag, *Trip to Hanoi*; and *They Have Been in North Viet Nam*.

24. *International Travel Statistics: 1957*, 93; *International Travel Statistics: 1960*, 102–103; *International Travel Statistics: 1961*, 124. In 1962, the National Tourist Office recorded 37,946 arrivals, which was virtually identical to the 37,783 recorded in 1961. The number fell to 28,905 in 1963, and then continued to fall in 1964 (26,282) before increasing in 1965 to 28,938. However, given that the 1965 arrivals grew after March, which is the month during which the United States landed its first official combat troops in Danang, the annual figure for 1965 almost certainly represented an increase in the number of war-related visitors (journalists, contractors, etc.) whose primary objective was hardly traditional tourism. *International Travel Statistics: 1962*, 109; *International Travel Statistics: 1963*, 128; *International Travel Statistics: 1964*, 57; *International Travel Statistics: 1965*, 56. American visitors outnumbered those from France for the first time in 1959. *International Travel Statistics: 1959*, 90.

25. *International Travel Statistics: 1967*, n.p. See also Le Thai Khuong, *Du Lich Ky Nghe Tam Dang tai Viet-Nam*, 74.

26. *International Travel Statistics: 1969*, n.p.; *International Travel Statistics: 1970*, n.p. The precise figure for 1970 was 72,474, of whom 47,481, according to the Vietnam National Tourist Office, arrived for purposes of "Holiday/Recreation." The rest were said to be in the RVN for "Business/Family" (13,473) or "Mission/Meeting" (11,520).

27. *International Travel Statistics: 1964*, 57; Associated Press, "What War? Tourists Get Viet Pitch," n.d., folder 37, box 1, MMC, VA.

28. *Saigon: A Booklet of Helpful Information for Americans in Vietnam* (1958), 5–6.

29. *Saigon: A Booklet of Helpful Information for Americans in Vietnam* (1962), 5.

30. "Saigon Beckons the Tourist," 30 March 1967, folder 24, box 17, DPC: U6, VA; the article was a syndicated reproduction of Stewart Harris, "Saigon Still Attracts the Tourists," *Times* (London), 27 March 1967.

31. Clement, *The Future of Tourism in the Pacific and Far East*, iii.

32. This was true, as well, of the Bao Dai administration during the First Indochina War. See *Vietnam as a Tourist Centre*, 2, 65.

33. An example of this discursive construction is a short guide to Nha Trang published by the National Tourist Office in the late 1950s that noted the Diem government's annual allocation to Mieu Sinh Trung, an old pagoda outside the city that was built under Gia Long to commemorate "the valiant feats of officials and soldiers who had shed their blood for the unity of Viet Nam," thus associating the Saigon regime with this patriotic undertaking. *Nha-Trang*, 7, 20.

34. For a fascinating exception to war driving away tourists — the case of Spain in the

1930s and, to a lesser extent, 1940s — see Holguín, "National Spain Invites You," 1399–1426.

35. *Visit Fascinating Vietnam*, 2, 14.

36. Gregory et al., *A Glimpse of Vietnam*, 93. For another example of this dichotomy, see *Tourism in Vietnam*, folder 9, box 18, DPC: U6, VA, 2–3.

37. *Your Guide to Vietnam*, folder 17713: Ho So v/v Soan Thao va An Hanh Cac Sach Nam 1959–62 (File about Compiling, Printing, and Publishing Books, 1959–62), Phu Tong Thong De Nhat Cong Hoa (Papers of the President's Office of the First Republic), Trung Tam Luu Tru Quoc Gia II (Archive Center No. II), Ho Chi Minh City, Vietnam, 2. I am grateful to Matt Masur for providing me with a copy of this document. The same language appeared earlier in *Vietnam: Communication, Tourism, and Transport*, 38.

38. *Saigon*, folder 5, box 1, JBC, VA, 1. The edition of the guide in my possession dates to no earlier than 1965; one of the hotels listed by the authors was the Astor, which was built that year. On the hotel's construction, see Denby Fawcett, "Pearl of the Orient," *Saturday Review* (8 October 1966): 70.

39. For a reference to "Free Vietnam," see, e.g., *Vietnam: Communication, Tourism, and Transport*, 132.

40. *Your Guide to Vietnam*, 1. Elsewhere in the publication, the authors referred to "approximately 12 million people living in South Vietnam and 13 million in the northern sector," again implying that the southern government ("South Vietnam") enjoyed more official legitimacy than its northern counterpart (the "northern sector"). Ibid., 1. The only reference in the guidebook to "North Vietnam" was a brief allusion, in a clearly apolitical context, to a style of lacquer work that was "a specialty of North Vietnam." Ibid., 12.

41. Ibid., 6.

42. Ibid., 2. Elsewhere, Saigon was referred to as "the capital city of Free Vietnam" and the "capital of the Free Republic of Vietnam." Ibid., 5, 8.

43. *Visit Fascinating Vietnam*, 1.

44. For an overview of American representations of the regroupees' plight, see Jacobs, *America's Miracle Man in Vietnam*, 127–71.

45. *Visit Fascinating Vietnam*, 2.

46. Ibid., 8–9.

47. *Life in Vietnam*, vol. 79 (24 September 1966), folder 3, box 1, GHC, VA, 44, 46.

48. *Your Guide to Vietnam*, 2, 9.

49. *Visit Fascinating Vietnam*, 2–3, 5.

50. *Your Guide to Vietnam*, 2. The same phrase was used in *Vietnam: Communication, Tourism, and Transport*, 38.

51. *Visit Fascinating Vietnam*, 14.

52. Gregory et al., *A Glimpse of Vietnam*, 20.

53. Ibid., 21–22.

54. Ibid., 22–23. The "gang of brigands" was a reference to the Cao Dai and Hoa Hao religious sects, and the "river pirates" were the Binh Xuyen syndicate.

55. Ibid., 35.

56. Ibid., 38–39.

57. *A Guide to Viet-Nam.*

58. Nevertheless, they reminded their audience, " 'The Balcony of the Pacific,' as Viet-Nam is often called by Western visitors, is not only in a strategic position in Southeast Asia, it is also, and above all, an enchanting, hospitable land." Ibid., 1, 39. Virtually identical language appeared in other tourism publications; see *Visit Fascinating Vietnam*, 14, which added, "Your trip to the Orient will be incomplete if you miss 'life-seeing' in Vietnam."

59. For more on the AFV, see Morgan, *The Vietnam Lobby*.

60. John Muth, "Free for All," 22 July 1962, folder 6, box 4, DPC: OM-AFV, VA. The announcement was effective, although the extent of that effectiveness is uncertain; see Fay MacKnight to American Friends of Vietnam, n.d., folder 6, box 4, DPC: OM-AFV, VA. MacKnight was a reader who requested a complimentary copy of the guide.

61. Louis Andreatta to Milton Horowitz, 28 March 1962, folder 18, box 15, DPC: OM-AFV, VA.

62. "Newly Available," n.d., folder 18, box 15, DPC: OM-AFV, VA; Gilbert Jonas to Louis Andreatta, 17 August 1960, folder 18, box 15, DPC: OM-AFV, VA; Louis Andreatta to Milton Horowitz, 28 March 1962. When the AFV contacted the embassy about publications it could include in the teaching kit in December 1961, its counselor suggested, among other titles, *Tourism in Vietnam*, and he indicated that the embassy would try to secure copies for this pedagogical purpose. Tran Van Dinh to Louis Andreatta, 2 January 1962, folder 18, box 15, DPC: OM-AFV, VA; Louis Andreatta to Tran Van Dinh, 5 January 1962, folder 18, box 15, DPC: OM-AFV, VA.

63. Louis Andreatta to Barbara Meddock, 26 July 1962, folder 18, box 15, DPC: OM-AFV, VA; Louis Andreatta to the editor of *Social Education*, 21 April 1962, folder 18, box 15, DPC: OM-AFV, VA; Louis Andreatta to Jeanne Singer, 11 April 1962, folder 18, box 15, DPC: OM-AFV, VA; Louis Andreatta to the editor of *Orient–Occident*, 20 June 1962, folder 18, box 15, DPC: OM-AFV, VA; Louis Andreatta to Milton Horowitz, 28 March 1962.

64. Louis Andreatta to Nathan M. Talbott, 20 March 1963, folder 18, box 15, DPC: OM-AFV, VA; "Teachers Packet — Proposed Free Distribution," n.d., folder 18, box 15, DPC: OM-AFV, VA.

65. Louis Andreatta to William Henderson, 20 December 1962, folder 24, box 1, DPC: OM-AFV, VA.

66. Indeed, the appeal of pictorial representations of Vietnam to young children was

evident in guidebooks sent home to their families by American military personnel. See, e.g., "Suz" to Michael Mittelmann, 25 October 1965, folder 37, box 1, MMC, VA; and Michael Mittelmann to "Everybody," 18 July 1965, folder 37, box 1, MMC, VA.

67. Student to American Friends of Vietnam, 2 March 1962, folder 8, box 8, DPC: OM-AFV, VA.

68. Kirtland, *Finding the Worth While in the Orient*, 253. For more on early perceptions of Vietnam and the Vietnamese, including the role of the environment in shaping the Vietnamese people, see Bradley, *Imagining Vietnam and America*, 45–72.

69. *Tourists' Guide to Saigon, Pnom-Penh, and Angkor*, 7.

70. One author, who elsewhere admiringly referred to the U.S. library in Saigon as a "symbol of freedom," rewrote the history of the French war altogether by simply designating the Viet Minh struggle against France a "civil war." Smith, *Southeast Asia*, 154, 158.

71. Olson, *Olson's Orient Guide*, 972–73.

72. Ibid., 973.

73. Kane, *Asia A to Z*, 409–10, 414.

74. Saunders, *The Cultural Cold War*, 35, 247; John M. Crewdson and Joseph B. Treaster, "CIA Established Many Links to Journalists in U.S. and Abroad," *New York Times*, 27 December 1977. Saunders wrote that several CIA agents employed by Fodor's "floated about Europe," although the source she cited, the *Times* article listed above (actually, Saunders misidentified the *Times* report as published on 25 December), did not contain such information. If there were other sources on which she relied, she did not identify them. I am grateful to Elaine Tyler May for bringing Saunders's work on Eugene Fodor to my attention.

75. Fodor and Fisher, *Fodor's Guide to Japan and East Asia 1962*, 25.

76. Robert C. Fisher, "Vietnam: New Nation, Old War," in ibid., 579–80, 583. Fisher's essay was retained until 1966, although revisions were made to it regularly. Even when it was replaced with an introduction by Peter Arnett in 1967, portions of Fisher's essay were incorporated into Arnett's text. See Fodor and Fisher, *Fodor's Guide to Japan and East Asia 1967*, 587–88.

77. Peter G. Arnett, "Vietnam: In the Grip of Turmoil," in Fodor and Fisher, *Fodor's Guide to Japan and East Asia 1968*, 585–86. In 1971, the conflict was still being classified in the guidebook as a "war between the Communists and the Free World." Peter G. Arnett, "Vietnam: In the Grip of Turmoil," in Fodor and Fisher, *Fodor's Japan and East Asia 1971*, 585.

78. *Tourism in Vietnam*, 13.

79. Ibid., 5.

80. *Saigon Round Up* (8 November 1963), folder 34, box 7, WCC, VA, 34.

81. *Visit Fascinating Vietnam*, 5.

82. For "lovely" hostesses and waitresses, see the advertisement for Dong Khanh

Hotel, *Visit Fascinating Vietnam*, 18; and the advertisement for Tahiti, *La Semaine a Saigon/Seven Days in Saigon*, vol. 241 (29 June–5 July 1963), 61. For "charming" hostesses, see the advertisements for Las Vegas and the Sporting Bar, *Saigon Round Up*, 27, 30; and the advertisement for the Monaco Bar, *La Semaine a Saigon/Seven Days in Saigon*, 43. For "lovely and charming" hostesses, see the advertisement for The Ocean, *La Semaine a Saigon/Seven Days in Saigon*, 5. For "attractive" hostesses, see the advertisement for My-Phung, *La Semaine a Saigon/Seven Days in Saigon*, 31. For "lovely English speaking hostesses," see the advertisement for the Sugar Cane Bar, *Saigon Round Up*, 21.

83. Tregaskis, "Vietnam Visit," 42.

84. George C. Scott, "Sorry About That," *Esquire* (December 1965): 211.

85. Fodor and Fisher, *Fodor's Guide to Japan and East Asia 1962*, 10, 591–92.

86. Clement, *The Future of Tourism in the Pacific and Far East*, 155. Among researchers, it was not just Americans who sought to gender Vietnam. A 1970 Vietnamese study, which featured an illustration of two women in *ao dai* on its front cover, opened with a studio photograph of a Vietnamese woman above the caption "Vietnam Beauty." Le Thai Khuong, *Du Lich Ky Nghe Tam Dang tai Viet-Nam*, 1. Of course, some Americans preferred Vietnamese women *without* their "traditional dress." Reflecting on the "slack" business caused by Saigon being declared off-limits to most GIS, an American journalist in 1971 spotlighted the "bar after bar" in the center of the city with "extraordinarily lovely looking girls peering out of the doorways and windows," wondering whether, "if the native women had been less attractive," so "many Americans would have stayed in Vietnam so long." E. J. Kahn Jr., "A Pentagon-Shaped Cemetery, Dry Elephant Tails, and Other Wonders of the Mysterious East," *New York Times*, 18 April 1971.

87. Advertisement for the Pacific Area Travel Association, *Holiday* (October 1962): 58–59.

88. Vietnamese-generated covers featuring women included *Visit Fascinating Vietnam*; *Viet Nam* (n.d.), folder 5, box 1, JBC, VA; *Dalat*; and *Saigon*. While more of a narrative introduction to life in Saigon than a traditional tourism document, *Saigon in the Flesh*, which was aimed at foreigners, took its title to heart by, quite literally, placing on its cover a young, busty Vietnamese woman in a swimsuit and high heels. Doan Bich and Le Trang, *Saigon in the Flesh*. Perhaps the best example of foreign-produced publications that featured Vietnamese women on their covers are the first two editions of the pocket guides created by the U.S. Department of Defense discussed in chapter 2: OAFIE, *A Pocket Guide to Viet-Nam*, DOD PG-21; and idem, *A Pocket Guide to Vietnam*, DOD PG-21A.

89. Scott, "Sorry About That," 210–11.

90. Hoganson, *Fighting for American Manhood*.

91. Jerry Burris, "Saigon Gears Up for Tourists, Investors," *Honolulu Advertiser*, 20 June 1973. Given the government's later crackdown on "Saigon's ladies of the

night" in an effort to "beautify South Vietnam's capital and attract the more desirable type of tourist," unregulated prostitution in the RVN appeared to have its limits. Police routinely began arresting "women whose dress" was considered "too revealing" or who solicited men on the streets. The effect on international tourism was substantial. "They caused trouble sometimes, but they were good for business," a waiter at one of Saigon's most popular hotels observed of the prostitutes who sought clients at his establishment. "They've gone now—and so have the customers. Business is down 80 per cent." Associated Press, "Saigon's Ladies of Night Find Their Day Fading," *New York Times*, 4 November 1973.

92. *Glimpses of French Indo-China*, in Military Intelligence Division; "Regional File," 1922–44; French Indo-China file, 1000–1190, French Indo-China, RG 165, NA, 4, 7. I am grateful to David Biggs for bringing this document to my attention.

93. "Letter From the Ambassador in Vietnam (Durbrow) to the Assistant Secretary of State for Far Eastern Affairs (Robertson)," 15 December 1958, in U.S. Department of State, *Foreign Relations of the United States, 1958–1960*, 105–107.

94. Pym, *The Road to Angkor*, 22, 33, 37.

95. Wolfstone, *The Golden Guide to South and East Asia*, 291.

96. Entry for 10 July 1964, Louis Connick Diary, "BV Connick, Louis," New-York Historical Society, New York. Courtesy of the New-York Historical Society.

97. Robert C. Fisher, "Vietnam: New Nation, Old War," in Fodor and Fisher, *Fodor's Guide to Japan and East Asia 1965*, 579, 584.

98. James Reston, "Saigon Seems as Far From War as It Is From U.S.," *New York Times*, 17 August 1965. For another commentary on the war's relative absence from the city, see Wesley Pruden Jr., "I Was Already Homesick for an Alien City," *National Observer*, 31 May 1965, folder 3, box 26, DPC: U6, VA.

99. Robert C. Fisher, "Vietnam: New Nation, Old War," in Fodor and Fisher, *Fodor's Guide to Japan and East Asia 1966*, 579, 584.

100. Peter G. Arnett, "Vietnam: In the Grip of Turmoil," in Fodor and Fisher, *Fodor's Guide to Japan and East Asia 1967*, 584–85. By 1974, the editors were forced to "surrender to the inevitable," counseling "purely and simply, *don't go!*" Fodor and Fisher, *Fodor's Japan and East Asia 1974*, 22. It would be decades—not until the twenty-first edition of its Southeast Asia guidebook in 1997—before Vietnam again drew the publishers' attention. See Mauldin et al., *Fodor's Southeast Asia*.

101. Smith, *Southeast Asia*, 154.

102. Travel Research International, *Pacific Visitors Survey*, 14, 21, 23.

103. Ibid., 90.

104. *Viet Nam* (1967), folder 6, box 1, JPC, VA, 1.

105. *An Introduction to Vietnam*, 41.

106. *Vietnam Du Lich Giao Thong*, 16.

107. Arnett, "Vietnam," in Fodor and Fisher, *Fodor's Guide to Japan and East Asia 1967*, 585.

108. Interview of George Moudry and Sharon Moudry, 30 September 2004, Minneapolis.

109. Seymour Topping, "Touring the Troubled but Still Exotic Orient," *New York Times*, 9 August 1964.

110. "Saigon Attracts Intrepid Tourist," *New York Times*, 26 December 1965. Tourists such as the Fosters were "viewed as curiosities by their countrymen who live and work in Vietnam," the newspaper added.

111. Topping, "Touring the Troubled but Still Exotic Orient." While the war scared away many American civilians from Southeast Asian destinations outside Vietnam, it did, however, attract military personnel on "R and R" trips to a number of regional cities. Hong Kong, for one, enjoyed a brief surge of tourist arrivals in 1965 until political sensitivities curbed the American military presence, and Bangkok drew hundreds of thousands of Vietnam-based Americans seeking hot water, alcohol, and sex. For two contemporaneous accounts, see ibid.; and Terence Smith, "Bangkok Magnet for Vietnam GIS," *New York Times*, 1 May 1968.

112. Fawcett, "Pearl of the Orient," 71.

113. Ibid., 70.

114. Arnett, "Vietnam," in Fodor and Fisher, *Fodor's Guide to Japan and East Asia 1967*, 585. On the frustration of the veteran travel writer and tour leader John C. Caldwell with this problem, which by 1966, in combination with concerns for personal safety, led him to conclude that "Vietnam is out for tourists for some time, perhaps several years, to come," see Caldwell, *Far Pacific Travel Guide*, 288. For his earlier coverage of Vietnam, see idem, *Far East Travel Guide*, 217–20; and idem, *Far East Travel Guide*, rev. ed., 210–14.

115. Kahn, "A Pentagon-Shaped Cemetery."

116. Fawcett, "Pearl of the Orient," 70–71. The airline itself entered the guidebook industry and, in 1973, published a volume on Asia and the Pacific that covered the RVN. Unlike nearly all other guidebooks prior to that time, it also contained a very brief entry on the DRV. The lack of serious attention afforded the latter section, however, was evident in the authors' identification of northern Vietnam's principal language as Korean. *The Real Pacific*, 181. More reliable coverage of the DRV could be found in the volume published by the *Far Eastern Economic Review*; see Jones, *Golden Guide to South and East Asia*, 317–18.

117. Fawcett, "Pearl of the Orient," 71; *Saigon*, 1. On the National Tourist Office's listing of the My Canh Floating Restaurant, see *Saigon*, 17.

118. R. W. Apple Jr., "Quiet Spot in Vietnam," *New York Times*, 26 February 1966. Dalat, by contrast, was "cool, roomy, and clean" and "smell[ed] of pine boughs." Ibid.

119. Arnett, "Vietnam," in Fodor and Fisher, *Fodor's Guide to Japan and East Asia 1967*, 585.

120. "The Worst City in the World?" *Newsweek* (29 December 1969): 38.

121. Fawcett, "Pearl of the Orient," 70–71. The tourism literature of the 1950s used hunting in the RVN as one means of enticing foreigners to visit. A National Tourist Office guidebook, for example, sought to explain why southern Vietnam, with a moderate year-round climate in the central highlands, was a more agreeable destination for hunters than "hot flat countries." *Hunting in Viet-Nam* (n.d.), 8. See also *Hunting in Viet-Nam* (1957), folder 14, box 14, DPC: OM-AFV, VA; and *An Outline of Game Shooting in Vietnam*, which referred to Vietnam as "a paradise for hunters."

122. Apple, "Quiet Spot in Vietnam." For the brochure, see Dalat Tourist Office, *Dalat*, 5.

123. "The Positive Approach," *Newsweek* (12 June 1967): 37.

124. Harris, "Saigon Still Attracts the Tourists."

125. Thieu, quoted in Terence Smith, "First GI's in Pullout Leave Saigon," *New York Times*, 8 July 1969. On the RVN's hopes for increased tourism after 1973, see Fox Butterfield, "Thieu Announces Eight-Year Program of War Recovery," *New York Times*, 21 May 1973; Richard Joseph, "Saigon: Fresh, Bright New Tourist Prospect," *Vietnam Report*, vol. 2, no. 7 (1 April 1973): 14–15; Burris, "Saigon Gears Up for Tourists, Investors"; and idem; "Come and Fly Me," *Time* (4 June 1973): 16. In 1971, a committee of the Asian Parliamentarians' Union (APU), believing that the RVN had largely "overcome the Communists' military threat," urged the promotion of tourist visits from APU and other nations. "Invest in RVN Now, APU Advised," *Viet-Nam Bulletin*, vol. 5, no. 1 (4 January 1971): 10–11. As noted earlier, it was not until 1974 that Hanoi created a tourism department, though the authorities had indirectly promoted the north's scenic potential before that time. (For a number of books published in Hanoi that contained annexes with information about "beauty spots" and other attractions in the DRV, see *Vietnam Today*, 171–76; *Viet Nam: A Sketch*, 139–43; and *The Democratic Republic of Vietnam*, 189–204.) With the war's official end in 1975, tourism remained a low priority. While there were in fact thousands of international arrivals — by late in 1977, the authorities had signed agreements with travel agencies in western Europe, Japan, and Australia to promote group travel to the new Socialist Republic of Vietnam — foreign tourists were relatively sparse until the early 1990s, with most having arrived from allied socialist states. Lynch, *All-Asia Guide*, 573.

126. Tregaskis, "Vietnam Visit," 42.

127. Scott, "Sorry About That," 316, 321.

128. Fawcett, "Pearl of the Orient," 72. For a more complicated view of Vietnamese political opinion — in this case from an Australian woman who hitchhiked through portions of southern Vietnam before the Tet Offensive — see Letters, *The Surprising Asians*, 214–15.

129. Warner, *Asia Is People*, 102–4, 106. Warner did not indicate precisely when she visited Vietnam, but she wrote that "very soon" after she and her husband left

"an unsuccessful attempt was made to overthrow the President" in a coup d'état. Ibid., 102. Her book was first published in Australia in 1961, and the only coup attempt prior to that time occurred in November 1960.

130. Lange, Vietnam Notes (1958).

131. Ibid.

2. EDUCATING PRIVATE RYAN

Source of second epigraph: David L. Sartori to Edward N. Peterson, 9 March 1969, Edward N. Peterson Letters, 1968–69, River Falls sc 90, Folder: Sartori and Thorson Letters from Vietnam; whs, River Falls.

1. United Press International, "Viet Reds Capture 2 ncos; 1 Escapes," 26 July 1962, folder 4, box 20, dpc: u3-pmi, va; David Halberstam, "2 gis Mark Yule in Vietnam with Buffalo Feast at Outpost," *New York Times*, 26 December 1962. See also "American Depicts Vietcong Jailing," *New York Times*, 9 January 1963. The fate of the second Vietnamese was not reported.

2. Interview of Martin Brady, 25 June 2003, Oral History Project, mbc, va.

3. oafie, *A Pocket Guide to Viet-Nam*, dod pg-21, 1, 102–103, 105–106. The pocket guide is dated 6 December 1962, but 1963 is listed elsewhere as the official year of publication: see *Monthly Catalog of United States Government Publications*, 2384.

4. oafie, *A Pocket Guide to Viet-Nam*, dod pg-21, 1.

5. Franklin, *Vietnam and Other American Fantasies*, 50. See also idem, "When Did the Vietnam War Begin?" Franklin drew for this material on Gillen, "Roots of Opposition."

6. B. P. Flint Jr. for the Record, Subject: "Visit of Committee Men to Army Aviation Units [at] Nha Trang, Viet Nam," 23 April 1962, Report of Southeast Asia Subcommittee file, accession no. 64-a2021, box 4; rg 330, na. See also A. A. Jordan Jr. for the Record, Subject: "Bendetsen Team Visits, Vietnam, 16–17 April," 20 April 1962, Report of Southeast Asia Subcommittee file, accession no. 64-a2021, box 4, rg 330, na.

7. A. A. Jordan Jr. for the Record, Subject: "Bendetsen Team Visits, Vietnam, 16–17 April."

8. B. P. Flint Jr. for the Record, Subject: "Visit of Bendetsen Committee to macv Headquarters, Saigon, Viet Nam," 23 April 1962, Report of Southeast Asia Subcommittee file, accession no. 64-a2021, box 4, rg 330, na.

9. Office of the Secretary of Defense for the Record, Subject: "'Observations' during the Southeast Asia Trip," 20 April 1962, Report of Southeast Asia Subcommittee file, accession no. 64-a2021, box 4, rg 330, na. This specific observation was made of military personnel in Hawaii.

10. oafie, *A Pocket Guide to Viet-Nam*, dod pg-21, 1.

11. Ibid., 2–3. This section did not appear in the pocket guide's second edition.

12. Ibid., 94–103.

13. Ibid., 108.

14. Ibid., 106.

15. The most comprehensive source on the political-education campaign in the American armed forces, especially the U.S. Army, is DeRosa, "A Million Thinking Bayonets"; see also idem, *Political Indoctrination in the U.S. Army from World War II to the Vietnam War.*

16. In the context of the Cold War, this meant framing international affairs as a simple story of good versus evil or, in the vernacular of the era, of freedom versus totalitarianism. On OAFIE's objective to explain affairs at an "eighth grade level of understanding," see E. W. Maxson to Leland B. Kuhre, 29 December 1954, Decimal File, 1953–54, Decimal File 461: 461 (General), 1 January 1954 — Section I, OAFIE, box 22, RG 330, NA.

17. OAFIE, *Armed Forces Information Pamphlet: Information Materials*, 8.

18. Ibid., 6–7.

19. John A. Hannah to the Secretary of the Army, Secretary of the Navy, and Secretary of the Air Force, 31 July 1953, reprinted in ibid., 4.

20. Subcommittees of the Committee on Expenditures in the Executive Departments and of the Committee on Education and Labor, *Investigation of Publication Sponsored by the Department of the Army Entitled "Army Talks,"* 24. Although *Armed Forces Talk* was produced by the Army, it was distributed to all of the U.S. armed forces.

21. Ibid., 17, 25, 29–30, 46. This theme would later prove popular among right-wing political activists: see, e.g., McGirr, *Suburban Warriors*, 131, 165.

22. Subcommittees of the Committee on Expenditures in the Executive Departments and of the Committee on Education and Labor, *Investigation of Publication Sponsored by the Department of the Army Entitled "Army Talks,"* 21, 38, 43.

23. Ibid., 37.

24. Wade M. Fleischer to James F. Collins, 3 February 1954, Decimal File, 1953–54, Decimal File 461: 461 Armed Forces Talk, 1 January 1954 — Section I, OAFIE, box 22, RG 330, NA. See also DeRosa, "A Million Thinking Bayonets," 195–97.

25. OAFIE, *Armed Forces Information Pamphlet: Information Materials*, 5.

26. William L. Barriger to Harlan N. Hartness, 29 October 1953, Decimal File, 1953–54, Decimal File 461: 461, 1 January 1951 — Section III (Overseas Theaters), OAFIE, box 22, RG 330, NA.

27. For an analysis of several Pentagon-produced films from the 1960s and 1970s, see Springer, "Military Propaganda," 95–114.

28. On the use of OAFIE publications in public schools, see, for one example among many, R. A. Fredrickson to OAFIE, 5 August 1955, General Subject Files, Decimal File 461: Armed Forces Talk, Section I — General (1 January 1955–December 1956), accession no. 60-A1251, OAFIE, box 21, RG 330, NA. For their use in educating students about the situation in Vietnam in particular, see Eleanor H. Gentry

to OAFIE, 13 December 1955, and OAFIE to Mrs. Herbert C. Gentry, 3 January 1955, General Subject Files, Decimal File 461: Armed Forces Talk, Section I—General (1 January 1955–December 1956), accession no. 60-A1251, OAFIE, box 21, RG 330, NA. On the education of missionaries, see, for just one example, Genevieve Greer to OAFIE, 10 May 1955, General Subject Files, Decimal File 461: Armed Forces Talk, Section I—General (1 January 1955–December 1956), accession no. 60-A1251, OAFIE, box 21, RG 330, NA. On requests to reprint OAFIE materials in local newspapers, see Edward Fink to the editor-in-chief, *Armed Forces Talk*, 26 January 1955, General Subject Files, Decimal File 461: Armed Forces Talk, Section I—General (1 January 1955–December 1956), accession no. 60-A1251, OAFIE, box 21, RG 330, NA. For OAFIE publications serving as scripts for public lectures, see Richard L. Ernst to the editor-in-chief, *Armed Forces Talk*, 13 November 1953, Decimal File, 1953–54, Decimal File 461: 461, 1 January 1951—Section III (Overseas Theaters), OAFIE, box 22, RG 330, NA; and Joseph J. Mona to OAFIE, 21 February 1953, Decimal File, 1953–54, Decimal File 461: 461 (Armed Forces Talks), 1 January 1953—Section I, OAFIE, box 23, RG 330, NA. On OAFIE publications serving as the basis of public-service radio and television programming, see Richard L. Ernst to the editor-in-chief, *Armed Forces Talk*, 13 November 1953, and John J. Struckus to the editor-in-chief, *Armed Forces Talk*, 15 May 1953, Decimal File, 1953–54, Decimal File 461: 461 (Armed Forces Talks), 1 January 1953—Section I, OAFIE, box 23, RG 330, NA.

29. OAFIE, *Armed Forces Talk: Your Safety*, 3.

30. See, e.g., OAFIE, *Armed Forces Talk: It's Your Future*; idem, *Armed Forces Information Pamphlet: Your Insurance, Savings, and Retirement*.

31. OAFIE, *Armed Forces Talk: Who Will Win the Olympics?* 11.

32. OAFIE, *Armed Forces Talk: Communism*, 11.

33. OAFIE, *Armed Forces Talk: Truth*, 2; idem, *Armed Forces Talk: Communist Propaganda*; idem, *Armed Forces Talk: Your Defense Against Enemy Propaganda*; idem, *Armed Forces Talk: Rumor Has It*.

34. OAFIE, *Armed Forces Talk: The American Way of Life*; idem, *Armed Forces Talk: The ABC's of Democracy*; idem, *Armed Forces Talk: What's Right with the United States*.

35. Fabriano Bertocci to the editor-in-chief, *Armed Forces Talk*, 27 January 1955, General Subject Files, Decimal File 461: Armed Forces Talk, Section I—General (1 January 1955–December 1956), accession no. 60-A1251, OAFIE, box 21, RG 330, NA; Fred B. Harrison Jr. to the editor-in-chief, *Armed Forces Talk*, 22 June 1953, Decimal File, 1953–54, Decimal File 461: 461 (Armed Forces Talks), 1 January 1953—Section I, OAFIE, box 23, RG 330, NA.

36. Joseph J. Mona to OAFIE, 21 February 1953.

37. William Rehr to the editor-in-chief, *Armed Forces Talk*, 27 November 1953, Deci-

mal File, 1953–54, Decimal File 461: 461 (Armed Forces Talk), 1 January 1953 – Section II, OAFIE, box 23, RG 330, NA.

38. Clair E. Towne to Brilsford P. Flint Jr., 23 October 1962, Chief of Information, General Correspondence, 1960, 1962, 260/32(RP) Pamphlets, August (62) file, box 23, RG 319, NA.

39. Alvin H. Niemann to OAFIE, 9 February 1955, General Subject Files, Decimal File 461: Armed Forces Talk, Section I — General (1 January 1955–December 1956), accession no. 60-A1251, OAFIE, box 21, RG 330, NA. As for the captain's concern about possible repercussions, OAFIE dismissed them as unfounded: "You do both the Air Force and the FBI an injustice when you express the fear that you will be 'fired' for 'possessing dangerous ideas.' Neither is engaged in the business of thought control. You need worry *only* if your words and deeds endanger the security of our Country." H. E. L. Zastrow to Alvin H. Niemann, 1 March 1955, General Subject Files, Decimal File 461: Armed Forces Talk, Section I — General (1 January 1955–December 1956), accession no. 60-A1251, OAFIE, box 21, RG 330, NA. For an example of a reader's criticism that OAFIE was engaged in precisely the sort of propaganda it denounced when undertaken by the Soviets, see Ivan Ronald Levin to the editors, *Armed Forces Talk*, 8 July 1953, Decimal File, 1953–54, Decimal File 461: 461 Armed Forces Talk, 1 January 1953 – Section II, OAFIE, box 23, RG 330, NA.

40. OAFIE, *Armed Forces Talk: The Free World's Allies*, 9.

41. In another example of this discursive denationalization, a 1958 booklet issued jointly by the U.S. Operations Mission to Vietnam and the American Women's Association of Saigon explained that the 1954 Geneva Accords "placed all of Tonkin, and the part of Annam north of the seventeenth parallel, in communist Viet Minh (also called Viet Cong) hands, leaving control of the rest of Viet Nam to the Vietnamese." The "Vietnamese," in this formulation, were solely those forces opposed to the Viet Minh. *Saigon: A Booklet of Helpful Information for Americans in Vietnam* (1958), 3.

42. OAFIE, *Armed Forces Talk: The Situation in Southeast Asia*, 3, 10. The information in this issue "was presented very well," wrote one serviceman to the editor of *Armed Forces Talk*. Irwin Richman to the editor, *Armed Forces Talk*, 9 October 1953, Decimal File, 1953–54, Decimal File 461: 461 Armed Forces Talk, 1 January 1953 — Section II, OAFIE, box 23, RG 330, NA. The publication's frank concession of an economic basis for U.S. involvement in Indochina, which was echoed by President Eisenhower in a news conference in April 1954, was one from which American policymakers and military educators would retreat — publicly, at least — in later years. On the news conference, see "The President's News Conference of April 7, 1954," no. 73, *Public Papers of the Presidents of the United States: Dwight D. Eisenhower, 1954*, 382.

43. OAFIE, *Armed Forces Talk: The War in Indochina*, 2, 3, 5.

44. OAFIE, *Armed Forces Talk: Total Rule*.

45. OAFIE, *Armed Forces Talk: The War in Indochina*, 13–15.

46. Rocky Versace to "My Friends," 1962, Tere Rios Versace Papers, mss. 268, box 1, folder 8 (Tere Versace: General Correspondence, 1946–62), WHS, Madison.

47. Rocky Versace to "Mom, Dad, and Kids," 18 October 1963, Tere Rios Versace Papers, mss. 268, box 1, folder 9 (Tere Versace: General Correspondence, 1963), WHS, Madison. Versace possessed a copy of *A Pocket Guide to Viet-Nam*, DOD PG-21: see Record of Personal Effects — Outside Combat Areas for Humbert R. Versace, 13 November 1963, Tere Rios Versace Papers, mss. 268, box 1, folder 1 (Rocky Versace: Biographical Material and Memorabilia, 1951–63), WHS, Madison.

48. On films before 1965 that dealt in some capacity with Vietnam — a topic that has received remarkably little attention from historians drawing on archival research — see Adair, *Hollywood's Vietnam*, 18–19; Auster and Quart, *How the War Was Remembered*, 13–22; Berg, "Losing Vietnam," 41–68; Devine, *Vietnam at 24 Frames a Second*, 1–27; Lanning, *Vietnam at the Movies*, 38–44; Muse, *The Land of Nam*, 23–34; Smith, *Looking Away*, 99–136; and Whillock, "The Fictive American Vietnam War Film," 303–12.

49. Jack Warner Jr. to Steve Trilling, 19 August 1954, file no. 2017, "Jump into Hell" Collection, WBA. I am grateful to Daniel Rosen of Warner Bros. for allowing me to view one of the studio's archival copies of *Jump Into Hell*.

50. It is unfortunately not possible to fully gauge service members' contemporaneous responses to the Vietnam pocket guides, as the official subject files of the Office of Armed Forces Information and Education from 1963 to 1966, which housed correspondence from readers, were destroyed in July 1994, according to the National Archives and Records Administration. My effort to locate documents elsewhere, such as the records of the Army staff, was only partially successful. Shortly after the 1963 pocket guide was published, for example, information officers in Hawaii, the Ryuku Islands, and Vietnam reportedly expressed their opinion that the guidebook was "a very fine document packed with pertinent information." Likewise, Dorothy Whipple, the director of cultural affairs for the U.S. Information Service in Vietnam, found, together with a Vietnamese colleague, that "the approach is excellent and the pamphlet as a whole was well done," according to a secondhand report. James P. Mulcahy to Robert B. Smith, 1 April 1963, Chief of Information, General Correspondence, 1963–64: 205–04 REF Publications Files (Pamphlets), COFF 31 December 1963 RES FRC January 1965 file, box 44, RG 319, NA. At least one serviceman used his "U.S. Army handbook for Vietnam," as well as an article in *National Geographic*, to familiarize himself with Vietnamese history in writing to an educator in the United States. See Gary Thorson to Edward N.

Peterson, n.d., Edward N. Peterson Letters, 1968–69, River Falls SC 90, Sartori and Thorson Letters from Vietnam folder, WHS, River Falls.

51. The visual imagery of later editions would assume a decidedly more martial cast.

52. Robert Feighny to Helen Feighny, 22 April 1964; Folder 1: Letters to His Wife, 1–50, Robert E. Feighny Papers, 1964–65, KSHS.

53. William Tuohy, "Sometimes It's Bad, Sometimes It's Good," *Newsweek* (18 January 1965): 29.

54. OAFIE, *A Pocket Guide to Viet-Nam*, DOD PG-21, 94.

55. OAFIE, *A Pocket Guide to Vietnam*, DOD PG-21A, 66.

56. OAFIE, *A Pocket Guide to Viet-Nam*, DOD PG-21, 103–104; OAFIE, *A Pocket Guide to Vietnam*, DOD PG-21A, 71.

57. Associated Press, "Protest Reported in Dalat," *New York Times*, 4 April 1966. On later concerns about the U.S. military presence in Saigon, see Richard M. Nixon to Henry A. Kissinger, 12 November 1969, NPMS, NSCF, AMHSF, box 1008, Haig's Vietnam File — Volume 3, November–December 1969 (2 of 2), NA.

58. OAFIE, *A Pocket Guide to Viet-Nam*, DOD PG-21, 97, 102; OAFIE, *A Pocket Guide to Vietnam*, DOD PG-21A, 68, 70. The coastal town of Vung Tau was still referred to as Cap St. Jacques in both guides, but this may have been because, as the 1966 edition noted, it "is now officially called Vung Tau but is also still known by its former French name." OAFIE, *A Pocket Guide to Vietnam*, DOD PG-21A, 72.

59. OAFIE, *A Pocket Guide to Viet-Nam*, DOD PG-21, 99.

60. OAFIE, *A Pocket Guide to Vietnam*, DOD PG-21B, 4, 15, 30, 57, 71.

61. Ibid., 63, 65.

62. Ibid., 21.

63. Ibid., 73.

64. Edward G. Lansdale to Colonel A. A. Jordan Jr., 27 March 1962, Report of Southeast Asia Subcommittee file, accession no. 64-A2021, box 4, RG 330, NA. The literature touching on Lansdale is vast. For an important recent "mythography," see Nashel, *Edward Lansdale's Cold War*.

65. OAFIE, *A Pocket Guide to Anywhere*, DOD PAM 2–5, 1. For the first edition, see *OAFIE, A Pocket Guide to Anywhere*, PG-13.

66. OAFIE, *A Pocket Guide to Anywhere*, DOD PAM 2–5, 2–4.

67. OAFIE, *A Pocket Guide to Viet-Nam*, DOD PG-21, 1–2. Contrast this insistence on the U.S. military's contribution to a "telling blow for democracy" and its support for "freedom-loving people" with the opinion of the Defense Department analysts who authored the Pentagon Papers: "Ngo Dinh Diem presided over a state which, for all the lip service it paid to individual freedom and American style government, remained a one party, highly centralized familial oligarchy in which neither operating democracy . . . nor the prerequisites for such existed." *The Pentagon Papers*, I: 324.

68. See, for example, OAFIE, *A Pocket Guide to Viet-Nam*, PG-21, 1, 106–108; and OAFIE, *A Pocket Guide to Vietnam*, DOD PG-21A, iii, 1.

69. The fact that the documents were reviewed by more senior officials before publication suggests that there was an element of conscious deception at work.

70. OAFIE, *A Pocket Guide to Viet-Nam*, DOD PG-21, 19. In the second edition, this sentence was changed to "The French assumed control over the province of Cochin China in 1863." OAFIE, *A Pocket Guide to Vietnam*, DOD PG-21A, 13.

71. OAFIE, *A Pocket Guide to Viet-Nam*, DOD PG-21, 19–20. This paragraph was excised from the 1966 publication.

72. Ibid., 20.

73. Ibid., 20–21. The implication that the Communist-led revolutionaries were "pretend[ers]" was perhaps most obvious in the pocket guide's third edition. Under a photograph of Ho Chi Minh meeting with a French delegation after World War Two, a caption stated, "Posing as nationalist, Ho Chi Minh met with French in 1946." OAFIE, *A Pocket Guide to Vietnam*, DOD PG-21B, 13.

74. "The Final Declaration on Indochina," in U.S. Department of State, *Foreign Relations of the United States, 1952–1954*, 1541. OAFIE's dismissal of the accords' relevance to the United States was evident elsewhere in its pocket guides. In a section in the 1966 edition (which was slightly different from the 1963 edition) entitled "Help for a Sister Republic," the authors wrote that "after the Geneva accords of 1954 divided Vietnam, a U.S. Military Assistance Advisory Group . . . became the only outside source of military aid for South Vietnam. Its mission was to improve the military effectiveness of the South Vietnamese Armed Forces." OAFIE, *A Pocket Guide to Vietnam*, DOD PG-21A, 19; see also OAFIE, *A Pocket Guide to Viet-Nam*, DOD PG-21, 24. This contravened the accords' prohibition of "the introduction into Viet-Nam of foreign troops and military personnel as well as of all kinds of arms and munitions." "The Final Declaration on Indochina," 1540.

75. OAFIE, *A Pocket Guide to Viet-Nam*, DOD PG-21, 21.

76. Herring, *America's Longest War*, 55. For an important analysis of the 1955 referendum, including Diem's promotion of democratic rhetoric within southern Vietnam and his use of the plebiscite as a means of avoiding the mandated 1956 reunification elections, see Chapman, "Staging Democracy," 671–703.

77. "Despatch From the Ambassador in Vietnam (Reinhardt) to the Department of State," 29 November 1955, in U.S. Department of State, *Foreign Relations of the United States, 1955–1957*, 592–93.

78. "Intelligence Brief Prepared by the Office of Intelligence Research, Department of State," 7 February 1956, in U.S. Department of State, *Foreign Relations of the United States, 1955–1957*, 639.

79. "Memorandum from the Chairman of the Vietnam Task Force (Cottrell) to the President's Military Representative (Taylor)," 27 October 1961, in U.S. Department of State, *Foreign Relations of the United States, 1961–1963*, 507.

80. Hanes, quoted in Jacobs, *America's Miracle Man in Vietnam*, 274.

81. OAFIE, *A Pocket Guide to Viet-Nam*, DOD PG-21, 22–23. This paragraph was substantially altered and expanded in the 1966 guidebook, with colorful language added about the "Communists in Hanoi" expecting "South Vietnam to collapse and fall into their hands like ripe fruit," only to be "frustrated by its growing prosperity." See OAFIE, *A Pocket Guide to Vietnam*, DOD PG-21A, 18–19.

82. OAFIE, *A Pocket Guide to Viet-Nam*, DOD PG-21, 23.

83. OAFIE, *A Pocket Guide to Vietnam*, DOD PG-21A, 15.

84. Absent from the 1966 edition of the guidebook was the reference to the "legality" of the RVN's government being "confirmed" in the October 1955 referendum; see OAFIE, *A Pocket Guide to Viet-Nam*, DOD PG-21, 21; and OAFIE, *A Pocket Guide to Vietnam*, DOD PG-21A, 14.

85. The white papers are U.S. Department of State, *A Threat to the Peace*, folder 11, box 7, DPC: U11, VA; and U.S. Department of State, *Aggression from the North*. The investigative journalist Izzy Stone published a widely circulated critique of the latter document when it was released in 1965; see I. F. Stone, "A Reply to the White Paper," *I. F. Stone's Weekly* (8 March 1965): 1–4.

86. Walt W. Rostow to Dean Rusk, 13 July 1961, Papers of President Kennedy, NSF, Countries, box 193A, Vietnam, General, 7/5/61–7/13/61, JFKL The reference to the position's fragility is from Kahin, *Intervention*, 471. Kahin referred to "many American officials" being "aware of the fragility of the 'aggression from the North' rationale," which he attributed to "successive administrations [finding] it useful in dealing with American and world audiences." In actuality, northern Vietnamese leaders pleaded with the southern revolutionaries not to engage in armed struggle in the late 1950s and in 1960. Top officials in Hanoi, with the exception of leading southern members of the Politburo such as Le Duan, wished to keep the opposition to Diem political. For scholarly accounts of the important role played by southerners in advocating Hanoi's support for armed resistance to the Saigon authorities, see ibid., 93–121; and Brigham, "Why the South Won the American War in Vietnam," 97–116.

87. *The Pentagon Papers*, I: 242–43.

88. "Telegram from Ambassador Eldridge Durbrow in Saigon to Secretary of State Christian A. Herter," 7 March 1960, *U.S.–Vietnam Relations*, book 10, 1254–57, reprinted in Porter, *Vietnam*, 201.

89. "Cablegram from Elbridge Durbrow, United States Ambassador in Saigon, to Secretary of State Christian A. Herter," 16 September 1960, in *The Pentagon Papers*, II: 635.

90. "Founding Program of the National Liberation Front of South Vietnam," Liberation Radio/South Vietnam, 13–14 February 1961, Foreign Broadcast Information Service Daily Reports, reprinted in Gettleman et al., *Vietnam and America*, 189. The platform built on the Ten-Point Manifesto released shortly after the

NLF's formation in December 1960. For the manifesto, see Tran Van Giau and Le Van Chat, *The South Viet Nam Liberation National Front*, 27–29.

91. *The Pentagon Papers*, I: 341. "My" in "My-Diem" is the Vietnamese term for "America."

92. "Founding Program of the National Liberation Front of South Vietnam," 192. On NLF neutralism and evolving views on the issue in Hanoi, see Brigham, *Guerrilla Diplomacy*.

93. OAFIE, *A Pocket Guide to Vietnam*, DOD PG-21A, 20. The 1971 pocket guide removed this paragraph's moderately harsh evaluation of Diem and replaced it with a much milder assessment. See OAFIE, *A Pocket Guide to Vietnam*, DOD PG-21B, 20–21.

94. OAFIE, *A Pocket Guide to Viet-Nam*, DOD PG-21, 2, 21, 22, 30.

95. Buzzanco, *Vietnam and the Transformation of American Life*, 69.

96. OAFIE, *A Pocket Guide to Vietnam*, DOD PG-21A, 20.

97. Penniman, *Elections in South Vietnam*, 38.

98. Bradley, *Imagining Vietnam and America*, 73–106.

99. For an analysis of how such expansionist objectives underlay U.S. assimilation policies directed at American Indians in the 1870s and 1880s, see Laderman, " 'It Is Cheaper and Better to Teach a Young Indian Than to Fight an Old One,' " 85–111.

100. OAFIE, *A Pocket Guide to Vietnam*, DOD PG-21A, 20–22.

101. Scigliano, *South Vietnam*, 145.

102. *The Pentagon Papers*, II: 204.

103. Vann, quoted in Herman and Chomsky, *Manufacturing Consent*, 181. Vann was the subject of Neil Sheehan's Pulitzer Prize–winning book, *A Bright Shining Lie*.

104. General Pham Xuan Chieu, quoted in Young, *The Vietnam Wars*, 167.

105. Heinl, "The Collapse of the Armed Forces," 30.

106. OAFIE, *A Pocket Guide to Vietnam*, DOD PG-21B, 12; *The Pentagon Papers*, I: 22.

107. OAFIE, *A Pocket Guide to Vietnam*, DOD PG-21B, 16.

108. *The Pentagon Papers*, I: 247.

109. OAFIE, *A Pocket Guide to Vietnam*, DOD PG-21B, 20–21.

110. Dean Rusk to Ellsworth Bunker, Subject: "Big" Minh, 8 July 1967, Papers of Lyndon Baines Johnson, President, 1963–69, NSF, CF—Vietnam, box 65, Elections, 1 G (1), 6/1/67–8/12/67 (1 of 2) folder, LBJL.

111. Dean Rusk to Ellsworth Bunker, Subject: Au Truong Thanh, 8 July 1967, Papers of Lyndon Baines Johnson, President, 1963–69, NSF, CF—Vietnam, box 65, Elections, 1 G (1), 6/1/67—8/12/67 (1 of 2) folder, LBJL. It is worth noting that the State Department's commitment to Thanh's inclusion in the election was entirely pragmatic: "We believe there are definite advantages . . . to allowing [the] Thanh candidacy to stand and to let him campaign freely on peace issues.

This would constitute important evidence to the world that the voters had a real choice in these elections, without entailing real risk of his winning."

112. For more on the 1967 election, see McAllister, "A Fiasco of Noble Proportions," 619–51; and Herman and Brodhead, *Demonstration Elections*. For analyses highly favorable to the Johnson administration's public position, see Penniman, *Elections in South Vietnam*; and Penniman, *Decision in South Vietnam*.

113. OAFIE, *A Pocket Guide to Vietnam*, DOD PG-21B, 16; on the embassy cable, see note 77.

114. *The Pentagon Papers*, I: 246.

115. OAFIE, *A Pocket Guide to Vietnam*, DOD PG-21B, 16.

116. *The Pentagon Papers*, I: 329.

117. OAFIE, *A Pocket Guide to Vietnam*, DOD PG-21B, 17; *The Pentagon Papers*, I: 341.

118. OAFIE, *A Pocket Guide to Vietnam*, DOD PG-21B, 19.

119. *The Pentagon Papers*, I: 243–44.

120. OAFIE, *A Pocket Guide to Vietnam*, DOD PG-21B, 12.

121. *The Pentagon Papers*, II: 22; OAFIE, *A Pocket Guide to Vietnam*, DOD PG-21B, 14.

122. OAFIE, *A Pocket Guide to Vietnam*, DOD PG-21B, 5–6.

123. Ibid., 4.

3. THE "HUE MASSACRE"

1. Florence and Storey, *Vietnam*, 6th ed., 319. The lists of names were also mentioned in Dodd and Lewis, *Vietnam*, 249.

2. Dunlop, *Fodor's Exploring Vietnam*, 1st ed., 114. Or, as described by the Moon and Footprint guidebooks, "VC and NVA forces went on a rampage" in an effort to "settle old scores." Buckley, *Vietnam, Cambodia and Laos Handbook*, 255; Colet and Eliot, *Vietnam Handbook*, 176. On the figure of "at least" 2,800 killed, see Népote and Guillaume, *Vietnam*, 134. On the estimate of 3,000 victims, see Buckley, *Vietnam, Cambodia and Laos Handbook*, 255; Colet and Eliot, *Vietnam Handbook*, 176; Dodd and Lewis, *Vietnam*, 249–50; Dunlop, *Fodor's Exploring Vietnam*, 1st ed., 114; and Florence and Storey, *Vietnam*, 6th ed., 319. On the figure of 14,000, see Lesser, *Vietnam*, 181. In addition to the above citation to Dunlop, stated or implied "North Vietnamese Army" responsibility for all or at least a share of the killing appeared in Buckley, *Vietnam, Cambodia, and Laos Handbook*, 255; Colet and Eliot, *Vietnam Handbook*, 176; and Dodd and Lewis, *Vietnam*, 249–50. The Lonely Planet guidebook simply attributed the executions to the "Communists"; see Florence and Storey, *Vietnam*, 6th ed., 319.

3. Dunlop, *Fodor's Exploring Vietnam*, 1st ed., 114.

4. Dodd and Lewis, *Vietnam*, 249; Florence and Storey, *Vietnam*, 6th ed., 319; Colet and Eliot, *Vietnam Handbook*, 176.

5. Buckley, *Vietnam, Cambodia, and Laos Handbook*, 255. *Fodor's Exploring Vietnam*

noted that the victims' "fate was either execution by firing squad, decapitation, or being buried alive." Dunlop, *Fodor's Exploring Vietnam*, 1st ed., 114. The Footprint guidebook also mentioned decapitation. Colet and Eliot, *Vietnam Handbook*, 176.

6. Florence and Storey, *Vietnam*, 6th ed., 319. The existence of the mass graves was also reported in Dodd and Lewis, *Vietnam*, 249–50.

7. Buckley, *Vietnam, Cambodia, and Laos Handbook*, 258.

8. Ibid., 255.

9. Porter, "The 1968 'Hue Massacre,'" 11.

10. Ibid., 2. The study was entered into the *Congressional Record* by Senator George McGovern in February 1975 in his stated hope that "each [m]ember of Congress will make the effort to look behind these hysterical misinterpretations of history, and to project the possibilities for the future on more rational grounds"; see *Congressional Record*, 94th Cong., 1st sess., 19 February 1975, 3515–19.

11. On the dispute over Turner's memory, see Greenberg, *Nat Turner*; and the documentary film *Nat Turner: A Troublesome Property* (2003).

12. Porter alleged that the "specific mission" of the Tenth Political Warfare Battalion was "to discredit the National Liberation Front without regard to the truth." Porter, "The 1968 'Hue Massacre,'" 2.

13. Pike, *The Viet-Cong Strategy of Terror*, 42. The portions of the document dealing specifically with Hue were also published in edited form as idem, *Massacre at Hue*. See also "Communist Political Executions at Hue in the 1968 Tet Offensive — A Documented Report," March 1968 [*sic*; the date is incorrect], folder 14, box 13, DPC: U5, VA, 8–9. In this last manuscript, the author — it is unclear whether it was Pike — ominously suggested to people in the RVN and "other countries" that the study could help "readers assess realistically the consequences of Communist authority." Pike's published study for the U.S. Mission was not his first public foray into the Hue Massacre. In November 1969, he traveled to Vietnam and spoke with a number of journalists about what he believed happened in the city. Porter, "The 1968 'Hue Massacre,'" 6.

14. Douglas Pike, "The Bitter Story of Hue," *Reader's Digest*, vol. 97 (September 1970): 105–109. On the mass circulation of *Reader's Digest*, see Sharp, *Condensing the Cold War*, xiv.

15. Hunt, "Images of the Viet Cong," 56. On concerns expressed about Pike's work during the period between the Tet Offensive and the publication of his 1970 monograph, see Minear, "Douglas Pike and the NLF," 44–47.

16. Douglas Pike to Patricia Way, 11 November 1988. I am grateful to Grover Furr of Montclair State University for furnishing me with a copy of this document.

17. On Porter and the Khmer Rouge, see Hildebrand and Porter, *Cambodia*; and Subcommittee on International Organizations of the Committee on International Relations, *Human Rights in Cambodia*, 34–53. By 1978, as the evidence for wide-

spread atrocities grew more compelling, Porter retreated from his initial skepticism and accepted Khmer Rouge responsibility for the horrific human-rights situation in Cambodia.

18. Hunt, "Images of the Viet Cong," 56. This is not to say that the conventional narrative itself has been rejected by nearly all scholars. But, as Hunt noted, those subscribing to it have generally cited the journalist Don Oberdorfer's *Tet!*, "a device that evades rather than resolves the problem of documentation," Hunt concluded, given that Oberdorfer's "treatment of the 'Hue Massacre' is just warmed over Pike." Hunt, "Images of the Viet Cong," 57. (A recent exception that cites both Pike and Porter is Willbanks, *The Tet Offensive*, 99–103.) Ngo Vinh Long's research on the Hue Massacre remains unpublished, but he discussed his findings in a 2002 radio interview with Daniel C. Tsang, an abridged transcript of which was published as Ngo Vinh Long, "Vietnam Today," 459–64. For the original radio program, see http://www.kuci.org/dtsang/subversity/Sv020702.ram (accessed 19 June 2007). Ngo Vinh Long also discussed his research with me in a private conversation at the 2004 annual meeting of the American Historical Association in Washington, D.C. Lending further support to the critique of the conventional narrative, Bui Tin, a veteran of the People's Army of Vietnam (PAVN) and well-known critic of the postwar government, offered a published account in 2002 that ascribed the atrocities to the chaos and hysteria of the revolutionaries' retreat from Hue. He wrote that Colonel Le Minh of the NLF estimated that two thousand people were killed, though Tin acknowledged uncertainty about the actual figure. Bui Tin, *From Enemy to Friend*, 66–68.

19. According to Marilyn Young, "All the accounts agree that NLF rather than North Vietnamese units were responsible for the executions." Young, *The Vietnam Wars*, 219. Or, as Pike concluded, "virtually all killings were done by local communists [*sic*] cadres and not by the PAVN troops or Northerners or other outside communists." Pike, *The Viet-Cong Strategy of Terror*, 32.

20. In a private communication in 1988, Pike acknowledged that "there are differences of interpretation as to the number," and that he "think[s] about 1,200 [were executed] but it could be less, for there are many [residents of Hue] who simply vanished." Pike to Way, 11 November 1988. On the figure of three hundred to four hundred executions, see Young, *The Vietnam Wars*, 217, who cited the contemporaneous research of Len Ackland. Young was presumably referring to the interviews reported in Porter and Ackland, "Vietnam," 1414–17. But elsewhere, citing an unpublished study, Ackland was reported to have learned from U.S. and Vietnamese officials that approximately seven hundred Vietnamese were killed by the insurgents, and that this figure was generally consistent with Ackland's own investigations into the matter. Chomsky and Herman, *The Washington Connection and Third World Fascism*, 346–47. (My own work in this study owes a considerable debt to Chomsky and Herman's important scholarship on the ideological frame-

work that gave the narrative of the Hue Massacre meaning.) More recently, Ngo Vinh Long concluded that 710 persons were executed in Hue. Ngo Vinh Long, "Vietnam Today," 464.

21. Pike, *The Viet-Cong Strategy of Terror*, 31. Another prominent proponent of the bloodbath theory, Stephen T. Hosmer, similarly concluded that the "savagery and indiscriminate nature of much of the repression in Hue seemed uncharacteristic of the Viet Cong's Security Service." Hosmer, *Viet Cong Repression and Its Implications for the Future*, 76.

22. Porter, "The 1968 'Hue Massacre,' " 10.

23. Ibid., 8–9.

24. Ngo Vinh Long, "Vietnam Today," 464.

25. Porter and Ackland, "Vietnam," 1415–16. In addition, Porter wrote in a letter to the *New York Times* in 1987 that "[m]any of [the executions] were apparently revenge killings by Buddhist activists and the former Hue police chief, who fled from the military suppression of the Buddhist struggle movement in 1966 and returned with Communist forces at Tet." Gareth Porter, "Little Evidence of 1968 Tet Massacre in Hue," letter, *New York Times*, 29 October 1987.

26. Storey and Robinson, *Vietnam*, 6th ed., 319. Images of mass graves — whether oral or visual — apparently hold considerable symbolic power in American consciousness. Perhaps this power derives from the oft-shown footage of Jewish victims of the Nazis buried in mass graves during World War Two. Whatever the source, it is an image that has been exploited by American policymakers and propagandists alike. For example, in his major November 1969 speech on the Vietnam war in which he discussed the Hue Massacre — the speech is addressed later in this chapter — Richard Nixon, at the last minute, added a reference to the mass graves in or near Hue. While the reference appeared in the version he read on the evening of 3 November, the allusion was absent from the official text distributed to the press earlier in the day; see Office of the White House Press Secretary, "Text of the Address by the President on Vietnam, Delivered to National Television and Radio Audiences from the White House, November 3, 1969 (Embargoed for Use until 9:30 p.m. EST)," 3 November 1969, NPMS, PPF, President's Speech File, 1969–74, box 52, November 3, 1969, Vietnam Speech (1 of 5) folder, NA.

27. The final production was actually more restrained — but in certain respects less critical — in its representation of the Hue Massacre than an earlier draft of the script. In the film, Joker, who is a correspondent for *Stars and Stripes*, and a photographer, Rafterman, are sent to central Vietnam to cover the ongoing combat between the United States and the Vietnamese revolutionaries. Joker's commanding officer does not mention any NLF atrocities in doling out the assignment. Much closer to the story by Gustav Hasford on which it was based, however, the January 1986 draft has Joker being given a task that is clearly identified as propa-

ganda: Captain January orders him to "make sleeping sounds here tonight and head up to Hue in the morning. We've had reports the vc have executed hundreds of civilians, maybe thousands. They've uncovered several mass graves. Walter Cronkite is due *here* tomorrow so *we'll* be busy. But your job is important, too. We need some good, clear photographs. And some hard-hitting captions. Get me photographs of indigenous civilian personnel who have been executed with their hands tied behind their backs, people buried alive, priests with their throats cut, dead babies — you know what I want. Then get me some good feature stuff on the fighting with good body counts. And remember: we're writing our own report cards in this country. Don't be afraid to give us a few A's." As for the victims, Captain January tells Joker, "Don't even photograph any naked bodies unless they're mutilated." Draft script, *Full Metal Jacket*, January 1986, Script Collection, MHL, 42–43. (The pagination of the draft script was not always precisely chronological or consistent given the apparent insertion of pages from earlier drafts; this scene, for example, covered three pages in the document but was numbered for only two.) By way of comparison, see Hasford, *The Short-Timers*, 51. In Hasford's novel, none of the bodies in the mass grave has hands tied behind their back, although the "green ghouls" had assured Joker that they had "seen such corpses elsewhere." Joker thus borrowed "some demolition wire from the Arvin [ARVN] snuffies and, crushing the stiff bodies with my knee until dry bones crack, I bind up a family, assembled at random from the multitude — a man, his wife, a little boy, a little girl, and, of course, their dog. As a final touch I wire the dog's feet together." Hasford, *The Short-Timers*, 107. These actions by Joker do not appear in Kubrick's final production. Also in the novel, when Joker is assigned by Captain January for duty as a rifleman and no longer as a journalist, Joker (as the narrator) relates, "I say good-bye to Chili Vendor and Daytona Dave and Mr. Payback and I tell them that I'm glad to be a grunt because now I won't have to write captions for atrocity photographs they file away or tell any more lies because there's nothing more the lifers can threaten me with. 'What are they going to do — send me to Viet Nam?' " Ibid., 119. When the film was released in 1987, at least one critic took Kubrick to task for being insufficiently critical of the revolutionaries' atrocities. "In one scene," wrote David Denby in *New York* magazine, "the corpses of executed citizens of Hue lie in neat rows, their lime-whitened bodies disturbingly beautiful. But the shock is hollow. The script barely registers that it was the North Vietnamese who executed the citizens; nor do the filmmakers link the deaths with any political force or idea. The sardonic and gruesome little bits add up to no more than an atmosphere of portentous disgust. Years after the war, Kubrick cultivates the awestruck mood of a stoned hippie exclaiming, 'Hea-*vy!*' " David Denby, "Death Trap," *New York* (13 July 1987), *Full Metal Jacket* clippings file, MHL, 55.

28. Porter, "The 1968 'Hue Massacre,' " 3–4. Vennema later wrote a book on the events in Hue that apparently differed considerably from his earlier firsthand

observations, which he had recorded in an unpublished manuscript. Vennema, *The Viet Cong Massacre at Hue*. For doubts about the reliability of the book, see Chomsky and Herman, *The Washington Connection and Third World Fascism*, 433, n. 193.

29. Porter, "The 1968 'Hue Massacre,' " 4–6, 8.

30. Griffiths, *Vietnam Inc.*, 137.

31. Robert Shaplen, "Letter from Saigon," *New Yorker* (23 March 1968): 122. U.S. officials requested that the State Department's Bureau of Intelligence and Research undertake a critique of Shaplen's article. The analysts concluded that his "perceptiveness and general objectivity" were "well reflected" in much of the piece, and while they did fault several of his conclusions, his comments on the destruction of Hue were not among them. Fred Greene to W. Averell Harriman, 12 March 1968, Papers of Lyndon Baines Johnson, President, 1963–69, NSF, CF — Vietnam, box 98, News Media Coverage of Vietnam, 7 D (2), 12/67–3/68 folder, LBJL.

32. Journalist Don Tate, quoted in Porter, "The 1968 'Hue Massacre,' " 8.

33. Chomsky and Herman, *The Washington Connection and Third World Fascism*, 351–52.

34. Young, *The Vietnam Wars*, 219.

35. Oriana Fallaci, "Working Up to Killing," *Washington Monthly*, vol. 3, no. 12 (February 1972): 40; Karnow, *Vietnam*, 544.

36. Porter and Ackland, "Vietnam," 1416. According to Edward Herman and Gareth Porter,

> Len Ackland and Don Oberdorfer have documented cases of individuals who were executed when they tried to hide or otherwise resisted the NLF in the early occupation. But these acts seem to have reflected individual decisions by NLF soldiers and cadres, rather than any policy decision to execute large numbers. According to residents of Hue, interviewed by Len Ackland in 1968, the number of executions early in the occupation was small. In the later phase, when the NLF was being forced out under military pressure, some officials and anti-Communist political leaders, earlier marked for 're-education,' were executed, but the numbers still appear to be a very small fraction of the propaganda claims. And there is no evidence in documents, graves, or from individual witnesses which suggests any large and indiscriminate slaughter of civilians by the NLF at Hue." Herman and Porter, "The Myth of the Hue Massacre," 10.

37. Schell, *The Military Half*, 198. Quang Ngai province was the site of the Son My (My Lai) massacre in March 1968.

38. Ibid., 391–92.

39. Michael D. Sallah and Mitch Weiss, "Rogue GIs Unleashed Wave of Terror in Central Highlands," *Blade* (Toledo, Ohio), 19 October 2003.

40. Turse, " 'Kill Anything That Moves.' " See also Nick Turse and Deborah Nelson, "Vietnam Horrors: Darker Yet," *Los Angeles Times*, 6 August 2006; Nick Turse, Deborah Nelson, and Janet Lundblad, "Verified Civilian Slayings," *Los Angeles Times*, 6 August 2006; Deborah Nelson and Nick Turse, "Lasting Pain, Minimal Punishment," *Los Angeles Times*, 20 August 2006; and Deborah Nelson and Nick Turse, "A Tortured Past," *Los Angeles Times*, 20 August 2006.

41. "Excerpt from the Official Text of Ngo Dinh Diem on 'The Policy of the Government of the Republic of Viet Nam with Regard to Former Resistance Members,' " in Pham Van Bach et al., *Fascist Terror in South Viet Nam*, 80.

42. Ibid., 80–81.

43. Florence and Storey, *Vietnam*, 6th ed., 384.

44. Kaufman, *Vietnam*, 159.

45. Interview no. 11, 4 June 2000, War Remnants Museum, Ho Chi Minh City.

46. Rousso, "Did the Purge Achieve Its Goals?" 100. "More than a quarter of these took place before the Allied invasion, half between 6 June 1944 and the Liberation, and only a fourth afterward, when the jurisdiction of a legal Purge went into effect. In other words, the major part of these executions was perpetrated while the war was still on and in a climate of disorder, civil war, and insurrection." Rousso, "Did the Purge Achieve Its Goals?" 100. For more on the executions and imprisonment of alleged collaborators in France, see Conan and Rousso, *Vichy*; Koreman, *The Expectation of Justice*; and Lottman, *The Purge*.

47. Rousso, "Did the Purge Achieve Its Goals?" 102. Executions made up only one element of the purge — there was also imprisonment, the denial of civil rights, dismissal from the civil service, or, for women accused of "horizontal collaboration," public humiliation such as being paraded naked through the streets — which one scholar referred to as "the mildest . . . in western Europe." Koreman, *The Expectation of Justice*, 102.

48. I examined Gray et al., *France*; Mindlin, *Let's Go: France*; and Fisher, *Fodor's France 2001*. It is worth noting that Daniel Robinson, the author of the first edition of the Lonely Planet guidebook for Vietnam, was also the co-author of the publisher's guidebook for France. For more on the European executions with specific reference to retribution in Vietnam, see Chomsky and Herman, *After the Cataclysm*, 38–39.

49. See, e.g., Gray et al., *France*, 359, 363, 369, 492, 722, 745, 759; Mindlin, *Let's Go: France*, 11, 126, 181, 229, 243, 464, 472, 492, 494, 496, 498, 502, 649; and Fisher, *Fodor's France 2001*, 231–32, 234–35, 652.

50. See, e.g., Dunlop, *Fodor's Exploring Vietnam*, 1st ed., 47; Florence and Storey, *Vietnam*, 6th ed., 342, 439; and Yang, *Let's Go*, 784. The Lonely Planet guidebook's use of the term was inconsistent. In some instances, "liberation" — or some derivation of the word — was placed in quotation marks; in others, it was not. Moreover, across time there had been changes to the same entries.

51. The first high-level American report on the executions I have seen is Walt W. Rostow to Lyndon B. Johnson, 24 February 1965 [*sic*; 1968]; Papers of Lyndon Baines Johnson, President, 1963–69, NSF, CF — Vietnam, box 70, General Military Activity, 2 C (7), 2/21–29/68 folder, LBJL. The memorandum contained an account by an unnamed embassy official "who was in Hue 16–17 February and who had previously served in and frequently visited Hue."

52. Walt W. Rostow to Lyndon B. Johnson, 25 February 1968, Papers of Lyndon Baines Johnson, President, 1963–69, NSF, CF — Vietnam, box 70, General Military Activity, 2 C (7), 2/21–29/68 folder, LBJL. It is unclear whether the statement was ever released. A top-secret cable on 27 February indicated that its issuance was approved, but one of the copies of the memorandum cited above contained a handwritten note which said that "as of 3/4/68 statement not made." Below the approval on the cable was another handwritten note: "send it to Bunker [indecipherable] & Thieu in message [indecipherable: rather?] [indecipherable] straight release." White House Situation Room (Wotring) to Lyndon B. Johnson, 27 February 1968, Papers of Lyndon Baines Johnson, President, 1963–69, NSF, CF — Vietnam, box 70, General Military Activity, 2 C (7), 2/21–29/68 folder, LBJL.

53. George Christian to Lyndon B. Johnson, 22 August 1967, Office Files of Fred Panzer, box 427, Viet-Nam Information Group folder, LBJL. I am indebted to John Wilson of the Lyndon Baines Johnson Library for locating and providing me with a copy of this document. On the attention of the Vietnam Information Group to the Hue executions, see Talking Notes no. 7, 29 February 1968; Talking Notes no. 8, 6 March 1968; Talking Notes no. 11, 19 March 1968; and Talking Notes no. 16, 30 April 1968, Papers of Lyndon Baines Johnson, President, 1963–69, NSF, CF — Vietnam, box 100; Public Relations Activities, 7 E (4)b, 2/68–4/68 folder, LBJL; Talking Notes no. 17, 6 May 1968, Papers of Lyndon Baines Johnson, President, 1963–69, NSF, CF — Vietnam, box 101, Public Relations Activities, 7 E (5), 5/68–6/68 folder, LBJL; and Talking Notes no. 25, 30 July 1968, Papers of Lyndon Baines Johnson, President, 1963–69, NSF, CF — Vietnam, box 101, Public Relations Activities, 7 E (6), 7/68–8/1968 folder, LBJL.

54. On William F. Buckley's use of the Hue Massacre to defuse moral indignation over the atrocities in Son My, see William F. Buckley Jr., "North Vietnam's Execution Warrant," 21 December 1969, folder 2, box 14, DPC: U5, VA.

55. Indeed, the U.S. ambassador to Indonesia, Francis J. Galbraith, placed those calling for an American withdrawal from Vietnam in the same moral universe as "those who are guilty of the atrocity at My Lai" in that both were "afflicted by the same inability to feel the plight of the people of South Vietnam." Francis J. Galbraith to Richard M. Nixon, 8 December 1969, NPMS, WHCF, Subject Files: Speeches (Ex), box 106, SP 3–56/Nationwide TV and Radio Address re: Vietnam at Wash. Hilton Hotel, November 3, 1969 (3 of 3) folder, NA. When Henry

Kissinger brought Galbraith's letter to Nixon's attention in a memorandum ex-
cerpting the correspondence of several U.S. ambassadors, Nixon wrote "excellent" in the margins next to the excerpted portion of Galbraith's letter. It was the
only ambassadorial correspondence for which he provided a written comment.
See Henry A. Kissinger to Richard M. Nixon, 21 January 1970, NPMS, WHCF,
Subject Files: Speeches (Ex), box 106, SP 3–56/Nationwide TV and Radio Address
re: Vietnam at Wash. Hilton Hotel, November 3, 1969 (3 of 3) folder, NA.

56. Subcommittee to Investigate the Administration of the Internal Security Act and
Other Internal Security Laws of the Committee on the Judiciary, *The Human Cost
of Communism in Vietnam*, 2. A number of Eastland's introductory comments to
the compendium were lifted verbatim — but without attribution or any acknowledgement of the source — from a manuscript prepared by the RVN diplomat Ta
Quoc Tuan. Others were slightly revised. For Ta Quoc Tuan's manuscript, see Ta
Quoc Tuan, "The Vietnamese Communist Terrorism," January 1970, folder 14,
box 13, DPC: U5, VA.

57. Subcommittee to Investigate the Administration of the Internal Security Act and
Other Internal Security Laws of the Committee on the Judiciary, *The Human Cost
of Communism in Vietnam*, 2–3. Excerpts from Hosmer's and Honey's studies were
reprinted in the document; their estimates appeared on pages 62–63 and 112,
respectively. Eastland's statement that "virtually every serious student of Vietnamese affairs" was in agreement about the bloodbath hypothesis was false. While
the word "virtually" admittedly lent the statement a certain degree of ambiguity,
many academic scholars of Vietnam and Asia had challenged, in the years preceding the senator's allegation, the likelihood of a massive bloodletting following an
American defeat. See, e.g., Committee of Concerned Asian Scholars, Cornell
University, "Twelve Questions on Vietnam," May 1970, folder 6, box 8, DPC:
U3-AA, VA.

58. For his part, Richard Nixon went back and forth over whether he should identify
the total as being in the "millions" or merely the "hundreds of thousands" in a
speech for which he was preparing in April 1972. The president, who was discussing the matter with Henry Kissinger, ultimately decided that it would be "better
to say" that only "hundreds of thousands" would be killed. Conversation no. 333–
21, Executive Office Building, 26 April 1972, Nixon White House Tapes, NPMS,
NA. Two and a half years earlier, Nixon had told Sir Robert Thompson, the British
counterinsurgency specialist, that "500,000 people in Vietnam would be massacred" following a revolutionary victory, according to a memorandum of conversation of the meeting. Memorandum of conversation, "The President's Remarks
to Sir Robert Thompson Concerning the Vietnam Situation," 17 October 1969,
NPMS; NSCF, Presidential/HAK MemCons, MemCon — The President, Sir Robert
Thompson et al., October 17, 1969 folder, NA.

59. Richard Nixon, "Address to the Nation on the War in Vietnam," 3 November

1969, no. 425, *Public Papers of the Presidents of the United States: Richard Nixon, 1969*, 902. Bill Safire had recommended to the president the addition of the following one-liner or theme: "With the atrocity of Hue clearly in mind, we want to 'stop the killing' in a way that allows nobody to start the killing." William Safire to Richard M. Nixon, 29 October 1969, NPMS, WHCF; Subject Files: Speeches (Ex), box 106, SP 3–56/Nationwide TV and Radio Address re: Vietnam at Wash. Hilton Hotel, November 3, 1969 (1 of 3) folder, NA. By the time Safire's memorandum was received, however, the sentiment had already made it into the president's speech; see draft of address, 28 October 1969, NPMS, PPF, President's Speech File, 1969–74, box 53, November 3, 1969, Vietnam Speech (3 of 5) folder, NA.

60. Typed note and attachment from Sven Kraemer to Alexander M. Haig, 1 November 1969, NPMS, NSCF, AMHSF, box 1008, Haig's Vietnam File — Volume 3, November–December 1969 (2 of 2) folder, NA.

61. See, e.g., Lieutenant-Colonel Sweitzer to Alexander M. Haig, 6 November 1969, NPMS, NSCF, AMHSF, box 1008, Haig's Vietnam File — Volume 3, November–December 1969 (1 of 2) folder, NA; and "Lora S." to Alexander M. Haig, 7 November 1969, NPMS, NSCF, AMHSF, box 1008, Haig's Vietnam File — Volume 3, November–December 1969 (1 of 2) folder, NA.

62. On the Nielsen figures, see Henry Rahmel to Herbert Klein, 20 November 1969, NPMS, WHCF, Subject Files: Speeches (Ex), box 106, SP 3–56/Nationwide TV and Radio Address re: Vietnam at Wash. Hilton Hotel, November 3, 1969 (3 of 3) folder, NA. On the hundreds of thousands of letters, telegrams, and postcards to the White House, see Herbert G. Klein to Pope Hill, 24 January 1970, NPMS, WHCF, Subject Files: Speeches (Gen), box 106, SP 3–56/Nationwide TV and Radio Address re: Vietnam at Wash. Hilton Hotel, November 3, 1969 (2 of 2) folder, NA. Klein added that in addition to the 400,000 individual correspondents, "hundreds of thousands of names were signed to petitions."

63. Tom McCall to Richard M. Nixon, 12 November 1969, and "Governor McCall's Statement on President Nixon's Vietnam Message," 3 November 1969, NPMS, WHCF, Subject Files: Speeches (Ex), box 107, SP 3–56/PRO, [11/4/69] — 11/13/69 folder, NA.

64. W. R. Smedberg III to Richard M. Nixon, 4 November 1969, NPMS, WHCF, Subject Files: Speeches (Ex), box 107, SP 3–56/PRO, [11/4/69] — 11/13/69 folder, NA.

65. "President on Solid Ground in Search for Vietnam Peace," editorial, *Orlando Sentinel*, 5 November 1969, NPMS, WHSC, Subject Files: Speeches (Ex), box 106, SP 3–56/Nationwide TV and Radio Address re: Vietnam at Wash. Hilton Hotel, November 3, 1969 (1 of 3) folder, NA. The sentiment echoed a statement by Clark Clifford, the former secretary of defense, that was brought to Nixon's attention

two weeks before the 3 November address: "If we pull out of South Vietnam there will be the most incredible blood bath since Hitler killed 6 million Jews." Patrick J. Buchanan to Richard M. Nixon, 20 October 1969, NPMS, WHSC, Subject Files: Speeches (Ex), box 106, SP 3–56/Nationwide TV and Radio Address re: Vietnam at Wash. Hilton Hotel, November 3, 1969 (1 of 3) folder, NA. In October 1972, Nixon went even further, claiming in a conversation with his national-security staff that the slaughter following a U.S. withdrawal and "Communist takeover" would be "worse than anything we've seen in this century." Conversation no. 377–7, Executive Office Building, 29 October 1972, Nixon White House Tapes, NPMS, NA.

66. Thomas J. Burke et al. to Richard M. Nixon, 26 November 1969, NPMS, WHSC, Subject Files: Speeches (Gen), box 113, SP 3–56/Con, 11/669–2/16/70 folder, NA.

67. George McT. Kahin, "History and the Bloodbath Theory in Vietnam," op-ed, *New York Times*, 6 December 1969. On the concern in the White House that some of the figures cited by Nixon in the speech might have been a "problem," see the sources identified in note 61. For Kahin's book, which was released in a revised edition in 1969, see Kahin and Lewis, *The United States in Vietnam*.

68. The reference to a "Roman circus" was Bryce Harlow's; see Bryce N. Harlow to Richard M. Nixon, 3 December 1969, NPMS, NSCF, AMHSF, box 1004, My Lai Incident (2 of 2) folder, NA.

69. Henry A. Kissinger to Richard M. Nixon, 4 December 1969, NPMS, NSCF, AMHSF, box 1004, My Lai Incident (2 of 2) folder, NA. This suggestion actually originated with Henry Kissinger's deputy, Alexander M. Haig, who proposed to Kissinger that the White House perhaps do "what we can unofficially to contribute to the backlash"; see Alexander M. Haig to Henry A. Kissinger, 4 December 1969, NPMS, NSCF, AMHSF, box 1004, My Lai Incident (2 of 2), NA.

70. Henry A. Kissinger to Richard M. Nixon with attachment ("Communist Terror Tactics in South Vietnam"), 4 December 1969, NPMS, NSCF, AMHSF, box 1004, My Lai Incident (2 of 2) folder, NA.

71. Patrick J. Buchanan to Henry A. Kissinger with "Questions and Answers" for Richard M. Nixon, 5 December 1969, NPMS, NSCF, AMHSF, box 1004, My Lai Incident (1 of 2) folder, NA. See also "Questions on My Lai," n.d., NPMS, NSCF, AMHSF, box 1004, My Lai Incident (1 of 2) folder, NA.

72. Richard Nixon, "The President's News Conference of December 8, 1969," no. 481, *Public Papers of the Presidents of the United States: Richard Nixon, 1969*, 1003–1004.

73. Richard Homan, "Pentagon Briefs Lawmakers on Hue Massacre," *Washington Post*, 9 December 1969. Perhaps tellingly, and to the apparent disappointment of some lawmakers, the Defense Department's thirty-minute slide presentation only

contained two photographs of the Hue victims. "Don't you have any more photos of atrocities in Hue?" Ichord asked Lieutenant Colonel Arno L. Ponder. "I'm quite surprised you have so few." Ibid.

74. Patrick J. Buchanan to Richard M. Nixon, 25 August 1970, NPMS, NSCF, Name Files, box 809, Buchanan, Patrick J. folder, NA. Nixon's response was handwritten on the document.

75. *Congressional Record*, 91st Cong., 1st sess., 21 April 1969, 9826. Several weeks later Rarick revisited the atrocities in Hue; see ibid., 7 May 1969, 11666–67.

76. Ibid., 29 September 1969, 27549.

77. Ibid., 10 December 1969, 38223.

78. Hammond, *Public Affairs: The Military and the Media, 1968–1973*, 225, 232. Hammond, in his two-volume official history for the U.S. Army, did not acknowledge the critiques of the Hue Massacre, claiming instead that "enemy forces within the city began systematically to execute province officials, policemen, technicians, student leaders, and anyone else who might pose a threat to Communist aims, in the end consigning more than 4,000 persons to mass graves in and around the city." Idem, *Public Affairs: The Military and the Media, 1962–1968*, 359. See also idem, *Reporting Vietnam*, 117–18, 191.

79. Video Recording no. 342-USAF-48733, "Viet Cong Massacre in Hue, Vietnam, 1968," RG 342, NA.

80. Ta Quoc Tuan, "The Vietnamese Communist Terrorism," 1, 8, 11. Douglas Pike's study of the Hue Massacre was approvingly quoted; see ibid., 2.

81. "In Memory of Hue, Tet 1968," *Viet-Nam Bulletin*, Viet-Nam Info Series no. 28 (Washington, D.C.: Embassy of Viet-Nam, April 1970): 2, 4, 7, 10. For the original table compiled by Pike, see *The Viet-Cong Strategy of Terror*, 30–31.

82. American Friends of Vietnam, "Communist Terrorism in Vietnam," 1969, folder 1, box 14, DPC: U5, VA. The reprinted publication is Untitled (New Delhi: India Vietnam Humanitarian League, 1969).

83. National Student Committee for Victory in Vietnam, "The Massacre at Hue," March 1970. The pamphlet is available on microform through the New York Public Library.

84. American Youth for a *Just* Peace, Proposal for the Convening of a National Student Conference on Vietnam and World Freedom, 1970, folder 6, box 8, DPC: U3-AA, VA. The other two issues were the "POW issue" and the "North Vietnamese invasion of Laos and Cambodia." It was later disclosed by Allen Tate Wood, co-chair of American Youth for a *Just* Peace, that his group was essentially an appendage of the Unification Church of the Reverend Sun Myung Moon. See Allen Tate Wood, "My Four and One Half Years with the Lord of the Flies," http://www.freedomofmind.com/resourcecenter/groups/m/moonies/moonflies.htm (accessed 29 August 2004).

85. Porter and Ackland, "Vietnam," 1414–17.

86. Ibid., 1415.

87. Excerpts were also reprinted in other publications. See, e.g., "Would U.S. Withdrawal Really Mean a Bloodbath?" *Minneapolis Tribune*, 23 November 1969.

88. Tran Van Dinh, "Fear of a Bloodbath," *New Republic* (6 December 1969): 12–13. Tran Van Dinh wrote again of his brother and nephew being killed by "direct U.S. bomb hits" in a 1989 article on the city of Hue in *National Geographic*. In the same piece, he inexplicably noted, without qualification, "U.S. estimates" that "2,800 civilians were executed by Viet Cong firing squads and were buried in mass graves," including several of his relatives and friends. "My questions about this terrible event were answered with saddened silence in Hue," he continued, "although Nguyen Van Dieu, the director of foreign affairs of the Binh Tri Thien People's Committee, gave me a commemorative history of the battle in which Le Minh, the commander of the communist forces attacking Hue, admitted that his troops had committed atrocities. 'We were unable to control brutal actions by individual soldiers,' Le Minh wrote. 'The leaders, including myself, must bear the responsibility.'" Tran Van Dinh, "Hue: My City, Myself," *National Geographic*, vol. 176, no. 5 (November 1989): 600.

89. Tom Wicker, "Mr. Nixon's Scary Dreams," *New York Times*, 12 May 1970. The *Times* also published, in its Sunday magazine in October 1972, a forum on the bloodbath theory that specifically drew on the Hue atrocities. See John S. Carroll, "The Past Warns That a Great Many Innocent People Will Be Executed," *New York Times Sunday Magazine* (15 October 1972): 38, 40–46; and Richard Barnet, "Bloodbath? That's What We Are Causing Now," *New York Times Sunday Magazine* (15 October 1972): 39, 48–56. Also important to the debate was the response by Gareth Porter, as well as the reply by John Carroll that followed Porter's letter; see D. Gareth Porter, "Bloodbaths, or Allegations?" *New York Times Sunday Magazine* (26 November 1972): 29, 112–13. Giving further attention to the matter, also in October 1972 the *Times* ran opposing pieces (yet under the same headline) by Porter and Robert F. Turner on the bloodbath hypothesis; see Robert F. Turner and D. Gareth Porter, "Bloodbaths in Vietnam: The Reality and the Myth," op-eds, *New York Times*, 24 October 1972.

90. William F. Ward to the editor, *New York Times*, 14 May 1970, folder 3, box 11, DPC: OM-AFV, VA. For Wicker's response, see Tom Wicker to William F. Ward, n.d., folder 3, box 11, DPC: OM-AFV, VA.

91. *Congressional Record*, 91st Cong., 2d sess., 21 May 1970, 16502–503, 16508. In fact, George McT. Kahin, with whom Porter worked closely at Cornell University, had referred to the executions as transpiring in "heat-of-battle conditions" in his December 1969 commentary in the *New York Times*. See Kahin, "History and the Bloodbath Theory in Vietnam."

92. *Congressional Record*, 21 May 1970, 16503.

93. Anita Lauve Nutt, "On the Question of Communist Reprisals in Vietnam," in

Subcommittee to Investigate the Administration of the Internal Security Act and Other Internal Security Laws, *The Human Cost of Communism in Vietnam*, 34–44.

94. Subcommittee to Investigate the Administration of the Internal Security Act and Other Internal Security Laws, *The Human Cost of Communism in Vietnam*, 83–99.

95. Subcommittee to Investigate Problems Connected with Refugees and Escapees of the Committee on the Judiciary, *Problems of War Victims in Indochina, Part III*, 48–49.

96. *Congressional Record*, 92nd Cong., 2d sess., 3 May 1972, 15580.

97. Porter had written, with George McT. Kahin, a broader but, with respect to the Hue Massacre, less developed rebuttal of the "bloodbath argument" in 1970; see George McT. Kahin and D. Gareth Porter, "The Administration's Bloodbath Argument," July 1970, folder 9, box 13, DPC: U8, VA.

98. D. Gareth Porter, "Hue 1968: A Study in USIA/Saigon Political Warfare," April 1973, folder 13, box 13, DPC: U5, VA. Porter's critique was a draft of his study ultimately published in 1974 in the *Indochina Chronicle*; see Porter, "The 1968 'Hue Massacre.'"

99. Chomsky and Herman, *Counter-Revolutionary Violence*, 27–29. For earlier attention by Herman to the Hue Massacre, see Herman, *Atrocities in Vietnam*, 38–39.

100. William Sarnoff, quoted in Bagdikian, *The Media Monopoly*, 33–34. Sarnoff told Ben Bagdikian that this account of what had transpired, which drew on the testimony of Claude McCaleb, publisher of Warner Modular, did not coincide with his own, but he refused to elaborate. See ibid., 34. On the suppression of *Counter-Revolutionary Violence*, see ibid., 32–35; and Barsky, *Noam Chomsky*, 160–62. Several years later, Chomsky and Herman's work on the Hue Massacre was published, in revised and expanded form, in Chomsky and Herman, *The Washington Connection and Third World Fascism*, 345–54. For their prefatory note on *Counter-Revolutionary Violence*, see ibid., xiv–xvii.

101. "How Hanoi Will Treat Its Enemies: Interview with Douglas Pike," *U.S. News and World Report* (21 April 1975): 20.

102. *Congressional Record*, 94th Cong., 1st sess., 6 May 1975, 13097; see also Ashbrook's claims about the atrocities at 13098. Ashbrook again took to the floor to criticize the press a week later. *Congressional Record*, 94th Cong., 1st sess., 14 May 1975, 14393.

103. *Congressional Record*, 100th Cong., 2d sess., 1 August 1988, 19685.

104. *Congressional Record*, 101st Cong., 2d sess., 21 March 1990, 4948–49; ibid., 28 March 1990, 5566–67. Representative Don Ritter, who was responsible for Toan Truong's commentary being placed into the *Congressional Record* on 21 March, years earlier did the same with an interview of the author and Army veteran Al Santoli that, like the piece in the *New York Times*, similarly addressed the Hue Massacre. "The North Vietnamese and Viet Cong attacked civilian populations," Santoli told the *Washington Times*. "They massacred more than 3,000

people at Hue — buried people alive. This is something Hitler would have done and they became viewed as agrarian-reform liberators." ibid., 99th Cong., 1st sess., 8 May 1985, 11198.

105. Reed Irvine, "How the Media Helped Defeat Us," *AIM Report*, April 1975, http://www.aim.org/publications/aim_report/1975/75_04-4.html (accessed 27 February 2004). Irvine erred in referring to My Lai as a "village." In fact, it was one of several hamlets that make up the village of Son My. On Irvine elsewhere citing the Hue Massacre as illustrative of media bias, see idem, "Savaging El Salvador," *AIM Report*, February 1982, http://www.aim.org/publications/aim_report/1982/02b.html (accessed 27 February 2004); idem, "Hue Massacre of 1968 Goes Beyond Hearsay," letter, *New York Times*, 22 September 1987; and Stephen Goode, "Irvine Fights War of Words to Correct Media's First Draft," *Insight on the News* (17 March 1997), http://www.insightmag.com/news/1997/03/17/Pictur eProfile/Irvine.Fights.War.Of.Words.To.Correct.Medias.First.Draft-214542 .shtml (accessed 27 February 2004). The Accuracy in Media documentary is *Television's Vietnam: The Impact of Media* (1985). The Hue Massacre was also featured, although without oral commentary on the subject, in *Television's Vietnam: The Real Story* (1984). For the PBS treatment of the atrocities, see episode 6 ("Tet 1968") of *Vietnam: A Television History* (2004).

106. Clifford, "Forgotten Massacre at Hue," 28; see also the letters in response to Clifford's article in *Vietnam*, vol. 15, no. 3 (October 2002): 8, 63. Clifford briefly articulated a similar position in "Missed in My Lai," letter, *San Francisco Chronicle*, 23 March 2003.

107. Gerard Jackson, "Hue: The Massacre the Left Wants Us to Forget," *New Australian*, vol. 66 (16–22 February 1998), http://pandora.nla.gov.au/pan/10189/ 20021026/www.newaus.com.au/news29b.html (accessed 28 February 2004). For another example of Jackson's fulminations on the issue, in which he accused journalists and "the left" of "immorality, hypocrisy, blind political bigotry, and [a] capacity for hatred" for "swill[ing] the embarrassment of the Hue massacre down their collective memory hole," see Gerard Jackson, "The Media, Abu Ghraib, and the Forgotten Massacres," *BrookesNews*.com (24 May 2004), http://www.newaus .com.au/042305_Abu_Ghraib.html (accessed 23 September 2004).

108. Cawley, "The War About the War," 79.

109. Mackubin Thomas Owens, "Vetting the Vet Record," *National Review Online* (27 January 2004), http://www.nationalreview.com/script/printpage.asp?ref=/ owens/owens200401270825.asp (accessed 12 March 2004).

110. Greg Lewis, "A Quarter Century of Disinformation," *Washington Dispatch* (2 March 2004), http://www.washingtondispatch.com/article_8268.shtml (accessed 29 August 2004). For the nationally syndicated radio host Hugh Hewitt's criticism of Kerry for ignoring the atrocities in Hue, see Hugh Hewitt, "The

Kerry Files, Volume II," *Daily Standard* (19 February 2004), http://www.weekly standard.com/Content/Public/Articles/000/000/003/751gbmvt.asp (accessed 29 August 2004).

111. Phong Trao Giao Dan Viet Nam Hai Ngoai, *Tham Sat Mau Than o Hue*, xi.

112. Frankum and Maxner, *The Vietnam War for Dummies*, 122. For an online adaptation, see "Escalating the Vietnam War: The Tet Offensives of 1968," http://www.dummies.com/WileyCDA/DummiesArticle/id-1657.html (accessed 27 February 2004).

113. Phong Trao Giao Dan Viet Nam Hai Ngoai, *Tham Sat Mau Than o Hue*, xii.

114. Le Huu Dan, *Tuyen Tap Su That*, 7. The author's charge about Buddhist monks not being killed under the Pol Pot regime must be understood in light of the fact that Buddhism was constitutionally outlawed in Democratic Kampuchea. Thus, in formal terms, there were no Buddhist monks during most of the reign of the Khmer Rouge. Kiernan, *The Pol Pot Regime*, 55–59, 446. That said, after assuming power in 1975 the Pol Pot government, according to eyewitnesses, massacred and persecuted monks and former monks. See, e.g., Chanthou Boua, "Genocide of a Religious Group," 227–40; and Kiernan, "The Cambodian Genocide—1975–1979," 344–45.

115. Free Vietnam Alliance, "1968 Tet Offensive Commemoration," http://www.fva .org/0498/news3.htm (accessed 27 February 2004).

116. Vietnamese Canadian Federation, "Edmonton: Commemorative Service for Victims of the 1968 Hue Massacre," *Bulletin*, vol. 14, no. 1 (1998), http://ww.viet federation.ca/newsletters/BLT98A.html (accessed 27 February 2004).

117. For Ngo The Linh's site, see http://ngothelinh.topcities.com/Hue.html (accessed 27 February 2004). The figure of "7,600 civilians murdered" was presumably a misreading of Douglas Pike's total estimate for the number of civilians executed, wounded, missing, and inadvertently killed "due to accident of battle" in Hue. See Pike, *The Viet-Cong Strategy of Terror*, 30–31.

118. Memorandum from Mimi Nguyen, 17 October 2003. I am grateful to Mimi Nguyen for providing me with a copy of this document. The name of the exhibition was ultimately changed to "What's Going On? California and the Era of Vietnam." For press coverage of the affair, see Pueng Vongs, "Vietnamese Slighted in Vietnam War Exhibit," *CaliToday* (4 November 2003), http://news.ncmonlineA1.com/news/ view_article.html?article_id=5cd7175cb57b97fb83228d2c2b286a1a (accessed 27 February 2004); Joyce Nishioka, "Inclusive or Exclusive?" *AsianWeek* (21 November 2003), http://news.asianweek.com/news/view_article.html?arti cle_id= a5d28dfof1f884b0bd046c14f1adbfc2 (accessed 3 March 2004); Vanessa Hua, "Oakland Museum Show Stirs Trouble," *San Francisco Chronicle*, 19 December 2003; and Carol Pogash, "In Imperfect Compromise, Exhibit Tells of Vietnam Era," *New York Times*, 7 September 2004. The exhibition and the case of Mimi Nguyen are also

treated in Dao, "What's Going On with the Oakland Museum's 'California and the Vietnam Era' Exhibit?"

119. On the museum's response to the protest over Nguyen's dismissal, see Nishioka, "Inclusive or Exclusive?"; Hua, "Oakland Museum Show Stirs Trouble"; and Pogash, "In Imperfect Compromise, Exhibit Tells of Vietnam Era."

120. For the text of the petition and a link to the signatures and comments, including those of Que H. Le (no. 101) and Lien Ton That (no. 200) discussing the Hue Massacre, see http://www.petitiononline.com/111403/petition.html (accessed 13 March 2004).

121. MacCannell, *The Tourist*, 137–38.

122. In referring to an "official" historical narrative, I do not mean to imply that there is a single Vietnamese perspective of the American war; there is not. Rather, I am referring to the dominant narrative of the conflict that has appeared in the discourses of most museum exhibits and at many war sites and memorials throughout the country.

123. Evan Thomas with Ron Moreau and Andrew Mandel, "The Last Days of Saigon," *Newsweek* (1 May 2000): 36.

124. Dunlop, *Fodor's Exploring Vietnam*, 1st ed., 114.

125. Lesser, *Vietnam*, 181. The origins of the claim that "14,000 people [were] massacred" is uncertain.

126. Florence and Storey, *Vietnam*, 5th ed., 462. Interestingly, these words, which first appeared in the third edition of the Lonely Planet guidebook, were removed from the sixth edition. Storey and Robinson, *Vietnam*, 3d ed., 199; idem, *Vietnam*, 4th ed., 201; Florence and Storey, *Vietnam*, 6th ed., 456–57.

127. Kennedy and Williams, "The Past Without the Pain," 138.

128. Similar to my findings in Vietnam, Andrew McGregor found Western "travelers" — as opposed to "tourists" — "particularly loyal" to the Lonely Planet series during his interviews with foreigners in Tana Toraja, Indonesia. McGregor, "Dynamic Texts and Tourist Gaze," 35. On the distinction between "travelers" and "tourists," see ibid., 31–32.

129. Kennedy and Williams, "The Past Without the Pain," 151.

130. While not empirically addressing the issue of tourists' reception of the texts, and thus their mediation of tourists' experiences, an interesting analysis of discourses in guidebooks to twentieth-century Saigon is Chi, "Necessary Fictions." On representations of the American war in more recent Vietnam guidebooks, see Laderman, "Shaping Memory of the Past."

131. Cohen, "The Tourist Guide." Cohen identified the "four principal elements" of the communicative component of the guide's role as selection, information, interpretation, and fabrication. Ibid., 14–16.

132. Bhattacharyya, "Mediating India," 375–76, 378, 381.

133. Of the 94 tourists I interviewed throughout Vietnam in June 2000, 74 percent were using a guidebook published by Lonely Planet; of the total number of people using a guidebook — 10 of the 94 people I spoke with were not — 83 percent had one from the Lonely Planet series. (These could have been the publisher's volume for either Vietnam, Southeast Asia, Hanoi, or Ho Chi Minh City. There have also appeared separate Lonely Planet volumes for cyclists and food connoisseurs.) In 2002, an even greater percentage (83, or 66 out of 80 interviewees) were actively using, or had read before visiting Vietnam, a guidebook published by Lonely Planet. I must caution, however, that these findings should not be construed as scientific, although I suspect they are reasonably accurate (or perhaps even too conservative) for independent Western travelers. I cannot claim to have interviewed a representative sample of Western tourists, if such was even possible, although I did make an effort to speak with as wide of a cross-section of individuals as possible. One notable exception, which almost certainly would have altered the above percentages, was my inability to interview large numbers of package tourists; their fixed, tight schedules made interviews logistically almost impossible, so with only a few exceptions they were not included in these findings.

134. Interview of Robert Storey, 30 May 2000, Jiafeng, Taiwan. It is worth noting that the director of the IRC was the Cornell University historian David Marr, a U.S. Marine Corps intelligence officer from 1959 to 1964 and an individual who is today acclaimed as one of the leading Western scholars of twentieth-century Vietnam.

135. Novick, *That Noble Dream*.

136. Lembcke, *The Spitting Image*, 184.

137. Holguín, " 'National Spain Invites You,' " 1418.

138. Herman and Porter, "The Myth of the Hue Massacre," 12. The point was illustrated in 1972 in a column by Raymond Cromley; referring to the "citizens of Hue [who] remember the Communists with hatred to this day," Cromley conceded that "although the Saigon government perhaps would win no popularity contests in Hue, the Communists are disliked and feared far more." Ray Cromley, "Murder Backfires on Reds," 24 August 1972, folder 12, box 14, DPC: U5, VA.

139. Colet and Eliot, *Vietnam Handbook*, 176.

140. Herman and Porter, "The Myth of the Hue Massacre," 12.

141. Instances of the Hue Massacre being cited as evidence of exceptional Communist brutality have been legion. For two recent examples, see James Webb, "History Proves Vietnam Victors Wrong," *Wall Street Journal*, 28 April 2000; and Mike Philipps, "Museum Reminder that War Is Dirty Business," *Cincinnati Post*, 24 April 2000, http://www.cincypost.com/news/2000/view042400.html (accessed 29 August 2004). See also William Branigin, "Village of My Lai Now a Memorial," *Washington Post*, 21 April 1985; Barbara Crossette, "Where Tet Meant Death, Life Goes On," *New York Times*, 26 August 1987; and the responses to Crossette's

article by Reed Irvine and Gareth Porter (Irvine, "Hue Massacre of 1968 Goes Beyond Hearsay"; Porter, "Little Evidence of 1968 Tet Massacre in Hue").

142. Colet and Eliot, *Vietnam Handbook*, 176.

143. Hunt, "Images of the Viet Cong," 55. Pike's original reference, which he claimed not to be interested in producing as a "word picture," was to "Vietnamese communists as fiendish fanatics with blood dripping from their hands" — thus Hunt's placement of "fiends" in quotation marks. Pike, *The Viet-Cong Strategy of Terror*, 3.

144. One former tour guide from Hue that I interviewed, who spent approximately two years as an English-speaking guide in central Vietnam, estimated that perhaps "2 out of 10" tourists with whom she worked would ask her about the Hue Massacre. The guide requested that her identity remain confidential.

145. There have been numerous studies of the war's treatment in American textbooks. For a recent analysis of high-school history texts, see Loewen, "The Vietnam War in High School American History," 150–72. A more recent examination of surveys of the war than David Hunt's previously cited analysis is Hunt, "War Crimes and the Vietnamese People," 173–200. The literature on the war's representation in American culture is too vast to identify here. For a small sampling of these works, see Franklin, *Vietnam and Other American Fantasies*; Beattie, *The Scar That Binds*; Rowe and Berg, *The Vietnam War and American Culture*; and Jeffords, *The Remasculinization of America*.

146. Williams, *Problems in Materialism and Culture*, 38–39.

147. Franklin, *Vietnam and Other American Fantasies*, 3.

4. THE NEW MODERNIZERS

1. Florence and Storey, *Vietnam*, 5th ed., 185. The use of "color," as well as light and darkness, as a symbol of Vietnam's capitalist transformation extends beyond travel guidebooks. See, for example, Crossette, *The Great Hill Stations of Asia*, 207–208. I am grateful to Chuong-Dai Vo for bringing Crossette's book to my attention.

2. Florence and Storey, *Vietnam*, 5th ed., 184. By way of contrast, the authors did not characterize as exemplary, nor did they even acknowledge, the country's "marginalized urban working class" toiling in locally owned private enterprises whose standards were "even more deplorable" than those of state firms. Kolko, "China and Vietnam on the Road to the Market," 438. See also idem, *Vietnam*, and "Vietnam since 1975." The latter appeared as a postscript in idem, *Anatomy of a War*.

3. Florence and Storey, *Vietnam*, 5th ed., 184.

4. Ibid., 185.

5. Rutherford, *Vietnam*, 16.

6. Lesser, *Vietnam*, v, 16.

7. Dunlop, *Fodor's Exploring Vietnam*, 1st ed., 8.

8. For statistical information about visitor arrivals in Vietnam, see the website of the Vietnam National Administration of Tourism at http://www.vietnamtourism .com. On possible problems associated with the figures, see Biles et al., " 'Tiger on a Bicycle,' " 14.

9. Interview no. 9, 31 January 2002, Hoa Lo Prison, Hanoi.

10. Klein, *Cold War Orientalism*; McAlister, *Epic Encounters*.

11. Tai, *The Country of Memory*.

12. Florence and Storey, *Vietnam*, 5th ed., 43–44. Contrary to Lonely Planet's assertion, Gabriel Kolko claimed of postwar Vietnam, "Whatever the rhetoric, there was far more pragmatism than ideology guiding the economy, and many sections of the nation pursued their own, often quite different, economic strategies." Kolko, *Vietnam*, 25.

13. Among the works that have contributed to my understanding of modernization theory and international history are Latham, *Modernization as Ideology*; Nashel, "The Road to Vietnam," 132–54; and Engerman et al., *Staging Growth*.

14. Lichtenstein, "Market Triumphalism and the Wishful Liberals," 103.

15. As one instance of crediting capitalism with much of Vietnam's presumed resuscitation, the Lonely Planet guidebook stated, "Vietnam might well have collapsed had it not been for Soviet aid and recent capitalist-style reforms," the latter replacing the "party's unpopular ideology, including collectivization and centralized planning." Florence and Storey, *Vietnam*, 5th ed., 44. The sentiment parroted the conventional wisdom, which held that capitalist policies in combination with Vietnam's "entrepreneurial spirit" were responsible for much of its economic growth under *doi moi*. For a reference to the country's "entrepreneurial spirit," see Dunlop, *Fodor's Exploring Vietnam*, 1st ed., 13.

16. Yang, *Let's Go*, 722, 777. The line about "suffering impatiently through 10 years of high socialism" appeared in the guidebook as a specific reference to Ho Chi Minh City.

17. In charting and analyzing the twenty-first century guidebooks' embrace of Vietnam's postwar capitalist turn, which is the objective of this chapter, it is important to be clear about what I am not arguing. I am not suggesting that Vietnam prior to *doi moi* was a socialist paradise in which meaningful economic reforms were unnecessary. By all accounts it was an impoverished, devastated, and often inefficiently managed state, and most Vietnamese and international analysts agree that reforms of various sorts were imperative. Neither am I asserting that the Vietnamese leadership was composed of fully competent planners ably directing the economy, rendering substantial change unwarranted. There are, most would concur, ample grounds on which to criticize leading government and party officials.

18. Florence and Storey, *Vietnam*, 5th ed., 44.

19. Ebashi, "The Economic Take-off," 38. See also Luong, "Postwar Vietnamese Society," 9.

20. Florence and Storey, *Vietnam*, 5th ed., 44; Kolko, *Vietnam*, 44; Vu Tuan Anh, "Economic Policy Reforms," 28. Kolko's finding about growth in 1985 seems inconsistent with the data recorded by Ebashi; see Ebashi, "The Economic Take-off," 39.

21. Buckley, *Moon Handbooks*, 74.

22. Kolko, *Vietnam*, 27. See also Ebashi, "The Economic Take-off," 38–39.

23. Buckley, *Moon Handbooks*, 74.

24. Ibid., 77.

25. It should be noted that the guidebook made no mention of the fact that the leverage held by the IMF as a result of Vietnam's foreign debt allowed the institution to exercise "central influence" over the country's economic reforms since at least the 1980s. Kolko, *Vietnam*, 33. Given the increasing attention by critics of corporate globalization to the IMF and the imposition of capitalist policies, such a disclosure would have seemed relevant.

26. Kolko, *Vietnam*, 44.

27. Babson, quoted in Pilger, *Hidden Agendas*, 329.

28. This argument was posited in Kolko, *Vietnam*, 22–23.

29. Ibid., 24–25. As a number of scholars have noted, inattention to historical or political context in describing economic development issues is common among modernization theorists. For an important analysis of this phenomenon, see Cullather, "Development?"

30. Florence and Storey, *Vietnam*, 5th ed., 42–44.

31. Ibid., 44.

32. Lonely Planet's implied view of the wartime southern economy largely corresponded to what Christian Appy and Alexander Bloom designated the "myth of economic modernization." Appy and Bloom, "Vietnam War Mythology and the Rise of Public Cynicism," 57–58.

33. The section in the guidebook's historical synopsis dealing with Vietnam "since reunification" was better, as it acknowledged "the legacy of a cruel and protracted war that had literally fractured the country; there were high levels of understandable bitterness (if not hatred) on both sides, and a mind-boggling array of problems. War damage extended from the unmarked minefields to war-focused, dysfunctional economies, from vast acreages of chemically poisoned countryside to millions of people who had been affected physically or mentally. The country was diplomatically isolated and its old allies were no longer willing or able to provide significant aid. Peace may have arrived, but in many ways the war was far from over." Florence and Storey, *Vietnam*, 5th ed., 33.

34. Kolko, *Vietnam*, 24. The phenomenon is not unique to economic history. A number of former southern insurgents have complained since 1975 about the manner in which their contribution to the war effort has been minimized by officials in

Hanoi seeking to bolster the party's legitimacy. See, e.g., Ngo Vinh Long, "The Tet Offensive and Its Aftermath," 89–123; and Brigham, "Why the South Won the American War in Vietnam," 97–116.

35. Martini, "(When) Did the Vietnam War End?" See also Martini's important study, *Invisible Enemies*.

36. Parkes, *Southeast Asia Handbook*, 947. While also implicitly embracing the capitalist reforms, the Indochina guidebook of the same publisher did a much fairer job in articulating the conflict's repercussions for postwar Vietnam; see Buckley, *Moon Handbooks*, 68–69. Unfortunately, however, the information appeared only in the guidebook's "History" section. Its omission from the "Economy" section may have divorced it in the minds of many Western tourists from the country's postwar economic dilemmas.

37. Yang, *Let's Go*, 731. The authors erroneously suggested that the capitalist reforms began following the Eighth Party Congress in 1996. Actually, they were instituted at least ten years earlier. The miscalculation carried the potential to mislead tourists in, for instance, Ho Chi Minh City, who may have mistakenly ascribed economic responsibility for the "beggars, thieves, and prostitutes" that the guidebook noted are abundant in the metropolis to its "suffering" under "high socialism," not the leadership's embrace of capitalism. Ibid., 777.

38. Frank, *One Market Under God*, ix.

39. Buckley, *Moon Handbooks*, 77.

40. Ibid., 78.

41. Florence and Storey, *Vietnam*, 5th ed., 45; Dunlop, *Fodor's Exploring Vietnam*, 1st ed., 14.

42. Nguyen Xuan Oanh, quoted in Helen Jarvis, "New Foreign Investment Law," *Direct Action* (13 April 1988): 12. A slightly different version of this quote appeared in Pilger, *Heroes*, 281. For more on Nguyen Xuan Oanh, see Kolko, *Vietnam*, 25–26, 32–33; and Pilger, *Hidden Agendas*, 330–31.

43. "Industrial Producers Head for Rural Areas to Cut Costs, Boost Employment," *Viet Nam News*, 1 April 2002. Hao justified the shift in production to exploit lower labor costs as "not solely for economic purposes" but, additionally, as "part of a larger strategy to develop a strong socio-economy in the countryside."

44. On the "race to the bottom," see, among others, Brecher and Costello, *Global Village or Global Pillage*; Klevorick, "Reflections on the Race to the Bottom," 459–67; Mehmet, "Race to the Bottom," 148–61; Mehmet and Tavakoli, "Does Foreign Direct Investment Cause a Race to the Bottom?"; Singh, "Labour Standards and the 'Race to the Bottom' "; and Tonelson, *The Race to the Bottom*.

45. Dunlop, *Fodor's Exploring Vietnam*, 2d ed., 196; Florence and Storey, *Vietnam*, 5th ed., 44.

46. Florence and Storey, *Vietnam*, 5th ed., 44, 526. On comparable claims by other

guidebooks concerning rice production and exports as an empirical affirmation of *doi moi*, see Yang, *Let's Go*, 790; and Lesser, *Vietnam*, 222.

47. Kolko, *Vietnam*, 104–6; Seth Mydans, "Clustering in Cities, Asians Are Becoming Obese," *New York Times*, 13 March 2003.

48. A further relevant disclosure would have been the effects of the global commodity market's vagaries on agricultural producers. While the price of rice rose from 189 dollars a ton in 1990 to 315 dollars a ton in 1995, it fell to 174 dollars a ton in 2000, adversely affecting rural incomes, particularly in mono-crop areas. Luong, "Postwar Vietnamese Society," 16; idem, "Wealth, Power, and Inequality," 90–91.

49. Gerard Greenfield asserted that only 4 percent of coffee grown in Vietnam was consumed domestically. Greenfield, "Vietnam and the World Coffee Crisis," 10.

50. Gresser and Tickell, *Mugged*, 9–11, 18. For additional evidence on the losses of coffee farmers, see United Nations Country Team Viet Nam, *International Economic Integration, Competitiveness, and Rural Livelihoods in Viet Nam*, 5; Luong, "Postwar Vietnamese Society," 16; and idem, "Wealth, Power, and Inequality," 90.

51. Florence and Jealous, *Vietnam*, 7th ed., 417; Dunlop, *Fodor's Exploring Vietnam*, 2d ed., 134, 138.

52. Florence and Jealous, *Vietnam*, 7th ed., 417.

53. Florence and Storey, *Vietnam*, 6th ed., 573; Florence and Jealous, *Vietnam*, 7th ed., 544.

54. Jerald Horst, "Vietnamese Fight to Export Seafood," *Times-Picayune*, 11 July 2002; Jerald Horst, "Vietnam's Shrimp, Fish Exports Grow," *Times-Picayune*, 17 October 2002.

55. Seth Mydans, "Americans and Vietnamese Fighting Over Catfish," *New York Times*, 5 November 2002.

56. Elizabeth Becker, "Delta Farmers Want Copyright on Catfish," *New York Times*, 16 January 2002.

57. On the appellations given to the Vietnamese fish, see Ngo Hong Hanh, "Catfish Export Triumph Irks American Fishermen," *Vietnam Investment Review*, 9 July 2001.

58. "The Vietnamese Invade," *Economist*, 6 October 2001.

59. Mydans, "Americans and Vietnamese Fighting Over Catfish."

60. Advertisement quoted in John McCain, "McCain: Catfish Import Barrier Puts International Trade Agreements at Risk," press release, 18 December 2001, http://mccain.senate.gov/index.cfm?fuseaction=Newscenter.ViewPressRelease&Content _id=279 (accessed 27 May 2005); see also Mydans, "Americans and Vietnamese Fighting Over Catfish."

61. Berry, quoted in Dan Morgan, "Vietnamese Catfish Rile Southern Lawmakers," *Washington Post*, 10 September 2001.

62. U.S. Embassy, quoted in McCain, "McCain." For a scientific evaluation of the claims of contaminated catfish drawing on Vietnamese exports to both the United

States and Laos that found the American producers' claims to apparently be without merit, see Schecter et al., "Are Vietnamese Food Exports Contaminated with Dioxin from Agent Orange?"

63. American shrimpers, like catfish farmers, also sought relief from Vietnamese imports, complaining that they were suffering from "unfair trade." Vietnam was thus one of six countries named by the Southern Shrimp Alliance when it filed an antidumping petition with the Department of Commerce and the U.S. International Trade Commission in December 2003. Associated Press, "U.S. Shrimpers Seek a Duty on Imports," *New York Times*, 1 January 2004. In July 2004, the Bush administration ruled preliminarily that Vietnam (as well as China) was dumping shrimp in the United States, and it thus imposed tariffs of 12.11 percent to 93.13 percent on the Vietnamese imports. Elizabeth Becker, "Bush Accuses Vietnam and China of Dumping Shrimp on U.S. Market," *New York Times*, 7 July 2004. The U.S. International Trade Commission agreed in January 2005, imposing tariffs on Vietnam and several other Asian and Latin American states. John McQuaid, "Panel Slaps Tariffs on Shrimp Imports," *Times-Picayune*, 7 January 2005.

64. Associated Press, "Tariffs Ordered on Catfish and Computer Chips," *New York Times*, 18 June 2003; see also Elizabeth Becker, "Vietnam: Fish Trade Dispute," *New York Times*, 28 January 2003.

65. Berry, quoted in Suzi Parker, "Whiskered Catfish Stir a New Trade Controversy," *Christian Science Monitor*, 3 October 2001.

66. Tina Rosenberg, "Why Mexico's Small Corn Farmers Go Hungry," editorial observer, *New York Times*, 3 March 2003. See also Fanjul and Fraser, "Dumping Without Borders"; and Elizabeth Becker, "U.S. Corn Subsidies Said to Damage Mexico," *New York Times*, 27 August 2003. There are, of course, exceptions. When the office of the United States trade representative, prompted by the 125-year-old herring canning industry of Maine, "agreed to requests from Maine to join a World Trade Organization protest over a European ban on calling anything other than European sardines by that name," the government "hastily abandoned its plans to defend American herring exports after Congress moved to back the same kind of ban on labels for imported catfish," Jeffrey H. Kaelin, a lobbyist for seafood legislation, told the *New York Times*. Becker, "Delta Farmers Want Copyright on Catfish."

67. Mark Landler, "Widening Economic Gap Keeps Vietnam Divided," *New York Times*, 21 April 2000. In referring to threats to established American industries, I am making a clear distinction between workers, on the one hand, and owners and executives on the other. U.S. foreign economic policy has been driven far more, I would argue, by concern for the latter. Low wages outside the United States have negatively affected American workers — jobs have been exported, and there have

been downward pressures on wages and benefits—while increased profits and bonuses have accrued to those exploiting cheaper labor abroad.

68. Dodsworth et al., *Vietnam*, 11; Kolko, *Vietnam*, 56.

69. Kolko, "China and Vietnam," 435. The data for Vietnam are from 1993. For the United States, Kolko consulted the 1997 *World Development Report* of the World Bank. By 1997, the top quintile in the United States had surpassed the top Vietnamese quintile, with the former receiving 46.4 percent and the latter receiving 44.5 percent. However, the top Vietnamese quintile still earned (or, more appropriately, consumed) a larger share than its counterparts in other major capitalist powers—for example, the United Kingdom (43.2 percent in 1995), France (40.2 percent in 1995), Germany (38.5 percent in 1994), and Japan (35.7 percent in 1993)—and a host of developing states, such as Bangladesh (42.8 percent in 1995–96) and Indonesia (41.1 percent in 1999). World Bank, *World Development Indicators 2002*, 74–76. Some of the surveys employed by the World Bank referred to the distribution of income and others to the distribution of consumption. The latter, which was used to deduce the figure for Vietnam, is typically more equal than income distribution. On this and the impossibility of "strict comparability," see the World Bank qualifications at ibid., 77. It should also be noted that wealth inequality tends to be even more skewed than income inequality. To my knowledge, no data from the 1990s exist for Vietnam, but in the United States in the early twenty-first century, the wealthiest 1 percent of households controlled approximately 38 percent of the national wealth, while the bottom 80 percent of households controlled only 17 percent. Mishel et al., *The State of Working America 2002–2003*, 277.

70. National Center for Social Sciences and Humanities, *National Human Development Report 2001*, 44, 46.

71. Kawachi and Kennedy, *The Health of Nations*, 6–7, 51, 56–57, 158–59, 168. For a variation of Kawachi and Kennedy's argument that focuses on the consequences of "relative deprivation" for the well-being of the middle class, see Frank, *Falling Behind*.

72. Asian Development Bank, *Indigenous Peoples/Ethnic Minorities and Poverty Reduction*, 17. A later World Bank study actually found ethnic minorities making up 29 percent of the country's poor. See ibid., 27.

73. Ibid., 17.

74. Wagstaff and Nguyen, *Poverty and Survival Prospects of Vietnamese Children under Doi Moi*, 1, 8–9, 11. In fact, there are indications that in some areas of the Central Highlands and Northern Highlands, infant mortality actually increased between 1989 and 1994. Asian Development Bank, *Indigenous Peoples/Ethnic Minorities and Poverty Reduction*, 28.

75. Wagstaff and Nguyen, *Poverty and Survival Prospects of Vietnamese Children under Doi Moi*, 24–25.

76. Ibid., 1, citing World Bank, *Vietnam*. On the demise of Vietnam's public-health services following the introduction of the capitalist reforms, see also Segall et al., "Economic Transition Should Come with a Health Warning."

77. Musgrove, *World Health Report 2000 — Health Systems*, 155; the study is cited in Kolko, "China and Vietnam," 439.

78. World Bank, *Vietnam: Growing Healthy*, 1, 186.

79. Ibid., 1, 51, 158–59, 191.

80. Ibid., 41, 191. Conversely, the poor were over-represented among the users of commune health centers, which generally provided less comprehensive care. See ibid., 41.

81. Ibid., 47. For more on the increasing polarization of public-health services, see Deolalikar, "Access to Health Services by the Poor and the Non-Poor."

82. World Bank, *Vietnam: Growing Healthy*, 188, 190–91.

83. A notable exception was the guidebook published by Footprint, which, I found — at least relative to other publications — was rarely used by tourists in Vietnam. While not without problems, the authors of the guidebook shunned much of the celebratory language that appeared in the other texts, and they seemed to take seriously the reforms' negative effects on a considerable portion of the populace in appraising the changes under *doi moi*. Nevertheless, they suggested and accepted as natural that the "reforms will need to be both deeper and wider." Colet and Eliot, *Vietnam Handbook*, 401.

84. Buckley, *Moon Handbooks*, 71–73; Parkes, *Southeast Asia Handbook*, 947–48.

85. Yang, *Let's Go*, 777.

86. Dunlop, *Fodor's Exploring Vietnam*, 1st ed., 12–14. While the impoverished were heavily concentrated in rural areas of the country, the incidence of poverty in urban areas nevertheless remained at approximately 15 percent, according to one study. Asian Development Bank, *Indigenous Peoples/Ethnic Minorities and Poverty Reduction*, 27. On a broader regional level, one scholar found the top income quintiles in 1997–98 earning from 7.9 to 14 times more than the respective bottom quintiles in the seven socioeconomic regions of the country (the Northern Highlands, Red River Delta, North Central Panhandle, South Central Coast, Central Highlands, South East, and Mekong Delta). Luong, "Wealth, Power, and Inequality," 87. Employing earlier data, Ngo Vinh Long reported in 1997 that, depending on the region, the incomes of wealthy households in rural areas were eleven to fourteen times greater than the incomes of poor households. Ngo Vinh Long, "A Letter from Vietnam," 97.

87. Dodd and Lewis, *Vietnam*, xi, 59, 413–14; Rutherford, *Vietnam*, 53–54.

88. Lesser, *Vietnam*, 9, 170.

89. Florence and Storey, *Vietnam*, 5th ed., 44. The sixth and seventh editions were improved — although not in the economic synopsis — with the addition of a special boxed section by Philip Taylor on *doi moi* that addressed — within an evaluation

that was still arguably more celebratory than critical in several important respects—a number of the reforms' negative effects. Florence and Storey, *Vietnam*, 6th ed., 34–35; Florence and Jealous, *Vietnam*, 7th ed., 32–33.

90. Florence and Storey, *Vietnam*, 5th ed., 103. In the sixth edition, the claim was slightly changed to "not such a huge problem any more." Florence and Storey, *Vietnam*, 6th ed., 97. A portion of the health section of the seventh edition was further revised. It stated, "The significant improved [*sic*] in Vietnam's economy has brought with it some major improvements in public health." Florence and Jealous, *Vietnam*, 7th ed., 89.

91. Florence and Storey, *Vietnam*, 5th ed., 526.

92. Swinkels and Turk, *Strategic Planning for Poverty Reduction in Vietnam*, 3; Ponce et al., "Will Vietnam Grow Out of Malnutrition?" 257.

93. Cited in World Bank, *Vietnam: Growing Healthy*, 27. The Vietnam Living Standards Survey of 1998 provided slightly different figures of 36 percent and 35 percent, respectively. Ibid., 27.

94. Ibid., 28. Whereas the rate of stunting had fallen "impressively" in recent years, the rate of wasting had actually increased, a trend owing, according to the World Bank, to the rate of stunting declining faster than the rate of underweight malnutrition. Ibid., 28.

95. Ibid., 29–30.

96. Luong and Unger, "Wealth, Power, and Poverty in the Transition to Market Economies," 121.

97. Luong, "Wealth, Power, and Inequality," 86–87.

98. See, e.g., the World Bank data cited in Luong, "Wealth, Power, and Inequality," 86–87.

99. Kolko, "China and Vietnam," 436–37.

100. Ibid., 439.

101. National Center for Social Sciences and Humanities, *National Human Development Report 2001*, 63–64.

102. Kolko, "China and Vietnam," 439.

103. National Center for Social Sciences and Humanities, *National Human Development Report 2001*, 43. On criticism of the methodology employed by the World Bank in its determination of national poverty levels, which the critics maintain had likely led to a substantial underestimation of the extent of global income poverty and to the incorrect inference that it had declined, see Sanjay G. Reddy and Thomas W. Pogge, "How *Not* to Count the Poor," Institute for Social Analysis, Columbia University, 29 October 2005, http://www.socialanalysis.org (accessed 3 November 2006).

104. ADB, quoted in Kolko, "China and Vietnam," 439. Hy Van Luong made the same point in Luong, "Postwar Vietnamese Society," 19.

105. National Center for Social Sciences and Humanities, *National Human Develop-*

ment Report 2001, 68. See also Swinkels and Turk, *Strategic Planning for Poverty Reduction in Vietnam*, 1.

106. IMF, quoted in Kolko, "China and Vietnam," 439.

107. Dr. Le Thi Quy, quoted in Pilger, *Hidden Agendas*, 332.

108. Nguyen Huy Thiep, *The General Retires and Other Stories*, 122. I am indebted to Mark Bradley, who brought this story to my attention, for his perceptive insights on its significance.

109. For one example, see Kay Johnson, "Vietnamese Flock to New Exhibit on Old Communist Hardships," Deutsche Presse-Agentur, 15 August 2006.

110. Ian Stewart, "A Legacy of Discontent: Vietnam Grapples with Peasant Unrest," Associated Press, 27 October 1997.

111. Jeremy Grant, "Vietnamese Club Together Against Golf," *Financial Times* (London), 4 January 1997.

112. Verena Dobnik, "Nike 'Treats Women Like Slave Labour,'" *Daily Telegraph* (Sydney), 29 March 1997.

113. Jim Hill, "Nike Plant Shuts After Workers Protest," *Sunday Oregonian* (Portland), 27 April 1997. The same newspaper subsequently carried a Bloomberg News story reporting that "fewer than 1,000 workers" had struck, but it failed to explain the discrepancy. Jason Folkmanis, "Nike Plant in Vietnam Reaches Wage Pact," *Oregonian* (Portland), 2 May 1997.

5. MEMORY AND MEANING

1. George Bush, "Inaugural Address," 20 January 1989, *Public Papers of the Presidents of the United States: George Bush, 1989*, I: 3.

2. George Bush, "Address to the Nation Announcing Allied Military Action in the Persian Gulf," 16 January 1991, *Public Papers of the Presidents of the United States: George Bush, 1991*, I: 44.

3. George Bush, "Remarks to the American Legislative Exchange Council," 1 March 1991, *Public Papers of the Presidents of the United States: George Bush, 1991*, I: 197.

4. Ronald Reagan most famously referred to the war as a "noble cause" in August 1980. Reagan, quoted in Turner, *Echoes of Combat*, 63.

5. Unless otherwise indicated, all comments from visitors are from the "Impressions" books at the museum, and all emphases are in the original. I relied on the comment books used at the site in March 2002 (which contained entries from January through March), a comment book from 1998 that had earlier appeared in the room devoted to the photography of Ishikawa Bunyo, and a selection of comments from throughout the 1990s. I am grateful to the directors of the museum for making copies of these documents available to me.

6. Richter, *The Politics of Tourism in Asia*, 4–11; Endy, *Cold War Holidays*.

7. Interview of Huynh Ngoc Van, vice-director of the War Remnants Museum,

12 March 2002, Ho Chi Minh City. There is considerable confusion with respect to the institution's former English-language names. The site opened on 4 September 1975. According to Huynh Ngoc Van, from 1975 until 1990 it was called, in Vietnamese, the Nha Trung Bay Toi Ac My Nguy, which roughly translates as the Exhibition House of Crimes of America and Its Puppet. However, I have been unable to confirm this English-language name with any contemporaneous source. A number of journalists and writers have reported that the institution was originally called the Museum of American War Crimes. However, to Vietnamese there is a difference between an "exhibition house," the purpose of which is to exhibit, and a museum, which also engages in functions such as research and conservation. A short piece in the *Economist* was probably most accurate. It referred to the English-language name of the institution as the Exhibition House of American and Chinese War Crimes, claiming that "Chinese" was dropped in 1990. "Spot the Crime in Vietnam," *Economist*, 3 December 1994. The same claim is found in Colet and Eliot, *Vietnam Handbook*, 242. It is doubtful, however, that "Chinese" existed in the name before the brief conflict between Vietnam and China in 1979. Before its rechristening as the War Remnants Museum (Bao Tang Chung Tich Chien Tranh) in 1995, the institution was called the Exhibition House of Aggression War Crimes (Nha Trung Bay Toi Ac Chien Tranh Xam Luoc). This name appeared in the *Economist* article cited earlier and was confirmed to me by the anthropologist Christina Schwenkel, who possessed a pre-1995 English-language pamphlet from the museum containing the appellation. E-mail communication from Christina Schwenkel, 4 August 2003. (A 1991 article in the *Los Angeles Times* used the slightly different Exhibition House of Aggressive War Crimes. Alvin Shuster, "Twenty Years Later, Back to Saigon," *Los Angeles Times*, 17 May 1991, folder 7, box 24, DPC: OM-CN, VA.) Huynh Ngoc Van indicated that the name was most recently changed to make it suitable to the opinions of people everywhere, as Vietnam, she said, had opened itself to the world since 1990. Since my last visit in 2002, the museum has undergone substantial renovation.

8. "Tourist Numbers Up at [Ho Chi Minh] City's War Remnants Museum," *Viet Nam News*, 10 February 2003, hppt://vietnnamnews.vnagency.com.vn/2003–02/10/Stories/04.htm (accessed 24 June 2003). According to the press report, visits increased from 207,000 persons in 2001 to 270,000 in 2002, 40 percent of whom were Japanese.

9. While I base this claim on my interviews during 2000 and 2002 with over 170 tourists throughout Vietnam, I must caution that my findings should not be construed as scientific, although I suspect they were reasonably accurate for independent Western travelers. I cannot claim to have interviewed a representative sample of Western visitors, if such was even possible, although I did make an effort to speak with as wide a cross-section of individuals as I could. One notable exception was my inability to interview large numbers of package tourists. Their fixed,

tight schedules made interviews almost impossible logistically, so with only a few exceptions, they are not included in these findings.

10. Unless indicated otherwise, all references to the exhibits at the museum were recorded by me in March 2002. I also conducted research at the museum in June 2000, and I visited as an interested tourist in February 1998. A number of changes had been made during that time — for example, by March 2002 the museum had begun displaying a series of drawings by Vietnamese children on war and peace and, by June 2000, it had installed a large collection of photographs by Ishikawa Bunyo and the Requiem exhibit — but I did not discern a substantial difference in the exhibits' general tone.

11. McNamara with VanDeMark, *In Retrospect*, xx. McNamara's statement generated widespread debate, much of it inspired by the mistaken belief that he was making a moral judgment about the war. He was not. For one of the more insightful exchanges on the publication of *In Retrospect*, see the roundtable essays by Chomsky, Just, Rostow, Wicker, Yoder, and Young in *Diplomatic History* 20, no. 3 (Summer 1996): 439–71.

12. In the film, Cecile Moore asked, "Daddy, what is war?" Her father, Harold Moore, responded: "War is, uh, well, it's . . . it's something that shouldn't happen, but, but it does. And, um, it's when some people in another country, or any country, try to take the lives of other people. And then soldiers like your daddy have to — you know, it's my job to go over there and stop 'em." This concerned Cecile. "Are they gonna try to take your life away, Daddy?" she wondered. Yet Gibson's character was confident: "Well, yes, Cecile, they're gonna try. But I'm not gonna let 'em." *We Were Soldiers* (2002).

13. Alneng, " 'What the Fuck Is a Vietnam?' " 476. There is scholarly uncertainty about the number of Vietnamese fatalities caused by the American war. The Vietnamese Ministry of Labor, War Invalids, and Social Affairs estimated in April 1995 that approximately three million soldiers and civilians had perished. More recently, drawing on Vietnam Life History Survey data, several scholars concluded (with important qualifications) that approximately one million Vietnamese suffered war-related deaths from 1965 to 1975. See Hirschman et al., "Vietnamese Casualties During the American War."

14. Tai, "Situating Memory," 3.

15. On the "official view" of the U.S. intervention, see, e.g., Kimball, *To Reason Why*, 25–50. The museum exhibits contained a number of grammatical errors, awkward statements, or uses of tense that I have chosen to revise for clarity, consistency, and flow. By way of illustration, the original version of the first quote said, "In August 1953, President Eisenhower, while briefing the Domino Doctrine said Burma, India, and Indonesia would be easily oppressed if the communists got victory in Indo-China. He emphasized that the U.S. economic and military aid to the anti-communist forces in Indo-China was the best way against the severe

threat toward the U.S. security." As both passages in this paragraph were attributed by the curators to Peter A. Poole's *The United States and Indochina*, it is likely that the quotes were English retranslations of a Vietnamese translation of Poole's original English-language text.

16. In fact, Ishikawa Bunyo's photographs, installed in the museum in 1998, also portrayed the "in country" experiences of American soldiers, although not as extensively as the Requiem exhibit. The latter collection has been published as Faas and Page, *Requiem*.

17. The site was still being referred to as the "War Crime [*sic*] Museum" in the brochures I obtained in March 2002 from the following travel agencies: Tropic Tour, Delta Adventure Tours (Saigontourist Travel Service Company), T. M. Brother's Tour (Hoan Hao Tourist Company), and Sinh Office (Tran Dang Trading and Tourist Company).

18. As I base this analysis in part on my interviews of foreign tourists during research trips in 2000 and 2002, I wish to reemphasize the caveats in note 9. With respect to the limitations in interviewing package tourists, it should be noted that many tour companies do not place the War Remnants Museum on their regular itineraries, adding a visit only if specifically requested by those enrolled in the tour. Telephone interview of Tu Nguyen, U.S. representative for Trails of Indochina, 27 September 2001; and interview of the director of a Vietnamese tour company who requested confidentiality, March 2002, Ho Chi Minh City.

19. Intrepid Travel, *Asia* (2000–2002): 4, 117; Intrepid Travel, *Asia* (2002–2003): 4, 113; Intrepid Travel, *Asia* (2003–2004): 112.

20. Jerome McFadden, "Vietnam Builds Back," *Morning Call* (Allentown, Penn.), 19 September 1999, folder 1, box 1, DVC, VA.

21. Reg Henry, "Nation Puts Its Past on View," *Pittsburgh Post-Gazette*, 30 April 2000, http://www.post-gazette.com/headlines/20000430viettours5.asp (accessed 16 December 2002).

22. Appy and Bloom, "Vietnam War Mythology and the Rise of Public Cynicism," 55–56.

23. See, e.g., Franklin, *Vietnam and Other American Fantasies*, 27–28.

24. Marie Javins, "Southeast Asia on a Hamstring—2000," http://www.bootsnall .com/travelogues/marie/mar06.shtml (accessed 22 September 2004). Javins wrote in her online journal: "The War Remnants Museum is a monument to the atrocities of war—and not just any atrocities, but specifically the atrocities committed by the Americans against the North Vietnamese."

25. Interview no. 73, 20 March 2002, War Remnants Museum, Ho Chi Minh City.

26. Interview no. 74, 20 March 2002, War Remnants Museum, Ho Chi Minh City. He was using the Vietnam volume published by Rough Guides.

27. Storey and Robinson, *Vietnam*, 4th ed., 201.

28. Parkes, *Southeast Asia Handbook*, 960.

29. Dunlop, *Fodor's Exploring Vietnam*, 2d ed., 176; Kaufman, *Vietnam*, 186.

30. Vu The Binh, *Vietnam Tourist Guidebook*, 2d and 3d eds. The first edition of the guidebook acknowledged the War Remnants Museum but did not, unlike with several other museums and historical attractions, provide any substantive information about it. The site's name ("War Crimes Exhibition"), address, and telephone number were simply listed in a catalog of museums in Ho Chi Minh City. Vu The Binh, *Vietnam Tourist Guidebook*, 1st ed., 113. Museum attendance rankings were provided in an interview with Trinh Thi Hoa, director of the Museum of Vietnamese History — Ho Chi Minh City, 7 March 2002, Ho Chi Minh City.

31. Vu The Binh, *Non Nuoc Viet Nam*, 559; Tai, *Hallowed Ground or Haunted House*, 1. I am grateful to Hue-Tam Ho Tai for providing me with a copy of this publication.

32. Biles et al., "Tiger on a Bicycle," 14–16. As the authors noted, the marketing of Vietnam as an international tourism destination had been promoted by both state-owned tourism companies and, especially, foreign tour operators. And, they wrote, the effort to attract "top end" visitors — as opposed to backpackers and other budget tourists — had "meant that much historic imagery familiar to the West, particularly relating to the harsh side of colonialism and Vietnam's wars of independence, is now being erased in an attempt to 'sanitize' Vietnam as a tourist destination for wealthy travelers." Ibid., 15.

33. *Vietnam Discovery* (February 2002): 1.

34. Ibid. (March 2002): 1. In both issues, the slogan was accompanied by the following statement: "The war is long gone. Listen to what people are saying NOW about Vietnam and you'll understand why so many tourists are flocking to this awe inspiring land, made of legends, exquisite landscapes, sunny smiles, and a unique cultural identity." Unlike the Vietnam National Administration of Tourism's English-language guidebook, the inaugural issue of *Vietnam Discovery* included a brief, one-paragraph profile of the War Remnants Museum and featured the site in its "Maps and Listing" handout. Ibid. (February 2002): 30.

35. Interview of Huynh Ngoc Van, 12 March 2002.

36. Interview of Robert Storey, 30 May 2000, Jiafeng, Taiwan; Storey and Robinson, *Vietnam*, 3d ed., 198–99. The same language was used in the fourth and fifth editions but was altered when a new author, Mason Florence, revised the sixth edition.

37. The statement on the caption read, "The American soldier laughed satisfactorily while carrying a part of the body of a liberation soldier just . . . hit by shells from a grenade-launcher. In my feelings I wondered whether he could have been a monster or a human being[.] In 1967. Infantry Division 25. In Tay Ninh." The photograph and text appear in Ishikawa, *The War for the Liberation of Vietnam*, 76–77. The photograph has also been published in Ishikawa, *War and Man*, 36–37. In the latter volume, however, the accompanying text says, "Liberation Front Soldier Broken into Pieces: The 25th Division in Tay Ninh Province, 1967." For compa-

rable touristic reactions to the same photograph, see Javins, "South East Asia on a Hamstring — 2000"; and Brian Wizard, "Viet Nam 1999," http://www.brianwizard.com/samples/vietnam1999.htm (accessed 22 September 2004).

38. Interview of Robert Storey, 30 May 2000.

39. Kaufman, *Vietnam*, 2d ed., 186.

40. Among the numerous exhibits acknowledging Vietnam's wartime division was the large quotation cited earlier in Vietnamese with an English caption that said, "The U.S. policy gradually strongly supported [the] Diem regime, eliminated French influence, and changed South Vietnam into a bunker against communism." Another exhibit noted of the Geneva Accords: "All the sides participating in the conference, in principle, recognized the independence, unification, and the territorial integrity of Vietnam. The negotiation[s] between [the] two parts of the country began on July 20, 1955[,] and the general election would be held in July 1956. The 17th parallel was the temporary military border in Vietnam." Also recognizing the country's division, a large painted map showed the "arrangement of [the] U.S. Army and its allied forces in South Vietnam in April 1969." Adjacent to this map was a chart with a caption that began, "Forces of the United States, its allies, and the former Saigon government in South Vietnam during the highest phase (April 1969)."

41. I write "seeming embrace" because, while the larger narrative at the site implicitly accepted this framework, the curators did not use the jargon (that is, "American imperialists" and "puppet government") attributed to the "Communist government" by the writer for Fodor's. Other Vietnamese institutions, such as the Museum of Vietnamese Revolution in Hanoi, have been more blunt than the War Remnants Museum, however.

42. Colet and Eliot, *Vietnam Handbook*, 242.

43. The two exhibits to which I refer — both of which were viewed in October 2002 — were the museum's displays on the Vietnam Veterans Memorial and a small section of "A Different Kind of War," an exhibit devoted to nuclear warfare and deterrence. The former included several statistics on the human cost of the war, although its focus was limited to the people of the United States.

44. Nor, for that matter, had the Smithsonian's record of ultimately shunning balanced examinations of U.S. and international history, such as its treatment of the nuclear destruction of Hiroshima and Nagasaki. Among other sources on this issue, see Dubin, *Displays of Power*, 186–226; Hogan, "The Enola Gay Controversy," 200–232; Linenthal and Engelhardt, *History Wars*; Luke, *Museum Politics*, 19–36; and Wallace, *Mickey Mouse History and Other Essays on American Memory*, 269–318.

45. Ford, *Frommer's Washington, D.C. from $80 a Day*, 169. The reference to "more than 58,000 fallen heroes" was from Sillett et al., *Moon Metro*, 23. Also consulted for guidebook treatments of these American sites were Brown and Cranmer, *The*

Rough Guide to Washington, D.C.; Cashion, *Fodor's U.S.A.*; Driesen et al., *Fodor's Washington, D.C.*; Flanagan, *Let's Go: Washington, D.C.*; and Harger, *Washington, D.C.*

46. Flanagan, *Let's Go: Washington, D.C.*, 113. For the list of guidebooks consulted, see note 45.

47. Interview no. 41, 13 March 2002, War Remnants Museum, Ho Chi Minh City.

48. For more on this issue, see Franklin, *M.I.A., or, Mythmaking in America.*

49. The exceptions were Oliver Stone's *Heaven and Earth* (1993), which was based on the life of Le Ly Hayslip, and *Hearts and Minds* (1974), the award-winning documentary by Peter Davis.

50. Interview no. 60, 17 March 2002, War Remnants Museum, Ho Chi Minh City.

51. Others wished to acknowledge their participation in the antiwar movement, as if to remind the curators that the American killing in Vietnam was not done in their names. A Californian who visited in March 2002, for example, wrote, "I have re-lived the horror of my student years. My only consolation is knowing that I protested the blood bath that my country inflicted. I hope to never have to do that again but I would, and it seems it may be necessary. America is slow to learn from its recent past."

52. Jeffords defined the remasculinization of America as "the large-scale renegotiation and regeneration of the interests, values, and projects of patriarchy now taking place in U.S. social relations." Jeffords, *The Remasculinization of America*, xi.

53. "Doves Recoil but Hawks Tend to See 'Massacre' as Just Part of War," *Wall Street Journal*, 1 December 1969.

54. "Many Disbelieve My Lai Reports," *Minneapolis Tribune*, 21 December 1969; see also "Poll Finds Doubters on Mylai," *Washington Post*, 22 December 1969, which reported the findings of the Minnesota poll published the day before in Minneapolis. Some respondents who called the allegations false did not deny the incident. Instead, they said that it should not be classified as "murder." Other Minnesotans were in flat denial. For a genealogy of the American press coverage of the atrocities, including the first public hints of the story in September 1969, see Hersh, *My Lai 4*, 128–43. Hersh's reporting on Americans' reactions to the incident is also valuable; see ibid., 151–70.

55. "Doves Recoil but Hawks Tend to See 'Massacre' as Just Part of War."

56. Ibid.

57. Ibid.

58. "The War: New Support for Nixon," *Time*, 12 January 1970, http://www.time .com/time/magazine/article/0,9171,942132,00.html (accessed 6 July 2007).

59. "Doves Recoil but Hawks Tend to See 'Massacre' as Just Part of War." In the Minnesota poll cited earlier, 4 percent of the six hundred respondents "stated they would rather not believe it, that American soldiers wouldn't do that sort of thing." Another 43 percent said "they were horrified and couldn't believe a massacre had

occurred." Fifteen percent indicated that "they didn't and still won't believe the report is true." "Many Disbelieve My Lai Reports."

60. Pat Buchanan to Henry A. Kissinger with "Questions and Answers" for the President, 5 December 1969, NPMS, NSCF, AMHSF, box 1004, My Lai Incident (1 of 2) folder, NA.

61. Richard Nixon, "Address to the Nation on the War in Vietnam," 3 November 1969, no. 425, *Public Papers of the Presidents of the United States: Richard Nixon, 1969,* 902.

62. On the ideology of "empire-building" in Indochina as part of a continuum dating from the "Indian-hating" of earlier centuries, see Drinnon, *Facing West.*

63. On the human rights violations in the Central Highlands, see Amnesty International, "Viet Nam," in *Amnesty International Report 2002* (Amnesty International Publications, 2002), http://web.amnesty.org/web/ar2002.nsf/asa/viet+nam!Open (accessed 14 October 2004).

64. The dates of the meeting appear to be incorrect. Kerry met with Do Muoi during a trip to Vietnam from 31 May to 1 June 1993, but I have been unable to locate any source placing Kerry in Vietnam from 15 July to 18 July of that same year.

65. O'Neill and Corsi, *Unfit for Command,* 168. See also Jerome R. Corsi and Jeffrey M. Epstein, "Kerry Honored by Vietnamese Communists," *WinterSoldier* .com, http://ice.he.net/freepnet/kerry/staticpages/index.php?page=200405311 40357545 (accessed 2 November 2004). On the photograph's significance to the veterans' case against Kerry, see O'Neill and Corsi, *Unfit for Command,* 7–8.

66. Corsi and Epstein, "Kerry Honored by Vietnamese Communists."

67. "A POW Story," *News Central,* 22 October 2004.

68. Jack Torry, "Viet Official Gives Glenn New Data on 2,000 MIAS," *Pittsburgh Post-Gazette,* 1 June 1993.

69. On the identification of the veterans' organizations, see Bruce Stanley, "U.S. Delegation Pushes Hanoi for More Help on MIAS," Associated Press, 31 May 1993; on the presence of the family members, see "U.S. Delegation Arrives in Hanoi for MIA Search," Agence France-Presse, 31 May 1993.

70. Jerome R. Corsi and Jeffrey M. Epstein, "Kerry Museum Photo Documented," *WinterSoldier*.com, http://ice.he.net/freepnet/kerry/staticpages/index.php?page =2004060419480799 (accessed 2 November 2004); see also O'Neill and Corsi, *Unfit for Command,* 172.

71. It is ironic that a photograph of Elmo Zumwalt Jr. appeared on the same wall as the photograph of Kerry, as among the veterans critical of Kerry's presidential run was James M. Zumwalt, son of the retired admiral. O'Neill and Corsi approvingly quoted the former Navy corpsman Bill Lupetti, who "happened upon" the photograph of Kerry in the museum (thus setting in motion the veterans' use of it), declaring that "the Communists are saying that everybody in that hall [the room containing the image] helped them win the war." By this logic, both James Zum-

walt's father and Robert McNamara made " 'heroic' contributions to the North Vietnamese victory," as O'Neill and Corsi elsewhere inferred of Kerry based on the presence of his photograph at the site. O'Neill and Corsi, *Unfit for Command*, 7, 168, 170. James Zumwalt's endorsement of the Swift Boat Veterans for Truth was affirmed in a 4 May 2004 letter reproduced in ibid., 188–95.

72. For two recent examples of the museum's appearance in the nation's editorial pages, see James Webb, "Purple Heartbreakers," *New York Times*, 18 January 2006; and Danielle Trussoni, "End Vietnam's Air War," *New York Times*, 18 June 2007. Also significant is Harrell Fletcher's traveling reproduction of many of the museum's exhibits, *The American War*, which by early 2007 had appeared in various arts venues in Texas, Virginia, New York, Massachusetts, Oregon, and California. For a book version of the project, see Fletcher, *The American War*.

73. According to an agreement between the Smithsonian and Kenneth E. Behring, the real-estate developer who donated $80 million to the institution for the creation of the exhibit, the National Museum of American History was to construct a permanent exhibition "highlighting the history and contributions of the American people (but focusing primarily on the military's role) in preserving and protecting freedom and democracy." The implication that the ongoing war in Iraq could be subsumed within this framework generated a complaint to the museum's management from Katherine Ott, chair of the site's branch of the Smithsonian Congress of Scholars. The decision to include the Iraq war under the title "The Price of Freedom," she wrote in a July 2004 memorandum, "presents a partisan view of the current war and is counter to our neutral public mission." If Ott lodged a similar complaint about the war in Vietnam, there was no mention of it in the press. Bob Thompson, "A Tug of War," *Washington Post*, 7 November 2004. For two scholarly reviews of the exhibition, see Burke, "The Price of Freedom Is Truth"; and Boehm, "Privatizing Public Memory."

74. Foner, *The Story of American Freedom*.

75. Bradley, *Imagining Vietnam and America*, esp. 10–44.

76. Tom Morganthau with Douglas Waller, Bill Turque, Ginny Carroll, and Andrew Murr, "The Military's New Image," *Newsweek* (11 March 1991): 50.

EPILOGUE

1. Robert F. Worth and James Brooke, "Body Is Said to be Japanese Held by Rebels," *New York Times*, 30 October 2004; "Koda Found Dead in Baghdad," *Daily Yomiuri* (Tokyo), 1 November 2004.

2. Noor Khan, "Italian Tourist Killed while Riding Motorcycle through Southern Afghanistan," Associated Press Worldstream, 11 April 2003; " 'Taliban' Kill Italian Tourist in Southern Afghanistan," Agence France-Presse, 12 April 2003; Carlotta Gall, "An Italian Tourist Is Slain by Taliban in Afghanistan," *New York Times*, 12 April 2003.

3. Lennon and Foley, *Dark Tourism*.

4. Stephen Khan, "Fearless Trekker Follows in Footsteps of Mogul Emperor," *Observer* (London), 3 February 2002. Stewart's travels were ultimately chronicled in his *The Places In Between*.

5. Declan Walsh, "Grandma's Gone to See Afghanistan," *Boston Globe*, 26 September 2004.

6. Wolfstone, *The Golden Guide to South and East Asia*, 291.

7. The notion is hardly inconceivable. Vietnam's growing popularity as a tourism destination was demonstrated when, in 2005, the World Travel and Tourism Council projected the country to be the world's seventh fastest-growing travel and tourism economy between 2006 and 2015. "Viet Nam in Top Ten for Tourism," *Viet Nam News*, 28 May 2005, http://vietnamnews.vnagency.com.vn/showarticle.php?num=01TRA280505 (accessed 5 June 2005).

8. Foner, *The Story of American Freedom*.

9. Olson, *Olson's Orient Guide*, 972–73.

REFERENCES

PRIMARY SOURCES

ARCHIVES

John Fitzgerald Kennedy Library, Boston, Massachusetts
    Papers of President Kennedy
Kansas State Historical Society, Topeka
    Robert E. Feighny Papers, 1964–1965
Lyndon Baines Johnson Library, Austin, Texas
    Office Files of Fred Panzer
    Papers of Lyndon Baines Johnson, President, 1963–69
Margaret Herrick Library, Academy of Motion Picture Arts and Sciences, Beverly
    Hills, California
    Clippings Files
    Script Collection
Minnesota Historical Society, St. Paul
    Marianne Hamilton Papers
National Archives II, College Park, Maryland
    Record Group 165: Records of the War Department General and Special Staffs
    Record Group 306: Records of the U.S. Information Agency
    Record Group 319: Records of the Army Staff
    Record Group 330: Records of the Office of the Secretary of Defense
    Record Group 342: Records of the U.S. Air Force Commands, Activities, and
        Organizations
New-York Historical Society, New York
    BV Connick, Louis
Nixon Presidential Materials Staff, National Archives II, College Park, Maryland
    National Security Council Files
    Nixon White House Tapes
    President's Personal File
    White House Central Files
Oakland Museum of California, Oakland
    Dorothea Lange Collection
Vietnam Archive, Texas Tech University, Lubbock
    David Venditta Collection

Douglas Pike Collection: Other Manuscripts — American Friends of Vietnam
Douglas Pike Collection: Other Manuscripts — Current News
Douglas Pike Collection: Unit 03 — POW/MIA Issues
Douglas Pike Collection: Unit 03 — Antiwar Activities
Douglas Pike Collection: Unit 05 — National Liberation Front
Douglas Pike Collection: Unit 06 — Democratic Republic of Vietnam
Douglas Pike Collection: Unit 08 — Biography
Douglas Pike Collection: Unit 11 — Monographs
Garth H. Holmes Collection
Jackson Bosley Collection
John Proe Collection
Martin Brady Collection
Michael Mittelmann Collection
Ronald Garrison Collection
William Colby Collection
Warner Bros. Archives, School of Cinema–Television, University of Southern
    California, Los Angeles
    "Jump Into Hell" Collection
Wisconsin Historical Society, Madison
    Tere Rios Versace Papers
Wisconsin Historical Society, River Falls
    Edward N. Peterson Letters, 1968–69

NEWSPAPERS, NEWSWIRES, AND PERIODICALS

Agence France-Presse
AsianWeek
Associated Press
Blade (Toledo)
Boston Globe
Christian Science Monitor
Cincinnati Post
Congressional Record
Daily Telegraph (Sydney)
Daily Yomiuri (Tokyo)
Department of State Bulletin
Deutsche Presse-Agentur
Direct Action (Surry Hills, New South Wales, Australia)
Economist (London)
Esquire
Europe Business Review
Financial Times (London)
Holiday

Honolulu Advertiser
I. F. Stone's Weekly
Independent (London)
Insight on the News
La Semaine a Saigon/Seven Days in Saigon
Life in Vietnam
Los Angeles Times
Michigan Alumnus
Minneapolis Tribune
Morning Call (Allentown, Pennsylvania)
Movie Gallery Video Buzz Magazine
Nation
National Geographic
National Observer
New Republic
Newsweek
New York
New York Times
New York Times Magazine
New Yorker
Observer (London)
Oregonian (Portland)
Orlando Sentinel
Pittsburgh Post-Gazette
Reader's Digest
Saigon Round Up
San Francisco Chronicle
Saturday Review
Sunday Oregonian (Portland)
Time
Times (London)
Times-Picayune (New Orleans)
Travel
United Press International
U.S. News and World Report
Viet-Nam Bulletin
Viet Nam News
Vietnam Discovery
Vietnam Investment Review
Vietnam Report
Wall Street Journal

Washington Monthly
Washington Post

U.S. GOVERNMENT DOCUMENTS

Clement, Harry G. *The Future of Tourism in the Pacific and Far East.* Washington, D.C.: Government Printing Office, 1961.

Monthly Catalog of United States Government Publications: Cumulative Index, 1961–1965, vol. 2. Washington, D.C.: Government Printing Office, n.d.

Office of Armed Forces Information and Education (OAFIE). *Armed Forces Information Pamphlet: Information Materials,* no. 1 (16 October 1953).

——. *Armed Forces Information Pamphlet: Your Insurance, Savings, and Retirement,* no. 4 (11 December 1953).

——. *Armed Forces Talk: Communism: The What and How,* no. 389 (2 November 1951).

——. *Armed Forces Talk: Communist Propaganda,* no. 401 (7 March 1952).

——. *Armed Forces Talk: It's Your Future,* no. 451 (24 July 1953).

——. *Armed Forces Talk: Rumor Has It,* no. 449 (1 July 1953).

——. *Armed Forces Talk: The ABC's of Democracy,* no. 416 (8 August 1952).

——. *Armed Forces Talk: The American Way of Life,* no. 392 (7 December 1951).

——. *Armed Forces Talk: The Free World's Allies,* no. 417 (15 August 1952).

——. *Armed Forces Talk: The Situation in Southeast Asia,* no. 453 (21 August 1953).

——. *Armed Forces Talk: The War in Indochina,* no. 439 (27 March 1953).

——. *Armed Forces Talk: Total Rule,* no. 444 (22 May 1953).

——. *Armed Forces Talk: Truth: Weapon and Shield,* no. 480 (18 November 1954).

——. *Armed Forces Talk: What's Right with the United States,* no. 429 (11 December 1952).

——. *Armed Forces Talk: Who Will Win the Olympics?* no. 408 (23 May 1952).

——. *Armed Forces Talk: Your Defense against Enemy Propaganda,* no. 424 (24 October 1952).

——. *Armed Forces Talk: Your Safety,* no. 426 (14 November 1952).

——. *A Pocket Guide to Anywhere,* DOD PAM 2–5, DA PAM 20–184, AFP 34–3–12. Washington, D.C.: Government Printing Office, 1956.

——. *A Pocket Guide to Anywhere,* PG-13, DA PAM 20–184. Washington, D.C.: Government Printing Office, 1953.

——. *A Pocket Guide to Vietnam,* DOD PG-21A, DA PAM 360–411, NAVPERS 93135A, AFP 190–4–3, NAVMC 2593A. Washington, D.C.: Government Printing Office, 1966.

——. *A Pocket Guide to Vietnam,* DOD PG-21B, DA PAM 360–411, NAVPERS 93135B, AFP 216–4, NAVMC 2593B. Washington, D.C.: Government Printing Office, 1971.

——. *A Pocket Guide to Viet-Nam,* DOD PG-21, DA PAM 20–198, NAVPERS 93135, AFP 190–4–3, NAVMC 2593. Washington, D.C.: Government Printing Office, 1963.

The Pentagon Papers: The Defense Department History of United States Decisionmaking on Vietnam, Senator Gravel ed. Boston: Beacon Press, 1971.

Public Papers of the Presidents of the United States: Dwight D. Eisenhower, 1954. Washington, D.C.: Government Printing Office, 1960.

Public Papers of the Presidents of the United States: George Bush, 1989. Washington, D.C.: Government Printing Office, 1990.

Public Papers of the Presidents of the United States: George Bush, 1991. Washington, D.C.: Government Printing Office, 1992.

Public Papers of the Presidents of the United States: Richard Nixon, 1969. Washington, D.C.: Government Printing Office, 1971.

Randall, Clarence B. *International Travel: Report to the President of the United States*. Washington, D.C.: Government Printing Office, 1958.

Subcommittee on International Organizations of the Committee on International Relations, U.S. House of Representatives. *Human Rights in Cambodia*, 95th Cong., 1st sess. Washington, D.C.: Government Printing Office, 1977.

Subcommittee to Investigate Problems Connected with Refugees and Escapees of the Committee on the Judiciary, U.S. Senate. *Problems of War Victims in Indochina, Part III: North Vietnam*, 92nd Cong., 2d sess., 16–17 August 1972. Washington, D.C.: Government Printing Office, 1972.

Subcommittee to Investigate the Administration of the Internal Security Act and Other Internal Security Laws of the Committee on the Judiciary, U.S. Senate. *The Human Cost of Communism in Vietnam*, 92d Cong., 2d sess. Washington, D.C.: Government Printing Office, 1972.

Subcommittees of the Committee on Expenditures in the Executive Departments and of the Committee on Education and Labor, U.S. House of Representatives. *Investigation of Publication Sponsored by the Department of the Army Entitled "Army Talks,"* 80th Cong., 2d sess., 20 April 1948. Washington, D.C.: Government Printing Office, 1948.

U.S. Department of State. *Aggression from the North: The Record of North Viet-Nam's Campaign to Conquer South Viet-Nam*. Department of State Publication 7839. Far Eastern Series 130. Washington, D.C.: Government Printing Office, 1965.

——. *Foreign Relations of the United States, 1952–1954, Volume 16: The Geneva Conference*. Washington, D.C.: Government Printing Office, 1981.

——. *Foreign Relations of the United States, 1955–1957, Volume 1: Vietnam*. Washington, D.C.: Government Printing Office, 1985.

——. *Foreign Relations of the United States, 1958–1960, Volume 1: Vietnam*. Washington, D.C.: Government Printing Office, 1986.

——. *Foreign Relations of the United States, 1961–1963, Volume 1: Vietnam, 1961*. Washington, D.C.: Government Printing Office, 1988.

———. *A Threat to the Peace: North Viet-Nam's Effort to Conquer South Viet-Nam*. Washington, D.C.: Government Printing Office, 1961.

TRAVEL GUIDEBOOKS, PAMPHLETS, BROCHURES, CATALOGS

Brown, Jules, and Jeff Cranmer. *The Rough Guide to Washington, D.C.*, 3d ed. London: Rough Guides, 2002.

Buckley, Michael. *Vietnam, Cambodia and Laos Handbook*, 2d ed. Chico, Calif.: Moon Publications, 1997.

———. *Moon Handbooks: Vietnam, Cambodia, and Laos*, 3d ed. Emeryville, Calif.: Avalon Travel Publishing, 2002.

Caldwell, John C. *Far East Travel Guide*. New York: John Day, 1959.

———. *Far East Travel Guide*, rev. ed. New York: John Day, 1961.

———. *Far Pacific Travel Guide*. New York: John Day, 1966.

Cashion, David S., ed. *Fodor's U.S.A.*, 27th ed. New York: Fodor's Travel Publications, 2001.

Colet, John, and Joshua Eliot. *Vietnam Handbook*, 2d ed. Bath: Footprint Handbooks, 1999.

Dalat. Saigon: National Tourist Office, n.d.

Dalat Tourist Office. *Dalat: An Ideal Vacationland of Vietnam*. Dalat: Town Hall of Dalat, n.d.

The Democratic Republic of Vietnam. Hanoi: Foreign Languages Publishing House, 1975.

Dodd, Jan, and Mark Lewis. *Vietnam: The Rough Guide*, 2d ed. London: Rough Guides, 1998.

Driesen, Jane, Julie Mazur, and Chris Swiac, eds. *Fodor's Washington, D.C.* New York: Fodor's Travel Publications, 2002.

Dunlop, Fiona. *Fodor's Exploring Vietnam*, 1st ed. New York: Fodor's Travel Publications, 1998.

———. *Fodor's Exploring Vietnam*, 2d ed. New York: Fodor's Travel Publications, 2002.

Fisher, Robert I. C., ed. *Fodor's France 2001*. New York: Fodor's Travel Publications, 2001.

Flanagan, Brian Wansley, ed. *Let's Go: Washington, D.C.* New York: St. Martin's Press, 2003.

Florence, Mason, and Virginia Jealous. *Vietnam*, 7th ed. Footscray, Victoria, Australia: Lonely Planet Publications, 2003.

Florence, Mason, and Robert Storey. *Vietnam*, 5th ed. Hawthorn, Victoria, Australia: Lonely Planet Publications, 1999.

———. *Vietnam*, 6th ed. Footscray, Victoria, Australia: Lonely Planet Publications, 2001.

Fodor, Eugene, and Robert C. Fisher, eds. *Fodor's Guide to Japan and East Asia 1962*. New York: David McKay, 1962.

———. *Fodor's Guide to Japan and East Asia 1964*. New York: David McKay, 1964.

———. *Fodor's Guide to Japan and East Asia 1965*. New York: David McKay, 1965.

———. *Fodor's Guide to Japan and East Asia 1966*. New York: David McKay, 1966.

———. *Fodor's Guide to Japan and East Asia 1967*. New York: David McKay, 1967.

———. *Fodor's Guide to Japan and East Asia 1968*. New York: David McKay, 1968.

———. *Fodor's Japan and East Asia 1971*. New York: David McKay, 1971.

———. *Fodor's Japan and East Asia 1974*. New York: David McKay, 1974.

Ford, Elise Hartman. *Frommer's Washington, D.C. from $80 a Day*, 11th ed. New York: Hungry Minds, 2002.

Glimpses of French Indo-China: A Great Tourist Country at the Beginning of 1938. Saigon: Office Central du Tourisme Indochinois, 1938.

Gray, Jeremy, Steve Fallon, Paul Hellander, Daniel Robinson, Miles Roddis, and Nicola Williams. *France*, 4th ed. Footscray, Victoria, Australia: Lonely Planet Publications, 2001.

Gregory, Gene, Nguyen Lau, and Phan Thi Ngoc Quoi. *A Glimpse of Vietnam*, 1957.

A Guide to Viet-Nam. Washington, D.C.: Embassy of Vietnam, n.d.

Harger, Laura. *Washington, D.C.* Footscray, Victoria, Australia: Lonely Planet Publications, 2001.

Hue Touristic Office. *Travelling and Tourism in Annam*. Hue: Bureau du Tourisme, n.d.

Hunting in Viet-Nam. Saigon: National Tourist Office, n.d.

Hunting in Viet-Nam. Saigon: National Tourist Office, 1957.

Intrepid Travel. *Asia*. 2000–2002.

———. *Asia*. 2002–2003.

———. *Asia*. 2003–2004.

An Introduction to Vietnam. Washington, D.C.: Embassy of Vietnam, 1969.

Jones, P. H. M., ed. *Golden Guide to South and East Asia*, 5th ed. Rutland, Vt.: Charles E. Tuttle, 1967.

Kane, Robert S. *Asia A to Z*. Garden City, N.Y.: Doubleday, 1963.

Kaufman, Deborah, ed. *Fodor's Vietnam*, 2d ed. New York: Fodor's Travel Publications, 2001.

Kirtland, Lucian Swift. *Finding the Worth While in the Orient*. New York: Robert M. McBride, 1926.

Lesser, Natasha, ed. *Vietnam*. New York: Fodor's Travel Publications, 1998.

Lynch, Michael, ed. *All-Asia Guide*, 10th ed. Rutland, Vt.: Charles E. Tuttle, 1978.

Mauldin, Chelsea, Conrad Little Paulus, and Deborah Washburn, eds. *Fodor's Southeast Asia*, 21st ed. New York: Fodor's Travel Publications, 1997.

Mindlin, Alexander F., ed. *Let's Go: France*. New York: St. Martin's Press, 2001.

Népote, Jacques, and Xavier Guillaume. *Vietnam*, 2d ed. Hong Kong: Odyssey Publications, 1999.

Nha-Trang. Saigon: National Tourist Office, n.d.

Olson, Harvey S. *Olson's Orient Guide*. Philadelphia: J. B. Lippincott, 1962.

An Outline of Game Shooting in Vietnam. Saigon: Review Horizons, n.d.

Parkes, Carl. *Southeast Asia Handbook*, 3d ed. Chico, Calif.: Moon Publications, 1998 [1999].

The Real Pacific: Hawaii to Hong Kong. New York: Bantam Books, 1973.

Rutherford, Scott, ed. *Vietnam*, 4th ed. London: Insight Guides, 1999.

Saigon. Saigon: National Tourist Office, n.d.

Saigon: A Booklet of Helpful Information for Americans in Vietnam, rev. ed. Saigon: American Women's Association of Saigon, 1958.

Saigon: A Booklet of Helpful Information for Americans in Vietnam, rev. ed. Saigon: American Women's Association of Saigon, 1962.

Sillett, Helen, Grace Fujimoto, Kim Marks, Erin Van Rheenen, Kevin McLain, Rebecca Browning, and Marisa Solís, eds. *Moon Metro: Washington, D.C.* Emeryville, Calif.: Avalon Travel Publishing, 2002.

Smith, Mary Benton. *Southeast Asia: A Sunset Travel Book*. Menlo Park, Calif.: Lane Books, 1968.

Storey, Robert, and Daniel Robinson. *Vietnam*, 3d ed. Hawthorn, Victoria, Australia: Lonely Planet Publications, 1995.

———. *Vietnam*, 4th ed. Hawthorn, Victoria, Australia: Lonely Planet Publications, 1997.

Tourism in Vietnam. Saigon: Review Horizons, 1957.

Tourists' Guide to Saigon, Pnom-Penh, and Angkor, 1st ed. Saigon: Imprimerie Nouvelle Albert Portail, 1930.

Viet Nam. Saigon: National Tourist Office, n.d.

Viet Nam. Saigon: National Tourist Office, 1967.

Viet Nam: A Sketch. Hanoi: Foreign Languages Publishing House, 1971.

Vietnam as a Tourist Centre. Saigon: National Office of Tourism, 1953.

Vietnam: Communication, Tourism, and Transport. Saigon: Thanh-Binh, 1959.

Vietnam Du Lich Giao Thong/Vietnam Tourism Guide. Saigon: Co So Xuat Ban Viet Nam Tu Do/Cosovido Publishing House, 1973.

Vietnam Today. Hanoi: Foreign Languages Publishing House, 1965.

Visit Fascinating Vietnam. Saigon: National Tourist Office, n.d.

Vu The Binh, ed. *Non Nuoc Viet Nam: Sach Huong Dan Du Lich*, In Lan Thu Bon. Hanoi: Tong Cuc Du Lich Trung Tam Cong Nghe Thong Tin Du Lich, 2002.

———. *Vietnam Tourist Guidebook*, 1st ed. Hanoi: Vietnam National Administration of Tourism, 1998.

———. *Vietnam Tourist Guidebook*, 2d ed. Hanoi: Vietnam National Administration of Tourism, 2000.

———. *Vietnam Tourist Guidebook*, 3d ed. Hanoi: Vietnam National Administration of Tourism, 2001.

Wolfstone, Daniel. *The Golden Guide to South and East Asia*. Hong Kong: Far Eastern Economic Review, 1961.

Yang, Pai C., ed. *Let's Go: The Budget Guide to Southeast Asia 1997*. New York: St. Martin's Press, 1997.

Your Guide to Vietnam. Saigon: National Tourist Office, n.d.

FILMS/VIDEO SOURCES

The Deer Hunter, dir. Michael Cimino, 1978.

Dr. Strangelove: or, How I Learned to Stop Worrying and Love the Bomb, dir. Stanley Kubrick, 1964.

Full Metal Jacket, dir. Stanley Kubrick, 1987.

The Hanoi Hilton, dir. Lionel Chetwynd, 1987.

Hearts and Minds, dir. Peter Davis, 1974.

Heaven and Earth, dir. Oliver Stone, 1993.

Jump Into Hell, dir. David Butler, 1955.

Missing in Action, dir. Joseph Zito, 1984.

Nat Turner: A Troublesome Property. Subpix, 2003.

News Central. Sinclair Broadcast Group, 2004.

Rambo: First Blood Part II, dir. George P. Cosmatos, 1985

Television's Vietnam: The Impact of Media. Accuracy in Media, 1985.

Television's Vietnam: The Real Story. Accuracy in Media, 1984.

Uncommon Valor, dir. Ted Kotcheff, 1983.

Vietnam: A Television History. WGBH Educational Foundation, 2004 [1983, 1986].

We Were Soldiers, dir. Randall Wallace, 2002.

FICTION

Hasford, Gustav. *The Short-Timers*. New York: Harper and Row, 1979.

Nguyen Huy Thiep. *The General Retires and Other Stories*, trans. Greg Lockhart. Singapore: Oxford University Press, 1992.

SECONDARY SOURCES

Adair, Gilbert. *Hollywood's Vietnam: From* The Green Berets *to* Full Metal Jacket. London: Heinemann, 1989.

Alneng, Victor. " 'What the Fuck Is a Vietnam?': Touristic Phantasms and the Pop-colonization of (the) Vietnam (War)." *Critique of Anthropology* 22, no. 4 (December 2002): 461–89.

Appy, Christian G. "Struggling for the World." In *Cold War Constructions: The Political Culture of United States Imperialism, 1945–1966*, ed. Christian G. Appy. Amherst: University of Massachusetts Press, 2000.

Appy, Christian, and Alexander Bloom. "Vietnam War Mythology and the Rise of

Public Cynicism." In *Long Time Gone: Sixties America Then and Now*, ed. Alexander Bloom. New York: Oxford University Press, 2001.

Asian Development Bank. *Indigenous Peoples/Ethnic Minorities and Poverty Reduction: Vietnam*. Manila: Asian Development Bank, 2002.

Auster, Albert, and Leonard Quart. *How the War Was Remembered: Hollywood and Vietnam*. New York: Praeger, 1988.

Bagdikian, Ben H. *The Media Monopoly*, 3d ed. Boston: Beacon Press, 1990.

Barsky, Robert F. *Noam Chomsky: A Life of Dissent*. Cambridge, Mass.: MIT Press, 1997.

Beattie, Keith. *The Scar That Binds: American Culture and the Vietnam War*. New York: New York University Press, 1998.

Berg, Rick. "Losing Vietnam: Covering the War in an Age of Technology." In *From Hanoi to Hollywood: The Vietnam War in American Film*, ed. Linda Dittmar and Gene Michaud. New Brunswick, N.J.: Rutgers University Press, 1990.

Bhattacharyya, Deborah B. "Mediating India: An Analysis of a Guidebook." *Annals of Tourism Research* 24, no. 2 (1997): 371–89.

Biles, Annabel, Kate Lloyd, and William S. Logan. "'Tiger on a Bicycle': The Growth, Character, and Dilemmas of International Tourism in Vietnam." *Pacific Tourism Review* 3, no. 1 (1999): 11–23.

Boehm, Scott. "Privatizing Public Memory: The Price of Patriotic Philanthropy and the Post-9/11 Politics of Display." *American Quarterly* 58, no. 4 (December 2006): 1147–66.

Borhan, Pierre. *Dorothea Lange: The Heart and Mind of a Photographer*. Boston: Bulfinch Press, 2002.

Bradley, Mark Philip. *Imagining Vietnam and America: The Making of Postcolonial Vietnam, 1919–1950*. Chapel Hill: University of North Carolina Press, 2000.

Brecher, Jeremy, and Tim Costello. *Global Village or Global Pillage: Economic Reconstruction from the Bottom Up*, 2d ed. Cambridge, Mass.: South End Press, 1998.

Brigham, Robert K. *Guerrilla Diplomacy: The NLF's Foreign Relations and the Viet Nam War*. Ithaca, N.Y.: Cornell University Press, 1999.

———. "Why the South Won the American War in Vietnam." In *Why the North Won the Vietnam War*, ed. Marc Jason Gilbert. New York: Palgrave, 2002.

Bui Tin. *From Enemy to Friend: A North Vietnamese Perspective on the War*. Annapolis, Md.: Naval Institute Press, 2002.

Burke, Carol. "The Price of Freedom Is Truth." *Radical History Review* 95 (Spring 2006): 235–45.

Buzzanco, Robert. *Vietnam and the Transformation of American Life*. Malden, Mass.: Blackwell Publishers, 1999.

Cameron, James. *Witness*. London: Victor Gollancz, 1966 [1965].

Cawley, Leo. "The War About the War: Vietnam Films and American Myth." In

From Hanoi to Hollywood: The Vietnam War in American Film, ed. Linda Dittmar and Gene Michaud. New Brunswick, N.J.: Rutgers University Press, 1990.

Chanthou Boua. "Genocide of a Religious Group: Pol Pot and Cambodia's Buddhist Monks." In *State-Organized Terror: The Case of Violent Internal Repression*, ed. P. Timothy Bushnell, Vladimir Shlapentokh, Christopher K. Vanderpool, and Jeyaratnam Sundram. Boulder, Colo.: Westview Press, 1991.

Chapman, Jessica M. "Staging Democracy: South Vietnam's 1955 Referendum to Depose Bao Dai." *Diplomatic History* 30, no. 4 (September 2006): 671–703.

Chi, Lily. "Necessary Fictions: A Tour of Guidebooks to Twentieth-Century Saigon." *Cabinet* 6 (Spring 2002): 42–48.

Chomsky, Noam. "Hamlet without the Prince of Denmark." *Diplomatic History* 20, no. 3 (Summer 1996): 450–55.

Chomsky, Noam, and Edward S. Herman. *After the Cataclysm: Postwar Indochina and the Reconstruction of Imperial Ideology*, vol. 2 of *The Political Economy of Human Rights*. Boston: South End Press, 1979.

———. *Counter-Revolutionary Violence: Bloodbaths in Fact and Propaganda*, module 57. Andover, Mass.: Warner Modular Publications, 1973.

———. *The Washington Connection and Third World Fascism*, vol. 1 of *The Political Economy of Human Rights*. Boston: South End Press, 1977.

Clifford Sr., James O. "Forgotten Massacre at Hue." *Vietnam* 14, no. 5 (February 2002): 26–32, 63.

Clinton, James W. *The Loyal Opposition: Americans in North Vietnam, 1965–1972.* Niwot: University Press of Colorado, 1995.

Cohen, Erik. "The Tourist Guide: The Origins, Structure, and Dynamics of a Role." *Annals of Tourism Research* 12, no. 1 (1985): 5–29.

Conan, Éric, and Henry Rousso. *Vichy: An Ever-Present Past*. Hanover, N.H.: University Press of America, 1998.

Crossette, Barbara. *The Great Hill Stations of Asia*. New York: Basic Books, 1999.

Cullather, Nick. "Development? It's History." *Diplomatic History* 24, no. 4 (Fall 2000): 641–53.

Dao, Loan. "What's Going On with the Oakland Museum's 'California and the Vietnam Era' Exhibit?" *Amerasia Journal* 31, no. 2 (2005): 88–106.

Deolalikar, Anil B. "Access to Health Services by the Poor and the Non-Poor: The Case of Vietnam." *Journal of Asian and African Studies* 37, no. 2 (July 2002): 244–61.

DeRosa, Christopher S. "A Million Thinking Bayonets: Political Indoctrination in the United States Army." Ph.D. diss., Temple University, 2000.

———. *Political Indoctrination in the U.S. Army from World War II to the Vietnam War.* Lincoln: University of Nebraska Press, 2006.

Devine, Jeremy M. *Vietnam at 24 Frames a Second: A Critical and Thematic Analysis of Over 400 Films About the Vietnam War.* Austin: University of Texas Press, 1995.

Doan Bich and Le Trang. *Saigon in the Flesh*. Saigon: Le Trang Publishing House, 1965.

Dodsworth, John R., Erich Spitäller, Michael Braulke, Keon Hyok Lee, Kenneth Miranda, Christian Mulder, Hisanobu Shishido, and Krishna Srinivasan. *Vietnam: Transition to a Market Economy*. Occasional Paper no. 135. Washington, D.C.: International Monetary Fund, 1996.

Drinnon, Richard. *Facing West: The Metaphysics of Indian-Hating and Empire-Building*. Norman: University of Oklahoma Press, 1997.

Dubin, Steven C. *Displays of Power: Memory and Amnesia in the American Museum*. New York: New York University Press, 1999.

Ebashi, Masahiko. "The Economic Take-off." In *Vietnam Joins the World*, ed. James W. Morley and Masashi Nishihara. Armonk, N.Y.: M. E. Sharpe, 1997.

Endy, Christopher. *Cold War Holidays: American Tourism in France*. Chapel Hill: University of North Carolina Press, 2004.

Engerman, David C., Nils Gilman, Mark H. Haefele, and Michael E. Latham, eds. *Staging Growth: Modernization, Development, and the Global Cold War*. Amherst: University of Massachusetts Press, 2003.

Faas, Horst, and Tim Page, eds. *Requiem: By the Photographers Who Died in Vietnam and Indochina*. New York: Random House, 1997.

Fanjul, Gonzalo, and Arabella Fraser. "Dumping without Borders: How U.S. Agricultural Policies Are Destroying the Livelihoods of Mexican Corn Farmers." Oxfam Briefing Paper no. 50. Oxfam International, 2003.

Fletcher, Harrell. *The American War*. Atlanta: J and L Books, 2005.

Foner, Eric. *The Story of American Freedom*. New York: W. W. Norton, 1998.

Fox, Len. *Friendly Vietnam*. Hanoi: Foreign Languages Publishing House, 1958.

Frank, Robert H. *Falling Behind: How Rising Inequality Harms the Middle Class*. Berkeley: University of California Press, 2007.

Frank, Thomas. *One Market Under God: Extreme Capitalism, Market Populism, and the End of Economic Democracy*. New York: Doubleday, 2000.

Franklin, H. Bruce. *MIA, or, Mythmaking in America*. New Brunswick, N.J.: Rutgers University Press, 1993.

———. *Vietnam and Other American Fantasies*. Amherst: University of Massachusetts Press, 2000.

———. "When Did the Vietnam War Begin?" Paper presented at the annual meeting of the American Historical Association, Washington, D.C., 10 January 2004.

Frankum Jr., Ronald B., and Stephen F. Maxner. *The Vietnam War for Dummies*. New York: Wiley Publishing, 2003.

Gettleman, Marvin E., Jane Franklin, Marilyn B. Young, and H. Bruce Franklin, eds. *Vietnam and America: A Documented History*, rev. ed. New York: Grove Press, 1995.

Gillen, Michael. "Roots of Opposition: The Critical Response to U.S. Indochina Policy, 1945–1954." Ph.D. diss., New York University, 1991.

Greenberg, Kenneth S., ed. *Nat Turner: A Slave Rebellion in History and Memory*. New York: Oxford University Press, 2003.

Greenfield, Gerard. "Vietnam and the World Coffee Crisis: Local Coffee Riots in a Global Context." *Sand in the Wheels*, ATTAC Weekly Newsletter, vol. 121 (27 March 2002): 9–15.

Gresser, Charis, and Sophia Tickell. *Mugged: Poverty in Your Coffee Cup*. Oxfam International, 2002.

Griffiths, Philip Jones. *Vietnam Inc.* New York: Macmillan, 1971.

Gruner, Elliott. *Prisoners of Culture: Representing the Vietnam POW*. New Brunswick, N.J.: Rutgers University Press, 1993.

Hammond, William M. *Public Affairs: The Military and the Media, 1962–1968*. Washington, D.C.: Center of Military History, U.S. Army, 1988.

———. *Public Affairs: The Military and the Media, 1968–1973*. Washington, D.C.: Center of Military History, U.S. Army, 1996.

———. *Reporting Vietnam: Media and Military at War*. Lawrence: University Press of Kansas, 1998.

Hass, Kristin Ann. *Carried to the Wall: American Memory and the Vietnam Veterans Memorial*. Berkeley: University of California Press, 1998.

Heinl Jr., Colonel Robert D. "The Collapse of the Armed Forces." *Armed Forces Journal* 108, no. 19 (7 June 1971): 30–38.

Herman, Edward S. *Atrocities in Vietnam: Myths and Realities*. Philadelphia: Pilgrim Press, 1970.

Herman, Edward S., and Frank Brodhead. *Demonstration Elections: U.S.-Staged Elections in the Dominican Republic, Vietnam, and El Salvador*. Boston: South End Press, 1984.

Herman, Edward S., and Noam Chomsky. *Manufacturing Consent: The Political Economy of the Mass Media*. New York: Pantheon Books, 1988.

Herman, Edward, and D. Gareth Porter. "The Myth of the Hue Massacre." *Ramparts* 13, no. 8 (May–June 1975): 8–13.

Herring, George C. *America's Longest War: The United States and Vietnam, 1950–1975*, 2d ed. New York: Alfred A. Knopf, 1986.

Hersh, Seymour M. *My Lai 4: A Report on the Massacre and Its Aftermath*. New York: Random House, 1970.

Hershberger, Mary. *Traveling to Vietnam: American Peace Activists and the War*. Syracuse, N.Y.: Syracuse University Press, 1998.

Hildebrand, George C., and Gareth Porter. *Cambodia: Starvation and Revolution*. New York: Monthly Review Press, 1976.

Hirschman, Charles, Samuel Preston, and Vu Manh Loi. "Vietnamese Casualties during the American War: A New Estimate." *Population and Development Review* 21, no. 4 (December 1995): 783–812.

Hogan, Michael J. "The Enola Gay Controversy: History, Memory, and the Politics of Presentation." In *Hiroshima in History and Memory*, ed. Michael J. Hogan. Cambridge: Cambridge University Press, 1996.

Hoganson, Kristin L. *Fighting for American Manhood: How Gender Politics Provoked the Spanish–American and Philippine–American Wars*. New Haven, Conn.: Yale University Press, 1998.

Holguín, Sandie. " 'National Spain Invites You': Battlefield Tourism during the Spanish Civil War." *American Historical Review* 110, no. 5 (December 2005): 1399–1426.

Hosmer, Stephen T. *Viet Cong Repression and Its Implications for the Future*, R-475/1-ARPA. Santa Monica, Calif.: RAND Corporation, 1970.

Hunt, David. "Images of the Viet Cong." In *The United States and Viet Nam from War to Peace: Papers from an Interdisciplinary Conference on Reconciliation*, ed. Robert M. Slabey. Jefferson, N.C.: McFarland and Company, 1996.

———. "War Crimes and the Vietnamese People: American Representations and Silences." In *Censoring History: Citizenship and Memory in Japan, Germany, and the United States*, ed. Laura Hein and Mark Selden. Armonk, N.Y.: M. E. Sharpe, 2000.

International Travel Statistics: 1957. Geneva: International Union of Official Travel Organizations; London: British Travel and Holidays Association, 1959.

International Travel Statistics: 1959. Geneva: International Union of Official Travel Organizations; London: British Travel and Holidays Association, 1961.

International Travel Statistics: 1960. Geneva: International Union of Official Travel Organizations, 1962.

International Travel Statistics: 1961. Geneva: International Union of Official Travel Organizations, 1963.

International Travel Statistics: 1962. Geneva: International Union of Official Travel Organizations, 1964.

International Travel Statistics: 1963. Geneva: International Union of Official Travel Organizations, 1965.

International Travel Statistics: 1964. Geneva: International Union of Official Travel Organizations, 1966.

International Travel Statistics: 1965. Geneva: International Union of Official Travel Organizations, 1967.

International Travel Statistics: 1967. ITS/CIR/69(1), vol. 21. Geneva: International Union of Official Travel Organizations, 1969.

International Travel Statistics: 1969. ITS/CIR/70(3), vol. 23. Geneva: International Union of Official Travel Organizations, 1970.

International Travel Statistics: 1970. ITS/CIR/72(1), vol. 24. Geneva: International Union of Official Travel Organizations, 1970.

Ishikawa Bunyo. *War and Man: Photo Document Vietnam*. Tokyo: Sowa Shuppan, 1989.

——. *The War for the Liberation of Vietnam (Chien Tranh Giai Phong Viet Nam)*. Ho Chi Minh City: Hoi Khoa Lich Su Thanh Pho Ho Chi Minh, 1995 [1977].

Jacobs, Seth. *America's Miracle Man in Vietnam: Ngo Dinh Diem, Religion, Race, and U.S. Intervention in Southeast Asia*. Durham: Duke University Press, 2004.

Jeffords, Susan. *The Remasculinization of America: Gender and the Vietnam War*. Bloomington: Indiana University Press, 1989.

Just, Ward. "McNamara's Complaint." *Diplomatic History* 20, no. 3 (Summer 1996): 462–66.

Kahin, George McT. *Intervention: How America Became Involved in Vietnam*. New York: Anchor Books, 1986.

Kahin, George McT., and John Wilson Lewis. *The United States in Vietnam*. New York: Dial Press, 1967.

Kaiser, David. *American Tragedy: Kennedy, Johnson, and the Origins of the Vietnam War*. Cambridge, Mass.: Harvard University Press, 2000.

Kaplan, Amy. " 'Left Alone with America': The Absence of Empire in the Study of American Culture." In *Cultures of United States Imperialism*, ed. Amy Kaplan and Donald E. Pease. Durham: Duke University Press, 1993.

Karnow, Stanley. *Vietnam: A History*, rev. ed. New York: Penguin Books, 1997.

Kawachi, Ichiro, and Bruce P. Kennedy. *The Health of Nations: Why Inequality Is Harmful to Your Health*. New York: New Press, 2002.

Kennedy, Laurel B., and Mary Rose Williams. "The Past without the Pain: The Manufacture of Nostalgia in Vietnam's Tourism Industry." In *The Country of Memory: Remaking the Past in Late Socialist Vietnam*, ed. Hue-Tam Ho Tai. Berkeley: University of California Press, 2001.

Kiernan, Ben. "The Cambodian Genocide—1975–1979." In *Century of Genocide: Critical Essays and Eyewitness Accounts*, 2d ed., ed. Samuel Totten, William S. Parsons, and Israel W. Charny. New York: Routledge, 2004.

——. *The Pol Pot Regime: Race, Power, and Genocide in Cambodia Under the Khmer Rouge, 1975–79*. Chiang Mai, Thailand: Silkworm Books, 1996.

Kimball, Jeffrey P. *To Reason Why: The Debate About the Causes of U.S. Involvement in the Vietnam War*. Philadelphia: Temple University Press, 1990.

Klein, Christina. *Cold War Orientalism: Asia in the Middlebrow Imagination, 1945–1961*. Berkeley: University of California Press, 2003.

Klevorick, Alvin K. "Reflections on the Race to the Bottom." In *Fair Trade and Harmonization: Prerequisites for Free Trade? Volume I: Economic Analysis*, ed. Jagdish Bhagwati and Robert E. Hudec. Cambridge, Mass.: MIT Press, 1996.

Kolko, Gabriel. *Anatomy of a War: Vietnam, the United States, and the Modern Historical Experience*, rev. ed. New York: New Press, 1994.

——. "China and Vietnam on the Road to the Market." *Journal of Contemporary Asia* 31, no. 4 (2001): 431–40.

——. *Vietnam: Anatomy of a Peace*. London: Routledge, 1997.

——. "Vietnam since 1975: Winning a War and Losing the Peace." *Journal of Contemporary Asia* 25, no. 1 (1995): 3–49.

Koreman, Megan. *The Expectation of Justice: France, 1944–1946*. Durham: Duke University Press, 1999.

Koshar, Rudy. *German Travel Cultures*. Oxford: Berg, 2000.

——. "'What Ought to Be Seen': Tourists' Guidebooks and National Identities in Modern Germany and Europe." *Journal of Contemporary History* 33, no. 3 (July 1998): 323–40.

Laderman, Scott. "'It Is Cheaper and Better to Teach a Young Indian Than to Fight an Old One': Thaddeus Pound and the Logic of Assimilation." *American Indian Culture and Research Journal* 26, no. 3 (2002): 85–111.

——. "Shaping Memory of the Past: Discourse in Travel Guidebooks for Vietnam." *Mass Communication and Society* 5, no. 1 (February 2002): 87–110.

Lange, Dorothea. "Remembrance of Asia." *Photography Annual 1964* (1963): 50–59.

Lanning, Michael Lee. *Vietnam at the Movies*. New York: Fawcett Columbine, 1994.

Latham, Michael E. *Modernization as Ideology: American Social Science and "Nation Building" in the Kennedy Era*. Chapel Hill: University of North Carolina Press, 2000.

Le Huu Dan. *Tuyen Tap Su That/Accounts of the Truth*. Fremont, Calif.: Xuat Ban Publishing, 1998.

Lembcke, Jerry. *The Spitting Image: Myth, Memory, and the Legacy of Vietnam*. New York: New York University Press, 1998.

Lennon, John, and Malcolm Foley. *Dark Tourism: The Attraction of Death and Disaster*. London: Continuum, 2000.

Le Thai Khuong. *Du Lich Ky Nghe Tam Dang tai Viet-Nam/Tourism in Vietnam*. Saigon: Nha Xuat Ban Minh-Ha, 1970.

Letters, Frances. *The Surprising Asians: A Hitch-Hike through Malaya, Thailand, Laos, Cambodia, and South Vietnam*. Sydney: Angus and Robertson, 1968.

Lichtenstein, Nelson. "Market Triumphalism and the Wishful Liberals." In *Cold War Triumphalism: The Misuse of History After the Fall of Communism*, ed. Ellen Schrecker. New York: New Press, 2004.

Linenthal, Edward T., and Tom Engelhardt, eds. *History Wars: The Enola Gay and Other Battles for the American Past*. New York: Metropolitan Books, 1996.

Loewen, James W. "The Vietnam War in High School American History." In *Censoring History: Citizenship and Memory in Japan, Germany, and the United States*, ed. Laura Hein and Mark Selden. Armonk, N.Y.: M. E. Sharpe, 2000.

Lottman, Herbert R. *The Purge*. New York: William Morrow, 1986.

Luke, Timothy W. *Museum Politics: Power Plays at the Exhibition*. Minneapolis: University of Minnesota Press, 2002.

Luong, Hy Van. "Postwar Vietnamese Society: An Overview of Transformational

Dynamics." In *Postwar Vietnam: Dynamics of a Transforming Society*, ed. Hy Van Luong. Lanham, Md.: Rowman and Littlefield; Singapore: Institute of Southeast Asian Studies, 2003.

———. "Wealth, Power, and Inequality: Global Market, the State, and Local Sociocultural Dynamics." In *Postwar Vietnam: Dynamics of a Transforming Society*, ed. Hy Van Luong. Lanham, Md.: Rowman and Littlefield; Singapore: Institute of Southeast Asian Studies, 2003.

Luong, Hy Van, and Jonathan Unger. "Wealth, Power, and Poverty in the Transition to Market Economies: The Process of Socio-economic Differentiation in Rural China and Northern Vietnam." In *Transforming Asian Socialism: China and Vietnam Compared*, ed. Anita Chan, Benedict J. Tria Kerkvliet, and Jonathan Unger. Lanham, Md.: Rowman and Littlefield, 1999.

MacCannell, Dean. *The Tourist: A New Theory of the Leisure Class*. New York: Schocken Books, 1976.

Martini, Edwin. *Invisible Enemies: The American War on Vietnam, 1975–2000*. Amherst: University of Massachusetts Press, 2007.

———. "(When) Did the Vietnam War End?" Paper presented at the annual meeting of the American Historical Association, Washington, D.C., 10 January 2004.

Masur, Matthew. "Hearts and Minds: Cultural Nation Building in South Vietnam, 1954–1963." Ph.D. diss., Ohio State University, 2004.

McAlister, Melani. *Epic Encounters: Culture, Media, and U.S. Interests in the Middle East since 1945*, rev ed. Berkeley: University of California Press, 2005.

McAllister, James. "'A Fiasco of Noble Proportions': The Johnson Administration and the South Vietnamese Elections of 1967." *Pacific Historical Review* 73, no. 4 (November 2004): 619–51.

McGirr, Lisa. *Suburban Warriors: The Origins of the New American Right*. Princeton, N.J.: Princeton University Press, 2001.

McGregor, Andrew. "Dynamic Texts and Tourist Gaze: Death, Bones, and Buffalo." *Annals of Tourism Research* 27, no. 1 (2000): 27–50.

McNamara, Robert S., with Brian VanDeMark. *In Retrospect: The Tragedy and Lessons of Vietnam*. New York: Vintage Books, 1996 [1995].

Mehmet, Ozay. "Race to the Bottom: The Impact of Globalization on Labor Markets — A Review of Empirical and Theoretical Evidence." In *Globalization and the Third World: A Study of Negative Consequences*, ed. B. N. Ghosh and Halil M. Guven. Basingstoke: Palgrave Macmillan, 2006.

Mehmet, Ozay, and Akbar Tavakoli. "Does Foreign Direct Investment Cause a Race to the Bottom? Evidence from Four Asian Countries." *Journal of the Asia Pacific Economy* 8, no. 2 (2003): 133–56.

Merrill, Dennis. "Negotiating Cold War Paradise: U.S. Tourism, Economic Planning, and Cultural Modernity in Twentieth-Century Puerto Rico." *Diplomatic History* 25, no. 2 (Spring 2001): 179–214.

Minear, Richard. "Douglas Pike and the NLF." *Bulletin of Concerned Asian Scholars* 2, no. 1 (October 1969): 44–47.

Mishel, Lawrence, Jared Bernstein, and Heather Boushey. *The State of Working America 2002–2003*. Washington, D.C.: Economic Policy Institute, 2002.

Morgan, Joseph G. *The Vietnam Lobby: The American Friends of Vietnam, 1955–1975*. Chapel Hill: University of North Carolina Press, 1997.

Muse, Eben J. *The Land of Nam: The Vietnam War in American Film*. Lanham, Md.: Scarecrow Press, 1995.

Musgrove, Philip, ed. *World Health Report 2000 — Health Systems: Improving Performance*. Geneva: World Health Organization, 2001.

Nashel, Jonathan D. *Edward Lansdale's Cold War*. Amherst: University of Massachusetts Press, 2005.

———. "The Road to Vietnam: Modernization Theory in Fact and Fiction." In *Cold War Constructions: The Political Culture of United States Imperialism, 1945–1966*, ed. Christian G. Appy. Amherst: University of Massachusetts Press, 2000.

National Center for Social Sciences and Humanities. *National Human Development Report 2001: Doi Moi and Human Development in Viet Nam*. Hanoi: Political Publishing House, 2001.

Ngo Vinh Long. "A Letter from Vietnam." *Challenge* 40, no. 1 (January–February 1997): 87–109.

———. "The Tet Offensive and Its Aftermath." In *The Tet Offensive*, ed. Marc Jason Gilbert and William Head. Westport, Conn.: Praeger, 1996.

Ngo Vinh Long with Daniel C. Tsang. "Vietnam Today." *Critical Asian Studies* 34, no. 3 (2002): 459–64.

Nguyen, Khuyen Vu. "Memorializing Vietnam: Transfiguring the Living Pasts." In *What's Going On? California and the Vietnam Era*, ed. Marcia A. Eymann and Charles Wollenberg. Berkeley: University of California Press, 2004.

Novick, Peter. *That Noble Dream: The "Objectivity Question" and the American Historical Profession*. Cambridge: Cambridge University Press, 1988.

Oberdorfer, Don. *Tet!* Garden City, N.Y.: Doubleday, 1971.

O'Neill, John E., and Jerome R. Corsi. *Unfit for Command: Swift Boat Veterans Speak Out Against John Kerry*. Washington, D.C.: Regnery Publishing, 2004.

Pacific Area Travel Association. *Sixteenth Annual Conference, United States of America, April 24th–27th, 1967: Report of Conference and Workshop Proceedings*. San Francisco: Pacific Area Travel Association, 1967.

Penniman, Howard R. *Decision in South Vietnam*. Washington, D.C.: Free Society Association, 1967.

———. *Elections in South Vietnam*, American Enterprise Institute–Hoover Policy Study 4. Washington, D.C.: American Enterprise Institute for Public Policy Research; Stanford, Calif.: Hoover Institution on War, Revolution, and Peace, 1972.

Pham Van Bach, Tran Cong Tuong, Do Xuan Sang, Pham Thanh Vinh, Luu Van Loi, and Le Van Chat. *Fascist Terror in South Viet Nam: Law 10–59*. Hanoi: Foreign Languages Publishing House, 1961.

Phong Trao Giao Dan Viet Nam Hai Ngoai/Vietnamese Laity Movement in the Diaspora. *Tham Sat Mau Than o Hue: Tuyen Tap Tai Lieu/The '68 Massacre at Hue: Documentation*. Reischstett, France: Dinh Huong Tung Thu, 1998.

Pike, Douglas. *Massacre at Hue*. Bangkok: South-East Asia Treaty Organization, 1970.

———. *The Viet-Cong Strategy of Terror*. Saigon: U.S. Mission, Viet-Nam, 1970.

Pilger, John. *Heroes*. London: Pan Books, 1989.

———. *Hidden Agendas*. New York: New Press, 1998.

Ponce, Ninez, Paul Gertler, and Paul Glewwe. "Will Vietnam Grow Out of Malnutrition?" In *Household Welfare and Vietnam's Transition*, ed. David Dollar, Paul Glewwe, and Jennie Litvack. Washington, D.C.: World Bank, 1998.

Poole, Peter A. *The United States and Indochina: From FDR to Nixon*. Hinsdale, Ill.: Dryden Press, 1973.

Porter, D. Gareth. "The 1968 'Hue Massacre.'" *Indochina Chronicle* 33 (24 June 1974): 2–13.

Porter, D. Gareth, ed. *Vietnam: A History in Documents*. New York: Meridian/New American Library, 1981.

Porter, D. Gareth, and Len E. Ackland. "Vietnam: The Bloodbath Argument." *Christian Century* 86, no. 45 (5 November 1969): 1414–17.

Pratt, Mary Louise. *Imperial Eyes: Travel Writing and Transculturation*. London: Routledge, 1992.

Pym, Christopher. *The Road to Angkor*. London: Robert Hale, 1959.

Richter, Linda K. *The Politics of Tourism in Asia*. Honolulu: University of Hawaii Press, 1989.

Rosendorf, Neal Moses. "Be El Caudillo's Guest: The Franco Regime's Quest for Rehabilitation and Dollars after World War II via the Promotion of U.S. Tourism to Spain," *Diplomatic History* 30, no. 3 (June 2006): 367–407.

Rostow, W. W. "Vietnam and Asia." *Diplomatic History* 20, no. 3 (Summer 1996): 467–71.

Rousso, Henry. "Did the Purge Achieve Its Goals?" In *Memory, the Holocaust, and French Justice: The Bousquet and Touvier Affairs*, ed. Richard J. Golsan. Hanover, N.H.: University Press of New England, 1996.

Rowe, John Carlos, and Rick Berg, eds. *The Vietnam War and American Culture*. New York: Columbia University Press, 1991.

Saunders, Frances Stonor. *The Cultural Cold War: The CIA and the World of Arts and Letters*. New York: New Press, 1999.

Schecter, Arnold, Marian Pavuk, Rainer Malisch, and John Jake Ryan. "Are Vietnamese Food Exports Contaminated with Dioxin from Agent Orange?" *Journal of Toxicology and Environmental Health: Part A* 66, no. 15 (8 August 2003): 1391–1404.

Schell, Jonathan. *The Military Half*. In *The Real War*. Cambridge, Mass.: Da Capo Press, 1988.

Schmitz, David F. *Thank God They're on Our Side: The United States and Right-Wing Dictatorships, 1921–1965*. Chapel Hill: University of North Carolina Press, 1999.

Scigliano, Robert. *South Vietnam: Nation Under Stress*. Boston: Houghton Mifflin, 1964.

Segall, M., G. Tipping, H. Lucas, T. V. Dung, N. T. Tam, D. X. Vinh, and D. L. Huong. "Economic Transition Should Come with a Health Warning: The Case of Vietnam." *Journal of Epidemiology and Community Health* 56, no. 7 (2002): 497–505.

Semmens, Kristin. *Seeing Hitler's Germany: Tourism in the Third Reich*. Basingstoke: Palgrave Macmillan, 2005.

Sharp, Joanne P. *Condensing the Cold War: Reader's Digest and American Identity*. Minneapolis: University of Minnesota Press, 2000.

Sheehan, Neil. *A Bright Shining Lie: John Paul Vann and America in Vietnam*. New York: Vintage Books, 1988.

Siegenthaler, Peter. "Hiroshima and Nagasaki in Japanese Guidebooks." *Annals of Tourism Research* 29, no. 4 (October 2002): 1111–37.

Singh, Ajit. "Labour Standards and the 'Race to the Bottom': Rethinking Globalisation and Workers' Rights from Developmental and Solidaristic Perspectives." *Oxford Review of Economic Policy* 20, no. 1 (Spring 2004): 85–104.

Smith, Julian. *Looking Away: Hollywood and Vietnam*. New York: Charles Scribner's Sons, 1975.

Sontag, Susan. *Trip to Hanoi*. New York: Farrar, Straus, and Giroux, 1969 [1968].

Springer, Claudia. "Military Propaganda: Defense Department Films from World War II and Vietnam." In *The Vietnam War and American Culture*, ed. John Carlos Rowe and Rick Berg. New York: Columbia University Press, 1991.

Stewart, Rory. *The Places in Between*. London: Picador, 2004.

Sturken, Marita. *Tangled Memories: The Vietnam War, the AIDS Epidemic, and the Politics of Remembering*. Berkeley: University of California Press, 1997.

Suran, Justin David. "Coming Out Against the War: Antimilitarism and the Politicization of Homosexuality in the Era of Vietnam." *American Quarterly* 53, no. 3 (September 2001): 452–88.

Swinkels, Rob, and Carrie Turk. *Strategic Planning for Poverty Reduction in Vietnam: Progress and Challenges for Meeting the Localized Millennium Development Goals (MDGs)*. World Bank Policy Research Working Paper no. 2961. Hanoi: World Bank, 2003.

Tai, Hue-Tam Ho, ed. *The Country of Memory: Remaking the Past in Late Socialist Vietnam*. Berkeley: University of California Press, 2001.

——. *Hallowed Ground or Haunted House: The War in Vietnamese History and Tourism*. Contemporary Issues 3. Cambridge, Mass.: Fairbank Center for East Asian Research, Harvard University, 1994.

———. "Situating Memory." In *The Country of Memory: Remaking the Past in Late Socialist Vietnam*, ed. Hue-Tam Ho Tai. Berkeley: University of California Press, 2001.

Taylor, Telford. *Nuremberg and Vietnam: An American Tragedy*. Chicago: Quadrangle Books, 1970.

They Have Been in North Viet Nam. Hanoi: Foreign Languages Publishing House, 1968.

Tonelson, Alan. *The Race to the Bottom: Why a Worldwide Worker Surplus and Uncontrolled Free Trade Are Sinking American Living Standards*. Boulder, Colo.: Westview Press, 2000.

Tran Van Giau and Le Van Chat. *The South Viet Nam Liberation National Front*. Hanoi: Foreign Languages Publishing House, 1962.

Travel Research International. *Pacific Visitors Survey: A Consumer Marketing Study of Tourists to the Pacific*. San Francisco: Pacific Area Travel Association, 1967.

Trouillot, Michel-Rolph. *Silencing the Past: Power and the Production of History*. Boston: Beacon Press, 1995.

Turner, Fred. *Echoes of Combat: The Vietnam War in American Memory*. New York: Anchor Books, 1996.

Turse, Nicholas. " 'Kill Anything That Moves': United States War Crimes and Atrocities in Vietnam, 1965–1973." Ph.D. diss., Columbia University, 2005.

United Nations Country Team Viet Nam. *International Economic Integration, Competitiveness, and Rural Livelihoods in Viet Nam*. Discussion Paper no. 1. Hanoi: Office of the United Nations Resident Coordinator, 2002.

Untitled. New Delhi: India Vietnam Humanitarian League, 1969.

Vennema, Alje. *The Viet Cong Massacre at Hue*. New York: Vantage Press, 1976.

Vu Tuan Anh. "Economic Policy Reforms: An Introductory Overview." In *Vietnam in a Changing World*, ed. Irene Nørlund, Carolyn L. Gates, and Vu Cao Dam. Richmond, Surrey: Curzon Press, 1995.

Wagstaff, Adam, and Nga Nguyet Nguyen. *Poverty and Survival Prospects of Vietnamese Children under Doi Moi*. Washington, D.C.: World Bank, 2002.

Wallace, Mike. *Mickey Mouse History and Other Essays on American Memory*. Philadelphia: Temple University Press, 1996.

Warner, Peggy. *Asia Is People*. London: Angus and Robertson, 1962.

Whillock, David Everett. "The Fictive American Vietnam War Film: A Filmography." In *America Rediscovered: Critical Essays on Literature and Film of the Vietnam War*, ed. Owen W. Gilman Jr. and Lorrie Smith. New York: Garland Publishing, 1990.

Wicker, Tom. "A Theological War." *Diplomatic History* 20, no. 3 (Summer 1996): 445–49.

Willbanks, James H. *The Tet Offensive: A Concise History*. New York: Columbia University Press, 2007.

Williams, Raymond. *Problems in Materialism and Culture*. London: Verso, 1980.

World Bank. *Vietnam: Growing Healthy, A Review of the Health Sector*. Hanoi: World Bank, 2001.

——. *World Development Indicators 2002*. Washington, D.C.: World Bank, 2002.

World Tourism Organization. *Tourism Development Master Plan: Socialist Republic of Vietnam (VIE/89/003): Summary Report*. Madrid: World Tourism Organization, 1991.

Yoder Jr., Edwin M. "A Very Subdued Confession." *Diplomatic History* 20, no. 3 (Summer 1996): 456–61.

Young, Marilyn B. "The Closest of Hindsight." *Diplomatic History* 20, no. 3 (Summer 1996): 440–44.

——. *The Vietnam Wars, 1945–1990*. New York: HarperPerennial, 1991.

Zinoman, Peter. *The Colonial Bastille: A History of Imprisonment in Vietnam, 1862–1940*. Berkeley: University of California Press, 2001.

Cawley, Leo, 112–13

CBS, 112–13

Central Highlands (Vietnam), 38, 43–44, 135, 140, 146, 201n121, 235n74

Central Institute for Economic Survey, 140

Central Intelligence Agency (CIA), 32, 197n74

Chetwynd, Lionel, *The Hanoi Hilton*, 2, 122, 166, 190n2 (introduction)

child malnutrition, 145–46, 237n93

Cholon (Saigon/Ho Chi Minh City), 33–34

Chomsky, Noam, 119; *Counter-Revolutionary Violence*, 110–11, 224n100

Christopher, Warren, 180

CIA (Central Intelligence Agency), 32, 197n74

Cimino, Michael, *The Deer Hunter*, 9, 96, 166

Clay, William, 155

Clifford, Clark, 220–21n65

Clifford, James, 112, 225n106

Cochin China, 69

coffee, 51, 134–35, 233n49

Cohen, Erik, 118, 227n131

Colburn, Lawrence, 156

Cold War: freedom vs. totalitarianism, trope of, 203n16; guidebooks as reinforcement of ideology of, 50, 68, 88; modernization ideology of, 126–27, 187; NSC-68 and, 57; solidarity fostered by travel during, 12; tensions during, 57

Cold War Holidays (Endy), 12

Colligan, Francis J., 18

colonialism: anticolonial movement and, ix; contact zone of, 8–9, 191n21; French, ix, 30–31, 35–36, 49–50, 69–70, 197n70. *See also* First Indochina War

commodity exports, 133–38, 233nn48–49, 234nn63, 66

communicative mediation, 118–19, 227n131

Communist Party, influence and control of, viii

Communists: American anti-Communist hysteria and, 56; anti-Communist campaign and, 103–4, 106–7, 222n74; Defense Department on, 58–59; nationalists vs., 84; neutralism as appeasement of, 76; in NLF, 53, 67, 75, 83, 187; nomenclature of, viii–ix; in Viet Minh, 60. *See also* Democratic Republic of Vietnam; OAFIE pocket guides

Congressional Record, 111, 212n10

contact zone, 8–9, 191n21

Copley News Service, 107

corn, 138

Corsi, Jerome R., *Unfit for Command*, 179, 245–46n71

Cosmatos, George P., *Rambo: First Blood Part II*, 9, 96, 166

Counter-Revolutionary Violence (Chomsky and Herman), 110–11, 224n100

Cromley, Raymond, 228n138

Cronkite, Walter, 114

Crowl, Richard, 73

Cu Chi tunnels, ix–x

Dac Lac province (Vietnam), 134–35

Daewoo, 149

Dai Linh (Vietnam), 48

Dalat (Vietnam): accessibility of, by air, 37; European atmosphere of, 26; hostility toward U.S. military presence in, 63; hunting in, 19, 42; mountain tribes of, 19; *New York Times* on, 200n118; popularity of, 22; safety of travel to, 62–63

guidebooks (*continued*)

in, 118–19; attractions highlighted in, 22–23; authority of, 118; backpackers and travelers vs. tourists and, 4–5, 227n128; for children's education, 29, 196n62, 196–97n66; Cold War ideology reinforced by, 50, 68, 88; on dangers of Vietnamese tourism during the war, 37–38, 199n100; on Diem, 25–28, 31–33; on DRV, 25, 195n40, 200n116; on the exotic and traditional vs. the modern, 24–26, 195n38, 196n58; on French colonialism, 30, 197n70; on French vs. Vietnamese history, 97–98, 217n48; historical consciousness and memory shaped by, 4, 7–8, 10–11; imperialism rationalized in, 3; on inequality, 143, 236n83; Let's Go, 6, 131–32, 143–44, 230n16, 232n37; on liberation of France vs. Vietnam, 98, 217n50; as mediating travel experience, 125–29, 230nn15–17, 231n25; on military tourism, 50–53, 62–65, 85; on modernization and anti-Communism, 23–26, 28–29; objectivity of, 8, 119; politicization of, 25–32; posters, 19, 22, 57; on refugees from northern Vietnam, 25; RVN legitimacy promoted in, 23, 194n33; scholarship on, 4, 7, 118, 227n131; scope of, 4; tourist behavior influenced by, 7–8; travelers targeted by, 4; trust in publisher brands of, 118, 227n128; on U.S. intervention in Vietnam, 30, 66–67, 197n70; on Vietnamese women, 33–35, 198n88; on the war, 23, 32–33, 197nn76–77; on War Remnants Museum, 117, 160–65, 242n34, 243n41. *See also* Fodor's; Lonely Planet; OAFIE pocket guides

Guide to Viet-Nam, A, 28–29, 196n60

Gulf War (1991), 151, 182, 185

GVN. *See* Government of Vietnam

Haig, Alexander M., 221n69

Haiphong (Vietnam), 81

Hamilton, Marianne, 193n23

Hammond, William M., 222n78

Hanes, John, 73

Hannah, John A., 54–55

Hanoi, 16, 123–24

"Hanoi Hilton" (Maison Centrale; Hoa Lo Prison), 1–3

Hanoi Hilton, The (Chetwynd), 2, 122, 166, 190n2 (introduction)

Harness, Forest A., 55–56

Harris, Stewart, 43

Hasford, Gustav, *The Short-Timers*, 214–15n27

Hearts and Minds (Davis), 9, 244n49

Heart to Heart International, 178

Heaven and Earth (O. Stone), 244n49

Heck, Michael, 156

Heinl, Robert, 81

Herman, Edward, 120; *Counter-Revolutionary Violence*, 110–11, 224n100; on Hue Massacre, 110, 120, 216n36, 224n100

herring, 234n66

Hershberger, Mary, 193n23

Herter, Christian A., 75

Hidden History of the Korean War (I. F. Stone), 57

Hiroshima, 159–60, 165, 243n43

Hitch-Hiker's Guide to Europe, 4

Hoa (ethnic Chinese), 140

Hoa Hao, 27–28, 196n54

Hoa Lo Prison (Maison Centrale; "Hanoi Hilton"), 1–3

Ho Chi Minh: declaration of Vietnamese independence by, 1, 59–60,

Military Assistance Command, Vietnam (MACV), 65

Missing in Action, 122

missing in action (MIA), 180

modernization theory, 126–27, 187, 231nn29, 32

Moon, Sun Myung, 222n84

Moon guidebooks, 88, 128, 131–32, 143, 149, 161, 211n2

Morning Call, 159

Morrison, Norman, 156–57

Moudry, George and Sharon, 39–40

movies. *See* Hollywood movies

Murphy, George, 105

Museum of Vietnamese Revolution (Hanoi), 156, 243n41

museums vs. exhibition houses, 239n7

Muth, John, 29, 196n60

My Canh Floating Restaurant (Saigon), 40, 42

My Lai massacre. *See* Son My massacre

Nagasaki, 165, 243n43

Nakamura Goro, 155, 157–58

napalm, 155–56

National Air and Space Museum (Washington, D.C.), 165

National Geographic, 38, 206n50, 223n88

National Human Development Report, 139, 147

National Institute of Nutrition, 145

nationalists vs. Communists, 84

National Liberation Front (Viet Cong). *See* NLF

National Museum of American History (Washington, D.C.), 165, 181, 188, 243n43, 246n73

National Review Online, 113

National Security Council, 57

National Student Committee for Victory in Vietnam (NSCVV), 107

National Tourist Office (NTO): on hunting, 42, 201n121; "International Tourist Year" (1967) guidebook, 38–39; Nha Trang guide published by, 194n33; O'Daniel's advice to, 20–21; posters by, 19; on risks to tourists, 22; on sex tourism, 35; on state development aided by tourism, 16; war ignored in literature of, 43; wartime goals of, 40–41; *Your Guide to Vietnam*, 25, 195n40. *See also* guidebooks, pamphlets, posters, brochures

Navy Log, 25

Nazi collaborators, 97, 217nn46–47

Nazis, 89, 97–98, 113, 214n26

Nazi tourism officials, 12

News Cafe (Hue), 6

Newsweek: on death and injuries to re-creating servicemen, 62; on NTO's failure to mention war, 43; on Persian Gulf War, 182; on Saigon's decline, 42; on Vietnam war, 117

New York Times: on bloodbath theory, 108–9, 223nn89, 91; on CIA agents employed by Fodor's, 197n74; on Dalat, 200n118; on Hue Massacre, 111; on Saigon's decline, 42; on Vietnamese exports, 136

Ngo Dinh Diem: assassination of, in U.S.-backed coup, 61, 77; Binh Xuyen defeated by, 27, 196n54; coup attempts against, 44, 48, 201–2n129; economy under, 130–31; election of, 71–72, 83; guidebooks on, 25–28, 31–33; OAFIE pocket guides on, 71–72, 77, 210n93; personalism adopted by, 49; progress under, 73–74; refugees resettled by, 27; religious sects defeated by, 27, 196n54; repression by, 32, 73, 77; terror used by, 16; unpopularity and authoritarianism

authorities, 67, 75, 95, 166; by vc, 117,
161, 163; of Vietnamese, 1, 95, 166
tourism: and martial fascination (dark
tourism), 183–88; politics of, 12,
17–18
tourism and rvn's legitimacy, 3, 15–45;
cultural propaganda of tourism, 28–
29, 43–45; gendering Vietnam, 33–
35, 198nn86, 88; hunting and, 19, 42,
201n121; marketing Vietnam, 18–
33, 194n33, 195n40, 196n58,
196n62, 196–97n66 overview of, 15–
18, 192n3; U.S. nation building in
Vietnam, 12–13, 45; U.S. foreign
policy objectives and, 16–20, 22, 24–
25, 31–32; wartime tourism, 35–43,
186, 200nn110–11, 201n125. *See also*
guidebooks, pamphlets, posters,
brochures
Tourism in Vietnam, 33–34, 196n62
tourism in Vietnam: air travel, 37, 41–
42; Americans' memory contested
via, 11–13; capitalist reforms' effects
on, 124; growth of, 247n7; history of,
10; military, 50–53, 62–65, 85, 186;
motivations and responses of tourists, 3, 190n4 (introduction); narratives of tourists at war-related sites
and in brochures, 117–18; numbers
of tourists, 3, 21–22, 48, 124,
194n24, 194n26; rvn government's
promotion of, 10, 15, 18, 21; U.S.
military in Vietnam and, 47–53; war
as barrier to, 10, 21–22, 36–37,
194n24; war-related, 10, 21, 39–40,
191 n.25, 194n24. *See also* guidebooks, pamphlets, posters, brochures; tourism and rvn's legitimacy;
War Remnants Museum
Towne, Clair E., 58
trade disputes. *See* catfish

Trails of Indochina, 241n18
Tran Trong Kim, 27
Tran Van Dinh, 108, 223n88
Tran Van Tung, 32
Travel magazine, 19–20
travel writing, 3–4, 11, 30. *See also*
guidebooks, pamphlets, posters,
brochures
Tregaskis, Richard, 19–20, 34, 43–44
Tri Quang. *See* Thich Tri Quang
triumphalism of the free market, 127
Trong Nhan, 106
Troop Information and Education Divi-
sion (TIED), 55–57
Tropic Tour, 241n17
Trouillot, Michel-Rolph, 11
Truman, Harry, 49
Truong, Toan, 111, 224n104
truth markers, 116
Turkey, 149–50
Turner, Nat, 89
Turner, Robert F., 223n89
Turse, Nicholas, 95

Uncommon Valor, 166
UNESCO (United Nations Educational,
Scientific, and Cultural Organiza-
tion), 29
Unfit for Command (O'Neill and Corsi),
179, 245–46n71
Unger, Jonathan, 146
UNICEF (United Nations Children's
Fund), 145
Unification Church, 222n84
unions, 55
United Nations Children's Fund
(UNICEF), 145
United Nations Educational, Scientific, and
Cultural Organization (UNESCO), 29
United States: Americans' criticism of,
177; anti-Communist hysteria in, 56;

United States (*continued*)

as benevolent power, 13; catfish in, 136; corn industry in, 138; as democracy vs. republic, 56, 203n21; Diem and, 61, 72, 77; France aided in Indochina by, 49, 69, 74; Ho Chi Minh and, 70–71, 156; humanitarian ambitions of, 25–26, 70, 102, 177–78; imperialism of, 7–8, 11, 78–79; income inequality in, 139, 235n69; interventionism of, 30, 49, 66–67, 74, 169, 182, 197n70; job and wages in, 234–35n67; liberal capitalism and, 17, 50, 152; liberal democracy of, 13; national identity of, 172–73, 182, 187–88; nation building in Vietnam by, 12–13, 45; on neutralism as Communist appeasement, 76; peace desired by, 83–84; presidential election of 2004 in, 9, 113–14, 178–81; punitive postwar policy of, toward Vietnam, 131; racial prejudice in, 55–56; RVN and, 10, 16, 21, 84; tourism and military of, in Vietnam, 47–48, 50–53; travel to Vietnam discouraged by, 41; Vietnamese aid and, 131; Vietnamese diplomatic relations with, 180; in War Remnants Museum, 156–58, 240–41n15, 243n43; wealth inequality in, 235n69. *See also* OAFIE pocket guides; Vietnam war; *and under other United States entries*

United States Department of Commerce: on good will generated by tourists, 22; on RVN as emerging market, 128; on RVN's tourism potential, 21; on Vietnamese women, 34

United States Department of Defense: on Hue Massacre, 103, 221–22n73; on military tourism, 50–53, 62–65,

85, 186; pamphlets on Communist propaganda, 58–59; *Pentagon Papers* and, 75–76, 80–81, 83–84, 207n67; pocket guides published by, 3, 48–50, 187, 198n88; propaganda campaign of, 49–51, 53, 186. *See also* OAFIE pocket guides

United States Department of State: on Au Truong Thanh, 82–83, 210–11n111; Bureau of Intelligence and Research, 216n31; on cultural diplomacy by American tourists, 18; on Duong Van Minh, 82–83; white papers of, on aggression by DRV, 74–75, 209n85

United States Embassy (Hanoi), 137

United States Information Agency (USIA), 89–90, 109

United States International Trade Commission, 234n63

United States Merchant Marine, on transport of French troops to Vietnam, 49, 74

United States Operations Mission to Vietnam (USOM), 21–22, 205n41

University of Michigan, ix–x, 190n4

USSR. *See* Soviet Union

VanDeMark, Brian, 240n11

Vann, John Paul, 80, 210n103

VC (Viet Cong), viii–x, 160. *See also* NLF; PAVN

Vennema, Alje, 92, 215–16n28

Versace, Humbert Roque ("Rocky"), 60–61

Veterans of Foreign Wars, 180

Viet Cong (VC), viii–x, 160. *See also* NLF; PAVN

"Vietcong: Purple Haze" (videogame), x

Viet Minh: Communists in, 60; French vs., 31, 71, 84, 197n70; Ho Chi

Scott Laderman is an assistant professor of history at the University of Minnesota, Duluth.

Library of Congress Cataloging-in-Publication Data
Laderman, Scott, 1971–
Tours of Vietnam : war, travel guides, and memory / Scott Laderman.
p. cm. — (American encounters/global interactions)
Includes bibliographical references and index.
ISBN 978-0-8223-4396-7 (cloth : alk. paper)
ISBN 978-0-8223-4414-8 (pbk. : alk. paper)
1. Tourism — Vietnam — History — 20th century. 2. Vietnam — History — 20th century. 3. Vietnam — Politics and government — 1945–1975. 4. Americans — Vietnam. 5. United States — Relations — Vietnam. 6. Vietnam — Relations — United States. I. Title. II. Series.
DS556.38.L33 2009
338.4′791597 — dc22   2008041776